THE NORDIC SERIES
Volume 9

Volume 1   *British Diplomacy and Swedish Politics, 1758-1773*
           by Michael Roberts

Volume 2   Henrik Ibsen, *Peer Gynt*, translated by Rolf Fjelde.
           A thoroughly revised version of Fjelde's translation,
           with new appendixes.

Volume 3   *The Finnish Revolution, 1917-1918*
           by Anthony F. Upton

Volume 4   *To the Third Empire: Ibsen's Early Drama*
           by Brian Johnston

Volume 5   *A History of Scandinavian Literature*
           by Sven H. Rossel

Volume 6   *Viking Art*
           by David M. Wilson and Ole Klindt-Jensen

Volume 7   *Finland and Europe: The Period of Autonomy
           and the International Crises, 1808-1914*
           by Juhani Paasivirta

Volume 8   *Socialism and Abundance: Radical Socialism
           in the Danish Welfare State*
           by John Logue

The publication of this book was assisted by
a bequest from Josiah H. Chase to honor his parents,
Ellen Rankin Chase and Josiah Hook Chase,
Minnesota territorial pioneers.

Scandinavia during the Second World War

edited by Henrik S. Nissen

translated by Thomas Munch-Petersen

The University of Minnesota Press □ Minneapolis

Universitetsforlaget
Oslo—Bergen—Tromsø

Copyright © 1983 by Universitetsforlaget.
All rights reserved.
Published by the University of Minnesota Press,
2037 University Avenue Southeast,
Minneapolis, Minnesota 55414 and
Universitetsforlaget, Kolstadgt. 1, Postboks 2959 Tøyen,
Oslo 6, Norway
Printed in the United States of America.

Library of Congress Cataloging in Publication Data
Main entry under title:

Scandinavia during the Second World War.

   (The Nordic series; 9)
   Bibliography: p.
   Includes index.
   1. World War, 1939-1945 – Scandinavia – Addresses,
essays, lectures. 2. World War, 1939-1945 – Finland –
Addresses, essays, lectures. 3. Scandinavia – History –
20th century – Addresses, essays, lectures. 4. Finland –
History – 1917-1945 – Addresses, essays, lectures.
I. Nissen, Henrik S. II. Series.
D754.S29S27   940.53'48   82-2779
ISBN 0-8166-1110-6   AACR2

Contributors

Ole Kristian Grimnes, lecturer in history, University of Oslo, Norway

Martti Häikiö, associate professor of political history and head of the Information Office, University of Helsinki, Finland

Ohto Manninen, research worker, Academy of Finland; associate professor of Finnish history, University of Helsinki, Finland

Karl Molin, associate professor of history, University of Uppsala, Sweden

Henrik S. Nissen, lecturer in contemporary history, University of Copenhagen, Denmark

Berit Nøkleby, former research fellow, Norway's Resistance Museum and Norwegian Research Council for Science and the Humanities

Aage Trommer, rector, University of Odense, Denmark

Preface

The Second World War had a profound and varied impact on Finland, Norway, Denmark, and Sweden. Under intense pressure from the great powers, the Nordic people had to struggle to preserve their societies, sometimes against overwhelming odds. The people of Denmark and Norway were put to a severe test, since these countries were occupied by the Germans during the war. Finland had to fight three wars. First it waged the Winter War, earning the admiration of the rest of the world for single-handedly resisting the Soviet attempt to conquer Finland; then it became a cobelligerent of Germany; and in the end it had to expel the *Wehrmacht* from its soil. Although faring the best among the four countries, Sweden was subjected to pressures from first one, then another of the great powers dominating the Nordic region, and stretched the concept of neutrality in order to stay out of the world war.

The policies adopted by the various Nordic governments during the war account for much of the history of these countries during this turbulent period. Yet the history is more than just the story of government policies. The population and particular groups within the population that lacked any official position or authority sometimes played a role that had an immediate and drastic effect on developments. Resistance activities in the form of strikes, aid to the Jews, clandestine newspapers, and so on, are well-known examples of the contributions made by the average person.

The aim of this book is to present readers of English with a short account of the history of the Nordic countries during the war years

and the early postwar period, taking into account the intensive research in this area that has been conducted in all four countries. The
volume is a joint effort by a team of seven historians. Although the
manuscript has been the subject of frequent discussions between the
authors, each author takes full responsibility for his or her chapter(s).
The authors have adopted an inter-Nordic approach, every chapter
covering all the Nordic states. At the same time, each chapter is
stamped with the author's specialist knowledge of a certain period
and country, so that the volume also features the topics that are
currently of most interest to historians in each of the Nordic states.

Iceland has, of course, participated in the institutionalized postwar
cooperation of the Nordic countries. However, Iceland is not covered
by this book, primarily because the problems it faced differed radically from those of the Nordic mainland. When we refer to the "Nordic"
countries in this book, we mean Denmark, Sweden, Norway, and
Finland, all of which countries faced the threat of being overrun by
dictatorships.

The book itself is a product of Nordic cooperation. It was made
possible by a grant from one of the institutions of Nordic cooperation, *Nordisk Kulturfond* (Nordic Cultural Fund). The *Oberst
Gustav Packalens Mindefond* (Colonel Gustav Packalen Memorial
Fund) contributed to the cost of translation. These grants were
given to and have been administered by *Udgiverselskab for Danmarks
Nyeste Historie* (Society for Contemporary Danish History).

Copenhagen 1983
Henrik S. Nissen

Contents

The Nordic Societies   3
  · Henrik S. Nissen

The Race for Northern Europe, September 1939-June 1940   53
  Martti Häikiö

Adjusting to German Domination   98
  Henrik S. Nissen

Operation Barbarossa and the Nordic Countries   139
  Ohto Manninen

The Beginnings of the Resistance Movement   182
  Ole Kristian Grimnes

Scandinavia and the Turn of the Tide   221
  Aage Trommer

Adjusting to Allied Victory   279
  Berit Nøkleby

Winning the Peace: Vision and Disappointment
  in Nordic Security Policy, 1945-49   324
  Karl Molin

Bibliographical Note   385

Index   401

MAPS

Denmark

Disposition of German troops in Denmark, 1 June 1944   226

Finland

Distribution of areas according to the 1939 treaty between the
Soviet Union and the Kuusinen government   68

Soviet troop concentrations and planned offensives before the
Winter War   70

Distribution of areas according to the Treaty of Moscow,
12 March 1940   87

The Finnish front, 1941-44   155

Fenno-Russian front lines in 1944   282

Russian advances in 1944   283

The war against the Germans in Lappland, 1944-45   287

Finnish boundaries before and after World War II   316

Norway

The German attack on Norway and Denmark, 1940   93

Norway's merchant marine   206

Disposition of German troops in Norway, 22 June 1944   247

Scandinavia during the Second World War

The Nordic Societies

by Henrik S. Nissen

During the Second World War Norway fought on the side of the Allies; Sweden remained neutral; Finland was at war with the Soviet Union in association with Germany; and Denmark, like Norway, was occupied by Germany, but claimed nevertheless a kind of neutral or at least nonbelligerent status. Despite the dramatic differences in the destinies of the four Nordic countries, there still exists a conviction in the rest of the world that the four countries constitute merely one society, oddly divided into four states.

This conviction has been supported by the governments of the four countries, which have repeatedly emphasized the existence of Nordic cooperation and a common Nordic culture. They did so before the war; they did so during the war insofar as it was politically feasible; and they did so again after the war, when cooperation was institutionalized, even though the attempt to form a neutral defensive alliance among the three Scandinavian kingdoms failed in 1948. This perseverance of the Nordic governments was not just a reflection of an old romantic dream about a union of the separated Nordic peoples. For each of the countries there have been political advantages to be gained from promoting the image of an informal though genuine alliance. At least the great powers were led to believe that applying severe pressure on one of the four Nordic countries would inevitably cause the other three to lose all sympathy for the aggressor. The great powers concerned were able to cope with this loss, because the Nordic states, when put to the test, hardly ever came to each other's assistance to any measurable degree. In their foreign policies, the Nordic countries have always acted contrary to the Napoleonic doctrine: they have been united on the march, separated in battle.

Given the varying destinies of the Nordic countries in 1939-45, what sense is there in treating the wartime histories of these four countries in one book, especially one that strives for an integrated presentation instead of just collecting four different stories under one cover? To answer this question, we must look at some of the reasons why the surrounding world believes there is uniformity, if not unity, among the Nordic countries. Presumably the idea was not created solely by the propaganda of solidarity presented by the four governments.

The geographical position of the Nordic countries, of course, is one factor that contributes to the impression of uniformity. The Scandinavian peoples are neighbors, situated between $4°30'$ and $32°49'$ eastern longitude and between $54°34'$ and well above $71°11'$ northern latitude. From our point of view, however, there are other geographical facts that are more important. Denmark has a common border with Germany, a border which on the eve of the Second World War was the only uncontested Versailles-frontier of the Third *Reich*. Finland borders on the Soviet Union and had won its independence from Russian rule during the years of the Bolshevik revolution. Finland's frontier of 1939 was at one point only twenty-five miles from Leningrad. Norway forms the northeastern coast of the Atlantic and was therefore in terms of blockade-warfare of strategic naval importance. The economy of the country was largely dependent on shipping, a fact that would make it a catastrophe to be involved in a war against Great Britain. Sweden, of course, took a certain interest in the maintenance of the independence of its Nordic neighbors, since they constituted a ring of buffer states around the Swedish kingdom. Since the four small countries are neighbors, their destinies in the great-power conflict were strongly intermingled; a crisis for one country could, and did, have dangerous repercussions for the others. However, the bare facts of geography also forced them to pursue different foreign policies.

Another reason for regarding the Nordic states as one society is that the languages of the three Scandinavian kingdoms are so similar that they can be thought of as three related dialects. The languages differ enough to make the mass media of each country unused if not unusable in the other two. The dictionaries between the three languages are few, and for good reason thin. They are not used much, but misunderstandings by untrained listeners and readers are frequent.

If not in other ways, then at least in their language the Finns are unique among the Nordic peoples. Their language has nothing whatsoever in common with those of their north Germanic and Slavic neighbors. There is a Swedish-speaking minority, but this fact has been a cause of problems in Finnish domestic politics rather than a cultural bridge to Scandinavia. The Swedish-speaking minority has traditionally been situated mainly in the western and southern coastal regions of Finland, and once formed an upper class of landowners and academics.

Historical Overview of the Nordic States

Norway

Norway had been under the Danish crown for more than 400 years, from the late fourteenth century until 1814. During that time the Norwegian landed nobility had vanished and had not been replaced by a Danish aristocracy. This had given rise to a large stratum of well-situated freeholders in Norwegian agriculture. In the last hundred years before the separation from Denmark, the administration of Norway had been in the hands of a class of high officials who were Norwegian by birth. These officials, like the clergy, had obtained degrees from the University of Copenhagen and mixed socially with the rising bourgeois class of well-to-do timber merchants and shipowners.

At the end of the Napoleonic Wars, in the later stages of which the Danish-Norwegian kingdom had sided with France, the Danish king was forced to cede Norway to Sweden. In Sweden one of Napoleon's marshals, Bernadotte, was chosen as crown prince and elegantly turned the foreign policy of his new country against his previous master.

The Danish crown prince, Christian, who was viceroy in Norway, met in May 1814 in Eidsvold with representatives of the Norwegian propertied classes and set up a Norwegian constitution, which was at that time one of the most democratic in the world. Whatever the motives behind this act, the attempt in this way to establish Norwegian independence did not fully succeed. Norway was united with Sweden for almost one hundred years, and its foreign policy

was conducted from Stockholm. The Eidsvold constitution nevertheless remained in force and became both a pillar of Norwegian
independence and a symbol of Norwegian patriotic aspirations.
  The later decades of the nineteenth century, the Norwegian parliament, *Stortinget,* became the scene of a prolonged struggle. On
one side was the cabinet, supported by the crown (i.e., the Swedish
king) and the minority party, *Høyre* (Right); on the other side was
the majority party, *Venstre* (Left). The latter eventually succeeded
in establishing a true parliamentary government (i.e., the cabinet in
Christiania, later Oslo, became responsible to parliament). On this
basis, Norway in 1905 unilaterally declared the union with Sweden
to be dissolved. A Danish prince became king of Norway after a
referendum. Under the name of Haakon VII he was still king during
the Second World War.

Finland

  Finland had belonged to the Swedish crown since the beginning
of the Middle Ages. This very sparsely populated country lagged far
behind the other parts of Scandinavia in economic development. In
many respects, however, it followed the same development as
Sweden. After the introduction of Christianity, Finland became a
part of the Swedish archbishopric of the Church of Rome, forming
a portion of the frontier of western Europe in relation to the Greek
Orthodox Church. The Lutheran reformation in Sweden during the
sixteenth century also extended to Finland.
  The geographical position of Finland made it the regular battlefield in Russo-Swedish wars, and its border with Russia repeatedly
shifted backward and forward during the centuries. After the end of
Sweden's period as a great power at the beginning of the eighteenth
century, Finland took part in the rudimentary parliamentary experi-
ments of the Diet of Four Estates, which ruled Sweden and Finland
for the greater part of the century. The shift in the balance of power
in the Baltic made itself felt at last in 1809, when Sweden handed
over Finland to the Russian tsar. Finland was not incorporated into
Russia but formed a grand duchy directly under the tsar. The Finnish
constitution including the diet was guaranteed by the tsar, and even
though this left the executive power exclusively in the hands of the
grand duke, it formed a legalistic shield against russification.
  Like the other Nordic countries, Finland experienced a revival of
nationalism during the nineteenth century. It did not give rise to

demands for national independence, since attention was focused on the Finnish language. In administration, in the courts, and in all schools above the grammar-school level, the language used was Swedish, which was not understood by about 90% of the population. Since the middle of the nineteenth century, language has been a nearly constant issue in politics, and it has occupied a prominent place in Finnish history books.

It was only during the last years of the nineteenth century and until the achievement of Finnish independence that the question of the preservation of the country's autonomy overshadowed (and partly mingled with) the internal strife over language. The brutal policy of russification during these years transformed the movement for national independence from the concern of a small group of romantic academics into a mass movement. In 1906, after the Russian defeat by Japan, the tsar was obliged for a short time to accede to Finnish demands for a restoration of autonomy and for constitutional reform. The antiquated four-estate diet was replaced by a unicameral parliament based on universal and equal suffrage (for women as well as men). Perhaps the most remarkable feature of the new parliament was that the Labor party—supported by smallholders and workers in the industries that were only now beginning to appear—won eighty of the 200 seats. But the Russian government soon reverted to its former policy of repression. Some of the leading members of the movement for independence were imprisoned and others were exiled.

In the turmoil of the Russian and Bolshevik revolutions Finland won total independence. It was at once flung into a civil war between Reds and Whites. The Whites were led by Carl Gustav Mannerheim, who had served as a general in the Russian army. They won a quick victory and were helped by a German army corps, whereas some Russian soldiers—the number is in dispute—stationed in Finland fought on the Red side. Nearly every village in Finland had its victims of either Red or White terror—or both. The mutual accusations have made these years a very delicate subject in Finnish historiography, and even the name of the struggle, "civil war" or "war of liberation," is in dispute.

There were plans for a monarchical form of government as late as the autumn of 1918, when partly out of *Staatsraisson* and partly out of gratitude toward the German *Reich* the crown was offered to a German prince. However, the fortunes of war shifted and a republican constitution, which was thought to be more agreeable to the western great powers, was adopted. After the civil war the desire for a strong central authority was perhaps the reason for the rather strong presidency that was introduced. The Finnish presidency represents something of a middle ground between the American executive and the powerless western European head of state. Finland's president—according to the constitution—was to be indirectly elected by universal suffrage. He possessed a suspensive veto over legislation, but the constitution stated that the government was parliamentary, the supreme authority resting with the people as represented in parliament, for which elections were to be held by the method of proportional representation. In other respects, the constitutional laws of independent Finland were not very different from the provisions of 1906.

The consequences of the civil war included the presence of a group of exiled communists in the Soviet Union and the existence of a sense of gratitude toward Germany among the Finnish upper class, but the wounds of the civil war were either suppressed or healed to an astonishing degree in the two following decades. The deviations in Finnish politics from liberal and pluralistic democracy demonstrated the difference between Finland and the other Nordic countries, as when the camouflaged Communist party was outlawed in 1930 or during the early thirties when the violence of the Lapua movement (semi-fascist and extreme rightist) was widely sanctioned.

Denmark

The extent of the lands ruled by the Danish crown has progressively diminished through the centuries. In the middle of the seventeenth century the southern part of the Scandinavian peninsula was ceded to Sweden. As already mentioned, the union with Norway was dissolved after the Napoleonic Wars. In 1864 Bismarck's Prussia solved in its own way its dispute with Denmark over possession of Holstein and Schleswig, two small German duchies located on Denmark's southern border and hitherto ruled by the Danish king. The war of 1864 was the last time Denmark resorted to armed defense, undoubtedly overestimating the fighting effectiveness of the Danish army and relying on assistance from the great powers or from Sweden-Norway. The war ended in defeat for Denmark. As a result, Bismarck was able to incorporate both duchies into the emerging German *Reich*. This was a tremendous blow to the Danish monarchy.

One-third of its population and the part of the country with the most highly developed economy had been lost, and the ability of the country to preserve its existence as a sovereign state was placed in jeopardy.

The population in the northern half of Schleswig was predominantly Danish, and for the next forty years it sustained a national struggle in spite of the seeming hopelessness of its cause. Public opinion in Denmark supported this cause, but for reasons of security the Danish government had to adopt a very cautious attitude toward the German *Reich*. After the First World War, in which Denmark had been able to remain neutral by striking a subtle balance between belligerent pressures, the northern part of Schleswig was returned to Denmark after a referendum, leaving only small populations of national minorities on both sides of the new frontier. Thus Denmark, like the other three Nordic countries, became a state inhabited by essentially one nationality. The Schleswig settlement was part of the Versailles Treaty, and in view of the German attitude toward that peace treaty, the Danish government constantly feared that Germany would put in a claim to have it revised.

In the conduct of Denmark's foreign policy, there was one basic fact to be considered: the independence of the country was at the discretion of the German army. As long as Germany could be persuaded that an independent Denmark was in its own interests or at least not contrary to them, Denmark could remain tranquil. The chances of avoiding a German attack and occupation (or incorporation) did not depend on the Danish armed forces and could not be secured by an alliance with any other great power, much less by an alliance with the other Nordic countries. From 1871, when German dominance after the defeat of France was evident, to the end of the Second World War this knowledge of the vulnerability to German attack was the basis of the security policy of the different governments in Denmark; the weakness of Germany right after the First World War hardly caused any interruption in this attitude. The sometimes agitated controversies in Danish politics regarding the size of the armed forces were not caused by disagreement about the inability of the country to defend itself against a German attack. The question was what size and what sort of armed forces were best suited to preserve neutrality, that is, to secure the acceptance or at least toleration of Danish neutrality by Germany and—of secondary importance—by the other great powers.

Far out in the Atlantic, the Faroe Islands, Greenland, and Iceland were still politically more or less connected with Denmark. The Faroes were legally a county, but had their own legislative assembly, which had some authority over the internal affairs of the islands. A growing number of Faroe Islanders wanted national independence, but they did not constitute a majority among the voters. Danish possession of the colony of Greenland had been acknowledged by the United States when Denmark sold its West Indian islands during the First World War, and although Danish sovereignty over eastern Greenland had been contested by Norway at the beginning of the thirties, it had been confirmed by the international court at the Hague. The tiny population of Eskimoes was shielded in a rather paternalist way from the hazards of modernization, while the strategic importance of the huge island had hardly been acknowledged when the war broke out in 1939. Iceland had long been developing toward total independence. Although the Danish king had sovereignty over Iceland, this was the only bond that existed between the two countries, and it was just a question of time before this last tie would be broken. In the middle of the war Iceland took the matter into its own hands and became an independent republic.

Sweden

From what has been said in the previous pages, it is evident that the history of Swedish foreign policy cannot be written without constant reference to the three neighboring countries. Despite the gradual contraction of Sweden's boundaries after it fell from its position as the dominant power in the Baltic in the first decades of the eighteenth century, despite the cession of Finland a hundred years later, and despite the dissolution of the union with Norway still another hundred years later, Sweden remained the largest of the Nordic countries in area as well as in population.

The wars of the period when Sweden had been a great power had been fought outside Sweden proper, and since the Napoleonic Wars the country has managed to remain neutral. Sweden's geographical position was undoubtedly the main reason for the country's good fortune in this respect, and the armed forces of the country have never been really put to the test. Disputes over defense policy in Sweden have concerned the question of how and where to defend the country—whether to meet the enemy at the border or to adopt scorched-earth tactics and concentrate the defense of the country on one or a few fortresses. During times of crisis the question has been asked whether the right place to meet an enemy was on the borders of Sweden's Nordic neighbors, in 1864 on the southern border of Denmark and in 1939-40 on the eastern border of Finland. The answer of Swedish policymakers responsible for the security of their country has been that it was not. Sweden has therefore been shielded from direct confrontation with any of the great powers of Europe, and its neighbors have functioned as buffer states.

Before we go a little deeper into the political systems of the four countries, we shall examine some of the socioeconomic features that might be said to be the basis for and result of political developments.

The Economic Structure

The following pages will not attempt to provide a complete description of economic conditions in the Nordic countries during the 1930s. Some essential information will be given for the benefit of the reader who knows little about the Nordic countries, but the account will concentrate on features that were significant during the Second World War. The question of similarities and differences between the four countries will be central to the discussion, and comparisons with other countries will also be drawn occasionally.

A number of observations must be made before we proceed further. It is always difficult to obtain comparable statistics from different countries. Categories and methods of calculation vary from country to country, and attempts to fit one country's statistics into categories that are used in another unfortunately tend only to increase the degree of error. In this respect, the statistics produced by the four Nordic states during the 1930s are no exception. Accordingly, the data presented on the following pages do not necessarily provide a more precise picture of economic conditions than purely verbal statements do.

The population of the Nordic countries, like that of the rest of western Europe, grew rapidly during the nineteenth century. By the time of the Second World War their populations had reached the following levels:

Denmark	3.8 million (86.3 per square kilometer)
Finland	3.6 million (9.9 per square kilometer)
Norway	2.9 million (9 per square kilometer)
Sweden	6.3 million (13.9 per square kilometer)

In the course of the second half of the nineteenth century the Nordic countries had increasingly become a part of the world economy. The agrarian subsistence economy had given way to production for the market, and this development had been accompanied, as in other countries, by growing prosperity. The number of people employed in nonagrarian occupations clearly reflected this trend, but the figures also show that agriculture continued to play a very important role in the economies of the Nordic states.

Employment in the Most Important Occupations in 1940
(as a Percentage of the Total Employed Population)

Country	Agricultural, Forestry, and Fishing	Industry and Mining	Commerce and Transport
Denmark	28	32	20
Finland	58	18	6
Norway[a]	37	25	22
Sweden	25	37	21

[a]There was no census in Norway in 1940, so the figures for Norway are taken from 1930.

Agriculture and Forestry

In Norway, Sweden, and Finland, smallholders commonly worked also in the timber and transport industries, particularly during the winter months. Moreover, in Norway some smallholders were also engaged in fishing as a secondary economic activity. However, in Denmark farming was an exclusive and specialized activity, as is apparent from the quite decisive contribution to the Danish economy made by the 28% of the working population that was employed in agriculture. In comparison with the other Nordic countries, the level of productivity in Danish agriculture was especially high.

Agriculture in the Nordic countries was predominantly based on freehold farming. There were a considerable number of tenant farmers in Sweden and Finland, but they had increasingly obtained security of tenure through legislation. The use of paid agricultural laborers was small and was even declining during the interwar period. The total area under cultivation was divided between 285,000 holdings in Finland, 298,000 in Norway, 428,000 in Sweden, and 205,000 in Denmark. As is shown by the accompanying table, land was distributed quite equally among the farming population.

Whereas smallholders in Norway, Sweden, and Finland were to a considerable degree obliged, as we have seen, to engage in nonagrarian

Distribution of Land around 1930 According to the Size of Holdings

Country	Less than 10 Hectares	10-50 Hectares	50-100 Hectares	100 Hectares and Above
Denmark	16.5%	63.2%	10.7%	9.6%
Finland	33.4	52.1	8.4	6.1
Norway	62.2	35.5	1.9	0.4
Sweden	34.5	45.5	9.4	10.6

work for part of the year, a large proportion of Danish farms that were smaller than ten hectares were quite capable of supporting a family. This was partly because the yield per acre was somewhat higher in Denmark and partly because a portion of the production of smallholdings in Denmark was based on purchasing rather than growing fodder.

The existence of many small independent holdings was to some extent the result of deliberate political decisions, especially in Finland, where extensive land reforms had been carried out after the civil war. One consequence of this equal distribution of land was that there was no economically (or politically) significant landowning aristocracy in any of the Nordic countries.

During this period Norway and Sweden were developing toward self-sufficiency in the production of food but did not have much of a surplus for export; the export of agricultural produce still played a role in the Finnish Economy and the economic importance of agricultural exports was extremely great in the case of Denmark. The mechanization of agriculture had to some degree begun, but tractors were still so uncommon that they do not figure in the statistics. A characteristic feature of agriculture in the Nordic countries, and once again especially in Denmark, was the dominance of cooperative dairies and slaughterhouses for the processing and sale of agricultural produce. It is noteworthy that scientific advances in agriculture were brought into practical use with remarkable speed.

Some of the conditions that have been emphasized in the preceding paragraphs played a special role during the Second World War. First, strict food rationing would be difficult to administer and control because of the existence of many independent holdings, each of which would be able to sell its produce on the black market. Second, the ability of Danish agriculture to act as a large-scale supplier of animal fats (butter and bacon) depended on the importation of feedstuffs and fertilizers. This dependence was used, not to say exaggerated, in Denmark's wartime trade negotiations with the belligerents before the German occupation of the country, since it provided an argument for allowing Danish trade to pass through the blockade lines established by Britain and Germany.

Forestry played an especially important role in the economies of Norway, Sweden, and Finland. Among these three countries, the proportion of processed timber exports was highest in Norway and lowest in Finland. The pattern of ownership of the very large forest areas in the three countries (about 58 million hectares) explains why they did not distinguish between agriculture and forestry in their employment statistics.

	Publicly Owned Areas	Areas Owned by Private Parties Who Also Engaged in Agriculture	Areas Owned by Joint Stock Companies Whose Shares Were Held by Individuals or the State
Finland	41.5%	51.0%	7.5%
Norway	20.3	70.0	9.0
Sweden	23.8	27.1	49.1

The three countries jointly provided over 30% of world exports of sawn timber, 85% of wood pulp, 71% of cellulose, and 27% of paper.

Industry

Seen in terms of the proportion of the working population that it employed (as shown in the table on p. 12), industry was on its way to becoming the leading economic activity in the Nordic countries. In Denmark and Norway just under, and in Sweden just over, a third of the working population was employed in industry. The corresponding figure for Finland was only 18%. The various measures taken by the Nordic governments to combat the depression of the 1930s had contributed to the emergence of new, usually small, industrial enterprises that required little capital and employed rather few workers.

Sweden was the most industrialized of the Nordic countries. Two of every three industrial workers in Sweden were employed in enterprises that had more than fifty workers. Danish and Norwegian statistics did not use the same categories as their Swedish counterparts, but a rough estimate of the corresponding ratio for these two countries would be just under one in three industrial workers. By comparison, in the United States 83.2% of industrial workers were employed in enterprises with more than fifty workers.

The level of industrial productivity was similar in the three Scandinavian kingdoms, while Finland lagged somewhat behind. In 1935 workers in the most important branches of industry were producing goods valued at well over £600 (calculated in pounds sterling) ($2,940) per person per year in Norway and Sweden, whereas the corresponding figures for Denmark and Finland were respectively over £100 ($490) more and over £100 ($490) less. The data on the food industry are responsible for the high figure in the case of Denmark, since the fact that the raw materials constitute a very high proportion of the value of the finished product was not taken into account in the statistical calculations. If instead only the metal industry is examined, the figures are quite different. In Sweden each worker in the metal industry produced goods valued at about £530 ($2,597) per year, whereas the figures for Denmark, Norway, and Finland were about £500 ($2,450), £440 ($2,156), and £250 ($1,225) respectively. The figures for Finland are somewhat misleading: When converting the Finnish mark into other currencies, it was not taken into account that the former was greatly undervalued at this time. The figures therefore tend to give an excessively gloomy picture of economic conditions in Finland, but it is nonetheless clear that Finland was the least prosperous and economically the least developed of the Nordic countries.

The relative importance of the main branches of industry can be seen in the accompanying table, from which the handicrafts have been excluded. The figures show that a considerable proportion of industry was still based on the processing of the natural products of forestry and agriculture. However, the other branches of industry were winning ground during the interwar period, in part because of the protection afforded by import regulations and other measures taken by the state. In consequence, the new industries concentrated on supplying the home market to a greater extent than did the long-established ones, and the proportion of industrial production that was exported was declining in all four countries. Just before the Second World War Denmark exported only 12% of its industrial production and the corresponding figures for Finland, Norway, and Sweden were 40%, 42%, and 25% respectively. These figures are somewhat misleading, since they do not include Denmark's processed agricultural produce, while they do include processed timber products of the other three countries.

Distribution of Workers and Value of Goods in the Main Branches of Industry in 1935

Country and Industry	No. of Workers as % of Total Industrial Labor Force	Value of Goods Produced as % of Value of Total Industrial Production
Denmark		
Food industry[a]	20	43
Metal industry	29	26
Textile and clothing industry	20	10
Chemical industry	14	16
Finland		
Timber and paper industry	40	60
Metal and mining industry	18	14
Textile and clothing industry	17	12
Norway		
Metal and mining industry	30	26
Timber and paper industry	20	20
Textile and clothing industry	19	13
Sweden		
Metal and mining industry	34	30
Timber and paper industry	24	20
Textile and clothing industry	15	11

[a]The misleading nature of the data on the Danish food industry (see text) should be borne in mind in this context. For example, if the food industry is excluded, the figures would show that the metal industry employed 35% of the industrial labor force and accounted for 33% of the value of total industrial production.

The ability and willingness of industry to change its pattern of production and to innovate became an important factor in the survival of the economies of the Nordic states when the latter were cut off from the West, at first partially and then after 9 April 1940 almost completely.

Foreign Trade

The exports of the Nordic countries were still dominated by individual industries or products. Raw materials used in industry constituted an even greater part of their imports, but imports of finished products for domestic consumption were still important, despite the economic crisis and the growth of industrial production for the home market. The main exports of all the Nordic countries were products connected with their natural resources: agriculture, forestry, and mining. However, it would be misleading to compare their economic circumstances with those of the developing countries after the Second World War, since a growing proportion of these exports was made up of processed goods: bacon and butter instead of grain, machinery instead of iron ore, cellulose instead of timber.

Small countries with relatively highly developed economies generally support a fairly extensive foreign trade, and the Nordic states were no exception. Despite the growing level of self-sufficiency that was mentioned earlier, they were dependent on their imports and exports. It is difficult to state precisely the importance of foreign trade for the national economy, but some comparisons with other

Imports and Exports in 1938

Imports of Individual Products as % of Total Imports:			
Denmark	raw materials	fuel	finished goods
	46	15	39
Finland	raw materials and capital goods	foodstuffs	finished goods
	64	14	22
Norway	raw materials	ships and machinery	finished goods
	40	27	33
Sweden	raw materials	capital goods	finished goods
	60	11	29
Exports of Individual Products as % of Total Exports:			
Denmark	agricultural goods		industrial goods
	73		24
Finland	timber and paper		agricultural goods
	82		8
Norway	timber and paper	fish	agricultural goods
	24	19	8
Sweden	mining & metal ind.		timber and paper
	38		30

Value of Imports and Exports in 1936 (Calculated at the 1936 Rate of Exchange)

Country	Imports		Exports	
	Thous. of Pounds	Thous. of Dollars	Thous. of Pounds	Thous. of Dollars
Denmark	£66,330	$325,017	£61,600	$301,840
Finland	28,057	137,479	31,541	154,551
Norway	46,582	228,282	34,422	168,668
Sweden	84,175	412,458	85,619	419,553

countries will give an indication of this. If the figures for exports in 1936 are divided by the number of inhabitants, the value (in pounds sterling and U.S. dollars, at the 1936 rate of exchange) of exports from the Nordic countries per inhabitant is as follows:

Denmark	£16.6	$81.34
Finland	8.5	41.65

Norway	11.9	58.31
Sweden	13.6	66.64

The corresponding figures for five other countries are:

Netherlands	£11.2	$54.88
Czechoslovakia	4.2	20.58
Britain	9.4	46.06
Germany	5.8	28.42
United States	3.8	18.62

It is not only the extent of foreign trade that is significant here. A still more decisive factor was the identity of the Nordic countries' trading partners. Another consideration that had to be taken into account, especially during the war (when foreign trade became a question of obtaining supplies rather than selling exports), was that commerce was an aspect of neutrality policy. It is easy to see from

Exports in 1935 to the Nordic Countries' Most
Important Customers (as a Percentage of Total Exports)

Exporter	Britain	Germany	United States	Other Nordic Countries
Denmark	52	20	0.8	10
Finland	47	9	9	10
Norway	28	13	10	14
Sweden	25	14	12	15

Imports in 1935 from the Nordic Countries'
Most Important Suppliers (as a Percentage of Total Imports)

Importer	Britain	Germany	United States	Other Nordic Countries
Denmark	36	22	5	9
Finland	24	20	7	17
Norway	23	17	9	18
Sweden	19	24	13	11

the accompanying tables why the Nordic countries experienced problems during the first phase of the war in balancing between British demands that they should not breach the Allied blockade of Germany and German demands that they should. However, their problems increased greatly once the war spread to Scandinavia after

9 April 1940; the Nordic countries were then cut off from between a third and a half of their traditional foreign trade.

Military security was therefore not the only consideration that impelled the Nordic states to pursue a policy of neutrality. If they were forced to choose sides, and in this situation could also take their economic requirements into account, Norway would be the only Nordic state whose economic structure pointed the country in the same direction as did its defense considerations. Since 41% of Norway's total earnings of foreign exchange were provided by the Norwegian merchant marine on its overseas journeys, the German conquest of the Country meant that the Norwegian government-in-exile in London enjoyed an independent financial foundation, while Norway itself experienced severe economic and social problems.

The economic structure of the Nordic countries made them vulnerable to the shocks and pressures of wartime. The importance of foreign trade for their economies placed them in a weak negotiating position in relation to Germany once they had been cut off from commercial contact with the West. Their economies had advanced so far beyond the subsistence level that their governments found it necessary to strive to maintain normal economic activity, i.e., to obtain raw materials and to find markets for domestic products. However, the economic structure of the Nordic states also conferred some advantages on them in wartime. They disposed over a productive apparatus which it might serve German interests to preserve, and their industrial structure was such that it was relatively easy to convert a part of the productive apparatus to the manufacture of goods that could no longer be imported.

The Distribution of Wealth

Between the world wars the four Nordic countries were developing at a fairly even tempo, with Finland bringing up the rear, toward

National Income in 1929 and 1938 (Calculated at the 1929 Rate of Exchange)

Country	1929		1938	
	Millions of Pounds	Millions of Dollars	Millions of Pounds	Millions of Dollars
Denmark	£203	$988	£346	$1,198
Finland	85	414	125	609
Norway	143	696	187	910
Sweden	430	2,094	541	2,634

becoming relatively prosperous societies, comparable in this respect to the other countries of northwestern Europe. This is clear from the figures for national income in the last year before the Great Depression and in the last year before the Second World War. (See table on p. 19.)

For comparative purposes, here are the 1929 figures on the annual income per inhabitant for the Nordic and certain other western European countries:

Denmark	£58	$282
Finland	25	122
Norway	51	248
Sweden	70	340
Britain	87	423
Netherlands	61	297
France	48	234

As with most such tabulations, these figures are somewhat misleading. For example, the cost of living was lower in Finland than in the other countries, and an estimate of real incomes (if one were possible) would therefore reduce the difference. The statistics on national income likewise present difficulties, but there can hardly be any doubt that in the Nordic countries differences in income had been declining, albeit slowly, since around the turn of the century.

In 1936 about a third of the population in Denmark (1.2 million people) were required to pay income tax, that is to say received an annual income of more than 800 Danish *kroner* ($163). The lowest quarter of taxable income in Denmark was earned by just over half (56.6%) of the taxpaying population. The second, third, and fourth quarters of taxable income were earned by 24.4%, 14%, and 5% of taxpayers respectively. One should not rely too heavily on these figures to gauge the level of equality in Denmark, since they do not necessarily provide a precise accounting of the earnings of a population. (It is a well-known fact that not everyone who should be paying taxes does so.) Moreover, there may, of course, have been dramatic differences in income and standard of living among the 56.6% of taxpayers who constitute the least prosperous group among those paying income tax. On the other hand, the redistributive effects of social welfare are reflected only to a limited extent in the figures, which do not include the consequences of the progressive income tax.

In Finland only 371,000 individuals (that is, heads of family) earned enough ($22) to pay income tax. Of these, 52.3% had earnings in the lowest tax bracket and 6.4% in the second-lowest.

The consumption of certain items of food is one indicator of the level of equality in a society, since there are limits to the degree to which the rich can eat more than the poor. As can be seen from the accompanying table, the level of consumption was about the same in Britain as in the Nordic countries, and this indicates that the distribution of wealth was less equitable in Britain than in the Nordic states, since income per inhabitant was considerable higher in the former than in the latter. This conclusion is, of course, valid only if it is assumed that consumption would have been greater if the less well-off had had more money. The pattern of consumption during the postwar years of growing prosperity suggests that this assumption is indeed sound. Taken as a whole, these figures therefore suggest that there was a more equal distribution of incomes in the Nordic states than in, for example, Britain.

Consumption of Selected Foodstuffs and Tobacco in 1934 in Pounds per Inhabitant

Country	Milk[a]	Meat	Sugar	Coffee	Tobacco
Britain	98	139	94	1	3
France	70	75	48	9	3
Netherlands	83	91[b]	55	8	7
Denmark	102	145	113	15	5
Finland	123	63[d]	50	11	2
Norway	100[c]	77	61	13	2
Sweden	143[c]	82[d]	89	16	3

[a]Milk includes cream, butter, and cheese in terms of gallons of milk. Figures for Britain exclude Northern Ireland.
[b]Average for the years 1930-33.
[c]Relates to the year 1933.
[d]Rough estimate, based on the average for the years 1932-33.

The same picture is by and large presented by the figures for mortality and average life expectancy, which provide a serviceable measuring rod for the general level of health in a country.

	Average Life Expectancy (1931-35)	Mortality[a] (average for 1931-38)
Denmark	62.8 years	10.8 deaths
Finland	52.9	13.4
Norway	62.4	10.3
Sweden	61.1	11.7

Britain	61.6
France	56.7
Netherlands	62.7
United States	61.1

aNumber of deaths per year for each 1,000 people.

This sketch of the economic structure of the Nordic countries shows that on the whole they had been able to reach and maintain an economic level comparable to that in the rest of western Europe. It also shows that the distribution of incomes was such that wealth had not been accumulated in only a few hands and that the bulk of the population had shared in the growing prosperity. In the long term, the increase in national wealth that had occurred since the end of the nineteenth century had been divided proportionately among the different income groups and a gradual, albeit slow and modest, decline in economic inequality had taken place. This meant that the great majority of the population had reached a level of income and a standard of living that would previously have been regarded as middle class.

It is clear that the development of a state social welfare system helped prevent the economic depression of the 1930s from pushing any significant proportion of the population down to the starvation level. Social security legislation was, of course, not a new phenomenon, but during the economic crisis a far greater number of people than before became eligible for social welfare assistance. However, there was one new feature in the situation that was of essential significance. The public increasingly believed not only that the state had a responsibility to help those who were in real need because of age, sickness, or unemployment, but also that it was the citizen's right to receive assistance because such misfortunes were not self-inflicted. It was on this basis that the political struggles for the passage of social measures were fought in the 1930s.

The labor movement was so strong in Denmark, Norway, and Sweden that it largely succeeded in maintaining the real incomes of its members during the depression. However, workers who were not organized into trade unions, especially laborers in agriculture and forestry, were hit hard by the depression since they were exposed more than others to pressure over wages and a decline in their real incomes. Those who were unemployed for a long time also did not benefit from the stability of wages, and there was pressure from some nonsocialists who believed in the old liberal dogma that a decline in wages might reduce unemployment.

On the whole, despite state intervention and various forms of social security, unemployment was widespread, and during the worst years of the depression the percentage of unemployed workers in the Nordic countries was among the highest in Europe. In Denmark and Norway unemployment remained alarmingly high for some time after the outbreak of war. Sweden fared considerably better, probably more because of its economic structure and its pattern of production than because of its tentative attempts to pursue Keynesian economic policies. The corresponding Finnish statistics are very uncertain, partly because the proportion of Finnish workers who were organized was low, but there is reason to believe that unemployment started to decline at a somewhat earlier stage in Finland than in Denmark and Norway and that Finland generally recovered more quickly from the economic crisis.

Average Annual Unemployment as a Percentage of Organized Labor

Year	Denmark	Norway	Sweden
1932	31.7	30.8	22.4
1933	28.8	33.4	23.3
1934	22.1	30.7	18.0
1935	19.7	25.3	15.0
1936	19.3	18.8	12.7
1937	21.9	20.0	10.8
1938	21.4	22.0	10.9
1939	18.4	18.3	9.2

Unemployment did not affect all sections of the population or the economy with equal severity. The young and the old suffered most and women more than men, there being a great deal of so-called concealed unemployment among women. Unemployment was higher in remote areas than in urban centers; some occupations were severely affected, others almost not at all or only briefly; and the effects of seasonal fluctuations varied from place to place.

There is some evidence that the very high levels of unemployment in the Nordic countries were in large part due to the fact that their whole economies were involved in a process of structural change and that the depression both accelerated these changes and aggravated their social consequences.

Primarily because of their social policies, the Nordic countries were already described in the 1930s as "laboratories of the welfare state." This description is accurate since much political activity was directed at developing a social security system and at removing the idea of charity from its administration. However, the Nordic countries were class societies in the sense that private ownership of the means of production predominated and the majority of the population lived by selling their labor to those who could profit through buying it. They were class societies in the sense that some enjoyed an abundance while others suffered from want, even if hunger and cold were largely avoided. And they were class societies in the sense that a few enjoyed the lion's share of the cultural advantages offered by society. As in the rest of western Europe, compulsory universal education had long been in operation, and there was also a strong tradition of voluntary adult education. However, the social basis for the recruitment of students to a program of higher education, which was for all practical purposes free, had not changed much: it was still overwhelmingly the children of those with a university education who attended university themselves, and each year only about 5% of those leaving school went on to the university.

Nonetheless, there were two characteristics of the Nordic countries that did not fit in with the classical description of a capitalistic class society. First, there were strongly anticapitalist features in the ideology and the organization of production in the agricultural sector. Second, the social democratic workers' parties had achieved a position of power in the political leadership of these countries which had no parallel in other states.

The Political Structure

The Political Spectrum

Denmark, Norway, and Sweden were hereditary monarchies, whereas Finland, as we have seen, was a republic. In general, the citizens of the three Scandinavian countries believed that their heads of state enjoyed very little or no political influence. However, there had been quite recent examples of royal interventions for good or ill in politics.

The political system in all four countries was a multiparty parliamentary democracy. The cabinet exercised ultimate control over a formally apolitical central administration and enjoyed decisive influence over the introduction of new legislation. The cabinet was responsible to parliament, which was chosen in free elections by secret ballot and universal adult suffrage. In Denmark and Sweden

parliament (which was called the *Rigsdag* and the *Riksdag* respectively) was divided into two chambers, but by 1939 the upper chamber
had ceased to have the conservative effect on the passage of legislation that had originally been intended.

The driving forces in the parliaments of the four Nordic countries
were the political parties, which were based on national electors' organizations that enjoyed internal democracy. The party organizations
nominated their candidates for election, and party platforms had to
be submitted to and approved by party conferences at which the rank
and file membership was represented. The methods of election to
parliament in the Nordic countries were different forms of proportional representation. This ensured that the number of seats more or
less coincided with the percentage of votes a party received, although
this principle was somewhat modified in the interests of preserving
some connection between each member of parliament and a local
electoral district.

Local government was also directed and controlled by the elected
representatives of the people. The political parties were also active in
local government, and elections to local bodies were becoming increasingly politicized.

The electorates in the four Nordic countries were presented with a
political spectrum that ranged from nazi or quasi-nazi parties on the
extreme right to communist parties on the left. However, none of
these extremist parties had been able to acquire much political influence, and their electoral support was extremely limited. In Denmark the DNSAP, under the leadership of Frits Clausen, a physician,
received only 1.8% of the votes in 1939; in Norway National Unity
(*Nasjonal Samling*), led by Vidkun Quisling, obtained exactly the
same percentage of the popular vote in 1936; and in Sweden no nazi
party had won representation in the *Riksdag*. Once again, Finland
constitutes an exception. The fascist-inspired, ultranationalist IKL
(the Patriotic People's Movement) had had considerable influence,
especially at the beginning of the 1930s—more influence indeed than
was justified by its 8.3% of the votes. However, its influence was on
the wane during the last years before the war, and it obtained only
6.6% of the votes in the election of 1939.

Communists loyal to Moscow had also failed to make much impact on the political scene. At the last elections held before the
outbreak of war, they had gained only 2.4% and 0.3% of the votes
in Denmark and Norway respectively, whereas in Sweden the two

Results of the Last Elections Held in the Nordic States before World War II[a]

	Social Democrats	Radikale Venstre[c] (Radical Liberals)	Venstre (Liberals)	Konservative (Conservative)	Bondepartiet (Agrarian Party)
Denmark (1929)[b]	Social Democrats	Radikale Venstre[c] (Radical Liberals)	Venstre (Liberals)	Konservative (Conservative)	Bondepartiet (Agrarian Party)
% of popular vote	42.9	9.5	18.2	17.2	3
No. of seats	64	14	30	26	4
Norway (1936)[d]	Social Democrats (DNA)	Bondepartiet (Agrarian Party)	Venstre (Liberals)	Høyre (Conservative)	
% of popular vote	42.5	11.6	16	21.3	
No. of seats	70	18	23	36	
Sweden (1936)	Social Democrats (SAP)	Bondeförbundet (Agrarian Union)	Folkepartiet (Liberals)	Högern (Conservative)	
% of popular vote	45.9	14.3	12.9	17.6	
No. of seats[e]	112 (66)	36 (22)	27 (16)	44 (45)	
Finland (1939)	Social Democrats	Agrarian Union	Liberals	Conservative	Swedish People's Party
% of popular vote	39.8	28	3	13	8
No. of seats	85	56	6	25	18

[a]See text for data on nazi and communist parties.

[b]Other results: Retsforbundet (Justice Party, Georgists), 2% and 3 seats; Slesvigsk (German minority), 1% and 1 seat; National Samvirke (ultraconservative), 1.2% and no seats; Dansk Samling (Christian and antiparliamentarian), 0.5% and no seats.

[c]The names of the parties, especially in translation, do not always provide a very satisfactory guide to this position to the right or the left on the political spectrum. For example, the name of the Danish party, Radikale Venstre, means literally "Radical Left," but the party was not left-wing and was by no means radical. Its electoral support was drawn from the smallholders and from progressive liberals in the towns.

[d]Other results: Samfundspartiet (Social Party), 3.1% and 1 seat; Kristeligt Folkeparti (Christian People's Party, locally based), 1.4% and 2 seats.

[e]The figures in parentheses represent the number of seats held in the First (i.e., Upper) Chamber. When the two chambers were in disagreement, joint votes of both chambers were taken to resolve the issue.

communist parties together obtained 7.7% of the votes. Communist influence within the trade union movement was minimal, but during the worst years of the depression the Communists had been able to create a platform by organizing the unemployed. The Finnish Communist party was an exception. It had received 11-12% of the votes in the 1920s and had at that time considerable influence in the trade unions. In 1930, however, the party was prohibited, and very little is known about its activities in the 1930s. First the show trials in Moscow in the thirties, then the Nazi-Soviet pact, and finally the Russo-Finnish Winter War of 1939-40 made the Nordic people lose all sympathy for the Communists for a time.

There were no drastic changes during the 1930s in the degree of electoral support enjoyed by the large parties, but the political balance of power was so delicate that relatively small shifts could lead to fairly decisive alterations in the distribution of political influence. The belief that equal and universal suffrage would automatically provide an absolute majority for the social democrats had not been entirely abandoned by this time, but it had at least become clear that this would at best be a slow process. The Nordic social democratic parties were reformist, and the depression only intensified the electorate's demands for immediate results in the struggle against unemployment and for social amelioration. Parliamentary influence existed in order to be used, and, if possible, the reins of government too were to be captured and used, perhaps in cooperation with one or several of the nonsocialist parties.

The Labor Movement

At the outbreak of war, the social democrats were participating in the governments of all four Nordic countries. In 1929 the Danish Social Democrats formed a coalition with the Radical Liberals, with Thorvald Stauning as prime minister and Peter Munch of the Radical Liberals (*Radikale Venstre*) as foreign minister. In 1935 the two parties in the coalition also obtained a majority in *Landstinget* (the upper chamber of parliament), and they remained in power without any great changes in the composition of the ministry until 9 April 1940, the beginning of the German occupation, when the two main opposition parties were brought into the government. In Norway *Det Norske Arbeiderparti* (the Norwegian Labor party) formed a government under Johan Nygaardsvold in 1935, which was based on parliamentary cooperation first with the Agrarians and later especially with the Liberals. This government also remained in power until 9 April 1940. In Sweden the Social Democrats formed a government in 1932 with Per Albin Hansson as prime minister, Rickard Sandler as foreign minister, and Ernst Wigforss as finance minister. After a brief interlude out of power, in 1936 the Social Democrats returned, now in coalition with the Agrarians. In December 1939 this coalition was succeeded by a national government in which all four of the main parties were represented.

The Finnish Social Democrats also regained a role in government before the outbreak of war. In 1937 A. Cajander of the Liberal party formed a coalition with the Social Democrats and the Agrarians. Throughout the 1930s the Finnish Social Democrats had done well at parliamentary elections, but their influence had been weakened by their almost total isolation. The party had been obliged to fight a purely defensive struggle for its existence against the Lapua movement and its successors, and the party's organization was weak: it had relatively few members and the trade union movement from which it drew its support was very weak. After the civil war the central organization of the Finnish trade union movement had been dominated by communists. This organization was dissolved by a court ruling, and its successor, the FFC, which was formed in 1930 on the initiative of the Social Democrats, was slow in attracting support; in 1937 it had only 64,000 members. The corresponding figures for the other Nordic countries were 323,000 for Norway, 452,000 for Denmark, and about 850,000 for Sweden. The trade union movements of the three Scandinavian kingdoms were, in other words, far more powerful than their Finnish counterpart.

A few trade unions and local organizations were not subject to the central leadership, and individual branches, especially those serving white-collar and forestry workers and agricultural laborers, were not highly organized. However, the central organs of the trade union movement enjoyed an almost absolute monopoly over the safeguarding of workers' interests in relation to working conditions and wages. In Denmark, Norway, and Sweden this monopoly was strengthened by legislation concerning the resolution of industrial conflicts and the process of centralization was assisted especially by the introduction of ballots combining several different trades and concerning agreements of two or more years' duration between trade unions and employers' associations. It is clear that a price had to be paid for centralization. In particular, a greater gulf was created and communications became more difficult between the workers on the shop floor and those who negotiated and reached agreements on their behalf. However, the number of so-called wildcat strikes, that is, strikes that were not supported by the central leadership of the trade union concerned, was modest.

When the social democrats came to power, their new role as administrators of the whole of society and not just as leaders of the working class obliged them by what they saw as economic necessity to foster compromise between the two sides of industry. This created the basis for a clash of interests between the workers' party and the trade union movement. But this conflict did not assume serious proportions, because the labor movement was by and large a united movement with a political and an industrial wing. The political leadership was entitled to representation on the central organs of the trade union movement and vice versa. Many social democratic politicians had had a great deal of experience as trade union leaders or had been elected both to a senior post in a trade union and to parliament. However, if one attempts to distinguish between the two parts of the labor movement, one finds that there was a tendency for the party to be the stronger of the two.

The social democratic parties were mass parties with a nationwide network of local associations and a substantial party bureaucracy. However, the active involvement of the rank and file membership in party affairs was quite limited in most areas, and the recruitment of new members and the collection of subscriptions constituted a large part of the activities of local associations.

The labor movement's segregation from and hostility to the rest of society was disappearing by this time. The attempts it had made during the first years of its existence to build up organizations that would so to speak offer the working class a set of social relations in competition with the traditional relationships provided by bourgeois society were now in decline. Although the labor movement still had its own Boy Scout associations, sports clubs, choral societies, funeral associations, etc., they were no longer seen as instruments in the party's struggle against bourgeois society. The labor movement's involvement in voluntary adult education was expressed in the existence of large organizations offering a wide range of evening classes, courses of study, and so on. However, political education (or indoctrination) did not play a prominent role in the adult education offered by the labor movement. Moreover, the latter had to compete in this respect with the voluntary education programs provided by nonsocialist groups, and the individual's choice of a course was hardly determined by his or her political or class affiliations. Nor could the cooperative movement, the so-called third arm of the labor movement, rely on political affiliation to sell its wares. "The workers' shoe factory," "the workers' bakery," or whatever it was called had to sell its shoes or bread or other wares on the conditions set by capitalist society.

Although on a per capita basis the circulation of newspapers in the Nordic countries was among the highest in the world, far fewer people read the social democratic press than voted for the party. The typical worker voted for the social democrats and belonged to a trade union that was under social democratic leadership, but he read a newspaper of moderate liberal-bourgeois convictions; outside working hours, he wore clothes that were virtually indistinguishable from those of the director of his factory; and to the extent that his finances permitted it, he followed the tastes of the bourgeois middle class when furnishing his home. There was talk of an independent workers' culture in harmony with the modern industrial society among some intellectuals who belonged to the labor movement and in circles to the left of the social democrats, but their products of avant-garde art and architecture were bought by the prosperous middle class.

This general trend of development can be interpreted, depending on one's point of view, as a slow but certain ideological disarmament of the working class or as an integration of the workers into the life of the community. It was accompanied by a continual growth in the labor movement's influence on the political and economic decisions taken by the state. However these developments are regarded from the standpoint of the subject of this book, the most important point to be made is that these states did not contain a proletariat that saw itself or was seen by others as separated from, let alone in opposition to, society as a whole.

Nonsocialist Parties

In all the Nordic countries the social democrats were opposed by a nationalist conservative party and a bourgeois liberal party. The latter two parties had been formed in the nineteenth century, when they had been very hostile to each other because they were on opposite sides in the struggle over universal suffrage and parliamentarism. In their organization, they resembled the mass parties of the social democrats. Their electoral base was not identical in all four Nordic countries, but in general the conservatives asserted the interests of industry and cooperated with employers' associations and the organizations that represented industry and commerce. In Norway and Sweden, the Liberals (*Venstre* and *Folkpartiet* respectively) were the heirs of great democratic parties and continued to adhere to liberal principles, whereas the farmers had acquired parties of their own to defend their interests. However, in Denmark the export-oriented farmers were still represented by the Liberal party (*Venstre*); on the left the Radical Liberals (*Radikale Venstre*) had broken away from the Liberals at the beginning of the century, and the economic crises of the 1930s provided the impulse for the formation of an extremist agrarian party to the right of the Liberals. In Finland the Agrarian Union had successfully challenged the Social Democrats for the votes of the small farmers, whereas the Liberals had only been able to retain the support of a very small proportion of the electorate, though their position at the center of the political spectrum made their influence disproportionately great.

The opposition parties were faced with a persistent dilemma. On the one hand, they were obliged to try to influence legislation by entering into compromise agreements with the governing party. Only in this way could they protect the interests with which they were traditionally associated, and moderation also enabled them to compete with the social democrats for the support of voters at the center of the political spectrum. On the other hand, the opposition parties needed to establish a marked political profile so as to present a real political alternative to social democracy. If they chose the first course and entered into political agreements with the governing party, they experienced difficulties with their more extreme supporters. In the case of the agrarians, these might be farmers who had been hard hit by the depression, or in that of the conservatives, the youth wing of the party with its great enthusiasm for defense. None of this was unique; it was the usual dilemma faced by opposition parties. However, in the 1930s the problem became particularly distressing because both the conservative and agrarian rebels borrowed from the phraseology and practices, and also to some degree the ideas, of the fascist and nazi regimes.

The successful struggle of the trade unions to maintain the level of real wages and the extent of the benefits paid to the unemployed, which was believed to encourage idleness, aroused particular resentment. The farmers' frustration over their relative decline in status and income in comparison with industrial workers was augmented by their fears that because of the depression they would be unable to meet their debts and would be forced to sell their farms. Such apprehensions and resentment were expressed in Denmark by the LS, *"Landbrugernes Sammenslutning"* (The Association of Agriculturists), which obtained representation in the *Folketing* through its parliamentary arm, *Bondepartiet* (the farmers' party); in Norway by *"Bygdefolkets Krisehjelp"* (Emergency Assistance for Farmers); and to some extent in Finland by the Lapua movement. For such groups, and indeed for a much wider range of opinion than they represented, the cultivation of the native soil was more than a productive occupation, more than a way of life; it was also a moral value in itself. In their view, there was something fundamentally wrong with a system that allowed the moral norms and way of life constituted by agriculture to be threatened. Such sentiments could easily turn into an angry outburst attacking the social security system and parliamentary democracy in the same breath.

The extremely low level of defense spending during the 1930s had the same effect on young conservatives. In their view, the parliaments and cabinets of the Nordic countries had evinced an unpatriotic attitude in this respect, an attitude that made them unfit to rule. In this case too, some of the criticism spilled over to include the form of government, and the influence from the south was very clear at least in such matters as clothing and the form taken by meetings. Some of these currents of opinion were felt inside the established conservative parties, especially within their youth wings. Such views were more or less energetically resisted within the conservative parties, and this sometimes led to a formal schism and the formation of new parties like *Nationella Ungdomsförbundet* (The National Youth League) in Sweden, *Nationalt Samvirke* (National Union) in Denmark, and the IKL in Finland.

However, it had already become clear toward the end of the 1930s that the extremist movements were stagnating or on the decline. The improvement in economic conditions doubtless played a large role in this respect, but just as the Moscow show trials reduced the enthusiasm of the left for the Soviet Union's five-year plans, so the persecution of the Jews in Germany and the protracted civil war in Spain undermined the interest of young conservatives in fascist and nazi ideas. Both the liberal and the conservative parties were, of course, careful to use the sort of language that would retain the loyalty of their right wing. However, they did not withdraw their support for parliamentary democracy, and they clearly dissociated themselves from the extremists' rejection of equal, universal suffrage as the basis of the state.

The influence of the extremist wing is more apparent in what might be called a cultural countercurrent. It was popular, not to say modern, among much wider groups than avowedly antiparliamentary circles to speak about the moral decay and self-indulgence that were destroying the nation's youth. The growing materialism of society was contrasted with the simple way of life, sexual restraint, and low wages of earlier periods. During the 1930s it was possible to ask whether the right wing would, in its resentment and impotence, renounce its loyalty to democracy and, if the opportunity arose, use unparliamentary means to turn the clock back. This question would be answered when the Nordic countries were exposed to the pressures of war.

Organizations, Interest Groups, and Associations

A description of the formal constitutional rules and an account of the political parties (their strength, their position on the political spectrum, etc.) do not provide a complete understanding of the way the decision-making authorities and the population acted during the 1930s, let alone during the Second World War. A constitution laying down formal democratic rights and duties for the individual citizen does not in itself guarantee that political decisions are made in a democratic way. (Democracy is broadly defined in this context as a combination of free discussion and decision by the majority.) Nor do political parties which, in power or in opposition, compete for the support of the electorate ensure the existence of a democratic decision-making process. Both a democratic constitution and political parties are very important, perhaps even a necessary precondition, but what has been called a "democratic political culture" is also required.

The basic political attitude in the Nordic countries was such that only a very small proportion of the population thought that the form of government should (or perhaps even could) be different. Parliamentary democracy functioned because the great majority accepted without reflection a set of democratic political norms. How was this acceptance expressed, other than by purely passive acquiescence, and from where were these norms derived?

In reaching decisions and administering policies, the bodies recognized by the constitution—government by a cabinet, responsible to a majority in parliament, the national and local bureaucracy, and the political parties—had to take into account the interests of a number of organizations that were at least formally private but which exercised a far-reaching influence. Some of these organizations, like trade unions and employers' associations, have already been mentioned, but there were many more: large umbrella organizations for industry and commerce, associations for producers of a single commodity within one branch of the economy, organizations representing agricultural interests, and producers' and consumers' cooperatives.

These interest groups were not mentioned in the constitution, but no one would deny that they played a role in the politics and administration of the Nordic countries. In some cases, this role was the only justification for their existence. During the period 1914-39 there was a marked growth in the number and membership of organizations representing special interests. On the one hand, this growth was seen as a threat to the democratic political system; on the other hand, the power enjoyed by such organizations could in part be traced to the fact that the state had charged them with the administration of important sectors of social activity, especially in relation to the economy. Sometimes it was the state itself that was instrumental in the organization of some interest group, so that it could administer a scheme it had devised or so that it might have a partner with which to negotiate concerning future plans. An analogy is provided by feudal societies, in which the central authority delegated some of its functions because the resources of the state were insufficient to carry out all its administrative obligations. Similarly, after 1914 the relationship between the state's administrative resources and the tasks which it was thought necessary for the state to undertake was thrown out of balance.

The relationship between the state and the special-interest organizations in the Nordic countries therefore reflected both the emergence of new, strong social influences that sought to protect their own special interests and the great growth in the activities of the state. The latter was continually assuming new tasks, tasks it had not previously regarded (and in many countries still did not regard) as its responsibility. These developments have been explained by the greatly increased complexity of society. It is, of course, true that a money economy and involvement with the world market constitute a more complicated affair than production for one's own or local consumption in a primitive society. However, it must also be added that the degree to which the population of the Nordic countries was prepared to accept "the free play of market forces" and its social consequences declined drastically during the period 1914-39.

The demand that a certain undesirable effect be alleviated or that some development be regulated was often presented by an interest organization, which first influenced the form taken by state intervention and then participated in the administration of the scheme introduced by the state. A characteristic of most of these large, nationwide organizations was that they were, at least formally, democratic in structure. The leadership was chosen through elections that were often indirect and which sometimes involved several stages. As with the political parties, the leadership of the interest organizations also became professionalized to a considerable degree. The organizations built up bureaucracies, so that they could protect their members' interests and more effectively perform the administrative tasks they assumed in cooperation with the state. However, the emergence of a professional leadership and an extensive bureaucracy had its price. The leadership of a large organization was seldom changed, and when it was this development usually reflected disunity between a few prominent individuals at the head of the organization rather than a change of opinion or attitude among the rank and file membership.

One might doubt the genuineness of the democracy inside the great interest organizations and question whether their participation in political decisions was democratic, but the fact remained that the leadership was reelected or replaced within the organizations themselves. The leadership did not consist of anonymous directors, and was responsible for its actions to an assembly that represented the membership in a fairly direct way. The most important means of pressure that an organization disposed of in relation to the rest of society was that its leaders had the support or at least the acceptance of the membership. The closer the leadership was to the bottom of the pyramid, the grass roots as it were, the easier it was to replace it. This could occur at the annual general meeting, at which the leadership for the following year was elected by those present.

In addition to the economic interest groups, there were many other associations pursuing almost every conceivable objective. To list them all would be pointless and not altogether possible. Some associations were purely local and might disappear after a fairly short time; others were sections of nationwide organizations that often maintained independent contact with similar organizations in other countries. It would be difficult to find an objective, an interest, a hobby, or a cultural activity that had *not* given birth to an association of some kind.

The total membership of such organizations far exceeded the total population, because it was quite common for a person to belong to a dozen or so associations. The individual was, of course, more active in some of the organizations to which he or she belonged than in others, but each association had at least a committee of three to seven members, who found the purpose of the association sufficiently important to keep it going, and in all probability an annual subscription. It is difficult to establish clearly the number of people who did not belong to any association at all. Individual attempts to calculate the number at the local level produced figures as high as 40-50% when membership of trade unions and health insurance societies, which was virtually compulsory, was left out of the account. However, associations were not obliged to be registered, and an association might very well have existed for a long time and have functioned to the full satisfaction of its members without making an impact on the community as a whole. Under any circumstances, the existence of between twenty and thirty associations in every locality, each with its own objective, must have given every individual many opportunities to participate and to meet like-minded people.

Nearly all associations held an annual general meeting. Attendance tended to be the greatest when there was a good chance that a dispute would arise over the activities of the association. In principle it was quite possible for an individual to attend the annual general meeting of a trade union or cooperative dairy one evening and appear the very next night at the annual general meeting of a political party in his or her electoral district, of a cultural society of some kind, of a garden allotment association, of a housewives' association, or of a sports club. The agenda was always the same: a committee presented a report, because it was responsible for its actions to the members assembled at the annual general meeting; the committee for the next year was elected by equal and "universal" suffrage (it was frequently more difficult to get new applicants for the committee than to get committee members to continue in their posts); and proposals made by the committee or by individual members were debated and put to the vote.

There *were* more exclusive associations whose influence was supposed to derive from the members' social position, and there were also masonic and perhaps other lodges at which the staid middle class of the town could satisfy any need it might have for mysticism. But these were the exception. The overwhelming majority of associations had open enrollment policies.

The strength of this characteristic of the political culture is illustrated by its presence also in parts of the economic sector, in the agricultural consumers' and producers' cooperatives that enjoyed a dominant position, especially in Denmark. The history of the cooperative movement in Denmark, and to a lesser extent also in the other Nordic countries, is closely connected with the political struggle for universal suffrage and parliamentarism and with the educational activities of the folk high schools. The political and cultural struggle of the farmers who rose against the bourgeoisie during the last part of the nineteenth century also took the form of a fight for liberation from the commercial capitalists of the towns. The establishment of an independent credit and banking system for farmers, of cooperative dairies and slaughterhouses, of cooperative insurance companies and consumers' cooperatives can all be seen as economic initiatives, but the democratic organizational structure with equal votes for all members regardless of their economic position, which was gradually introduced in all these organizations, was probably largely a result of the farmers' struggle for cultural and political independence against the urban bourgeoisie and academically trained officials. At this time there were, as we have seen, few citizens of the Nordic countries whose families had lived in the towns for more than one generation, which in this context means that the effects of the farmers' democratic ideals were felt far beyond those circles that were employed in agriculture and directly influenced by agrarian culture in the 1930s.

As in the case of the description of the political system, this account of organizations may seem banal and greatly idealized. However, attention has been drawn to organizations because they represented an aspect of the political culture of the Nordic countries that was threatened during the Second World War. This network of democratic associations must be seen in two ways in relation to the problems faced by the Nordic countries during this period.

First, almost all citizens were presented with and encouraged to participate in the democratic way of managing affairs in all possible connections. Democracy was imbibed from birth and was the self-evident principle on which organizations were based. If the members of an association had learned that annual general meetings were not to be held, that the committee was to be self-perpetuating, and that the treasury was no concern of the rank and file, the result would undoubtedly have been consternation, public scandal, and resignations from the association. There were, as we have seen, exceptions, especially associations which proclaimed that they were apolitical, a claim which often meant in reality that their influence was conservative, perhaps even authoritarian. This was true, for example, of the Boy Scouts corps and some Christian organizations. In some cases, the reactions of these movements during the war are of special interest. But in general, involvement in an association, particularly for the thousands who were officers of an association, constituted a democratizing counterweight to the Victorian, bourgeois upbringing with its inculcation of the duty to obey and a belief in authority. Individuals who had themselves served on committees and participated in democratic meetings were better able to understand and to criticize the actions of parliamentarians. More immediately, during the Second World War, when democracy at the governmental and parliamentary level was under external and internal pressure, the involvement of so many individuals in associations provided a second line of defense for democracy.

Second, the societies of the Nordic countries were thoroughly organized in the fullest sense of the term. It is clear that social stratification made itself felt in the associations: the golf club and the skittles club did not draw their members from the same circles. However, the essential point to be made is that individuals were not only linked through their family, through work, or through the public authorities. Nearly all members of the population also had contacts or easy opportunities for making contacts with other people through the associations. One weapon in the Nazi *Gleichschaltung* of society, which has been called the atomization of society (that is to say, the isolation of the individual, with the state or party arranging all his or her contacts with others) had to remain ineffectual in societies that had not only a few centrally led organizations but also hundreds or thousands of local associations. When reason of state or plain duress made it necessary for the state to impose censorship on the normal conveyers of news, the press and radio, the associations became an essential channel for information and the formation of opinion. The attempts of the Nazis in Norway to regiment the associations and bring them under the party's control show that they knew what they were up against. The enormous growth in participation in the meetings of associations, which occurred in Denmark in the course of 1940, and the hastily established cooperation between Danish associations of all kinds at the local and national level indicate that the other side also realized what was involved.

Foreign and Defense Policy

Democratic Control

In principle, democracy also extended to the sphere of foreign policy. In principle, secret diplomacy had come to an end when parliamentary governments had become responsible to the elected representatives of the people not only for domestic but also for foreign policy. However, it was difficult to translate principle into reality. Even in domestic matters, important negotiations had to be conducted behind closed doors, but at least their outcome was immediately, or at least very quickly, made public. In foreign policy, secrecy has traditionally played a much greater role; indeed one or both of the parties involved in negotiations often demand that the negotiations be kept secret and that their outcome not be made public.

When democratic control finally began to make itself felt in the field of foreign policy, this was combined in Denmark, Norway, and Sweden with a pronounced respect for diplomatic secrecy. The parliamentary foreign affairs committees that became firmly established institutions in the course of the 1920s were pledged to secrecy, and they were, to a greater degree than other parliamentary committees, controlled by the foreign minister, who decided at his own discretion what information should be made available to the committee. On the other hand, it was clear that a country's foreign policy was strengthened if it enjoyed the support of all the important political parties. Other states could not then expect a change in foreign policy if a change in cabinet occurred (i.e., if one of the opposition parties came to power). This consideration might inspire the foreign minister to seek support for his policies in the parliamentary foreign affairs committee. There were differences between the parties over domestic policy in Denmark, Norway, and Sweden, but to a large extent there was a common view on the essentials of both security and trade policy. In Finland, the divergences between the parties over foreign policy were greater, and the fact that the popularly elected president exercised a personal influence over foreign policy meant that parliamentary control was weaker.

The public debate on topics related to foreign affairs revealed greater fluctuations of opinion than were apparent at the closed meetings of parliamentary committees. Moral judgments quite naturally also played a greater role in the statements of the mass media on foreign affairs. There was nothing to prevent a newspaper from, for example, dissociating itself very clearly from the actions of an aggressive great power, but governments felt obliged in the name of "reason of state" to base their decisions primarily on traditional considerations of national security and export markets. Moreover, there is no evidence to suggest that deliberations on foreign policy in the media had any great influence on electors when they cast their votes. In this respect, however, the Second World War provided politicians with some interesting experiences. Developments in Denmark were the most striking. The foreign policy pursued by the Danish government and parliament was based on cold realism. During the first part of the war public opinion afforded essential support for this policy, but in 1943 contributed to its collapse. The fundamental lesson that foreign policy could not be conducted without regard for public opinion was learned in all four Nordic countries.

The Nordic States and the League of Nations

Like the development of international relations in Europe, the foreign policy of the Nordic countries during the interwar period can be divided into two phases. The first lasted from the end of the First World War until the beginning of the 1930s and the second from the Great Depression and the Nazi assumption of power in Germany until the outbreak of the Second World War or perhaps until the Nordic states were drawn into the hostilities.

The first phase was characterized in the economic sphere by a liberal commercial policy which could be conducted largely within a recovering or expanding world economy, and in the field of security policy, by the quite exceptional weakness of the two great powers, Russia and Germany, which had decisively influenced the situation in northern Europe in the past.

As we have seen, the three Scandinavian kingdoms succeeded in remaining neutral during the First World War. At the end of this conflict neutrality was discredited in the eyes of the victors. The establishment of the League of Nations was in the interests of the small, neutral states, insofar as it could be seen as an attempt to create an international order based on law. However, it was also clear that membership in the League made neutrality in the classical sense of the term impossible. The Scandinavian countries, like the other weak, ex-neutral states, chose to resolve this dilemma by joining the League and devoting their efforts to making it a more universal organization directed at solving conflicts instead of an instrument in the hands of the victors for the maintenance of the status quo. In the view of the smaller states, one of the most important sections of the League's Covenant was article 16, which obliged the League's members to participate in economic and military sanctions against any state that it designated an aggresssor. Already in 1921 the ex-neutral states secured acceptance of the so-called Directives in which they reserved the right to decide whether or not to take part in military sanctions in each particular case.

It did not require much prescience to foresee that Russia and Germany would not remain weak indefinitely. A vital consideration for the small states was whether the League could develop into a sufficiently strong and flexible organization to accommodate the return of the dissatisfied states to the international arena as great powers. The modest influence enjoyed by the Nordic countries was largely employed in promoting the development of the League in such a direction. In practice, this meant that they usually adopted the same line as Britain. Their persistent efforts to act as a moral example to the great powers in the question of disarmament cost them nothing and were quite fruitless.

Finland's security problems were largely determined by the country's proximity to the Soviet Union; during these years the Finns sought closer contact with the Baltic states, and to some extent with the east European countries allied with France, rather than with the Scandinavian countries. A conflict between Sweden and Finland concerning sovereignty over the Åland islands, whose population spoke Swedish, was submitted to the League, which awarded the archipelago to Finland in 1921. However, Finland was obliged, as Russia had been since the Crimean War, to refrain from establishing military installations on the islands. The Åland question was raised again at the end of the 1930s, when Finland sought to fortify the islands in military cooperation with Sweden.

The Return to Neutrality

It became clear in the course of the 1930s that it was no longer profitable for the Nordic countries to conduct their security policy in association with the League. They reacted by gradually withdrawing from the collective security system and by reestablishing their neutral status. It is a matter of opinion as to when they took the decisive step in this process, but two events are undoubtedly of great importance in this regard. The first was the Anglo-German naval agreement of 1935, by which Britain renounced its military position in the Baltic and abandoned these waters to Russo-German rivalry. Once Germany had left the League and the Soviet Union had become a member, a policy that sought to strengthen the League became in reality a policy of support for Russia against Germany. The second event was the collapse of the attempt to impose sanctions on Italy during the Italo-Abyssinian war. In the summer of 1936, after sanctions had proved ineffective and had been formally brought to an end, the six ex-neutrals (Denmark, Norway, Sweden, the Netherlands, Spain, and Switzerland) and Finland issued a joint declaration proclaiming their future attitude toward article 16 of the League Covenant. They declared that they were free to decide whether to participate in any sanctions that the League might impose in the future and justified their attitude by referring to the Directives of 1921 and the fact that other of the Covenant's provisions (that is to say disarmament) had remained "a dead letter." The declaration was unilateral and did not therefore require a decision on whether it had to entail withdrawal from the League.

Differences in the attitudes of the Nordic countries emerged during the negotiations that preceded this declaration. Finland was more interested than the others in maintaining the obligatory character of article 16; Norway wanted a declaration that the states involved would under no circumstances participate in sanctions; and Denmark and Sweden adopted the intermediate view that participation in sanctions should remain optional. Finland's position, even though it was similar to Soviet policy toward the League, was determined by the possibility that sanctions might be imposed on the Soviet Union in the event of a Russian attack on Finland. However, neither Finland's position nor the moderate attitude of Denmark and Sweden changed the fact that sanctions were no longer viewed as a means of preventing war. Instead, the Nordic countries increasingly believed that the protection afforded and the obligations imposed by membership in the League were of less importance than the risk of being drawn into a conflict between the great powers through participation in sanctions.

Finland's Position between the Soviet Union, Germany, and Scandinavia

Once Germany had regained its position as a great power and Britain had withdrawn from the Baltic, Finland chose to draw closer to the Scandinavian countries and to follow them along the path back toward neutrality. The Finns hoped that the Soviet Union and Germany would hold each other in check. At the end of 1935 the Finnish prime minister, Toivo Kivimäki, emphasized this policy in a declaration to the Finnish parliament, or *Eduskunta.* The preconditions for such a policy were the existence of a real balance of power in the Baltic region and that both the Soviet Union and Germany had confidence in Finnish neutrality. The first of these preconditions disappeared with the Nazi-Soviet pact of August 1939, whereas the second did not exist and Finnish efforts to create it proved insufficient.

The Finnish right wing regarded the country's Scandinavian orientation with suspicion. This was due in part to an ideological aversion to the social democratic governments in the other Nordic countries and in part to the fact that such an orientation failed to produce the concrete results that could solve Finland's security problem. The right wing preferred to draw closer to Germany; only one section of the right wing found the existence of the Nazi regime to be an obstacle in this regard. It is difficult to estimate the strength of such attitudes, but they contributed to keeping alive the suspicions of the Soviet Union. At the same time, the aggressive tone that the Finnish Right adopted toward Russia was one of the reasons why the Swedish government was anxious lest a closer association with Finland should create doubt about Swedish neutrality. On the other hand, the Swedes also realized that closer ties between Finland and Scandinavia might contribute to maintaining Finnish neutrality, reduce Soviet suspicions, and therefore also reduce the risks of involvement in war for all the Nordic countries.

These problems are exemplified by the Finno-Swedish efforts in

1938-39 to secure the great powers' acceptance of a joint remilitarization of the Ålands. The Swedes made it a condition of their cooperation in this scheme that the Soviet Union, which was not a signatory
of the Åland Convention of 1921, should also consent to the remilitarization of the archipelago. This condition was in reality a demand
for an improvement in relations between Finland and the Soviet
Union. Despite the ideological rapprochement with the governments
of the other Nordic countries, resulting from the participation of
the Finnish Social Democrats in the Cajander government (the
so-called red-and-green cabinet) after 1937, the Soviet reply was
unequivocally negative: Moscow did not have confidence in the
ability or the will of the Finns to maintain their neutrality and
would regard a fortification of the Ålands as directed against Russia.

The Swedish government was unaware of the negotiations that
were taking place at the same time between members of the Finnish
government and Soviet representatives concerning the surrender to
Russia of a number of islands in the Gulf of Finland, perhaps in exchange for Soviet territory in eastern Karelia. Apart from the genuine
Soviet desire to increase the security of Leningrad, the negotiations
were probably also, perhaps even primarily, an attempt by the Russians to test the willingness of the Finnish government to improve
its relations with Moscow and to guarantee insofar as possible that
Finland would not be used as an avenue for a German attack on the
Soviet Union.

However, the exiled Finnish Communist leaders, who directed the
illegal Finnish Communist party from Moscow, contributed to
making a Finnish rapprochement with the Soviet Union more difficult. They may also have contributed to the unrealistic picture the
Soviet government formed of the balance of strength in Finnish
opinion between left and right.

It is extremely difficult to assess the factors behind the development of Russo-Finnish relations before the Second World War, because so little is known about Soviet deliberations and motives. As
a result, and also because the consequences for Finland and Scandinavia were so momentous, there has been much discussion about
"the might-have-beens."

Denmark and Germany

Denmark's position, like that of Finland, left the country vulnerable to domination by a single great power. However, in Den-

mark's case this fact was already clear by the mid-1930s, so the Danish government had time to adjust its policies accordingly. Moreover, this was not a new situation for the Danish government but merely a return to the state of affairs that had prevailed during the period 1870-1918. The situation was easier to cope with than before, because the frontier revision of 1920 had shown that Denmark could not be suspected of wishing to exploit a crisis in order to ally itself with Germany's enemies. On the other hand, the new border was a part of the Versailles settlement, and the German government was careful never to give any assurance that it regarded the frontier question as solved once and for all.

However, the Nazi regime saw this question as a minor problem, which could be deferred to a later date and which ought not to interfere with its activities at a time when more weighty matters were on the agenda. It has been maintained that the Nazi government ordered the German minority in northern Schleswig to remain passive, since its long-term plan envisaged not only a revision of the frontier but also the incorporation of the whole of Denmark, and perhaps more than that, into a greater Germanic *Reich*.

The Danish government chose to adopt a low, not to say flat, profile in relation to the dominant great power. At every opportunity — for example, when the possibility of changing the League Covenant was raised — the Danes took great care to avoid occasioning any discussion of the frontier question. The Danish government was at pains to influence the press to refrain from provoking the leaders of the Third *Reich* and organized Denmark's defenses in such a way that it must have been clear that it did not intend to resist a deliberate German attack. In view of the level of Danish armaments, it might be reasonable to describe Denmark and the straits that commanded the entry to the Baltic as a "military vacuum." However, after Britain's disengagement from the Baltic in accordance with the naval agreement of 1935, such a description would be inappropriate. The Danish straits and Danish territory were not a military vacuum but under the latent domination of the German armed forces. This reality was so clear that it had to some degree been recognized by London.

As the threat of war became ever more acute at the end of the 1930s, the Danish authorities based their considerations in the first instance on the experiences of the First World War. Both Stauning and Munch had been ministers at that time. Apart from the very first phase of the conflict, it had been foreign trade that had caused the greatest difficulties for Denmark during the First World War. It was a question of convincing both Germany and Britain that it was in their interests that Denmark maintain as much of its normal trade as possible. If Germany did not permit Danish exports of secondary agricultural produce to Britain, the latter would put an end to Danish imports of feedstuffs and therefore also to Danish exports to Germany. Conversely, if Britain included Denmark within its blockade of Germany, the production of bacon, etc., would naturally decline, but normal quantities of these commodities, perhaps even more, could still be exported to Germany. The extent to which this double game succeeded is uncertain, but Danish efforts to play it are clear enough. For example, the Danes exploited the conclusion of a nonaggression treaty with Germany in the spring of 1939, a treaty which they found unwelcome in most respects, in order to establish formally that the maintenance of Denmark's normal foreign trade in wartime would not conflict with neutrality.

Norway

The radical attitudes that characterized the Norwegian Labor party during the 1920s were the reason for the party's opposition to Norway's entry into the League of Nations, which was seen as an alliance of the capitalistic Western powers against the Soviet Union. However, even before Russia joined the League in the mid-1930s, this attitude within the Labor party had given way to a more positive, in some cases enthusiastic, espousal of the League. Nonetheless, Norway, like the other weak states already mentioned, was quick to withdraw from the system of collective security.

Norwegian foreign policy, of course, also had to take into account the country's interests in its merchant marine and fishing industry. Norwegian fishing interests led the nation into a conflict with Denmark concerning sovereignty over eastern Greenland. The dispute was settled by the International Court of Justice at the Hague in Denmark's favor, but not before it had created a wave of feeling in Norway which contributed to delaying the development of Nordic cooperation.

During the second half of the 1930s, when the danger of a war between the great powers was ever more apparent, Norway's primary objective was to preserve its neutrality. A plausible assessment of the balance between the great powers would suggest that Britain was the one most likely to present a threat to Norway's neutrality. The superiority of the British navy made a German attack on Norway improbable. Therefore, Norwegian policy on the one hand had to steer clear of British demands that might compromise the country's neutrality and on the other hand had to ensure that, if Norway were forced into the war, it should not be on what was significantly called "the wrong side." Not only economic and security considerations but also idiological aversion to nazism and fascism impelled Norway to choose the British side under such circumstances. This was, of course, as clear to London as it was to Oslo, and this meant that Norwegian neutrality encountered its greatest difficulties in relation to the Western powers. During the first months of the war the problems and episodes arising from the use of Norwegian territorial waters by German shipping provided striking examples of these realities.

Sweden

The interest that the Swedish foreign minister, Sandler, evinced in the possibilities of cooperating with Finland, and to a limited degree also with Denmark, on matters of defense, and the interest of the prime minister, Hansson, in the Danish border problem stemmed from more than a sentimental Scandinavianism. The maintenance of the neutrality, and in the last resort the independence, of the other three Nordic countries was clearly a Swedish interest.

In one respect, Sweden was of vital importance in the conflict between the great powers. Germany obtained much of its supplies of iron ore from the mines in the far north of Sweden. A portion of Swedish ore exports to Germany was sent by railway to the ice-free Norwegian port of Narvik and was then shipped to Germany, while the greater part was shipped from the Gulf of Bothnia during the warmer months of the year. Before the war Germany tried to obtain a contract from Sweden guaranteeing that deliveries of iron ore would continue in wartime, but the Swedes declined to give any such assurances.

It has been said with regard to the foreign policies of the Nordic countries during the last years of peace that Finland feared the Soviet Union, Denmark feared Germany, Sweden did not know which of the two to fear more, and Norway believed it need not fear either. If the Western powers are included in the calculation, it is clear that Sweden was in the favorable position of having each of its three neighbors under the military domination of a separate great power. Sweden thus was surrounded by these contending forces, and if the balance of power shifted, would have to adjust its policies accordingly.

Nordic Cooperation

The circle of ex-neutral countries was often called "the Oslo states" after a rather unimportant convention about customs duties that was concluded in 1930. These countries had many common concerns relating to the League, and they frequently agreed to adopt the same position on an issue. The three Scandinavian kingdoms constituted a special group within the circle of the Oslo states, and at any rate after the spring of 1935 Finland too belonged to this group. From the mid-1930s a firm tradition was begun, although no formal agreement was concluded, in which the foreign ministers of the four countries met every six months.

Historical works dealing with Nordic political cooperation at this time often express disappointment over the meager results achieved, a disappointment which is usually directed at the failure to establish cooperation in the field of defense. (Cooperation in this field was primarily manifested in negative declarations concerning the obligations of League membership.) However, these dashed hopes are only a small part of the inescapable sense of tragedy which European history during the 1930s gives to the modern observer, as it did to contemporaries.

The foreign ministers of the Nordic countries were repeatedly obliged to reiterate their governments' position on Nordic cooperation in the field of defense whenever the subject came up for discussion in the media. Their position was a negative one, but the very fact that the question was raised incessantly, if only to be buried immediately, is an indication of the strength of the vague support for Nordic cooperation which existed. Nevertheless, historians have been correct in pointing out that Nordic cooperation did not lead to spectacular results. However useful agreements concerning the validity of marriages, inheritance law, or the common designation of commodities for customs purposes might be, whenever discussion turned to security or economic matters it soon became apparent that it was the centrifugal forces that were the strongest. The economies of the Nordic countries did not complement each other, and in consequence negotiations about cooperation in "a difficult supply situation" (that is to say, during a wartime blockade) proved fruitless. Although they were neighbors, the Nordic countries were placed in the spheres of interest of different great powers, and even a united Nordic bloc did not have the resources to form an independent military factor except in association with one or more of the great powers.

It is, of course, difficult to assess the importance of Nordic political cooperation, but it is certainly conceivable that the individual countries would have been exposed to pressure from one or another great power to a greater extent than they were if this cooperative tradition had not existed, albeit to a limited degree. For example, it is doubtful whether Denmark could have resisted when Germany in 1938 wanted it to issue a real declaration of neutrality and to withdraw from the League, had Danish foreign policy not been formed in association with the other Nordic states. The four countries were able to negotiate joint neutrality rules, but they did so with the knowledge, acquired from the experiences of the First World War, that neutrality in the legal sense of the term was not respected by the great powers during wartime. Each of them knew that they would deviate from impartial, disinterested neutrality if the great power that dominated their area demanded it.

It is possible that the degree of cooperation established through the regular meetings of the four foreign ministers represented the most that could be achieved. When Munch suggested in the autumn of 1938 and in February 1939 that Nordic cooperation be institutionalized, so that the Nordic prime ministers and a number of parliamentarians should regularly participate in meetings, his proposal aroused opposition in Norway and no enthusiasm anywhere. It was not until after the Second World War, and after the Nordic countries had each gone its own way in the field of security policy, that this idea was realized. When Hitler, in reply to President Roosevelt's appeal, offered nonaggression pacts to a number of states in the spring of 1939, Munch made persistent efforts to induce the other Nordic countries to accept the offer. Their refusal to do so disappointed him, because it placed the Danish acceptance of the offer, an acceptance which he regarded as a "compelling necessity," in an unfortunately unneutral light. However, both his attempts to persuade the others and his disappointment show that Munch, who did not usually indulge in the construction of castles in the air, ascribed some importance to Nordic cooperation in the face of great power pressure.

Security policy should be conducted without illusion. It was difficult to explain clearly to the population that no outside help, whether from the great powers or the other Nordic countries, was to be expected. If wishful thinking could not be stifled, it had to be accepted that unrealistic hopes would flourish and that there would be agitation for Nordic cooperation on matters of defense. However, if all hopes were dashed by clear speaking, one of the feeble impediments that lay in the way of an aggressive great power was also removed. The very fact that it was conceivable that a great power or other Nordic countries might send troops to the defense of the Karelian isthmus or the frontier in Jutland might influence decisions in Moscow or Berlin. However, the defense policies of the Nordic countries did not encourage the belief that such action was possible, and this did not pass unnoticed in the capitals of the great powers.

Before we consider the defense policies of the Nordic countries, it must be noted that the Nordic foreign ministries had more to concern themselves with than renouncing the obligations of article 16 and dispelling the illusions that sprang from the feelings of solidarity among the Nordic peoples. The 1930s were also the years of the economic crisis, the period when states entirely abandoned liberal commercial policies. In endless negotiations, foreign trade had to be regulated at the national level through agreements in which reciprocity and balance of payments were carefully weighed. In terms of the amount of paper and man-hours consumed, trade policy was a far more central concern than security policy. These commercial problems created an administrative apparatus and afforded experience that could be drawn upon in wartime. However, they also gave the great powers some insight into the economic difficulties of the Nordic countries, an insight which could be used once economic warfare (the blockade, etc.) began.

Defense Policy

As mentioned earlier, the defense policies of the Nordic countries were essentially a domestic political matter. The conservative parties demanded a higher level of armaments, though not as high as that which the military experts regarded as absolutely necessary. The liberal parties wanted a somewhat lower level of defense spending, primarily in the interest of economy. As for the social democratic parties, disarmament was still on their platforms at the beginning of the 1930s. This line remained clear so long as the social democrats

THE NORDIC SOCIETIES □ 51

were in opposition to the rest of society. Defense was one of the instruments of coercion at the bourgeois state's disposal, and the Nordic labor movements had bitter and not especially remote experiences of the army having been used against them. The officer corps was notoriously right-wing in its sympathies, and included some members who associated with extremist groups; consequently, there seemed to be very good reasons for demanding the abolition of the armed forces.

Matters were seen in a somewhat different light when the social democrats themselves took office. In the first place, they had no majority in parliament and were therefore unable to carry out any policy that they could not persuade one or more of the nonsocialist parties to accept. Second, they had become ministers not in order to abolish the armed forces but to carry out social reforms and to combat the effects of the depression, and the possibility of achieving something in these respects could not be put at risk by cosmetic proposals relating to disarmament. Moreover, the social democrats came to power in the three Scandinavian kingdoms at a time when the international situation was becoming ever darker. Fascism and Nazism were on the march and contributed to the beginnings of a change in the attitude of the Nordic labor movements toward defense. Finally, it was debatable whether the Nordic countries were still bourgeois capitalist states, once they were ruled by the labor movement. We are dealing here with two separate phenomena that were simultaneously, albeit slowly, undergoing a metamorphosis. On the one hand, the bourgeois state was moving in the direction of more social welfare and bureaucratic regulation of the economy. On the other, the possession of power changed the social democrats as much as they changed the balance of power within the state. A reversal of position on an important political question could not occur overnight. However, during the last years of peace, as it became clear that war was imminent, the altered attitudes of the social democrats were expressed in increased defense spending.

Sweden had already introduced a new defense program by 1936 to replace the so-called disarmament plan of 1925. Denmark followed suit in 1937. In both cases, emphasis was placed on technical modernization. Norway, however, did not change its defense plan of 1932, which had in that year been described by the spokesmen for the majority in parliament as establishing limited but good defenses. The plan presupposed that the country would have what was called "a farsighted political leadership." Throughout this period, Finland's level of armaments was relatively high by Scandinavian standards. The experiences of the first years of the independent republic— the civil war and the war with the Soviet Union in the years 1920-21 — combined with a quite widespread or at any rate vociferous nationalism to make political opposition to defense spending suspect. However, the country's limited resources and the requirements of economic and social development naturally kept such expenditure within bounds.

In 1938 the following percentages of state expenditure were devoted to defense:

Denmark	ca. 10.0%
Finland	ca. 25.0
Norway	ca. 11.5
Sweden	ca. 17.5

In addition to the normal budgets for defense, increased grants for the purchase of war material were made, but the latter was to be acquired over a number of years and in consequence no drastic change in defense potential had occurred by the time that the material was needed by Finland and Norway.

Historical accounts of the period are full of reproaches that the Nordic countries were so ill-prepared for war. In the case of Norway, Sweden, and Finland, it is certainly true that the armed forces were not strong enough to fulfill the tasks set for them by the political leadership in 1940. However, even during the last years of peace, the attitude in Norway and Denmark and probably also in Sweden was that the nation's armed forces should not be expected to resist an attempt to conquer the country by a great power. Denmark stood by this attitude on 9 April 1940, even though it had come under domestic political attack in January of that year; Norway did not stand by this attitude, because the great power that attacked the country was not the one that was expected to do so; and Sweden was never put to the test.

The Race for Northern Europe, September 1939-June 1940

by Martti Häikiö

If one considers the relationship between the great powers and the Nordic countries during the period 1939-40, one can adopt the viewpoint of the former or the latter but hardly that of both at the same time. If one lays most emphasis on the fate of the four Nordic countries either separately or jointly, one can view this period of history as a time when neutrality was challenged and when each Nordic state reacted in a different way to the actual or potential aggression of a neighboring great power. But if events are examined from the viewpoint of the great powers, one must speak of "a race for northern Europe" in which a move by one great power provoked a countermove by the others, and so on. The great powers observed primarily each other, not the neutrality policies pursued by the small powers. Accordingly, although the main theme of this book is how the four Nordic countries coped with the various threats to their neutrality and how they emerged from the war as independent states with their social and political structures basically intact, a great deal of attention will have to be devoted in this chapter to the "race for northern Europe." Unless there is such a degree of unity among a group of small powers that the group constitutes a great power in itself, it is the great powers that make the ultimate decisions about war and peace.

The Nazi-Soviet Pact

The Second World War began when Britain and France declared war on Germany on 3 September 1939. Two days earlier, Germany had invaded Poland, a country with which the Allies had entered into a treaty of mutual assistance. One year before, in September 1938, the Allies had acceded to German demands that the so-called Sudetenland in Czechoslovakia be incorporated into Germany and had concluded the Munich agreement. However, in March 1939 Germany had already expanded beyond the area inhabited by a German-speaking population occupying the remainder of Czechoslovakia.

As a result of the tension in relations between the great powers which emerged in 1939, Britain and France attempted to establish a broad peace front. The purpose of this front was not to create a military alliance but rather to give a warning to Germany. However, the Soviet Union, which had been excluded from the Munich agreement, proposed to the Western powers that a treaty of mutual assistance should be concluded. The question of guarantees for other countries was raised in May in the course of the three-power negotiations between Britain, France, and the Soviet Union. The last-named wished to extend the system of guarantees which were to be given by these three powers to the Baltic region, that is to say to Finland and the three Baltic states. However, the Western powers, which were reluctant to enter into a mutual assistance pact from the start, thought it would be impossible to afford guarantees to other states, especially Poland and Romania, unless the countries concerned were prepared to accept such guarantees.

At the same time that the three-power negotiations touched upon the Baltic area in May 1939, German attention was also directed toward this region because of the German offer to the Nordic states to enter into nonaggression treaties with them. The Nordic countries had already made their negative attitude toward guarantees from outside powers quite plain in connection with the three-power negotiations, and now all but Denmark declined the German offer; Denmark believed that its strategic position did not permit it to reject this German proposal.

The attitudes of Finland and Sweden toward both the three-power negotiations and the German offer of a nonaggression treaty were determined to a great extent by considerations connected with their common plan for a refortification of the Åland Islands. In January 1939 Finland and Sweden had reached an agreement to fortify jointly the Åland archipelago, which had been demilitarized in 1856 and 1921 and which, though situated outside Stockholm, was under Finnish sovereignty. The Fenno-Swedish plan was discussed by the

League of Nations in May, and it finally became clear at this meeting that the Soviet Union was opposed to its execution. In consequence, Sweden did not take any steps to pursue it further and thought that the views of the other Baltic powers should be taken into consideration. However, Finland did not abandon the plan and sent its own troops to the Åland Islands beginning in October of that year.

The negative attitude of the Soviet Union in the Åland question was connected with the efforts it had made since the spring of 1938 to secure military bases on Finnish territory, changes in the Russo-Finnish frontier, and a mutual assistance treaty with Finland. The Finnish government, however, had adhered strictly to the policy of Nordic neutrality it had adopted, rejecting first the Soviet proposals to build a Soviet naval base on Finnish territory and to make frontier adjustments on the Karelian isthmus, which were suggested in the spring of 1938 by the Soviet representative Boris Jartsev, and then the similar proposals offered by the Soviet diplomat Boris Stein in the spring of 1939.

The Nordic countries had a basically negative attitude toward the nonaggression treaties, great-power guarantees, bases, and frontier changes proposed by the great powers. However, the policies of the leading great powers were determined by their mutual relations rather than by the attitudes of the smaller states. Thus in June 1939 Britain and France agreed in principle that guarantees should be extended to so-called third states against their express will.

At this time, negotiations between the Soviet Union and Germany were initiated. The Soviet Union preferred an agreement with the Western powers to one with Germany, but was not prepared to make compromises on any important point in order to secure an understanding with Britain and France. After the political negotiations between Britain, France, and the Soviet Union had gone aground on the question of how the concept of "indirect aggression" was to be defined—should each of the three powers, for example, have the right to regard its security as threatened by a trade agreement between Germany and one of its small neighbors—the Western powers and the Soviet Union tried to find a solution by simultaneously initiating military consultations about the forms that mutual assistance would take. However, the desire of the Soviet Union to get Poland to agree in advance to the entry of Russian troops onto Polish territory even before a German attack had occurred, a demand that Poland rejected, proved an insoluble problem in these negotiations, and they were broken off.

Finally, the Soviet Union signed a nonaggression pact with Germany in Moscow on 23 August. This treaty contained a secret, supplementary protocol, which defined the German and Soviet spheres of influence and the demarcation lines between them. For Germany, the Nazi-Soviet Pact ensured that there would be no two-front war, a point of vital importance to Berlin. For the Soviet Union, the pact gave a further breathing-space for rearmament and a clear German recognition of an extremely wide Russian sphere of influence.

Geheimes Zusatzprotokoll.
_____

Aus Anlass der Unterzeichnung des Nichtangriffs-
vertrages zwischen dem Deutschen Reich und der Union
der Sozialistischen Sowjetrepubliken haben die unter-
zeichneten Bevollmächtigten der beiden Teile in streng
vertraulicher Aussprache die Frage der Abgrenzung der
beiderseitigen Interessenssphären in Osteuropa erörtert.
Diese Aussprache hat zu folgendem Ergebnis geführt:

1. Für den Fall einer territorial-politischen Umgestaltung in den zu den baltischen Staaten (Finnland,
Estland, Lettland, Litauen) gehörenden Gebieten bildet
die nördliche Grenze Litauens zugleich die Grenze der
Interessenssphären Deutschlands und der UdSSR. Hierbei
wird das interesse Litauens am Wilnaer Gebiet beider-
seits anerkannt.

2. Für den Fall einer territorialepolitischen
Umgestaltung der zum polnischen Staate gehörenden Gebiete
werden die Interessenssphären Deutschlands und der UdSSR

The secret protocol of the German-Soviet Pact, 23 August 1939. (Dokument
229/F 19/182-83, Politisches Archiv des Auswärtigen Amtes, Bonn)

ungefähr durch die Linie der Flüsse Narew, Weichsel und
San abgegrenzt.

Die Frage, ob die beiderseitigen Interessen die
Erhaltung eines unabhängigen polnischen Staates erwünscht
erscheinen lassen und wie dieser Staat abzugrenzen wäre,
kann endgültig erst im Laufe der weiteren politischen
Entwickelung geklärt werden.

In jeden Falle werden bei **beide** Regierungen diese Frage
in Wege einer freundschaftlichen Verständigung lösen.

3) Hinsichtlich des Südostens Europas wird von
sowjetischer Seite das Interesse an Bessarabien betont.
Von deutscher Seite wird das völlige politische Desinter-
essement an diesen Gebieten erklärt.

4) Dieses Protokoll wird von beiden Seiten streng
geheim behandelt werden.

Moskau, den 23.August 1939.

Für die
Deutsche Reichsregierung:

In Vollmacht
der Regierung der
UdSSR:

СЕКРЕТНЫЙ ДОПОЛНИТЕЛЬНЫЙ ПРОТОКОЛ.

При подписании договора о ненападении между Германией и Союзом Советских Социалистических Республик нижеподписавшиеся уполномоченные обоих сторон обсудили в строго конфиденциальном порядке вопрос о разграничении сфер обоюдных интересов в Восточной Европе. Это обсуждение привело к нижеследующему результату:

1. В случае территориально-политического переустройства областей, входящих в состав Прибалтийских государств (Финляндия, Эстония. Латвия, Литва), северная граница Литвы одновременно является границей сфер интересов Германии и СССР. При этом интересы Литвы по отношению Виленской области признаются обоими сторонами.

2. В случае территориально-политического переустройства областей, входящих в состав Польского Государства, граница сфер интересов Германии и СССР будет приблизительно проходить по линии рек Нарева, Вислы и Сана.

Вопрос, является ли в обоюдных интересах желательным сохранение независимого Польского Государства и каковы будут границы этого государства, может быть окончательно выяснен только в течение дальнейшего политического развития.

Во всяком случае, оба Правительства будут решать этот вопрос в порядке дружественного обоюдного согласия.

3. Касательно юго-востока Европы с советской стороны подчеркивается интерес СССР к Бессарабии. С германской стороны заявляется с ее полной политической незаинтересованности в этих областях.

4. Этот протокол будет сохраняться обоими сторонами в строгом секрете.

Москва, 23 августа 1939 года.

По уполномочию Правительства СССР

V. Molotow

За Правительство Германии.

The treaty brought about an abrupt change in the balance of power in the Baltic region. Finland, Estonia, Latvia, and Lithuania, which had won their independence following the collapse of tsarist Russia, and to some degree Poland too, had based their foreign policies on the fundamental hostility between Germany and the Soviet Union. For Denmark, Finland, and Sweden, the pact meant that Britain would have even less opportunity or desire than before to intervene in the affairs of the Baltic area.

The Great Powers and the North in the Autumn of 1939

The outbreak of the Second World War at the beginning of September 1939 led to immediate declarations of neutrality from the Nordic countries. During the First World War and also, in the light of the experiences of the war years, during the interwar period, the Nordic states had tried to ensure that their commercial relationships could be maintained even when the great powers were at war. The efforts of the Nordic governments at the beginning of September were devoted to securing the continuance of their normal trade and to remaining outside the conflicts of interest of the great powers.

On 18 September the prime ministers and foreign ministers of the Nordic countries held a joint meeting in Copenhagen. This conference had been preceded by a meeting of the Oslo states in Brussels on 11 and 12 September in which they had discussed the legal and economic aspects of neutrality. In Copenhagen, the focus of interest was the problem of maintaining trade relationships with all countries, including the belligerents, as neutrality required. Inter-Nordic relations was another question that was touched upon. These negotiations between the neutral countries continued in October and November. A common feature of these efforts to establish a concrete basis for cooperation between the neutral states was that it was generally agreed that in view of the position and special circumstances of the countries concerned there was no point in trying to establish formal cooperation. An important result of the discussions, apart from the demonstration of mutual solidarity, was that the Nordic states agreed to adopt a common line toward the limitations on neutral foreign trade which were a part of Britain's strategy for economic warfare and which were expressed in the form of demands for export restrictions and the conclusion of war trade agreements.

Britain did not show much interest in Denmark and Finland in the war trade negotiations that were held with the Nordic states, but the Norwegian merchant marine and Swedish iron ore proved difficult problems in the discussions. During the previous autumn Britain had pursued the possibility of buying a larger proportion of Sweden's exports of iron ore, a commodity which was regarded as vital for Germany because it was an important raw material for the armaments industry. However, in these preliminary negotiations the Swedes were able to preserve their right to trade freely.

Iron ore was exported to Germany from Sweden via two main routes: throughout the year it was shipped from the ice-free Norwegian port of Narvik and through Norwegian territorial waters to Germany; and during the summer months, when the Baltic was ice-free, from Luleå, Oxelösund, and certain less important ports. After the outbreak of war, two separate considerations led to the British government to take an interest in the Norwegian coast: one was that the completion of a minefield across the North Sea of the kind which had been laid during the First World War and which was now again planned would involve laying mines in Norwegian territorial waters; and the other was that large quantities of Swedish iron ore reached Germany through the same territorial waters.

In the Anglo-Swedish war trade negotiations which began in September 1939 the Swedes tried to convince the British that ore exports to Germany had declined and warned that Sweden would break off the negotiations if the figures for 1938 were not accepted as the basis for future ore exports to Germany. The British Ministry of Economic Warfare believed that the disadvantages for Britain that would result from a collapse of the war trade negotiations were greater than any benefits that could be derived from having a free hand in relation to Sweden, and the War Cabinet therefore agreed on 2 November that the iron ore question should be dropped for the time being. However, Winston Churchill, the new First Lord of the Admiralty, raised the iron ore question again toward the end of November and asked the Ministry of Economic Warfare to provide a new account of the importance of Swedish iron ore for the German arms industry. The Ministry of Economic Warfare, which was extremely influential at this time because of the great importance attached to indirect forms of warfare, argued in the report it issued on 27 November that a complete cessation of ore exports from Sweden would lead to economic collapse in Germany in the spring of 1940 and therefore also to a shortening of the war.

At a meeting of the War Cabinet on 19 November, Churchill raised the question of extending the minefield across the North Sea, the so-called Northern Barrage, into Norwegian territorial waters. However, Churchill's colleagues thought that the laying of the Northern Barrage did not require contact with the Norwegians at that stage, since the completion of the other parts of the minefield would take at least nine months. Britain did not wish unnecessarily to alarm Norway, a country which had been told by London at the beginning of September that a German attack on Norway would be regarded as tantamount to an attack on Britain. The British government had delivered this communication partly because British naval superiority gave Britain the opportunity to conduct operations off the Norwegian coast and partly because Norway was an area of strategic importance for the security of the United Kingdom.

During this period, in which guarantees had been given to Norway and the iron ore problem had been discussed with Sweden, it had become clear that the region to the east of the Norwegian coast—the Norwegian interior, Sweden, and Finland—was of no immediate importance to British security. This British view of the situation in northern Europe had many parallels in the German attitude.

The German authorities fully realized the importance of iron ore imports from Sweden, and German policy toward northern Europe was consistently based on the assumption that continuing neutrality

on the part of the Nordic countries would best serve German interests in the area. The agreement reached with the Soviet Union concerning spheres of influence was consistent with this basic attitude
in an important way. The agreement was in itself an expression of
the fact that Germany was satisfied with the status quo in northern
Europe, with the opportunities it afforded for cooperation with the
Soviet Union, and would even accept a change in the status quo so
that the position in northern Europe became somewhat more favorable to the Soviet Union.

Northern Europe was, to be sure, taken into account in Germany's
strategic calculations and even figured as the possible scene of a flank-
ing attack in the war game of 1939, though it is hard to assess the
latter's historical significance. Just as the question of the importance
of the Norwegian coast was examined in Britain from time to time at
the initiative of the First Lord of the Admiralty, so in Germany
Grand Admiral Raeder, the commander of the German navy and
Churchill's counterpart in Germany, stubbornly insisted on emphasizing the significance of the Norwegian coast in maritime strategy.
However, like Churchill in Britain, Raeder encountered opposition
from the political leadership in Germany. During the autumn of
1939 Hitler repeatedly expressed the view that Germany had no
reason to intervene in the affairs of northern Europe or on the Norwegian coast and that the maintenance of the status quo was the best
alternative.

However, there was one great power in northern Europe, the
Soviet Union, whose immediate interests were very closely affected
by the situation in the Baltic. The Soviet Union felt threatened by
Germany and thus wished to obtain concrete security guarantees
against that country.

The Soviet-Finnish Negotiations

In 1938, quite independently of political arrangements in central
Europe, the Soviet Union had pursued its idea of obtaining security
guarantees, particularly along its own frontiers, and in the spring and
summer of 1939 it had tried to achieve this objective through
cooperation with the Western powers. As far as northern Europe was
concerned, the Soviet Union's efforts were concentrated on trying to
persuade Britain and France to agree that guarantees should be given
to the Baltic states and Finland. However, after the three-power

negotiations had failed, the Soviet Union concluded a nonaggression treaty with Germany, a treaty which included a definition of the border between the two countries' spheres of influence.

In September the Soviet Union moved to put into effect its own system of concrete security guarantees within its sphere of influence. On the basis of their agreement with Germany, the Russians occupied the eastern part of Poland in the middle of the month. Shortly afterward, Moscow initiated negotiations with Estonia and Latvia concerning military bases and political treaties. On 5 October, the day before the last organized units of Polish troops capitulated to the Germans, the Soviet Union invited Finland to enter into discussions on "concrete political questions." Estonia had signed a treaty with the Soviet Union on 28 September, Latvia did so on 5 October, and Lithuania concluded its treaty on 11 October, the same day that Finland decided to mobilize its armed forces.

When Stalin suggested to representatives of the German government on 25 September that no residual Polish state should be left in existence and also informed them that the Soviet Union, in accordance with the secret additional protocol of 23 August, intended to solve the question of the Baltic countries immediately, he had specifically mentioned Estonia, Latvia, and Lithuania, but not Finland. This omission may have meant that the Soviet plan of action in relation to Finland was, for the time being at any rate, different from that which Moscow regarded as necessary in the case of the Baltic states.

The Finnish attitude toward the Soviet invitation to enter into negotiations was from the start considerably more negative than that of the Baltic states. This attitude was a logical extension of the line Finland had adopted when, in the spring of 1938 and especially a year later in the spring of 1939, it had categorically rejected the Soviet proposals for international or bilateral security guarantees. Mobilization of the armed forces and the evacuation of people from the larger towns demonstrated the full extent of the tough Finnish attitude.

In the view of the Finnish government, the Soviet Union was aiming at the reabsorption of the Baltic states and Finland, countries which had achieved their independence from Russia twenty years before, and the Finns therefore prepared themselves for a continuation of their war of independence. At this stage, Soviet demands were limited. During the negotiations that were held in Moscow between 12 and 14 October, and in which the Soviet Union was represented by Stalin and Molotov and Finland by J. K. Paasikivi, the Russians dropped their original demand for a mutual assistance treaty. However, they maintained that as "minimum demands" for Leningrad's security they had to insist that Finland surrender to the Soviet Union the town of Hanko and the surrounding area on the south coast of Finland as a naval base and the port of Lappvik as an anchoring station for the Soviet navy, all the outer islands in the Gulf of Finland, Koivisto on the Karelian isthmus, the southern part of the Lipola-Koivisto district, and the western part of the Fishermen's peninsula on the Arctic coast. This was a total of 2,761 square kilometers, and as compensation Finland would receive an area of 5,529 square kilometers from Porajärvi to Repola north of Lake Ladoga. The Soviet Union was also prepared to guarantee that it would not oppose a remilitarization of the Åland Islands, provided that Finland acted alone on the archipelago.

Both the German and British governments made it quite clear to the Finns that no concrete military assistance was to be expected from them. In October the Finns twice got in touch with the Swedish government and tried to ascertain whether Sweden might, if necessary, participate in the defense of Finland. On 26 October Väinö Tanner, the Social Democratic minister of finance and a member of the Finnish delegation that had just come back from Moscow, wrote a letter to the Swedish prime minister, Per Albin Hansson, in which he described the demands the Soviet Union had presented to Finland. He went on to say that war might break out "if we refuse to accept the demands" and asked, "Is it at all possible that, in view of the fact that the dispute concerns the Hanko peninsula, Sweden might involve itself in this matter through affording effective military assistance to Finland?" Hansson's reply to this direct question was very clear: "You ought not to count on any such assistance."

At the end of October both the Soviet Union and Finland made some concessions, but these were not very significant and no progress could be made in the negotiations. Events took a new turn on the evening of 31 October when Molotov gave a speech to the Supreme Soviet in which he made public the Russian demands and accused the Finns of being unwilling to contribute to the security of Leningrad. However, this move was seen in Finland as part of a war of nerves, and it did not lead to the recall of the Finnish negotiators, who were again on their way to Moscow at this time, or to any changes in their instructions, which were to reject sharply the demands for bases and the destruction of frontier fortifications, to renew the earlier offer to surrender the eastern islands of the Gulf of Finland, to enlarge somewhat the area that the Finns were willing to cede on the Karelian isthmus, and to promise to enter into negotiations concerning the cession of the western part of the Fishermen's peninsula. It became clear during the course of the negotiations held on 3 and 4 November that it was not possible to reach an agreement even on the basis of the new Finnish proposals. Once again the concessions made by both sides were too small, and the negotiations that took place on 9 November on the basis of new instructions were without result. The immediate cause of the collapse of the negotiations was the unwillingness of the Finns to compromise on the question of Hanko (for example, by surrendering some islands in the vicinity of Hanko instead), and their view that the frontier changes on the Karelian isthmus that the Russians proposed were excessive.

The collapse of the negotiations was seen in very different ways in Finland and the Soviet Union. The Finns believed that the negotiations had only been broken off temporarily and that the danger of war had passed for the time being. This attitude was expressed in such measures as putting the reservists on leave, returning the evacuees to the towns, and reopening the schools. In a speech on 23 November the prime minister, Cajander, urged his countrymen to lead as normal lives as possible. However, the Finnish problem had not been shelved in Moscow. On 3 November Molotov had remarked to the Finnish delegates, after they had rejected what he regarded as the minimum Soviet demands, "We civilians do not seem to be able to get any further in this matter, and now it is time for the military to speak." It later became known that on 13 November, the same day the Finnish delegation left Moscow for the last time, the Russians began to assemble in Moscow a number of exiled Finnish Communists who could form an alternative Finnish government and with whom the Kremlin could conclude the kind of a treaty it wanted. The Finnish exiles seem to have been able to convince the Soviet leadership that they enjoyed considerable support in Finland, and it was on this belief that the political part of the Soviet plan was based.

While Finland was demobilizing, the Soviet Union was quickly preparing to take action. The success of the German *Blitzkrieg,* the easy occupation of eastern Poland, and the rapid submission of the

Baltic states to Soviet wishes had clearly created the impression in Moscow that in the case of Finland too it would be possible to secure a speedy and above all local solution to the problem.

The First Phase of the Winter War

In view of the balance of power between the great powers in northern Europe, the Russian attack on Finland had unexpected and lasting consequences, even though it is clear that Soviet objectives were of a local nature. During the seemingly calm period that followed the Polish campaign, this war in the far north attracted the attention of the great powers and for a time shifted the center of gravity of the great-power contest northward.

On 26 November 1939 the so-called Mainila incident occurred on the Fenno-Soviet frontier. Moscow asserted that Finnish artillery had opened fire across the border and that the Finns had in this way revealed their intention to attack the Soviet Union. However, according to Finnish sources, the incident was arranged by the Russians in order to secure a pretext for invading Finland.

The British ambassador in Moscow, Sir William Seeds, immediately noticed the rapid timetable that the Russians followed in their handling of this affair. According to the information he had received, the incident was said to have occurred at 3:45 P.M. on 26 November, and yet the Russians were still able, "after a thorough investigation," to present a protest note to the Finnish minister in Moscow at 8:30 P.M. That morning *Pravda* had carried a sharp attack on the Finnish prime minister, and as early as 27 November *Pravda* and *Izvestia* contained declarations from *Tass* and meetings of workers condemning the Finnish imperialists.

On 28 November the Soviet Union abrogated the Fenno-Soviet nonaggression treaty, and it broke off diplomatic relations with Finland on the following day. On 30 November Soviet troops attacked Finland, and Soviet airplanes bombed Finnish cities, including the capital, Helsinki. On 1 December the Kremlin established "The Democratic Republic of Finland" under the leadership of the exiled Finnish Communist O. W. Kuusinen, and on 2 December concluded with this government a treaty providing for mutual assistance and the exchange of territories. Under the terms of this treaty, the Soviet Union obtained a large part of the Karelian isthmus and gave the Kuusinen regime the purely Finnish parts of eastern Karelia in return.

Exiled Finnish Communist O. W. Kuusinen, head of "The Democratic Republic of Finland," signing a cooperation pact with the Soviet Union on 2 December 1939 as Stalin (right) and Molotov (far left) look on. (Puolustusvoimien Kuvakeskus, Helsinki)

Until January 1940 Moscow regarded the Kuusinen regime as the only legal government of Finland and thus claimed that it was not really at war with Finland.

In Helsinki, the Cajander ministry resigned at the beginning of December and was succeeded by a new government led by Risto Ryti, the governor of the Bank of Finland. The central figure in the new government was the former finance minister, Väinö Tanner, who now became foreign minister. The restoration of peace and the resumption of negotiations with the Soviet Union were essential parts of the new government's program. However, once it became apparent that this was impossible, the only remaining alternative for the government was to wage war as effectively as it could.

The question of obtaining outside help now became pressing. The government turned to Sweden, but once again received a negative response to its request for the dispatch of Swedish troops to Finland. On 3 December Finland referred the dispute to the League of Nations. The idea of condemning the Soviet Union appealed particu-

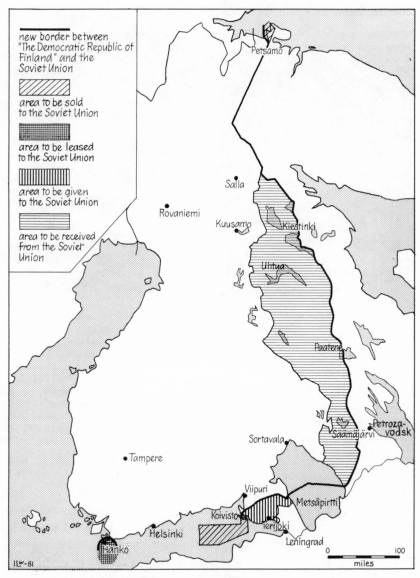

new border between
"The Democratic Republic of
Finland" and the
Soviet Union

area to be sold
to the Soviet Union

area to be leased
to the Soviet Union

area to be given
to the Soviet Union

area to be received
from the Soviet
Union

Petsamo

Salla

Rovaniemi

Kuusamo

Kiestinki

Uhtua

Paatene

Sortavala

Saamajärvi

Petroza-
vodsk

Tampere

Viipuri

Metsäpirtti

Koivisto

Terijoki

Helsinki

Leningrad

Hanko

0   100
miles

ILW-81

Distribution of areas according to the 1939 treaty between the Soviet Union and
the Kuusinen government. (Cartographer: Ingrid Lowzow)

larly to certain South American countries and to France. Britain too, which at first had adopted a more cautious attitude, soon voted with the others for the expulsion of the Soviet Union from the League in order to maintain a common front with France.

In France, the Soviet invasion of Finland had provoked a strong wave of anti-Soviet opinion, which the French government sought to exploit. In Britain, the War Cabinet and the chiefs of staff began to consider the larger strategic consequences of the Russian attack immediately after the outbreak of the Winter War. On 2 December the War Cabinet agreed that the Soviet advance into Finland would not necessarily harm the interests of the Western powers. A Russian move into the Balkans, on the other hand, would be a very worrisome development. These signs of incipient interest on the part of the Western powers and the world at large were of no practical importance, at least at this stage, since it was generally believed that Finland would be forced to surrender, in the same way that Poland had already been crushed by the *Blitzkrieg.* During the first two weeks of the Winter War Finland's fate was determined not in the corridors of foreign ministries but on its own eastern frontier.

The Russians concentrated their main assault on the Karelian isthmus, where a Finnish force of 13,000 men fought off the enemy until it was forced to retreat on 4-6 December. Similar retreats were carried out on the fronts farther north. On the basis of the experience gained during these retreats, the Finnish army was significantly reorganized, and the first Finnish counterattacks were begun as early as 4 December. However, the Soviet forces had also been regrouping, and on 6-7 December they made their first attempt to break through on the Karelian isthmus in the Taipale sector. About 84 batteries and 150 tanks took part in this attack, but it was repulsed, as was a renewed assault on 15-17 December, in which three Russian divisions participated. This so-called miracle at Summa, together with the *motti* battles and the Finnish victories at Suomussalmi and Raade, determined the nature of the struggle, and they soon became known around the world.

Once the first wave of the Soviet attack had been halted, there was more scope for diplomacy and political speculation, because it was now believed that the Finns could hold out for a long time and in this way tie down Soviet troops in the north and reduce the Russian menace in other regions. The Western powers were the first to become interested in the possibilities of exploiting the Finnish conflict.

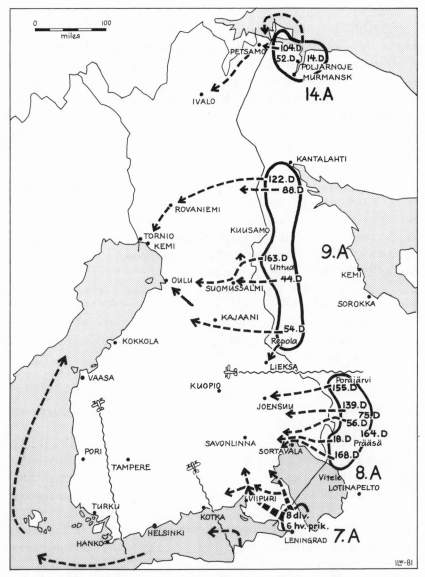

Soviet troop concentrations and planned offensives before the Winter War. Army (A) and Division (D) numbers are indicated. Under the 7th army in the Leningrad area there were 8 divisions and 6 tank brigades. (Cartographer: Ingrid Lowzow)

Allied Interest Is Aroused

When Halifax met the French ambassador in London, Corbin, on 11 December, he told him of a decision the War Cabinet had reached that day to examine the consequences for the Scandinavian countries of the Soviet attack on Finland and the opportunities open to the Allies of preventing any undesirable effects. Halifax emphasized that the best way of influencing opinion in the Scandinavian countries in the direction of the Allied cause was by assisting Finland as effectively as possible. From the Allied point of view, it would be much simpler if Sweden and Norway were drawn into the war, since so long as they remained neutral there was a risk that they might accept German or Russian protection, a development which would be unfortunate for the Western powers. In Halifax's view, these considerations justified a more active Allied policy in northern Europe.

Three days later Corbin called at the Foreign Office to outline the French attitude toward the situation in the North. The French government believed that the longer the Russians were tied down on the Finnish front the better, since it would then be so much harder for them to advance in the Balkans. It was not possible to know with certainty whether Soviet plans included an attack on Sweden and Norway and an advance to the Atlantic coast. However, if the Russians obtained a foothold on the Norwegian coast, this would have a catastrophic effect on the Allied blockage. The French government therefore proposed to London that the Western powers should hold internal discussions concerning assistance to Finland, since France wished to influence the Scandinavian countries and the United States through such assistance. France also suggested that the Allies try to strengthen the spirit of resistance in Sweden and Norway by sending military supplies to these countries. With regard to the method of proceeding, the French proposed that the Western powers should present a démarche in the Scandinavian countries which would encourage the latter to increase their assistance to Finland and to make plans to resist any eventual Soviet advance into Scandinavia. This note ought to be in two sections; the first part should contain an account of the assistance the Allies had given and intended to give to Finland, and the second should be an inquiry about the possibilities of establishing a joint Allied-Scandinavian organization to deal with aid for Finland.

The memorandum by Lord Halifax on the "Situation of Scandinavia and the possible results of the Russian invasion of Finland," which was completed by 15 December, laid the foundations for the new Allied policy in northern Europe. Halifax believed that the German attitude toward Scandinavia was the most important factor and that it was clear that if the Soviet Union made demands on Sweden, either because of Swedish assistance to Finland or after the latter had been conquered, Germany would be obliged to protect its own interests, interests which primarily related to iron ore but which included strategic bases. Germany might offer Sweden its "protection" and demand bases, just as the Soviet Union had done in the case of the Baltic states and Finland. Halifax thought that Sweden would not accede to such demands and would instead request Allied help. In Norway, Germany had no other interests to protect than those associated with the export of iron ore through Narvik, and it therefore seemed unlikely that Norway would be drawn into the conflict before Sweden. Moreover, Halifax believed that a clash at sea off the Norwegian coast was improbable, because British naval superiority in these waters was incontestable in relation to both the Soviet Union and Germany. Halifax thought that neither the Scandinavian countries nor Germany would become more closely involved in the Finnish conflict unless the Soviet Union were to make demands on Sweden or Norway. However, if the Russians continued their advance into Scandinavia, this would unavoidably lead to a race between the great powers in that area. As long as the Finnish war continued, it was possible that Germany would intervene, and the Allies ought to be prepared for such a development.

These British and French ideas concerning the situation in northern Europe were considered at a meeting of the Supreme War Council in Paris on 19 December. It was now that the iron ore question definitely emerged for the first time as the most important factor in Allied policy toward the North, since the situation in that part of Europe, because of the outbreak of the Winter War, had become more favorable to an attempt to solve this problem in a manner satisfactory to the Western powers. In Paris, the French had been studying extracts from a memorandum by the eminent German industrialist Fritz Thyssen, who maintained that Swedish iron ore was of critical importance for the German armaments industry. With the support of this memorandum, the French renewed their earlier proposal that the Allies undertake a démarche in Stockholm and Oslo, since assistance to Finland was seen as the best means of influencing the Scandinavian countries. In the view of the French government, the approach should also give expression to the willingness of the Western powers to become allies of the Scandinavian countries: the note should state that Britain and France were prepared to consider under what circumstances and in what form they could give Sweden and Norway an assurance of protection against the direct or indirect consequences of such assistance as they might afford to Finland.

On 20 December a subcommittee of the British War Cabinet, the Military Coordination Committee, recommended that all exports of iron ore be stopped and asked the chiefs of staff to consider dispatching troops to Narvik and northern Sweden. When the War Cabinet met two days later, it decided that the démarche proposed by the French offered a basis for closer relations with the Scandinavian countries and therefore also a political means of attaining these military objectives. The decisions of the War Cabinet on this occasion represented a definitive change of attitude toward northern Europe on the part of the highest political and military leadership in Britain.

German Interest in the North Is Aroused

The manner in which German interest in the North was aroused lends further support to the belief that the Soviet advance into Finland unleashed a race for northern Europe among the great powers. In Germany too, the outbreak of the Winter War and the first weeks of December brought about a clear change from passive and contented support for the status quo toward active planning for military operations.

It is legitimate to ask whether German policy toward northern Europe at this time was largely a creation of the commander of the German navy, Grand Admiral Raeder, and whether he regarded the involvement of Vidkun Quisling, the former defense minister in Norway and the leader of the extreme right-wing party *Nasjonal Samling,* in these plans merely as a means of securing his objectives, in the same way that giving assistance to Finland was viewed by France and Britain as an indirect means of drawing closer to Sweden and Norway.

In the war game that was played in 1939 before the outbreak of the Second World War, a front in the North had figured as one possibility in the imagined conflict with the Western powers. However, after the Polish problem had been resolved by force, an extension of the war to northern Europe seemed unnecessary to Hitler, and he concentrated his efforts on fruitless peace initiatives. Once these efforts had failed, Hitler's attention focused only on the coming land campaign in the west, and he took no interest in northern Europe, an area that could be regarded as having been pacified by the agreement between Germany and the Soviet Union.

Raeder, on the other hand, because of his position as commander of the German Navy, was constantly searching for opportunities to conduct the war at sea more vigorously, and his eyes fell upon the Norwegian coast. A German naval base on the Norwegian coast, for example at Trondheim, seemed to offer excellent opportunities for maritime operations against the Western powers, but to acquire such a base in a rugged and mountainous country in the shadow of British naval superiority and in the face of Norwegian resistance would be an extremely daring undertaking. Raeder was therefore interested in achieving his objective by indirect means. A week after the outbreak of the Winter War, at a "Führer conference" on 8 December, Raeder stated his full conviction of the urgent need to occupy Norway in order to acquire the bases in question, but he was less clear about the method than the ends.

During the autumn Raeder had even considered cooperating with the Soviet Union in order to obtain a base on the Norwegian coast. However, the connections with Berlin which the Norwegian businessman Viljam Hagelin, a representative of *Nasjonal Samling,* established in the autumn of 1939 opened up entirely new ways of approaching the Norwegian problem. In the second week of December, Quisling visited Berlin with the clear encouragement of chief nazi-ideologue Rosenberg. Quisling arrived in Berlin on 10 December, at the same time that the League of Nations was dealing with the question of aid to Finland. He met Rosenberg on the following day and gave him an account of British influence in Norway. Quisling claimed that the Norwegian government would, without resistance, agree to the limitations on neutrality and of German influence which Britain was proposing. He offered to prevent this danger by establishing a new government in Norway, which would invite German forces into the country. Rosenberg informed Hitler of these ideas. Quisling and Hagelin also met Raeder and other members of the naval high command and told them of a secret agreement between Britain and Norway concerning Allied bases in Norway. Raeder presented

Quisling's arguments to Hitler on 12 December and persuaded him to receive Quisling. Before the meeting between Hitler and Quisling took place, Raeder raised with Hitler, "so that the *Führer* would obtain a favorable impression of Quisling," the question of permission to begin planning for the conquest of Norway, either peacefully in the manner proposed by Quisling or by force.

Two days later, while Quisling and Hagelin were listening to Hitler say that he could not permit Britain to acquire bases in Norway, Raeder and Rosenberg were already having detailed discussions on the practical execution of Raeder's first alternative means of conquering Norway. Immediately after meeting with Quisling, Hitler instructed the German military authorities to begin preparations for the conquest of Norway.

Two factors connected with Quisling's visit to Berlin seem to be important: on the one hand, by speaking about a secret agreement between the British and Norwegian governments concerning Allied bases in Norway, Quisling furnished the Germans with a motive for intervention; and on the other, by speaking of a new government in Norway which would invite the Germans into the country, Quisling offered them an indirect method of securing their goals. Raeder had achieved his objective. However, Quisling had only provided Raeder with a means of winning acceptance for his ideas in Germany and of setting in motion preparations for intervention. An entirely different question was whether it was practical to act in collusion with Quisling, who might only have been seeking to promote the interests of his party. During the period of preparation that followed, Raeder took care that the initiative would remain in German hands throughout the operation, and Quisling was allowed no role in the preparations.

The interest of both the Western powers and Germany in northern Europe thus seems to have been aroused by the Soviet advance into Finland, and this interest was focused on the Norwegian coast, whose strategic importance seems to have been evident to both sides. The status quo in the North clearly was favorable to Germany, since as long as it persisted Germany received its supplies of Swedish iron ore. As for the Allies, northern Europe, a remote region in which large naval forces could be brought to bear, offered an opportunity for limiting the growth of German influence and the German arms industry. However, in December 1939 the continuance of Finnish resistance was still an essential and uncertain factor in the calculations of the great powers.

The Policies of the Scandinavian Countries and Finland

By the middle of December both the Western powers and Germany were actively preparing for an extension of the war to northern Europe, while the Soviet Union was already engaged in hostilities in that region. For Finland, the situation was quite clear: Finnish resistance had to be made effective by every means available.

Immediately after the meeting of the Supreme War Council on 19 December Harri Holma, the Finnish minister in Paris, was summoned for discussions with the French authorities. He was told that France had proposed to Britain that a joint Allied démarche be made in Stockholm and Oslo. According to his own testimony, Holma was authorized to inform his government that the Western powers had decided that "if Sweden and Norway enter our war, France and Britain would send troops to assist us." Aaro Pakaslahti, the head of the Political Department at the Finnish Foreign Ministry, replied to this report by asking "What can Helsinki do?" and by emphasizing that "we certainly need military assistance in the form of troops."

Even though the British, after learning of this French initiative, declared that the French had misled Finland, this exchange of telegrams between Paris and Helsinki had far-reaching consequences for Sweden and Norway. On 22 December Pakaslahti informed the Finnish ministers in Stockholm and Oslo of the report he had received from Paris and instructed them to pass the information on to the Swedish and Norwegian foreign ministers, Christian Günther and Halvdan Koht, respectively. "Britain and France will presumably undertake a démarche. Inform Günther and Koht that we know that the Western powers are planning to provide military assistance in the form of troops. Make it clear that we most certainly need effective military assistance from abroad." This request for assistance did not, however, represent the official policy of the Finnish government, but was an expression of the views of Holma and Pakaslahti. It was important, nonetheless, that Sweden and Norway were in this way obliged to adopt a position toward the démarche that was to be expected from the Allies before it had been made and indeed before the Western powers had formally decided that it would be made. Even though the final contents of the Allied note that was presented on 27 December largely coincided with the information conveyed by the Finns, the note did not have anything to say about the dispatch of troops.

This recruiting poster, distributed in February 1940, reads: "You should join up — our future is at stake. Join the volunteer corps." Twelve thousand Swedes joined the volunteer corps which was organized during the Finnish Winter War. (Krigsarkivet, Stockholm)

The Swedish government had succeeded in maintaining its unity when the Finnish request for assistance had been rejected. Now it had to meet a new threat from the West. On 23 December the Swedish government discussed the information received from Helsinki about Allied intentions and decided to stand by its previous attitude: "Günther sought to restrain both Finland and the Western powers." Sweden's objective was to avoid involvement in the war between the great powers, and it was now being drawn into this conflict on the one side by Finland and on the other by Norway, which was well known to be very pro-British. "Britain will never allow any other country to conquer Norway" had been Günther's summary of the basic belief among the Norwegians while he was Swedish minister in Oslo before the war.

On 25 December Günther traveled to Oslo to confer with his Norwegian counterpart, Koht. Günther believed that the Western powers would probably ask Sweden and Norway for permission to transport Allied troops across their territories. A positive response to this request would, he said, lead to German countermeasures that would involve the Scandinavian countries in the war between the great powers. The Swedish government was therefore resolved to give an unequivocally negative reply to the inquiry that it expected to receive. For his part, Koht said that Norway had had similar reports and had been preparing to adopt a cautiously neutral attitude, but after learning of Sweden's unambiguous position, he was entirely in agreement with it: "Norway cannot do anything else."

The Anglo-French note of 27 December, with its reference to Allied interest in the security of Sweden and Norway and to the willingness of the Western powers to assist Sweden, Norway, and Finland, gave the Scandinavian countries no reason to doubt the reliability of the information on Allied intentions which they had previously received from Finland. Koht and Günther spoke over the telephone on 30 December and agreed on a common attitude toward the Allied démarche: they would not enter into any agreement with the Western powers concerning assistance; but on the other hand, they would not put obstacles in the way of the transit of supplies or civilian technicians from Britain and France to Finland across Scandinavia.

The Swedes had also noticed the Finns' equivocal attitude toward assistance from the Western powers. The official foreign policy of Finland, as conducted by Foreign Minister Tanner, did not take into

The central archives of the Swedish Communist party, confiscated in a police raid in February 1940, being loaded into a car. During the Russo-Finnish war of 1939-40, the Communists were the highly suspect lone wolves of Swedish politics. (Arbetarrörelsens arkiv, Stockholm)

consideration the newly awakened interest of the Allies in the North, but the activities of Holma and Pakaslahti did. The Swedes believed that Holma was pursuing an active policy designed to "persuade the government to drive Sweden into an open conflict with both Russia and Germany"—to quote the words of Erik Boheman, the chief permanent official of the Swedish Foreign Ministry. Sweden therefore sought to influence the course followed by Finnish foreign policy.

The idea that Sweden could play a mediating role in any peace negotiations which might be initiated between Finland and the Soviet Union seems to have been discussed as early as 27 December, the very day that the Allied note was presented to Sweden and Norway. Madame Kollontai, the Russian minister in Stockholm, told Günther that, although she had received no instructions from her government on the matter, she personally hoped that it would prove possible to reestablish peace between Finland and the Soviet Union. Immediately after this conversation Günther discussed the possibilities of peace with the Finnish *chargé d'affaires* in Stockholm, Eljas Erkko. These first indications of incipient peace negotiations meant that Stockholm became the focus of the attention of the contending great powers as the diplomatic activities of the Western powers above all and of the Soviet Union sought to influence Swedish attitudes. The Allies tried to induce Sweden to enter the Finnish war, while the Soviet Union attempted to prevent this from happening. These were the diplomatic constellations that governed the course of events that ultimately led to the ending of the Winter War.

Sweden replied to the Allied note of 27 December on 4 January. The Swedish reply maintained that Sweden could best serve the Finnish cause by remaining neutral because, if it entered the conflict, this would immediately lead to German and Soviet countermeasures against Sweden, which might cause a Finnish collapse. Norway also returned a negative reply, though not until 15 January. However, during this period Allied plans had gained new depth, as serious examination of the problems associated with intervention in northern Europe had begun and as the machinery for the practical execution of Allied ideas had been set in motion.

The Norwegian Coast or the Swedish Orefields?

Although France had taken the initiative in proposing a change in Allied policy toward northern Europe, Britain was responsible for the practical preparation of the plan for intervention. At its meeting of 20 December the British Military Coordination Committee had accepted the view that Swedish iron ore was of such essential importance to Germany that an Allied occupation of the orefields could shorten the war. The committee asked the British chiefs of staff to examine the military implications of sending Allied troops to Narvik and northern Sweden. The size of this force was to be sufficient to retain control of the orefields against attack by Germany and/or the Soviet Union.

The various strands of the questions raised by the idea of resisting the Soviet advance, by the iron ore problem, and by the purely diplomatic action proposed by the French were first brought together at the War Cabinet's meeting on 22 December. It was quite clear to the British that a resolution of the iron ore problem was only

possible with Swedish cooperation, and that the only way of influencing the Swedes was by approaching the problem in an indirect
manner through exploitation of the Finnish war.

From then on, Allied policy followed two parallel but separate
lines: preparations for a more limited plan, based on laying a minefield or taking naval action in Norwegian territorial waters, and for
a more extensive plan involving intervention at the Swedish orefields. During January and February the British were obliged on
several occasions to consider the relationship between these two
plans, but by the end of that year the smaller plan was viewed in the
light of the larger.

On 3 January the War Cabinet decided to present a new note to
Norway concerning Norwegian territorial waters, after London had
concluded that action in these waters would not seriously damage
the prospects of carrying out the larger plan. The note expressed
anxiety over German activities off the Norwegian coast and informed
Oslo that the British government thought it was entitled to take
action in these waters if this proved necessary, a statement which
of course referred to action against the export of iron ore through
Narvik. The note, which formed part of the smaller plan, was presented to Norway on 6 January, and a copy was given to the Swedish
government at the same time for its information. On 13 January
these two Scandinavian countries received a third note, in which
Britain inquired about the possibilities of sending volunteers to
Finland across Norway and Sweden.

These last two notes met with as cool a reception from Norway
and Sweden as the démarche of 27 December had done. On 17
January the Swedish prime minister, Hansson, even declared publicly
that Sweden would not permit the passage of belligerent troops or
the establishment of foreign bases on its territory. The race for
northern Europe between the great powers, set in motion by the
Soviet Union, had placed Sweden in danger from three sides, but the
Swedish attitude was especially influenced by fear of a German
attack. By trying to mediate in the Fenno-Soviet conflict and by rejecting Allied approaches, Sweden sought to remove any grounds for
such an attack, and continuing to export iron ore to Germany, so as
to avoid provoking German countermeasures, formed a natural part
of this policy.

The strong opposition to Allied designs offered by the Scandinavian
countries from the middle of January on caused the Western powers

to abandon the smaller plan, which was limited to action in Norwegian territorial waters. As a result, still greater emphasis was placed on the role of Finland in the preparations that were being made for intervention at the orefields in northern Sweden. At the end of January 1940 the British War Cabinet intensified assistance to Finland. A remarkable hypothetical addition to the plan was the idea of a naval operation at Petsamo; this was originally proposed by the Finns and was then examined by the Allies at the suggestion of the French, but was ultimately rejected by the Western powers.

These preliminary studies of the possibilities of naval action off the Norwegian coast and to some degree also the Petsamo project emphasized the position the larger plan occupied in Allied policy toward northern Europe. After the smaller plan and the Petsamo venture had been rejected in January 1940, the idea of occupying the orefields gained new impetus.

The Allied Intervention Plan

On 12 December the War Cabinet had asked the chiefs of staff to prepare detailed plans for intervention in northern Europe. The military reports were ready on 16 January and were considered by the War Cabinet on 19 January. In the view of the chiefs of staff, two brigades would be enough for northern Sweden, but it could be assumed that Sweden would insist that the Allies also participate in the defense of southern Sweden. These tasks would require about 24,000 fighting men and about 80,000 men for supply and other supporting duties. A third measure, which was to be carried out at the same time and which was also prepared, was the occupation of Bergen, Stavanger, and Trondheim. The military believed that five battalions would suffice for this purpose.

After the War Cabinet had approved these guidelines on 19 January, the chiefs of staff drew up detailed plans for the operation in a lengthy report, entitled "Intervention in Scandinavia: Plans and Preparations," which was completed by 28 January. The chiefs of staff pointed out in their report that a campaign in Scandinavia would be more favorable to the Western powers than to Germany. The only potential German countermeasure that the Allies would find it difficult to deal with was a German air attack on southern Scandinavia. Troops had been reserved for the land defense of southern Sweden, but the Western powers wholly lacked the capacity to repel an attack by air. The chiefs of staff also prepared a special report on the relationship between aid to Finland and the larger plan. The fundamental idea in this report, "Allied Assistance to Finland," was the belief that the continuation of the Finnish war was advantageous to the Western powers and that the Soviet Union was tied down in the North.

The British chiefs of staff met the French high command at General Gamelin's headquarters on 31 January and discussed the drawing up of a common plan on the basis of the British proposals. The French emphasized that the Western powers ought to assist Finland, and argued for direct intervention there. The French believed that aid to Finland offered a means of securing the cooperation of the Scandinavian countries, a view which was accepted by the British War Cabinet at its meeting on 2 February. On this occasion, Sir Samuel Hoare, the Lord Privy Seal, argued that the Allies should force the hand of the Scandinavian countries by offering to give Finland extensive military assistance in the form of troops. The War Cabinet thought it was extremely important to prevent a Soviet conquest of Finland during the spring, and that this could only be done by trained troops in considerable numbers, which could reach Finland directly from Sweden and Norway or by passing through these countries. Thus Finland was once again allotted an organic role in the Allied intervention plan and was to be used as a means of persuading the Scandinavian countries to tolerate the occupation of the Swedish orefields by the Western powers.

At the meeting of the Supreme War Council in Paris on 5 February, the French officially abandoned their own intervention plans. The Supreme War Council now linked Allied policy toward northern Europe with the question of assistance to Finland, an attitude which meant that the Finnish war had to be kept going for as long as possible and that attempts to reestablish peace had to be frustrated. The British now began to prepare for intervention in Finland too. The chiefs of staff started to examine the question at the beginning of February and reported that, although in several respects it was extremely difficult to assist Finland, two to three Allied brigades, some part of which had originally been intended for northern Sweden, should be reserved for this purpose. However, more importance was attached to a close coordination of the diplomatic and military actions of the Western powers than to the number of troops that would be sent, since the whole problem of intervention in Finland really concerned the question of how to persuade the Scandinavian countries, above all Sweden, to accept the occupation of the orefields by Allied troops. From a diplomatic point of view it was important to secure Finnish consent to Allied intervention in the Winter War immediately. The British General Ling and the French General Ganeval were therefore sent to Finland to inform the Finns of the Allied plan.

The Ending of the Winter War

After their victories over the Russians in December, the Finns wished to resume negotiations with the Soviet Union, but the latter declined to do so. A discernible change in Fenno-Soviet relations first occurred in January, when Moscow abandoned the Kuusinen regime and entered into direct discussions with the Ryti-Tanner government. During February, as the Fenno-Soviet negotiations began in earnest, the Finns also had to consider the significance of the evident Allied interest in their decisions. Throughout the Winter War Tanner gave priority to the reestablishment of peace with the Soviet Union. The acquisition of Swedish assistance was the next best alternative, whereas aid from the Western powers—whose intentions were the subject of very contradictory reports from different sources in the course of February—was merely the third alternative, which he would pursue only if the first two failed to produce satisfactory results. Tanner visited Stockholm on a number of occasions in order to discuss these alternatives with Swedish leaders, and was consistently told that Sweden would neither enter the Finnish war itself nor permit the Western powers to send troops to Finland across Swedish territory. But at the beginning of February the peace terms that Moscow had put to Finland asked for much more than the Finns thought they could give.

From the Russian point of view, growing Allied interest in the Winter War constituted a serious change in the situation, but Soviet prestige still required that the war be brought to an honorable conclusion. The Russian attempt to secure a breakthrough on the Karelian isthmus was initiated on 1 February with artillery bombardments and minor attacks designed to probe the Finnish defenses. The main assault began on 6 February and was extended to the whole length of the isthmus front on the eleventh. The Soviet forces concentrated on the isthmus far exceeded the Finnish reserves, and this caused the Finns to retreat from their main defense line to an intermediate position. There was fighting along this new line on 17-26 February, and on the twenty-seventh the Finns began to fall back toward their inadequately prepared rear positions. The Finns believed that at the end of the war there were twenty-nine Soviet divisions, supported by at least nineteen tank battalions, in the front line on the isthmus. It was estimated that the Russians had 2,500 planes on Finnish territory, whereas the Finns never had more than 300 planes at any stage of the conflict. The Finns were also particularly worried by their lack of artillery and ammunition.

The political and military leadership in Finland obtained more detailed information on the assistance the Western powers proposed to provide from General Ling on 22 February and also from Gordon Vereker, the British minister in Helsinki, and from Holma, the Finnish minister in Paris, information which it was obliged to consider in the light of the ever-worsening situation at the front. The Finns thought that the contingent of 20-22,000 men mentioned by Ling was too small and that the date of its arrival, the end of March, was too late. On 23 February the Finnish *chargé d'affaires* in Stockholm, Erkko, once again put two clear questions to Foreign Minister Günther. First, was the Swedish government able to assist Finland with troops and material, and if so, when and on what scale? Second, what attitude would the Swedish government adopt toward "the passage across Swedish territory of such troops as other countries might send to assist Finland"? The Swedish reply was presented on the very next day: "the dispatch of Swedish troops, except for volunteers, or the granting of permission for the passage of troop formations from belligerent countries cannot be expected in the present situation." Prime Minister Hansson confirmed this attitude personally to Tanner on 26 February, and he also urged the Finns to accept the severe peace terms they had been offered. Tanner also met Swedish Foreign Minister Günther and Kollontai, on this visit to Stockholm, and he received similar advice from them. After he had returned home he declared that "the passage of Allied troops across Sweden is impossible. This matter is clear."

The Finnish rejection of the Allied offer of assistance was thus due partly to the limited scale of this assistance and partly to the unyielding attitude Sweden adopted to the passage of foreign troops. One factor that delayed the conclusion of peace was the earlier Finnish successes in the field: it was difficult to reconcile Finnish public opinion to the prospect of substantial cessions of territory in view of the publicity that had been given to the Finnish victories around the turn of the year.

The Soviet advance on the Karelian isthmus continued in March. The situation was greatly complicated by the Soviet attack over the ice of the Gulf of Viipuri, an attack which began on 2 March. Farther inland, the area around Tali became the center of a great struggle. The Russians succeeded in breaking through the Finnish positions on 8 March, and they crossed the Tali river on the following day. In view of the military situation, the scale of the assistance offered by the Western powers did not seem very impressive. The decision of the Finnish government and the foreign affairs committee of parliament on the best course of action to take was determined on the evening of 9 March by Commander-in-Chief Marshal Mannerheim, who expressed the view, with the support of the opinions of the commanders on the isthmus and of the various army corps, that the situation was untenable and that "continued hostilities can lead only to a weakening of the position and to further losses of ground." The government decided to accept the Soviet terms, and a peace treaty was signed in Moscow on 12 March.

The peace treaty imposed substantial losses of territory on Finland, which was obliged to cede to the Soviet Union the whole of the Karelian isthmus; the town of Viipuri and the islands and shores of the Gulf of Viipuri; the western and northern shores of Lake Ladoga and the towns of Käkisalmi, Sortavala, and Suojärvi; a number of islands in the Gulf of Finland; the area east of Märkäjärvi and the town of Kuolajärvi; and parts of the Fishermen's and Srednij peninsulas. Hanko and the surrounding waters were leased to the Soviet Union for thirty years. Finland also had to accommodate more than 400,000 refugees from the ceded areas of Karelia. All of them were settled in the remaining parts of the country, and it is remarkable that neither at the time nor after 1944 were any serious political difficulties caused by the Karelians or by those who had to give up considerable parts of their land to the new settlers.

The peace treaty was a severe economic blow to Finland, but its political consequences were perhaps of more importance. During the peace negotiations the possibility of continuing the war with Allied assistance had led some Finnish political leaders to imagine that peace was not a military necessity. Such attitudes combined with the peace terms, which were generally considered to be excessively severe,

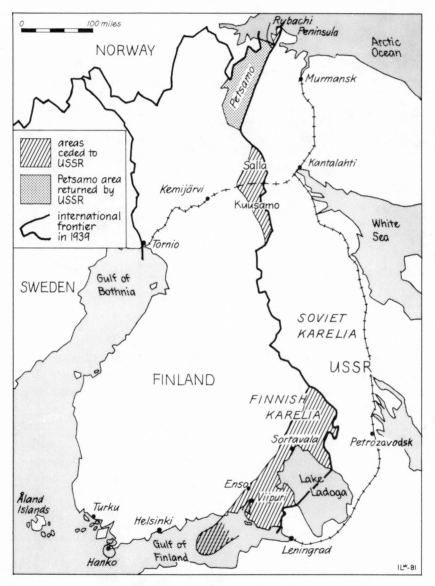

Distribution of areas according to the Treaty of Moscow, 12 March 1940. (Cartographer: Ingrid Lowzow)

Half a million Finnish people had to leave their homes in Karelia after the Peace of Moscow of 12 March 1940. (SA-kuva, Helsinki)

to create a willingness in Finland to seek to regain the lost territories with foreign help. In addition, the Winter War had other and still more important consequences for Finnish national feeling. Finland had by itself succeeded in resisting a Soviet attempt to conquer the country, and the self-confidence that this generated helped the Finns maintain their sovereign independence, first against the increased Soviet demands of the months following the Winter War, and later against German efforts to impose a complete alliance and a position of subordination on Finland after a new war with Russia had broken out.

From the Eastern Frontier of Finland to the Norwegian Coast

The Winter War and the great-power policies that brought it to an end had very tragic consequences for the Nordic countries. Over 23,000 Finns were killed, 45,000 wounded, and 420,000 evacuated from the ceded areas. However, once the Winter War was over Finland could begin to rebuild its economy, which had been damaged by the conflict. Denmark and Norway, on the other hand, which had previously been able to live in peace, were attacked by a great power almost as soon as the Finnish war was over.

After the conclusion of the Winter War, the Western powers, which had drawn up plans for the occupation of the orefields in northern Sweden, had to consider whether the political preconditions for intervention in northern Europe still existed. On 14 March the British prime minister, Neville Chamberlain, was of the opinion that the Peace of Moscow made it impossible to put the intervention plan into effect. The War Cabinet decided to abandon the plan and to begin to develop a new policy toward northern Europe. The purpose of aid to Finland had been to secure a change in the political attitudes of Norway and Sweden. In their communications to the Scandinavian countries, the Western powers now contented themselves with hinting at the possibility of using force; at the same time they reduced their military preparedness for action in Scandinavia. However, in contrast to the Western powers, which had clearly held the military and diplomatic initiative throughout the Finnish war, Germany was making deliberate preparations for an invasion of Denmark and Norway in the spring of 1940.

After Quisling left Berlin in December military preparations for the occupation of Denmark and Norway began in earnest in Germany. Nevertheless, throughout this period the preparations seem to have proceeded at a slower pace and on a smaller scale than the corresponding activities of the Western powers, a fact which emphasizes that it was the Allies who possessed the initiative from December to March. After March these positions were reversed. Another difference was that German plans were more realistic and limited in scope than those of the Western powers had been. Moreover, German plans were quite unconnected with the Finnish war, and Norwegian, and more particularly Swedish, cooperation played no part in them. Whereas the Allies had aimed at occupying the Swedish orefields by assisting Finland, the Germans merely intended to seize certain Norwegian ports. Although preparations for carrying out the "peaceful alternative" with Quisling's connivance continued, the emphasis on a purely military operation increased in the course of the planning.

By the middle of January a *Lagebetrachtung zur Studie Nord* had been drawn up by the *Arbeitsgemeinschaft Krancke,* which worked inside the German army headquarters. This report argued that it was vital, in order to neutralize British naval supremacy, that Germany be able to seize the initiative and to begin the operation undetected by the British. It was not thought likely that Britain was planning any operations in northern Europe. As for relations with the Soviet Union, it might be desirable to come to an agreement concerning spheres of influence in the North similar to that reached with regard to Poland, and it was emphasized that any deterioration in relations with Moscow because of the proposed move into Denmark and Norway had to be avoided at all costs.

On 27 January Hitler ordered that the hypothetical investigations of *Studie Nord* be transformed into active preparations for Operation *Weserübung,* and the highest military leadership was charged with the task of drawing up the main guidelines for the coming operations in Scandinavia. And on 5 February, the same day the Supreme War Council decided on Allied intervention in northern Europe, *Arbeits-stab Krancke* was set up to prepare the German operations and to serve as the nucleus of a future operational staff. However, just when the Western powers and Germany were, each unbeknownst to the other, undertaking these preparations, the first clash in Norwegian territorial waters occurred in connection with the so-called *Altmark* incident.

The German supply vessel *Altmark,* which had previously acted in support of the *Graf Spee* was on its way back to Germany from the Atlantic and lay off the Norwegian coast. The *Altmark,* which was within Norwegian territorial waters, was carrying about 300 prisoners taken from British merchant vessels. The Norwegian authorities did not interfere in the *Altmark's* journey, so Churchill, through the admiralty, ordered the captain of the destroyer *Cossack* to board the vessel. He did so on 16 February and in this way freed the prisoners.

The *Altmark* incident had a great influence on German preparations. At a meeting with Hitler on 23 February, Raeder pointed out that if British activity in Norwegian territorial waters could impede deliveries of Swedish iron ore to Germany, a British occupation of Norway would be much more catastrophic since it would present a threat to all German supplies of Swedish ore. On 1 March Hitler ordered the execution of Operation *Weserübung,* which had now been extended to include the occupation of the whole of Denmark and not just the northern part of Jutland, as envisaged in the plan of 27 January. The objectives of the operation were to prevent British activity in Scandinavia, to guarantee German access to Swedish iron ore, and to secure naval and air bases for the war against Britain.

According to the plans that were ready by 5 March, the operation, which involved technically difficult problems of transporting troops to Norway and coordinating the activities of the different branches of the service, was to be carried out in three waves, in the first of which armaments and supplies would be secretly shipped to the Norwegian ports to await the arrival of the troop transports. The *Luftwaffe* had an important role to play in the plan, since 220 bombers, over 100 fighters and reconnaisance planes, and about 500 transport planes had been reserved for the operation in order to ensure German air supremacy.

At the beginning of March the Germans, after learning of Allied efforts to induce Norway and Sweden to allow the passage of Allied troops, accelerated their preparations. On 6 March General Halder wrote in his diary that "England and France have demanded right of passage through Norway and Sweden. The *Führer* will act. On 10th. preparations finished. 15th. start *Weserübung.* Believes possible start of greater enterprise in west three days later." However, the ever more frequent reports of peace negotiations between Finland and the Soviet Union presented the Germans, like the Western powers, with a problem. On 12 March, the day on which the Fenno-Soviet peace treaty was concluded, General Jodl, the chief of staff at the German army headquarters, wrote, "The peace Finland-Russia deprives England, but us as well, of the political basis for action in Norway."

Hitler and the German military leadership began to look for a new justification for the Norwegian operation as soon as the Winter War had been brought to an end, a task that was easier for them than for the Allies, who had linked their plans so closely to assistance to Finland. The German naval authorities discovered that the Western powers had reduced their military preparedness for intervention in northern Europe, a circumstance which made the problem of finding a justification for the German operation still more difficult. However, the naval authorities declared that Britain would at some time or other attempt to interfere with German use of Norwegian territorial waters and consequently concluded that

Sooner or later Germany will have to face the question of carrying out *Weserübung.* The execution should therefore come as soon as possible—at least before 15 April, as thereafter the nights will be too short. There is a new moon on 7 April.

Nonetheless, the operation was more an expression of the German navy's desire to obtain bases than a preventive measure. The high level of preparedness within the German navy, which could not be maintained for a long time, was another argument that favored immediate action.

The military execution of the Allied plan had depended on political developments, but in the case of Germany the opposite was true. A preparedness for military action had been created, and the German war machine had been focused on operations in Norway. Not even a radical change in the political situation, like the Peace of Moscow, could deflect the execution of the plan that had been drawn up.

The Occupation of Denmark and Norway

After the Soviet Union had contented itself with a compromise peace with Finland, great-power activity in the North was restricted to the Norwegian coast. The Norwegians were receiving increasingly sharp communications from the Allies, who clearly indicated that action in Norwegian territorial waters was contemplated. The Norwegian government therefore prepared itself for action on the part of the Western powers rather than of Germany. Neither Norway nor Denmark, which as a neighbor of Germany was closer to its troop concentrations, made any attempt at political or military mobilization or to increase military preparedness. In consequence, the Germans were able to surprise Norway and Denmark and to seize the initiative in relation to Danish and Norwegian resistance. However, it was the Western powers that were the first to take action. Early on the morning of 8 April British naval units laid a minefield in Norwegian territorial waters near Narvik, and the Norwegian government was simultaneously informed of this measure in a diplomatic note. At the same time two brigades and one battalion of British troops were taken on board warships in Scotland, in case the Germans took countermeasures. The British navy had been alerted on the previous evening, and by the afternoon of 8 April British destroyers were ready to sail from the naval base in Rosyth.

In Denmark, King Christian X and the Stauning government had also learned of the Allied minefield off Narvik. This news, like the reports received on troop concentrations in Germany, including the frontier area in Schleswig, caused anxiety in Copenhagen, but did not lead to concrete action. On 9 April, after the Germans had occupied Copenhagen, the Danish government received a memorandum from

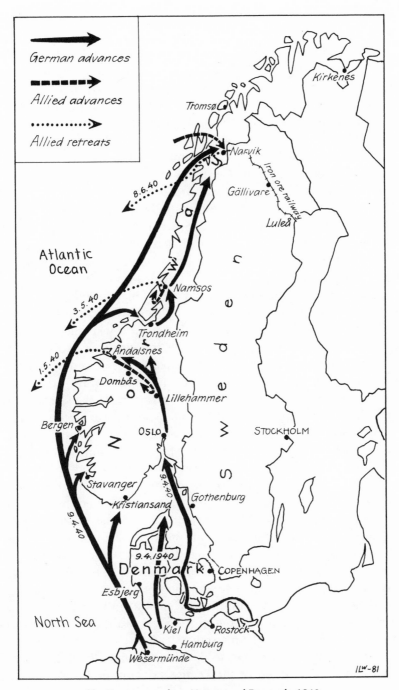

The German attack on Norway and Denmark, 1940

Germany, which stated that the aim of the German action was to thwart Allied designs and which requested the cooperation of the Danish government so that the disruptive effects of the occupation might be minimized. The Danish government was also given a thirteen-point program concerning the details of the German occupation policy. This program dealt not only with the ending of resistance but also with control over the mass media and such branches of the economy as were vital to the German war effort.

The capitulation of Denmark without resistance within a few hours raises, of course, the question of Denmark's foreign and defense policy before 9 April 1940. Since 1864 the Danes had based their foreign policy on the axiom that to preserve the existence of their own community as a social entity Denmark had to avoid war with Germany. During the First World War Denmark had acceded to German demands in order to avoid an open conflict. In the later 1930s and during the "Phony War" of 1939-40 Denmark had been aware of the possibility of German demands in wartime, but not in the form in which they occurred. The surprise was twofold. First, the Danes were expecting specific German demands and negotiations about those demands. Second, and more important, the Danes expected in general a far more limited action from the German side. Denmark was prepared to negotiate the handing over to the Germans of some naval bases and perhaps also of some strategic airfields. The total occupation of the country was a logical outcome of the capitulation policy, but it was not what the government had been expecting. Before the occupation Denmark did practically nothing to improve its defenses. Denmark did not believe that mobilization would increase its security. The numerous warnings about the growing German threat did not cause any major precautionary measures: parliament was not summoned and the party leaders were not informed until April. The aims of Danish policy can be summarized as being to preserve the normal functioning of Danish society as much as possible, and to avoid Danish involvement in the war. The former aim led to the so-called negotiation policy toward the Germans, and the latter to the fictional "neutrality" which the government tried to preserve, largely in order to bolster the morale of the Danish people and also to improve the Danish position in a postwar peace settlement.

The first important incident in the occupation of Norway occurred at Oscarsborg fort in Oslo fjord when the vessels under the command of Vice-Admiral Kummetz encountered heavy fire from the fort's coastal batteries. The heavy cruiser *Blücher,* which had been entrusted with the task of seizing the Norwegian government and royal family, was sunk, and the pocket-battleship *Lützow* suffered such damage that it had to return home. However, the Germans broke through, and the 163rd division captured Oslo. By the afternoon of 9 April the first German transport planes were already delivering troops to Oslo's airport, Fornebu.

The Germans took Trondheim without difficulty, and at Bergen they suffered only moderate losses, including that of the light cruiser *Königsberg,* which was first damaged by coastal artillery and later sunk by British planes. At Narvik, the Germans sank the Norwegian vessels *Eidsvold* and *Norge,* and the town was then taken by troops led by Lieutenant-General Dietl, the commander of the Alpine division. The German forces were not large: seven cruisers, fourteen destroyers, and about 10,000 men, of whom only 2,000 landed in the first assault. German successes were based not only on surprise and the weakness of resistance but also on the smooth cooperation that had been established between the *Luftwaffe,* the troops that landed in the first assault, the navy, and the army proper. German air supremacy was an especially important factor. Unlike Denmark, which clearly tried to avoid conflict with Germany at any price, Norway was in principle prepared to defend its neutrality. During the "Phony War" there was much discussion in Norway about the use of Norwegian territorial waters and neutrality regulations. In September 1939 Norway had increased its defense preparedness in the north of the country, but the government did not agree to the amount of mobilization that had been proposed by the military authorities on 5, 6, and 8 April.

The Norwegian decision to resist the invader was not, however, an unambiguous one. The sinking of the *Blücher* gave the government extra time to react, but the Danish example, together with the initial vague and ineffective mobilization orders, might have led — without Quisling — to an attitude similar to that in Denmark. The demand by Hitler, against the advice of his minister in Norway, Dr. Curt Bräuer, that the king accept Quisling as the head of government made it impossible for the Norwegians to cooperate with the Germans in the way that the Danes did.

One of the aims of the Western powers during the preceding winter had been to draw German forces to a remote theater of war where the Allies would find it easier than their enemy would to supply their forces. The Western powers had now succeeded in extending the war to such an area and had an opportunity to exploit their maritime supremacy. On 9 April the British War Cabinet was of the opinion that the Allies now had a better chance than before of occupying Gällivare iron ore fields in Sweden. The British minister in Oslo was immediately instructed to inform the Norwegian government that it could expect full British support.

Already on 10 April the British second destroyer flotilla, commanded by Warburton-Lee, sailed into Vestfjord and took by surprise the Germans who had captured Narvik on the preceding day. In the clash that ensued the British sank two destroyers as retaliation for the loss of two of their own destroyers, and later they sank three more German destroyers and the merchant vessel *Rauenfels,* which was carrying ammunition. On 13 April a British battleship and accompanying flotilla sank the remaining German destroyers at Narvik.

Political developments at the very beginning of the occupation had an important role in determining the nature of the conflict. The Norwegian government had time to issue a partial order for mobilization on the morning of 9 April before it withdrew to Hamar, north of Oslo. The Germans allowed Quisling to set up his government, and the latter cancelled the mobilization order. However, the Germans still negotiated with the king and his government and presented them, like their Danish counterparts, with a list of demands, among them that Quisling's regime be accepted. However, the king said he would rather abdicate than yield to these demands, and the government informed the Germans that it intended to continue the struggle for as long as possible. Even if the situation was very unclear to the ordinary Norwegian because the country's communication system was in German hands, the decision of the king and the government and the action of the *Storting* at Hamar and Elverum created a firm basis for resistance activities of the military formations as well as of separate small groups. The establishment of the Norwegian resistance movement starts with this decision. The fact that there was no single leadership, however, afforded no practical opportunity for coordinated activity then or later.

The Western powers landed at Namsos on 14 April and at Åndalsnes on 18 April, but the Allied contribution to the struggle on land was modest and very muddled. Their attempt to recapture Trondheim for the Norwegian government ended a fortnight later in an evacuation: the activities of the three branches of the service were ill-coordinated, the Allies lacked air bases and also proper bases for their troops on land, and above all they lacked real determination to occupy Norway. From 9 April on the Allies were determined only to help Norway to the extent that their limited resources allowed.

Once the limited extent of the counterattacks carried out by the Allies had become clear, the most important problem became the relationship of the Norwegian government to the occupying power. After the king had refused to accept the appointment of Quisling's government, the Germans tried to establish some other form of co-operation with the Norwegians. A so-called administrative council was set up, which was headed by I. E. Christensen. The German minister Bräuer accepted it, and the Norwegian Supreme Court approved of it, thus giving it its standing as an administrative, but strictly speaking not political, authority. However, soon afterward, on 24 April, the Germans appointed Hitler's *Gauleiter*, Joseph Ter-boven, as *Reichskommissar* in Norway and tried to bring the country under direct German rule.

On 24 May the Western powers decided that since they could not achieve their military goals in Norway, they should withdraw from the country and concentrate their forces on the western front. As a result, the Norwegian government resolved on 7 June to end hostilities on Norwegian soil and to continue the struggle from Britain. The king, the government, and what was left of the Norwegian navy and air force were evacuated to Britain. From now on Norwegian military and political efforts to wage war against Germany were to be a part of the similar efforts of the Western powers, above all Britain.

Adjusting to German Domination

by Henrik S. Nissen

When Erik Scavenius, who had been both prime minister and foreign minister of Denmark during the Second World War, summed up his experiences a few years after the war, he began by taking issue with the mistaken view that the foreign policy of Denmark was decided by its cabinet and parliament:

Among the factors whose interplay determines the nature of Danish foreign policy, the decisive one is the real balance of strength in the world about us, above all the balance of power among the adjacent great powers.

With his long experience (he had also been foreign minister during the First World War), he could have extended his statement to include the other Nordic states as well. In the summer of 1940, when under strong pressure he accepted the post of foreign minister in the national government headed by the Social Democrat Thorvald Stauning, it was difficult to detect any balance in the strength of the great powers that surrounded the Nordic countries. German domination was almost complete.

The situation had been different only three months earlier, but the audacious and successful execution of Operation *Weserübung* had decisively altered the position of the Nordic states. Germany's attack in the west on 10 May, its rapid victories and the defeat of France in June created complete and, to all appearances, lasting German supremacy on the European continent. The varying tempo at which the Nordic countries were subjected to German control illustrates the differences in their situations. As we have seen, Denmark was militarily subjugated in the course of a few hours. The military conquest of Norway took nearly two months, whereas Germany's growing mastery over Sweden, which was not expressed in direct military terms, reflected the course of operations in Norway. When the last Allied troops, along with King Haakon VII and the Norwegian government, left Norway, Sweden too was subjected to the military domination of the *Wehrmacht*. The Swedish government recognized this fact when it accepted German demands for an agreement that allowed German troops to use Swedish railways for traveling to and from Norway and between Trondheim and Narvik.

In the case of Finland, the German military presence in Scandinavia, notwithstanding Finnish sympathy for the Norwegians and Danes, provided a ray of hope that a certain balance between the great powers would again emerge. It was extremely difficult to interpret Soviet policy at that time. Was Moscow looking for security or did it contemplate a "Baltic" solution for Finland? In these circumstances, Finnish policy was not entirely clear, but one of its central characteristics was an attempt to draw closer to Scandinavia. Efforts in this direction were expressed before 9 April in a suggestion for cooperation among the four countries in the field of defense and during the summer of 1940 in a far-reaching proposal for Fenno-Swedish cooperation. The intention of the Finnish government was to underline Finland's neutrality, but at the same time the Finns built extensive fortifications along their new eastern frontier, fortifications that were to a considerable degree financed through Swedish loans. The Soviet veto on an alliance with Sweden, a veto which was justified on the same grounds as many other Soviet interventions in Finnish affairs, namely that it was designed to prevent a divergence from the terms of the peace treaty, suggested that the Russians sought a subordinate, not a neutral, Finland. However, there is some evidence that the Kremlin quite simply had no confidence in Finland's ability, quite irrespective of its will, to remain neutral if the Nazi-Soviet pact broke down. Thus the German military presence in Norway gave rise not only to hope in Finland but also to suspicion in Moscow.

Whereas Sweden in June agreed to allow the transit of German troops across its territory with pronounced anxiety as to the consequences of this divergence from neutrality, the conclusion in September of a similar arrangement in the case of Finland, an arrangement which also involved the transportation of weapons and even the stationing of German troops along the transit route, was greeted with relief, not to say enthusiasm, by the Finns. In the course of 1940 Finland was thus increasingly brought within the German military sphere of influence. During the preparations for Operation Barbarossa and throughout most of the Continuation War, Finland was naturally obliged to pay still greater attention to the wishes and representations of the *Wehrmacht,* regardless of Finnish efforts to foster the notion that Finland was fighting a separate war.

German military domination of the Nordic countries remained more or less unchallenged until the summer of 1944, and it was then once again in Finland that the change in the situation manifested itself. In the case of Sweden, the precise time when the declining strength of the *Wehrmacht* and the pace of Swedish rearmament reached such a point that Sweden no longer had to fear occupation is debatable, whereas Denmark and Norway clearly remained under German control until the end of the European war in May 1945.

However, the domination of Nazi Germany was not only a question of a military presence or the credibility of the military threat it presented. German hegemony also manifested itself in two other areas in different forms at different times, perhaps above all as a reflection of the fortunes of war in the great conflict. One of these areas was politico-ideological influence, and the other was the control of the economies of the Nordic states. In both these areas, the central question was the degree to which pragmatism governed German policy. At those times when German hopes of victory were strong, pragmatic solutions gave way before more or less imprecise, grandiose schemes which aroused alarm or despair in the Nordic countries. However, pragmatism once more gained the upper hand when it became clear that a long war was probable. But even then this development in German policy and administrative practice was often counteracted by the demands of ideology or propaganda for spectacular successes, frequently in the form of official declarations by the governments of the small countries. The explanation for developments in the relationship between the Nordic countries on the one hand and Germany on the other can often be found in the fact that Germany, even though it was a dictatorship, experienced insurmountable difficulties in coordinating its requirements on the political, economic, and military levels into a coherent policy. The constant struggle for power at the top of the Nazi hierarchy, which spread far down into the lower ranks of the German administration, at some times strongly influenced German policies toward the Nordic countries, in particular Denmark and Norway.

The adjustment of the Nordic countries to German domination assumed very different forms with regard to concrete issues, but it was always a reaction to stimuli from Berlin. The sometimes undisguised lack of coordination between the political, economic, and military aspects of German policy had no counterpart in the Nordic countries. German economic demands could influence the internal distribution of goods and upset the social balance to such a degree that the government's hold on the population was impaired. Moreover, the economic demands could affect politics, which in turn might later influence military developments. One common feature marked political developments in the Nordic countries during the period when German power was at its zenith: internal conflicts moved into the background. The pressure from without pushed political divisions aside, so that parties that had previously opposed each other strongly now served together in a coalition cabinet. Other bodies that had competed with and fought each other were now assembled in umbrella organizations or coordinated their activities. These developments did not occur overnight. In Denmark and Norway the spring and summer of 1940 were a time of confusion and clarification. In Finland the rapid growth in the membership of the newly established "Society for Peace and Friendship between Finland and the Soviet Union" showed that an opposition did exist. However, the overwhelming majority approved of the government's attempt to strike a balance between defeatism and revanchism, a balance that was strongly influenced by developments in the broader international situation.

Finland Is Caught between Scylla and Charybdis

As long as the archives in the Kremlin remain closed to scholars, all hypotheses about the Soviet Union's political objectives in Finland must rest on uncertain foundations. We do not know whether the Soviet Union was trying in the period that lasted from the Peace of Moscow of 13 March 1940 to the spring of 1941 (or perhaps only to the autumn of 1940) to "bolshevize" Finland or whether its policies were still determined by anxiety that Finland would allow itself to be used by Germany as a base for attacking Russia. At any rate, some of the Soviet interventions in Finnish affairs and some of the demands made on the Finnish governments clearly went beyond what the peace treaty allowed, even on a very far-reaching interpretation of its terms. Examples of Soviet encroachments of this kind are to be found in Russia's using the Finnish railway network for traffic to and from the naval base at Hanko; its interference in the question of who "ought" to be elected president; and its attempts to obtain the concession for exploiting the nickel deposits in the Petsamo region of northern Finland. Each new demand—and there were more, some more important and some less so, than those mentioned above— strengthened suspicions about Soviet political intentions in Finnish government circles. The more these suspicions grew, the more persistently the Finns sought to overcome the coolness in their relations with Germany which had prevailed during the Winter War.

The Finnish government itself contributed to this vicious circle. It was, to be sure, a national government, but it did not reflect proportionately the balance of strength in the Finnish parliament. The Right was clearly over represented, especially after a representative of the IKL was admitted to the government during the winter of 1940-41. The chairman of the "Society for Peace and Friendship between Finland and the Soviet Union" was arrested as early as the summer of 1940; in the autumn the society's newspaper was banned; and finally in November the organization itself was prohibited. One of the difficulties in assessing Finnish policy is that to a very great degree foreign policy issues of critical importance, such as the agreement with Germany concerning the transit of German troops from ports on the Gulf of Bothnia to northern Norway, were decided entirely without consulting the Finnish parliament. Indeed, even members of the cabinet were kept in the dark and presented with a *fait accompli.*

As far as it is possible to judge, the autumn of 1940 seems to have been the decisive period. Even if the Finnish government had the will to allay the suspicions of Moscow, it had not succeeded in doing so. The Russians were striving to obtain the concession to the Petsamo nickel mines. An Anglo-Canadian company held the rights to exploit these deposits, but this consideration was in reality of no importance after the German occupation of Norway. In August Soviet troop concentrations along the Finnish frontier were observed once again, and it is understandable that the nervousness of the Finnish government gave way to panic. It was at this time that the first signs of German interest in Finland became apparent. Contact was established through Joseph Veltjens, an arms dealer, who was able to inform the Finnish government in August, on the orders of Hermann Göring, that the German embargo on armaments exports to Finland had in effect been lifted. This decision had been made by Hitler, who believed that a Soviet attack on Finland was imminent. Permission to buy armaments in Germany was presented as a German *quid pro quo* for an agreement concerning the transit of German troops from the Gulf of Bothnia to northern Norway, and the Finnish government did not have an opportunity to ascertain how far-reaching German interests in Finland were, since the Germans kept it a secret that they were now contesting the provision in the Nazi-Soviet pact that assigned Finland to the Russian sphere of influence. However, Germany's newfound interest in Finland could not pass unnoticed in Moscow, so that although there was no official declaration of German interest in Finland, let alone any guarantees, and although the new turn in German policy was undoubtedly a relief for the Finnish government, the latter still had to consider the possibility of another bargain between Germany and the Soviet Union.

It was in these circumstances that the idea of Fenno-Swedish cooperation in the field of defense was again raised. In Sweden, it was above all the foreign minister, Christian Günther, and Conservative and military circles that took the greatest interest in this question. In their view, Sweden had even more to gain from such an alliance in the prevailing situation than before. As Günther had argued during the crisis in July and August, if the Soviet Union attacked Finland and its forces reached the Gulf of Bothnia, Germany would probably march into Sweden. An unequivocal Swedish declaration that a Soviet invasion of Finland would be regarded as a *casus belli* might perhaps deter the Russians and in this way also prevent a German attack on Sweden. The Swedish government did not accept Günther's suggestion, but in the somewhat calmer climate that emerged after August and September, first unofficial conversations and then negotiations proper took place between Swedish and Finnish politicians concerning cooperation between the two countries. The scope of the discussions quickly expanded to include foreign and economic policy, and they culminated in the suggestion of a union, of which the Swedish king would be head of state. The whole idea was received with skepticism, not to say distaste, by Swedish Social Democrats and most Liberals, and their opposition lent an air of unreality to the discussions. From the Swedish point of view the necessary preconditions for any agreement, if Swedish neutrality was not to be compromised, were that Finland accepted the frontiers of March 1940 and that the plan received the explicit approval of Moscow and Berlin.

It was on this latter point that the plan collapsed. At the beginning of December Molotov informed the Finnish minister in Moscow, Juho Kusti Paasikivi, and his Swedish colleague that the Soviet Union would regard the contemplated alliance as an open breach of the Peace of Moscow. Germany manifested an equally negative attitude, and this put an end to the plan. Germany had no reason to desire a strengthening of Sweden's neutrality and, what was surely more important, had a clear interest in seeing Finland forced to turn to Berlin in order to safeguard its security. The Soviet Union seems to have believed that a panic-stricken Finland would be more compliant, while any increase in its strength presaged a war of revenge. The shift in Soviet policy in response to the German threat had not yet occurred, and when it finally came, it was too late to influence Finland's relations with Germany.

The question of the Soviet Union's real intentions toward Finland during the period March 1940-June 1941 has been much discussed, in part of course because of the uncertainty Russian policy created in Finland at this time; but it has also been very important in relation to the problem of whether Finland could have pursued a different policy from the one followed. The right-wing bias in the composition of the Finnish government and its suppression of pro-Soviet opinion have already been mentioned. Another aspect of the situation is that the nature and extent of the transit agreement with Germany were kept secret. However, this does not of course change the fact that throughout this period the Finnish cabinet enjoyed the support of more than 90% of members of parliament. Not only the atmosphere after the Winter War and the awareness that spectacular victories had been won and hard peace terms imposed, but also the influence on public opinion exercised by the mass of evacuees from the Karelian isthmus, probably made a pro-Soviet policy impossible. With a hindsight founded in the necessities that became apparent in 1944 and later, one can conceive of a different policy in 1940. However, in 1940 and 1941 the effectiveness of the Red Army was constantly and grotesquely underestimated, while—and this was still more important—the strongest military power in the world showed a growing interest in Finland, landed troops on Finnish territory, and offered to supply material for Finnish rearmament. It could be argued that Finnish policy in the autumn of 1940 and afterward was not an attempt to adjust to German military domination, but rather that the *Wehrmacht*'s presence and interest in Finland constituted the support that the Finnish government sought in order to resist Soviet pressure. In the following years Finland had to try to prevent this support from becoming a fetter binding it to Nazi Germany.

Swedish Neutrality and the Transit Agreement with Germany

The German attack on Denmark and Norway ended the Swedish deliberations as to which great power was to be feared most. Germany constituted an immediate threat, and the German conquest of Norway and Denmark also deprived Sweden of two buffer states separating it from the great powers. Germany had already tried to exploit its new position of power in relation to Sweden during the campaign in Norway. In the Narvik area, Allied forces had pushed the German troops up toward the Swedish frontier, and Germany demanded that Sweden allow supplies to reach these troops by rail across Swedish territory. On 17 April the Swedish government agreed that medical supplies might be sent, but by 22 April the Germans had increased their demands to include armaments. They suggested that Swedish cooperation might take the following form: the Swedes would buy German armaments and in return deliver Swedish material to General Dietl in the Narvik area. The Swedish government refused and justified its attitude by referring both to its neutrality policy and to Swedish honor, which prevented the Swedish people from disregarding the plight of their Norwegian brothers. Although the Germans maintained their demands and indeed pressed them more vigorously in the course of May, the Swedish government continued to reject them despite strong warnings from the Swedish legation in Berlin. A not particularly serious attempt to remove the difficulty was made in the proposal that the Narvik area be neutralized under Swedish control.

The unity of the Swedish government over a rejection of the German demands began to crumble as it became clear that the Allies were withdrawing from Norway and that the German presence would therefore be permanent. With the capitulation of the Norwegian military forces in northern Norway on 10 June, one of the two arguments for refusing transit facilities disappeared. Günther and the minister of justice, Karl Gustav Westman, were now able to persuade the rest of the government that a continued rejection of the German demands would benefit no one and would in any case increase the risk of German aggression against Sweden. The cabinet recommended to parliament that it accept a transit agreement with Germany, and the question was discussed at a secret session at which only a small minority, consisting mainly of Social Democrats, spoke against acceptance. At a meeting of the cabinet afterward, Per Albin Hansson declared that acceptance involved a blow against neutrality, and he wrote in his diary the same evening: "And so our cherished and strictly maintained policy of neutrality was broken because of the realization that it was unreasonable to risk war in the present circumstances." His remarks show that a somewhat formal, legalistic conception of neutrality still retained its hold on the prime minister of Sweden.

During the negotiations that ensued, the Germans presented demands that would have placed the Swedish railways almost entirely at their disposal. However, the Swedish negotiators succeeded in limiting the scope of the agreement, and this was probably due primarily to the fact that there were limits to German needs, since transportation by sea was far more important, but it may also have been due in some degree to the fact that parts of the agreement were formulated in such vague terms that it was possible to make adjustments later. The agreement restricted German use of Swedish railways for transporting soldiers on leave to one train a day in each direction between Oslo and Trelleborg on the south coast of Sweden and one train a week in both directions between Narvik and Trelleborg. Each train could carry 500 soldiers on leave, but the agreement presupposed that the numbers of those traveling north and south would be in equilibrium. The passage of armaments was also permitted within the limits of what was technically possible. In reality, the agreement did not determine the extent to which the Germans made use of the Swedish railway system, partly because the agreement could be and was changed, and partly because the decisive factor was the German need for transit facilities and the consequent risk that the Germans would attack Sweden if their wishes were not met. However, during the last phase of the period of the transit agreement, which lasted until August 1943, this consideration was counterbalanced by the changing balance of strength in the great conflict. A total of about two million German soldiers, which was about 75% more than the terms of the agreement allowed, and 75,000 railway carloads of armaments crossed Swedish territory, constituting 2% of the total number of individuals and amount of freight that used the Swedish railway system during the same period.

From a military point of view, the passage of troops and material across Sweden can only have been of limited importance. However, the agreement was a political victory for Germany, because it demonstrated that Sweden had had to submit to the domination of the Third *Reich* in Scandinavia and that a neutral country must adapt itself to a Europe ruled by Nazi Germany. The agreement has perhaps

German soldiers being transported by rail across Swedish territory. Between July 1940 and August 1943, two million German soldiers were transported to Norway in this fashion. (Pressens Bild, Stockholm)

received undue emphasis in public discussion, an emphasis increased by the fact that at the time rumors circulated about the existence of other agreements which were being kept secret from the public, and these rumors were not denied by the authorities.

It was hardly respect for the strength of Sweden's defenses that induced the *Wehrmacht* in 1940 to exclude Sweden from the scope of *Weserübung,* but rather the sober calculation that, once Denmark and Norway were conquered and the Germans had established effective control of the Skaggerak, Sweden would in any case have to submit to Germany's wishes. The transit agreement proved the correctness of this calculation. Swedish rearmament was, however, intensified after 9 April 1940 to an extent that would have been inconceivable only a few years earlier. The Social Democratic party's aversion to defense spending had totally disappeared. To the extent that there was any competition between the parties during the political truce of these years, this competition concerned which party was the most nationalist in attitude and the most zealous in strengthening the country's defenses. Sweden could not of course prevent a German conquest, even if armed to the teeth, especially when the Germans had already occupied Norway. However, Swedish rearmament could increase the price the *Wehrmacht* would have to pay for overrunning Sweden to such a degree that an attack became less likely, on the assumption of course that German troops would continue to be engaged elsewhere. It is clear that on the basis of such calculations Swedish rearmament increased, while the resources that Germany had available for use against a recalcitrant Sweden declined during these years. The exact time when a German invasion of Sweden became impossible can be debated, though it should be taken into account that even a brief campaign would have led to a long-term interruption in the deliveries of Swedish iron ore to the German steel industry. However, there can be no doubt that in 1941 the *Wehrmacht* was still capable of occupying Sweden if sufficiently important German interests were in danger. This problem was therefore for both sides a calculation that involved many military, economic, and political factors. It was of decisive importance that both sides were aware of each other's interests and used the same standards in their calculations.

During the summer and autumn of 1940 the fact that an occupation of Sweden might unleash a Russian advance into Finland probably influenced German calculations. By the end of 1940 the situation thus seemed to have stabilized. However, only a few months later the substantial increase in the quantity of men and material moving northward indicated that great changes were imminent, as the buildup for Operation Barbarossa made itself felt. Regardless of Swedish thoughts on the matter, the German planners evidently assumed that the Swedish transport system was at their disposal.

On the morning of 22 June, as the great attack in the east began, the German diplomat Karl Schnurre presented the Swedish government with a note that explained the new situation and that contained a number of demands. Finland lent its support to the German démarche. However, three of these demands raised political difficulties. One was that German planes should have the right to fly over Swedish territory and should not be interned if they were forced to make an emergency landing in Sweden. The second was that German naval vessels should be able to remain in Swedish territorial waters for longer than the twenty-four hours permitted by international law. The third and most important of the demands, at least in terms of the political problems it caused inside Sweden, was that the 163rd infantry division, called *Division Engelbrecht* after the name of its commander, should be allowed to cross Sweden from Norway to Finland.

The German demands provoked the most serious political crisis in Sweden during the Second World War, a crisis which has been called "the midsummer crisis" by Swedish historians. All the Social Democratic ministers, except Hansson, immediately adopted the attitude that a negative response had to be given. The Social Democratic parliamentary party and a minority among the Liberals took the same view. The Conservatives and the Agrarians advocated acceptance of the German demands, and Günther was insistent that a favorable reply should be made. A decisive role was played by King Gustav V, who reportedly said that he would "take the consequences" if the cabinet gave a negative reply to the German requests. By this he could have meant that he would abdicate, and thereby foster a crisis in the government at a most inconvenient time, or that he would form a new cabinet without Social Democrats, an action that is clearly unconstitutional. It is hardly possible to say what finally induced the opponents of acceptance to give way—the attitude of the king, the danger that the national government might break up, or the firm promises they received that this would be a once-and-for-all concession which would not be given again. The decisive argument during the protracted discussions within the Social Democratic parliamentary party was probably the risk of a government without Social Democratic participation. In view of parliament's limited ability to control foreign policy, it was feared that such a government would pursue a more pro-German course.

Neither the acceptance of the other German demands nor the passage of the Engelbrecht division across Sweden can be said to have constituted a military threat or to have presented any real risk that Sweden's ability to maintain its independence would be reduced, but it was incontestable that Sweden had diverged from its persistently proclaimed neutrality. The opponents of acceptance of the German demands, who had been obliged to give way, were very eager to ensure that the promise that a concession had been made for the first and last time was kept. When the Germans presented several new demands of a similar kind in August, including the passage of a further infantry division from Norway to Finland, the government was united in rejecting them. However, by that time it was already clear that Operation Barbarossa would not be a brief campaign, and this consideration may also have influenced the Swedish government.

The tone of the German press toward Sweden in the autumn of 1941 was violent. It was said that the failure of the Swedes to participate in "the crusade against Bolshevism" showed that they were "a nation of pensioners" or, less delicately, "swine in dinner jackets." A press campaign of this kind might be the prelude to demands for new concessions or to something worse. The campaign may have been connected with suspicions that Sweden's neutrality policy would change if an opportunity presented itself. At a conference with the naval command on 22 January Hitler suggested that, if the Allies landed in Norway, Sweden might make common cause with them and receive Narvik and Petsamo as a reward.

The Allied raids on the Norwegian coast, which were of no immediate military significance, convinced Hitler that the coastline of Norway was of paramount importance in the war and instilled in him an exaggerated anxiety concerning an Allied invasion of Norway. The flood of diplomatic reports reaching Stockholm in February 1942, which contained warnings of an impending German attack on Sweden, were probably a consequence of Hitler's apprehensions in this respect. On 19 February Sweden began to mobilize; toward the end of the month mobilization was almost complete, with over 300,000 men under arms. Mobilization was followed by assurances that Sweden would defend its independence and neutrality against aggression, regardless of who the aggressor might be.

That neutrality that Sweden undertook to defend was only loosely linked to classical international law. It was a policy whose contents were determined purely by its objective, which was to keep Sweden out of the war. The divergences from classical neutrality as defined by international law, which Swedish policy undoubtedly involved, were defended with the argument that they were not due to any desire to favor one belligerent at the expense of another but were designed solely to serve Swedish interests and to preserve Sweden's independence. This defense of the concessions made to the Third *Reich* had two aims. One was to make Sweden's policy of neutrality and compliance acceptable to the Allies. The second was to maintain the credibility of Sweden's neutrality policy in the long term—even in an insecure postwar world. In a sense Sweden's neutrality policy can be said to have been a concrete manifestation of some of the ideas that had been present during the 1930s in the policies of the smaller states within the League of Nations. The basis of these ideas had been that international undertakings, whether they be membership in the League or neutrality, could not be allowed to oblige a small country to place its existence at risk when there was a threat of a conflict between the great powers. Danish policy toward Germany during the first months of the occupation was marked by some of the same features.

Denmark's "Policy of Negotiation"—on a Slippery Slope

Although military considerations often had political consequences both for the great powers and for Sweden and Finland, military requirements dominated the questions that have hitherto been discussed in this chapter. As for the two occupied Scandinavian countries, they presented Germany with military problems of a quite different character: Germany first had to carry out the occupation and later resist a possible Allied invasion. It can be said of Norway that the country's military problems were solved with the capitulation of the army on 10 June. The king and the government, and the small forces that were able to leave the country, continued the struggle only by giving as much assistance as possible to the British war effort. As for the Danish armed forces, between 9 April 1940 and their dissolution on 29 August 1943, they fulfilled the same function as the Swiss Guard in Rome, namely, they served as a symbol of sovereignty.

Politically, there was a great difference between the Danish and Norwegian reactions to German mastery of Scandinavia, a difference that was determined by military events. However, there are also certain similarities in these two reactions to German domination. In the summer of 1940, when it was possible to hope for but hardly to believe in the ultimate defeat of Germany, there were some political forces in Norway that began to try to bring their country more closely into line with what might be called "Danish conditions."

"Danish conditions," a term that was hardly used at the time, were marked above all by the existence of two sides that negotiated with each other concerning practical arrangements for practical problems. The two parties were far from equal in strength. Germany was always able to impose its wishes, but if it did, the process of negotiation would come to an end. As long as a Danish government, which enjoyed the support of the greater part of the population and which disposed of an administrative apparatus that loyally followed the policy that had been marked out, continued to function, its existence offered certain advantages to the occupying power. First, the country could be governed without having to call in more than a minimal number of qualified German administrators. Second, it was useful for propaganda purposes to be able to point to an occupied country in which "all went well." Finally, as long as the fiction of a sovereign Denmark was maintained, the German foreign minister, Ribbentrop, was able to keep the country under the authority of the German Foreign Ministry, and he watched zealously over "his" occupied area.

These were the cards that the Danish negotiators could play, although they were never used directly as arguments in discussion with the Germans. In the Danish reply to the German memorandum of 9 April, Foreign Minister Peter Munch had made a solemn protest at the violation of neutrality that had occurred and had not accepted the German demands. Instead, he had said that the Danish government "had decided, in view of the occupation that had taken place, to arrange conditions in the country." In order to sustain the protest he had made, Munch emphasized repeatedly during internal Danish discussions that there was no agreement or the like between Denmark and the occupying power, but only "*ad hoc* solutions" to individual problems. As far as possible, negotiations were handled by the

Danish Foreign Ministry, in order to underline the fact that it was a question of relations between two states and in this way to keep German control to some extent at arm's length. The Danish government had chosen not to fight and was not therefore at war with Germany. Nor, of course, was Denmark at war with the Allies, so long as the latter would accept that this was so.

The German memorandum of 9 April contained an assurance that Germany would not interfere with Danish sovereignty. In order to undermine any resistance that might be offered, German planes on the same day dropped leaflets all over Denmark, in which the *Wehrmacht* declared that the aim behind its action was to protect the neutrality of Denmark and Norway. Munch sought to combine these two German undertakings in such a way that Denmark could continue to assert its sovereignty and neutrality. The German attack was therefore described as having violated but not destroyed Danish neutrality. Denmark's position was extremely unclear in international law. The country was a sovereign state, but its sovereignty was undeniably doubtful after foreign troops had occupied it without the agreement of its government. Denmark was neutral, but its territory was being used by one belligerent as a base in its conduct of the war. The Danish ministers in London and Paris were not sent home, but their diplomatic status was only partially recognized. Danish merchant vessels that entered British ports, in most cases of their own free will, were not taken in prize, but on the other hand they were not regarded as neutral ships, being obliged, for example, to sail under the British flag. Denmark's remarkable status, which had no precedent in international law, undoubtedly provided some immediate advantages in negotiations with the Germans. In the longer term, Munch probably hoped that the United States, that most powerful of neutrals, would protect the interests of the small neutrals in the event of a possible compromise peace. Munch's support for the Danish minister in Washington, Henrik Kauffmann, who declared himself a "free envoy," may suggest that this was the case.

Negotiating positions and more or less fictitious legal arguments could not, of course, deflect the occupying power when really important interests, especially military ones, were at stake. German promises in memoranda and declarations were broken from one day to the next, and the story of the Danish policy of negotiation is a tale of a long series of Danish concessions to German demands. It is more difficult to demonstrate the positive results of this policy.

However, it was sometimes possible to persuade the Germans to reduce their demands or to accept a delay in the implementation of
Danish concessions, and the Danes were able on many occasions to
convince the Germans in private discussions before their demands
had been presented that the fulfillment of their wishes was imprac-
ticable or perhaps unfavorable to their own interests. This policy has
been called "the policy of negotiation." It is distinguished from collaboration, despite striking and at times humiliating concessions, by
the fact that it never linked Danish interests to the ultimate victory of
German arms. The policy of negotiation sought to protect Danish interests, often by finding solutions that accommodated German desires,
but never in such a way that an advantage for Denmark became a consequence of a favor to Germany. In this respect, it resembled Swedish
foreign policy during these years.

However, the policy of negotiation was also a policy that stood on
a slippery slope. With each little concession to the occupying power,
the Danish government lost a little more of what it wished to preserve, namely the country's independence and political integrity.
Hardly any of those who shaped Danish policy during these years had
any illusions that German promises of Danish independence after the
war would be kept if the Third *Reich* triumphed in the great conflict,
but each day won through continued negotiations was regarded as a
respite. Was there a limit to the concessions the Danes were willing
to make? This question was raised in January 1941, but it was not
until October 1941 that the leading politicians in the democratic
parties could agree on an answer, which naturally had to live a shad-
owy existence between deep secrecy and public awareness. Democratic politicians in Denmark agreed that German demands should be
rejected if they affected the democratic nature of the government,
that is to say its dependence on parliament; or if they related to
Danish participation in the war; or if they required special legislation
for the Danish Jews. These three points were set as the limit for the
policy of negotiation, though it is not possible to determine whether
they could have been maintained against the full pressure that the
occupying power could bring to bear, since so many other "inalien-
able" values were jettisoned during these years.

Among the occupied countries, Denmark's status was, as we have
seen, closely tied to the fiction of sovereignty, and the question of
the boundary between the jurisdiction of German and Danish courts
was therefore an extremely difficult problem. It was clear that

German soldiers should be tried in German courts and that Danes who committed offenses against other Danes should be tried in Danish courts and in accordance with the Danish penal code. The problem concerned Danes who committed offenses against the *Wehrmacht*. At one point, a solution was in sight to the extent that certain changes designed to make the Danish penal code more severe had been drafted, and it was intended that they should be agreed to in return for a renunciation by the *Wehrmacht* of its jurisdiction over Danish citizens. However, an official change in jurisdiction never materialized. Around the turn of the year 1940-41 a couple of Danish officers were arrested by the Germans and accused of espionage. In order to save their lives, parliament adopted the changes to the penal code which the Germans had previously demanded, and the two officers were handed over to be dealt with under Danish law, but no agreement about jurisdiction was ever concluded. Instead, *ad hoc* arrangements based on no set of guiding principles, arrangements which tended to be linked with yet further Danish concessions that often took the form of breaches of the democratic legal tradition, were the order of the day. The jurisdiction question has been emphasized in this connection as an example both of the connection between minor decisions in individual matters and larger questions of principle and of Denmark's irresistible slide down the slippery slope toward collaboration.

The German *Wehrmacht* was generally pragmatic in the demands it made on the Danish government. Its primary concern was the maintenance of unchallenged control in Denmark with the use of as few troops as possible. Political considerations did not at this time play much of a role, even when the pursuit of military requirements placed a strain on relations with the Danish government; this occurred, for example, when the Germans demanded the surrender of arms held in the Danish army depots. However, there were other official German bodies which saw it as their task to reap the political fruits of German domination in Scandinavia.

The Policy of Negotiation in Norway

Nazi Germany naturally pursued propaganda interests and these could be said to be a part of the war effort, but it was difficult to draw a clear line between general propaganda and attempts to influence the political system which had more long-term objectives. In the areas of both foreign and domestic policy, the Germans wished to see the Nordic states develop in the direction of what they called "positive adjustment." In the field of foreign policy, this meant that the smaller countries should prepare themselves for being parts of a Nazi-dominated Europe and for occupying within such a Europe a status which was more or less that of satellite states. In the field of domestic policy, "positive adjustment" should involve gradual change in the direction of autocratic regimes. There is one common feature in the Scandinavian reaction to such demands. Internal divisions gave way to an increasingly conscious defense of democracy. However, an insoluble problem emerged in this connection: some of the measures designed to strengthen the democratic political system or to prevent or delay German demands for drastic changes were in themselves undemocratic or perhaps direct encroachments on some of the institutions or rights that sustained democracy. This was yet another example of the recurrent difficulty democracy has experienced in maintaining its own principles when these principles are threatened. In 1940, 1941, and to some extent 1942 the democratic form of government was at a low ebb, since dictatorship seemed so effective. The victories of Nazi Germany had caused the limited admiration of "the strong man" which had been present during the 1930s to grow to a catastrophic degree. It was said that democracy devoted its time to talk and solved problems in half-hearted compromises.

In Norway, anger and despair over the occupation were naturally enough directed at the enemy, the Germans, but the Nygaardsvold government was the object of a not inconsiderable part of the resentment, because of the wholly inadequate state of the country's defenses on 9 April. In one sense, it can be said that the Nazi *Führer* in Norway, Vidkun Quisling, alleviated the ill-feeling against the government-in-exile, since the Norwegian population was faced with an easy choice between loyalty toward the king and government in London and on the other side Nazism as represented by Quisling, who was clearly a traitor to his country. Consequently, the attempt to set in motion a policy of negotiation in Norway was both brief and dramatic.

In April 1940 the establishment of the Norwegian Administrative Council, with purely administrative tasks, was accepted by both the Germans and, reluctantly, the Norwegian government. Its jurisdiction at that time was restricted to the areas that had been occupied by the Germans, but it was natural after the capitulation of the Norwegian army on 10 June to consider the possibility of extending its activities to the whole country and making its composition more representative, at least geographically. The main objective in view was to create in Norway that distance between the German administration and the population at large which already seemed to exist in Denmark. The German *Reichskommissar* Joseph Terboven was interested in the idea because he hoped to form a real Norwegian government. If he succeeded in doing so, the government-in-exile would be seriously weakened, and this would have consequences both in Norway and probably for control over Norwegian merchant vessels in neutral ports. The means of pressure at Terboven's disposal was above all the prospect of direct German rule, for example in the form of a protectorate, but the threat that Quisling would be given a political role was also a constant element in his tactics, even though Terboven at least did not believe that Quisling ought to occupy any place in Norwegian politics.

The German demands, which were supported by a wide-ranging propaganda campaign against the Nygaardsvold government, were that the *Storting* should annul the powers given to the government-in-exile, remove King Haakon VII and the Nygaardsvold ministry from office, and accept a *Riksråd* (State Council, another name for a ministry), which would receive full powers and rule until the end of the war, in reality, if not formally, with the approval of the German authorities. The Norwegian negotiators were gradually pushed back from one position to the next until they stood in the last ditch —where they were faced with the question of whether the king should be deposed. On 17 June, as the news of the fall of France spread, resistance to this concession ceased, and the presidential board of the *Storting* agreed to ask the king to abdicate. Moreover, the Norwegian negotiators consented to depose him if he did not respond to this call. The idea of a separate peace between Norway and Germany also figured in the negotiations, but it is characteristic of the discussions that almost all German promises were vaguely formulated or lacked real significance. For example, one of the most important German promises was that the post of *Reichskommissar* would be abolished and replaced by a "Plenipotentiary of the German *Reich*," the title which was held by the German minister in Oslo, Curt Bräuer, from 9 April until he was recalled a week later and which the German minister in Copenhagen, Cecil von Renthe-Fink, had received on 9 April. However, what difference there might be in the powers exercised by a *Reichskommissar* and a plenipotentiary was only hinted at.

King Haakon VII's reply was an unequivocal refusal. It was brought to Oslo from Stockholm by courier on 6 July, and the king read it out in a radio broadcast from the BBC in London on 8 July. This action made the Norwegian public suddenly aware of the negotiations that were being conducted. The king's reply, which was of course supported by the government-in-exile, provided an excellent basis for mobilizing a strong body of opinion against further compliance with German demands. However, although the outcome of the negotiations between the presidential board of the *Storting* and the Germans envisaged that the *Storting* should now be summoned in order to remove the king and the Nygaardsvold government from office, nothing in fact happened for the time being.

Instead, the new political order, which Terboven had achieved through negotiation or through threats, was rejected in Berlin. Quisling had powerful friends at the top of the Nazi hierarchy, and they were probably the ones who were able to insist on starting afresh, this time with the new objective of giving Quisling a place in the new political order in Norway. Late in July it became known within the different branches of the German administration in Norway that the post of *Reichskommissar* would not be abolished. Negotiations were resumed in September, and once again the Norwegians were strongly driven back from one position to the next under continuous pressure. The Germans now demanded that the contemplated *Riksråd* be composed in part of members of *Nasjonal Samling*, the Norwegian Nazi party. The *Storting,* which had assembled but not formally gone into session, drew back when the Germans insisted that a Nazi should occupy the Ministry of Justice. The negotiations did not formally fail, but instead were broken off on 25 September by Terboven. He also appointed a group of commissar-ministers who were to govern Norway and to be responsible to him. Non-Nazis were appointed only to the "economic" posts (the Germans could not abandon pragmatism entirely), and the other commissar-ministers embarked on an attempt to regiment and nazify Norwegian society. The Nazis became the only lawful party, and Terboven declared that the road to a place in the new Europe led through *Nasjonal Samling.*

It could be argued that political life ceased in Norway at this point until the liberation in 1945. After 25 September 1940 there was no longer any question of Norwegian adjustment to German domination, and resistance to nazification was the order of the day. However, applying a not-too-narrow definition of politics, it is probably more correct to say that during these years politics in Norway were carried out by other organs, administrative and statutory organizations, which were one by one forced into illegality — at least in the eyes of Terboven. The choice of the form of resistance, which limited itself to opposing demands that exceeded what an occupying power could require under international law, was also a political choice. Warnings against actions that resembled guerrilla warfare can also be seen as a response to German military domination. In any event, Norwegian administrators continued in the economic field to adapt the Norwegian economy to the existing situation so that catastrophe might be averted.

The negotiations for the formation of a *Riksråd,* a countergovernment, in the summer of 1940 have been universally described by Norwegian historians as a dark chapter in the country's political history, especially in contrast to the following period of popular resistance. In the summer of 1940, Germany seemed invincible, and Norwegian politicians, who had spent the whole of their previous careers attempting to satisfy the economic and social desires of the population, now had to act in accordance with democratic or national ideals. They quite simply doubted whether the population could resist Nazi coercion and Nazi promises that democratic principles and national sentiment would be respected. It was these doubts that would be put to shame in the following years.

National Sentiment and Democracy in Denmark

The political developments that Norway experienced between June and September 1940 had clear parallels in Denmark, but in the latter case they occurred over a longer period, from 9 April 1940 to 29 August 1943. Because a legal government was maintained in Denmark, certain features of these developments were far more blurred than in Norway, but others emerged much more clearly.

The predicament inherent in the policy of negotiation has already been described, and a number of concrete examples will be given below. This policy toward the occupying power also had a domestic political aspect, especially in 1940. It was the Stauning-Munch government which had to take responsibility for the decision reached on 9 April, and, although the ministry was immediately widened to include representatives of the two main opposition parties, the Conservatives and the Liberals, it quickly became clear that in the field of domestic policy a price would have to be paid for this apparent unity. A reactionary current against the social reforms of the previous decade was gaining strength and made its influence felt both within and outside the two former opposition parties. This current of opinion was expressed on the one hand in economic demands designed to produce a shift in the social balance and on the other in criticisms of parliamentary democracy. For the two former ruling parties, the first six months of the occupation were a period of defensiveness and at times of retreat before these forces.

In May, after protracted negotiations which on several occasions threatened to break up the government, the four governing parties concluded an economic agreement that ended the automatic adjustment of wages in line with inflation. Apart from the economic aspect of this agreement, the two former opposition parties wished to deal a blow to the power of the trade unions. The Social Democrats gave way in order to keep the cabinet of four parties intact. They feared that a government without Social Democrats would enact an even

A public concert sponsored by the *Wehrmacht* in an unsuccessful attempt to gain popularity with the Danish people. (Museet for Danmarks Frihedskamp 1940-45, Copenhagen)

more reactionary policy and that it would someday open the door to the Nazi party. However, calm did not by any means prevail within the government after the agreement was reached. Parts of the Conservative press conducted a campaign in favor of a government that would be less tied to the political parties and, it was asserted, therefore better able to achieve more impartial solutions to problems. At the end of June the leading politicians in the country conducted negotiations concerning the formation of a real national cabinet, in which the parties would be represented in proportion to their strength, and they held parallel discussions to establish close cooperation among the four parties. The negotiations were conducted in a tense atmosphere. The campaign for "apolitical" ministers continued; the Danish Nazis organized street demonstrations; and, last but not least, there was the influence of events in France in the days between the French request for an armistice and the founding of the Vichy regime. The outcome of the negotiations was the establishment of close cooperation among the parties in the Danish parliament that accepted the constitution, i.e., the parties that subscribed to parliamentary democracy, and the formation of a real national government. Stauning remained prime minister and the same four parties were represented in the government as before, but places were also found for three nonparty ministers: Erik Scavenius as foreign minister, Gunnar Larsen, an industrialist, as minister of transport, and a police official as minister of justice. The cooperation among the four parties (and the small Georgist party) was proclaimed in a declaration of faith in democracy and was institutionalized in the so-called Committee of Nine, which gradually came to serve as the real parliamentary basis for the government.

The first significant manifestation of the attitudes of the new government was the statement issued by Scavenius upon his assumption of office. In the future, this statement was to gain notoriety as the culminating verbal expression of the policy of adapting to German domination. The statement contained a tactically skillful reference to the parallels between Denmark's relations with Germany during the First World War and the present situation and a number of flattering remarks about Germany's victories, but the important point was a passage about Denmark's willingness to find its place in the new Europe under German leadership. The expectation that Denmark's traditional peaceful development would be respected was also expressed. The statement meant in plainer language — many thought it was already too plain—that Germany ought to accept the national government that had now been formed and refrain from attempting to promote its own supporters in Denmark, since the national government would provide Germany with that cooperation which its domination of Europe gave it the opportunity to demand. If Germany sought to impose a different government or a more direct German administration of the country, the only result would be that the Danish population would not be loyal to the new regime. The value of the national government in the field of foreign policy was that it lent credibility to Danish policy both in its efforts to adjust to German domination and in the limits it set for these efforts. The question, of course, was whether the Germans would yield to the temptations of pragmatism. The answer was determined in the first instance by the competing individuals and groups within the German government apparatus and in the last resort by Hitler, the ultimate, unpredictable decision maker.

In the following months leaders of opinion, politicians, and the occupying power were astonished by a mass phenomenon that can best be described as a national revival. Its first concrete manifestation was the *Alsang* (community singing), which began in July when a provincial town held a public meeting in one of its parks at which national songs were sung. The idea spread with extraordinary rapidity, and only two months later the movement had become so coordinated that *Alsang* was held in every town in the country on the same evening, the number of participants being estimated at 700,000. A more clearly articulated expression of the national revival was the establishment of an umbrella organization for the various political and nonpolitical youth organizations. It was more evident in this case that preparations were being made for a national and political battle for the minds of the Danish people, inspired partly by the nationality dispute in Schleswig between 1864 and 1920 and partly by the more recent struggle of the Norwegian people. The old king, Christian X, achieved an extraordinary level of popularity during these months. His birthday on 26 September, the day after Terboven established his new order in Norway, was the occasion of great popular tributes to him.

The national revival and the rapid increase in the king's prestige were significant developments in themselves, but their political importance was enhanced because both phenomena were linked to the defense of democracy and, to some extent, of the national government.

King Christian X taking his daily ride on his birthday in September 1940, escorted by university students (in white caps). That year his popularity rose to undreamed-of heights. (Museet for Danmarks Frihedskamp 1940-45, Copenhagen)

The Danish Nazis and certain rapidly declining groups that had allied themselves with them in the course of the summer did not belong to this movement in support of national and democratic ideas. Nor did extreme conservatives and the *Dansk Samling* party (see p. 26). Attempts to persuade the king to use his formal, but under constitutional practice highly doubtful, right to appoint a new cabinet were rebuffed, as were the efforts of the German minister, von Renthe-Fink, to create a greater distance between cabinet and parliament in this way. It was already clear to the Germans in January 1941 that although they could push certain individuals, like the Conservative leader John Christmas Møller, out of politics, any change in the parliamentary nature of the government could be achieved only with bayonets. There had been some German support in October and November for the idea that the Danish Nazis should take power, but the latter were now regarded as unserviceable, although they continued to receive economic assistance and protection from the occupying power. The extreme conservatives and *Dansk Samling*, like the Communists, were hopelessly isolated for the time being because of their opposition to the national government. However, it was from the extreme right and the extreme left, neither of which was bound by any ties of loyalty to the national government or to the policy of negotiation, that the later resistance movement was at first recruited.

The combination of national with democratic sentiment involved certain difficulties for the government, because the public now realized that the concessions the occupying power extracted from the government posed certain risks for democracy. Censorship, which was administered by the government under vigilant German supervision, was constantly a sore point. The impossibility of intervening against the provocations of the Danish Nazis was another. However, worse burdens were the flagrant breaches of Danish legal practice and the humiliating declarations made by the government concerning its close cooperation with Germany.

In connection with the German invasion of the Soviet Union, the Danish police interned the leading Communists in the country at the request of the Germans and in clear breach of the constitution. The *Rigsdag* followed suit a few months later by banning all "communist activity." As a result of its attitude toward the Nazi-Soviet Pact and the Finnish Winter War, the Danish Communist party was still so isolated that it could not cause any great unrest, but when the Germans forced the Danish government to accede to the Anti-Comintern

Danish Nazi demonstration, November 1940, an attempt to show the occupying power that they were ready to take over authority. The demonstration ended in street fighting with the incensed inhabitants of Copenhagen. (Museet for Danmarks Frihedskamp 1940-45, Copenhagen)

Pact in November 1941, this led to the first extensive public demonstrations, which took place in Copenhagen. Recruitment by the Germans for a special Danish unit of the *Waffen* SS, "Free Corps Denmark," was accompanied by a number of exceptionally strained declarations that this action enjoyed the approval of the Danish government. In reality, it was almost exclusively Nazis who joined the corps, which in any case was very unpopular. Its period on leave in Denmark in September 1942 was one of the irritants behind the last serious crisis before the policy of negotiation collapsed in the summer of 1943.

The crisis in October and November 1942 is called the "telegram crisis," because it was caused by a telegram from Christian X to Hitler thanking him for the best wishes he had sent to the king on the latter's birthday. The king's brief and formal reply was regarded as an affront, and even while the German 6th army was being bogged down at Stalingrad and Rommel's Africa Corps was pushed onto the defensive at El Alamein, Hitler spared the time to replace his Plenipotentiary in Denmark with Werner von Best, a member of the SS. After a protracted war of nerves the Danish negotiators were forced to retreat on one of the points that had been considered inviolable. The composition of the government was changed so that a majority of the ministers became "apolitical" (that is, they did not belong to any political party), and Foreign Minister Scavenius, despite his undoubted unpopularity both with the political parties and with the general population, assumed the post of prime minister. In fact, the new government carried out its policies during the nine-month period up to 29 August 1943 in close accord with the five parties that constituted its parliamentary basis. It did not use the emergency powers act which it had persuaded the *Riksdag* to pass in response to German demands. However, it pursued its policies under the influence of an ever stronger consciousness that the sands were running out for the policy of negotiation.

The Danish policy of negotiation toward Germany was not resistance in the sense that it sought to contribute to the Allied war effort. Nor, as we have seen, was it collaboration. And it was certainly not neutral in the classical sense of the term, since it afforded advantages to one belligerent which it was unable to grant to the other. The objectives of the policy of negotiation were clear enough. First, it sought to avoid Denmark's active participation in the war. Second, it tried to prevent or at least delay the introduction of Nazi or German rule in Denmark. The Danish government attempted to adjust to German domination to the degree necessary if these ends were to be attained, and its policy was a compromise between, on the one side, giving in to German demands and, on the other, the attitudes required if it was to retain the loyal support of the Danish people.

Defending Swedish Democracy in a Democratic Way

Although the situation faced by the national government in Sweden had some parallels in the fields of both foreign and domestic policy with conditions in Denmark, it was in some ways more difficult for the Swedish government to defend its actions, because German pressure was less obvious to the individual citizen. There was greater opportunity for open discussion of the problems of principle raised by the government's policies, but the self-evident reasons why the government had to try to restrain debate could not be publicly acknowledged while the risk of German aggression was thought to be great. It was therefore very much more difficult in Sweden than in Denmark to convince the public of the seriousness of the situation. In Denmark, which had a long-standing and deeply rooted fear of German might—indeed, one can almost speak of a national tradition of anti-German feeling—it proved difficult at first in spite of the occupation to arouse a sufficiently strong sense of national feeling in each individual citizen. In Sweden, where history had not produced a similar syndrome, the ground was more fertile for the growth of admiration for Germany, even though Nazism as an ideology suffered the same sad fate in Sweden as in Denmark and Norway. Although only a very small minority of Swedes hoped for the victory of Nazi Germany, there were relatively many who hoped that those aspects of Swedish culture and politics which they valued highly could survive within a Europe dominated by Germany. Moreover, another element in the confused picture presented by Swedish public opinion also contributed to the delicacy of the situation: the ingrained fear of Russia or Bolshevism within the Swedish upper classes. While Swedes were united in their support of the country's rapid rearmament and while, as we have seen, the most dramatic crises were caused by German demands and related to foreign policy, it was the government's infringements of, and the debate about, democratic liberties and rights like freedom of speech and of the press which most clearly illustrated the democratic dilemma in Sweden.

The problem was raised even before 9 April by a demand within the *Riksdag* for measures against the Communist press, an idea which grew out of indignation at the Communists' defense of the Soviet attack on Finland. The government had a committee draw up a proposal for taking steps against newspapers whose statements endangered the security of the realm. The outcome was a draft law in May 1940 which would give the government the power in the event of war or mobilization to introduce advance censorship and to forbid publication. Sweden's security position had undeniably changed since the new law was first conceived of, but because the proposal did not contain any provisions that could be said to be directed against any particular power, it passed through the *Riksdag* without much discussion. The proposal was clearly seen as an attempt to strengthen the country's defenses at a time when the risk that Sweden might be attacked was regarded as immediate.

Freedom of the press is, however, guaranteed by the Swedish constitution, and the adoption of the new law, like all constitutional changes, therefore had to be confirmed by a new *Riksdag* after an election. Elections were held in the autumn of 1940, and the proposal was presented again and debated in the spring of 1941. On this occasion, discussion was considerably more lively, and the dividing line on questions of principle was more sharply drawn. The proposal was still regarded as a part of the country's defense preparations, and disagreement centered on the usefulness and effectiveness of the new law. On the government side it was asserted, especially by the minister of justice, that the suppression of the opposition press would prevent excessive internal divisions and criticism at a time when all resources should be devoted to defending freedom. The opponents of the measure argued, on the other hand, that all interference with the free formation of opinion would lead to general ignorance and especially to general distrust of the information that was made public. The new law was adopted, but it was never put into operation, since the preconditions for its application, war or total mobilization, never occurred.

However, the committee had in its report pointed out that there were other ways of interfering with the press, including the so-called transportation ban, which had been placed on the statute book in March 1940. This law enabled the government to prevent newspapers that endangered the security of the realm or that could be said to be directly in the service of a foreign power from being carried on the state transport system. As the date of its adoption suggests, this law was clearly directed at the Communist press, which was indeed placed under a transportation ban from March 1940 until March 1943 and in the case of one Communist newspaper for a further six months. From April 1940 to January 1941 the pro-Allied or rather Anglophile weekly *Trots Allt* was affected by a transportation ban, and one reason for lifting it was that the journal gave assurances it would adopt a cautious tone. A Nazi newspaper was affected between April and October 1942. There can be no doubt that the application of the transportation ban was determined by the development of the international situation. After 22 June 1941, when the Germans repeatedly complained about Sweden's failure to participate in "the crusade against Bolshevism," the Swedish government was able to reply that the Communists were being kept in check in Sweden too.

As well as the measures mentioned above, the law concerning the freedom of the press already contained a clause that permitted the government to seize publications that gave cause for "misunderstandings with foreign powers." The clause could be applied without even going to court, but on the other hand it had not been used since the middle of the nineteenth century and was regarded by lawyers as *de facto* inoperative. However, it was now dusted off and employed in the government's efforts, not so much to guide opinion in Sweden as to satisfy the great powers, which needed to be convinced in the prevailing situation that the Swedish government was doing its duty. In 1940, 46 publications were seized, and a peak was reached in 1942 when 146 were confiscated. During the years 1940-43 a total of 315 publications were seized, 264 of them because they contained articles that might arouse the anger of the Axis powers. A more detailed examination of the confiscations clearly shows that they were due entirely to the development of the international situation. When the government considered this situation to be threatening, it increased the number of publications seized. As Karl Gustav Westman, the minister of justice, noted in his private diary, the confiscations could also be used as "a warning to the Swedish people, which thinks that the situation has now become less dangerous for us."

Westman's diary contains several entries which may suggest that his faith in the principle of the freedom of the press was rather slight. In his view, relations between states were now dictated by the naked exercise of power, and it seemed to him pointless to endanger the country's security out of respect for democratic principles. Democracy was a form of government that arose out of particular historical conditions and was not in itself an eternal value. However, it cannot be assumed merely because Westman left a diary that his views reflected those of the government as a whole. It is probable that most ministers saw the limitations imposed on freedom of speech as regrettable but unavoidable at a time when the great powers seemed to regard control of the press as a part of neutrality policy. The German minister in Stockholm was constantly complaining about the anti-German tone of the greater part of the Swedish press. The argument that a democratic government does not control the press but is kept on its democratic course by a free press did not go down well with the Nazis. As Hansson observed, "It is of no avail that we believe foreign policy and the freedom of the press should be seen as separate issues, since there are others who regard them as interconnected."

The opposition to the government's suppression of the free

Per Albin Hansson (second from right), prime minister and leader of the Social Democratic party, marching alongside the Liberal and Conservative party leaders in the Swedish May Day celebration of 1941. The words on the banner – "Freedom is the best of all" – are taken from a fifteenth-century song of liberty familiar to every Swede. (Arbetarrörelsens arkiv, Stockholm)

formation of opinion, which manifested itself in the spring of 1941, came mainly from Social Democrats and Liberals. They did not deny that the government was acting out of expediency, but they attacked ministers for having lost their faith in democracy, the very thing that rearmament was designed to defend. In their eyes, the suppression of the freedom of the press was a genuflection not only before the might of the great powers but also before totalitarian ideologies and methods. A considerable proportion of the Swedish press, including some papers that were not themselves interfered with by the authorities, supported the protests of the government's opponents.

Despite their doubtful nature from a democratic viewpoint, the transportation ban and the seizure of publications were at least known to the public. It is far more difficult to assess the degree of control imposed on that section of the mass media which reached the greatest number of people in this period, namely radio. *Sveriges Radio* (Swedish Radio) followed the government's political line in its presentation and choice of news. Whereas the illegal press in Norway reproduced the news from London after wireless sets were confiscated, and whereas Danes learned to sit with their heads right inside their radio loud speakers in order to listen to the BBC's Danish broadcasts, the Swedes were less strongly motivated to acquire a corrective to the news as presented by *Sveriges Radio*. In 1940 the government set up *Statens Informationsstyrelse* (SIS) (the state information board) with the task of preventing the publication of news that might embarrass other states, which usually meant Germany, through confidential communications to the editors of leading newspapers. If the latter did not respond to such representations or rebukes, more coercive measures could be employed. In September 1941 the SIS was supplemented by a press committee, which had the task of bringing about a closer cooperation with, and a closer supervision of, the press. The negative control of opinion was thus supplemented as far as possible by "advice," a practice that was also exposed to public debate and criticism.

The atmosphere that had placed limitations on the freedom of expression on the political agenda in the winter of 1940 also led to proposals that the government should have the power to dissolve political parties and organizations. Those who put these proposals forward had in reality the Communist party in mind, but the text of the new law, which was adopted in June 1940, was worded in more general terms. It stated that parties should be prohibited which sought to overthrow the country's form of government by violent means or whose activities threatened the security of the realm. A state of war or mobilization were not mentioned as preconditions for applying the law. The Conservatives, who had demanded that the Communist party be banned on several occasions during the 1930s, now had the wind in their sails, especially in the late summer and autumn of 1941, when the German army stood before Moscow. The Germans had not presented a demand, but it was argued that the prohibition of the Communist party might remove the ill-feeling that Sweden's passivity in the struggle against Bolshevism had caused in Germany. The representatives of the Conservative party within the government accordingly demanded that the new law should be invoked.

Social Democratic and Liberal ministers at first responded by adopting delaying tactics, but in October the Conservatives pressed their demand by threatening to leave the government unless it was met. In order to avoid this, the Social Democrats and the Liberals declared that they would accede to the Conservative demand, provided that the Swedish Nazi party was also banned. This was a rather astute tactical move. The Conservatives could not refuse without appearing to be defenders of Nazism, and so they accepted this condition. However, in November reports were received from Berlin which indicated that, while the Germans would welcome the prohibition of the Communist party, they would regard measures against the Swedish Nazis as an unfriendly act. This piece of intelligence was not quite enough to pacify the Conservatives, and the crisis within the government was not finally resolved before February 1942. The outcome of this episode was that the penalties for espionage and sabotage were made more severe.

Grossraum and the Economy

During the 1930s the Nordic countries had already been forced to regulate their foreign trade through bilateral agreements because of the depression. They had built up an administrative apparatus to issue import licenses and to control the expenditure of foreign currency. This apparatus could therefore be used to adjust their foreign trade to the new demands created by the outbreak of war. Their major concern was to ensure that their commercial activities should not undermine their neutrality, but of course they also wanted to protect their supplies in the face of the general shortage of goods and of the risks to maritime communications. During the first winter of the war Denmark, Norway, and Sweden all succeeded in concluding war trade agreements with both Germany and Great Britain, even though this was a difficult task because Britain sought to safeguard the effectiveness of its blockade and Germany to use the Nordic countries to circumvent that blockade. Finland was not able to reorganize its economy during the Winter War and financed its war effort by foreign credits and by recourse to the printing presses, that is to say by inflation. In the case of Finland, the reorganization of the economy to meet war conditions was therefore a task over and above the burdens imposed by the Peace of Moscow.

Weserübung changed the economic situation of the Nordic countries with one stroke. Germany totally closed the Skaggerak and severed virtually all commercial contacts between Scandinavia and the

West. Finland was still able to maintain some links through the port of Petsamo in the north, but its capacity was limited and trade through Petsamo required permission from both belligerents and was therefore subject to their control. At a later stage, Sweden managed to establish some trade with the outer world through Gothenburg, but this traffic was constantly exposed to difficulties and limitations from both Germany and Britain. The Gothenburg traffic was important to Sweden but never became extensive. Thus the outcome of the commercial situation was that after April 1940 the Nordic countries had to conduct virtually the whole of their foreign trade with Germany and German-dominated areas. The military dominance of the Third *Reich* was thus accompanied by firm German control of the economies of the Nordic states. The decisive question was therefore whether Germany would exploit its power to plunder the two occupied Scandinavian countries and to establish unequal terms of trade with Sweden and Finland.

The first months after April 1940 were a very difficult period of transition, but they also suggested that the German economic administrators were pragmatists. They clearly realized that in order to avoid the collapse of the Nordic economies Germany would have to deliver a number of commodities that had hitherto been imported from the West and to buy the exports of the Nordic states. There were immediate signs that prices were being adjusted in Germany's favor, but this adjustment was relatively modest, though the shortage of goods naturally encouraged inflation. However, other tendencies also became apparent in the summer of 1940. German planners began to take an interest in the peace that would follow Germany's triumph, which must have seemed to them very close, and there were many rumors about the form of the coming "Versailles in reverse." The stream of rumors was made no less confusing by the fact that different bodies within the German government competed with each other for the right to shape the new Europe. The ideas that emerged, and which were also put forward with greater or lesser clarity by individuals at the top of the Nazi hierarchy, pointed toward a German-dominated, planned European economy — a *Grossraumswirtschaft*.

The closest that such plans came to being put into a concrete form was in a move the *Auswärtiges Amt* made in relation to Denmark. It was a response to the statement Scavenius issued upon assuming the post of foreign minister, but it was probably rather an outcome of the power struggle between Ribbentrop and Göring. Karl Ritter, who had been working on grandiose but far from detailed plans within the *Auswärtiges Amt* since May, obtained Hitler's approval to initiate negotiations with Denmark for the establishment of a currency and customs union. This plan aroused consternation within the Danish government and the narrow circle of Danes who learned of it, but at first, at the end of July and the beginning of August, the Danes thought it would be too risky to reject the offer. Negotiations accordingly began, but within fourteen days Ritter, because of opposition from other branches of the German administration, felt obliged to make the conditions contained in the original offer considerably more severe. The Danish negotiators and the government were divided on the question of whether to continue the negotiations. This was not because it was already apparent that peace was still out of sight. The national revival, which of course had seized politicians as well as other Danes, probably played some role, but the draft treaty that Ritter had submitted to the Danish negotiators also had an effect. On the one hand, there could be no doubt that Denmark would lose all economic sovereignty if it signed the treaty, and on the other the draft was so inconsistent and sketchy that it was clear that German planning was not yet at such an advanced stage as the rumors had suggested.

In the course of the discussions the Danish negotiators had asked whether similar arrangements with the other Nordic countries were contemplated, and had received an affirmative answer. The voluntary and compulsory incorporation of Denmark and Norway respectively into the German *Grossraum* would oblige Sweden to follow suit. However, within only a few months it began to be clear that the grandiose German plans had been shelved until after the war. Pragmatism was in the ascendant for some time, because the preparations for the invasion of the Soviet Union were in progress. The more long-term adaptation of the economies of the Nordic countries to German requirements was a topic that nonetheless continued to crop up from time to time, as when the Germans attempted to establish production agreements between the German and Swedish timber industries, or to institute changes in the structure of pig breeding in Denmark, or to make large-scale investments in the Norwegian aluminum industry.

The guiding principle for the German representatives in the trade negotiations that were held each quarter was to secure as large deliveries as possible from the Nordic countries without causing such great upheavals as to destroy their capacity to deliver goods in the future. The German negotiators understood that drastic changes in the economic structure would disturb tranquillity and order, but they constantly pressed for a gradual adjustment of the Nordic economies. They closely watched the rationing system so that commodities which Germany could use were not consumed unnecessarily, but they also held in check the efforts of their own countrymen to exploit their monopoly position in order to extort exorbitant price increases for goods that the Nordic states had to import from Germany.

However, economic developments in the Nordic countries during these years closely reflected the political situation as well. Sweden managed the best and obtained the most favorable conditions, partly because it was not occupied and partly because it applied pressure on Germany by threatening to reduce iron ore exports. Finland, which was a valuable brother in arms, a euphemism for ally, was kept up to the mark by carefully calculated economic assistance. Supplies of armaments and corn in particular were used as instruments of pressure on Finland, which was allowed to maintain a substantial balance of payments deficit. Denmark supplied Germany with great quantities of agricultural produce, particularly of animal fats, a field in which Denmark provided one-twelfth of Germany's annual consumption, yet its own standard of living remained considerably higher than the German throughout the war. As for the Norwegians, they had to pay in the economic sphere too for their status as a directly administered region. The Norwegian standard of living declined more than in Denmark and Sweden and about as much as in Finland. Norway also received supplies of corn from Germany but was obliged to export a considerable part of its high-protein foodstuffs. The statistics do not, of course, contain figures for goods that were sold outside the official channels, that is, on the black market. This market did not play any great role in Denmark and Sweden, but in Norway and Finland it was almost a vital supplement to the official rations.

A comparison of the trade with Germany in the four Nordic states reveals more than their differing status. An analysis of the figures for imports and exports also shows that the various phases of the war exerted a strong influence in the economic sphere. When Germany was at the height of its power, Sweden had to agree to extend credit to the Germans, but at a later stage Sweden was able to threaten a stoppage of iron ore exports unless the debt was repaid in coal. Even more short-term changes in the figures were sometimes due to the course of the war: during the period when the forces for Operation Barbarossa were being assembled, German coal exports were far below the level that had been agreed, simply because the German railway system had no spare capacity. The relationship between Swedish iron ore exports, the import of coal from Germany, and the balance in the prices for these two commodities is illuminating. Sweden used coal in order to maintain its industry at full capacity, and a considerable part of Swedish industry was devoted to the country's rearmament. For each ship carrying Swedish ore for the German armaments industry, a vessel carrying coal returned—coal which was used to strengthen the policy of neutrality and the independence of Sweden's attitude toward Germany.

The problem of keeping the economy on its feet was not only a question of trade with Germany, although well-nigh any measure would have been in vain if the Germans had tried to thwart it. After the Germans had secured an adjustment of price levels to match the artificial overvaluation of the *Reichsmark* during the first years of their domination, they gradually agreed to cooperate in the fight against inflation. The general inflation of the war years was exacerbated by the great increase in public spending. The war effort in Finland, the *Wehrmacht's* extensive building program in Norway, the balance of payments deficit in Denmark, and the rapid pace of rearmament in Sweden all inexorably placed a heavy burden on the state budget and pumped more money into the economy. Various devices like price controls, rationing, and state subsidies were used to hold down prices, while higher taxes were imposed in a deliberate effort to take money out of the economy and the same end was served by private investment in state bonds. However, the method most frequently employed was interference with wage levels. Real incomes in Denmark fell by about 20%—somewhat less (10-12%) in Sweden and somewhat more in Norway and Finland. The effect on the social balance was a little greater than this figure suggests, since the black market favored those in a strong financial position and since the deterioration in the quality of many goods is not included in the figures for real incomes.

There is no doubt that the Nordic states, like all other European countries, became poorer during the war. The internal political struggle, which did not make much of an impact on the public consciousness, concerned the manner in which the burdens of the economic regression were to be distributed. It cannot be said that they were equally distributed. Some, particularly those in Denmark and Norway who produced for German orders, made large profits. Those in agriculture generally enjoyed an increased income, while those who were worst-placed suffered distress. However, in comparison with other countries that were occupied by Germany, the Nordic states coped reasonably well with the economic consequences of the war and suffered a less serious disruption of the social balance.

Index of the Cost of Living in 1939-45 (January-June 1939 = 100)

Year	Denmark	Finland	Norway	Sweden
1939	103	102	102	102
1940	127	121	119	114
1941	148	143	139	129
1942	153	168	147	140
1943	156	191	150	145
1944	158	201	153	143
1945	159	282	156	144

The figures in the accompanying table show that the Norwegian economy, despite more blatant German exploitation, largely developed along the same lines as the Danish and Swedish economies. This was due in some degree to the fact that the *Reichskommissar* allowed competent, non-Nazi Norwegians to administer the economy, but another factor was that in this as in other fields Terboven so to speak attended to the interests of "his" area when dealing with other branches of the German government.

The figures for the cost of living during the war, like statistics on production and incomes, reveal quite a similar picture for all the Nordic countries: a deterioration in 1940, 1941, and part of 1942, followed by a stabilization of the situation as the German economy prepared for a long war, in which the resources of the occupied countries would be exploited more rationally. However, it should be added that in the course of 1942 the reactionary Nazi Germany ceased to set the political tone. In 1940 and 1941 the reactionary political tendencies which Nazism embodied spread across national frontiers, even if the ideology itself had little appeal. At the end of 1942 the pendulum swung the other way all over Europe, even though Hitler's military domination still had two years to run.

The adjustment of the Nordic states to German domination was manifested in all areas of social life: in economic and social policy;

in the steps taken by the Nordic governments, under greater or lesser compulsion, to suspend some democratic liberties; and finally in public opinion, insofar as it can be discerned through the veil thrown over it by censorship. There are at least two clearly identifiable periods in the process of adjustment: the first, in which a German victory seemed inevitable, and the second, in which it slowly became apparent that it was simply a matter of time before Germany would be defeated. It is extremely difficult to fix the point at which public opinion realized that this change in the fortunes of war had occurred, since it was, of course, strongly influenced by wishful thinking. The few Nazis could, in their social isolation, maintain their faith in a German victory for a long time, whereas there were circles at the other end of the political spectrum in which to voice doubts about the certainty of Germany's ultimate defeat was almost regarded as treason. Every nuance of opinion was to be found between these two extremes. However, despite such differences, the internal cohesion of the population of all four countries was so strong that it constituted the essential basis for the policy that was followed, whether it was resistance in Norway, the policy of negotiation in Denmark, divergence from classical neutrality in Sweden, or resumption of the war against the Soviet Union in Finland. This internal cohesion was, of course, so strong because of the external threat, but it could hardly have been maintained if the social balance had been entirely disrupted.

Adjustment to German domination was a means of defending the societies that had been built up before the war. Those circles that thought they could exploit the situation in order to achieve changes in society did not get far. However, there were differences of opinion as to which aspects of the existing society were most important— national honor, the democratic system of government and democratic freedoms, or the social balance. A stronger realization that there was an essential interrelationship between them was one consequence of these years.

Operation Barbarossa and the Nordic Countries

by Ohto Manninen

In the summer of 1940 Adolf Hitler decided that preparations should be begun for a campaign aimed at crushing the Soviet Union, since he believed that the fall of Russia would undermine Britain's will to fight and persuade London to accept a negotiated peace. Such a course of action would also enable Germany to guarantee supplies of grain and oil for the rest of the war and to avoid the hazardous step of invading Britain. Taking over Russia and so broadening the German *Lebensraum* was an old idea of Hitler's. It was not easy for him to wage war against germanic Britain but rather easier to rally opinion against the Slavs, whom the National Socialists regarded as racially inferior.

The initiation of preparations for the Russian campaign altered the position of the Nordic countries in German eyes. Until that time the North had constituted the right flank of the western front. Now it also became the left flank of the eastern front, and its importance was enhanced by the fact that the shortest maritime route between Britain and the Soviet Union passed to the north of the Scandinavian peninsula. The significance of Finland for Germany was also increased. The Soviet Union could not be allowed to gain control of the nickel mines in Petsamo, which were important for the armaments industry. Moreover, the maritime communications between Britain and the Soviet Union could be interrupted from Finland by taking Murmansk and, at the same time, Archangel. Finland had succeeded in maintaining its independence during and after the Winter War, and Berlin therefore had good reason to do what it could to prevent the Soviet Union from incorporating Finland until such time as Germany was ready to launch the campaign in the east, or Operation Barbarossa, as this planned campaign was called from December 1940 on.

After August 1940 Germany gave discreet assistance to Finland. It delivered supplies of armaments to Finland from September on, with imaginary firms acting as intermediaries, and it sent men and material for the German forces in northern Norway through Finland. This transit traffic was of no importance to the German armed forces in Norway, since until June 1941 it amounted only to a fraction (less than one-tenth) of the traffic through Sweden, but it gave the Finns a sense of political security. Germany did not feel able to extend official political support to Finland, since it was not able to go to war with the Soviet Union before the spring of 1941. Germany therefore urged the Finns throughout the autumn of 1940 to accede to Soviet demands if the latter were not absurdly far-reaching.

In the case of Norway, Hitler feared that this country would be the object of a joint Anglo-Soviet assault. He decided to reinforce the troops in northern Norway and to strengthen the country's coastal defenses "so as to render a Soviet attack hopeless." In August the German army in Norway was assigned the task of taking Petsamo in the event of a Soviet attack on Finland. The plan for carrying out this undertaking was named Operation Renntier.

As early as the summer of 1940 Hitler believed that Finland would participate in his campaign in the east, since that country's continued existence would depend on the success of the German invasion of Russia. This belief was strengthened by Finnish efforts from the summer on to obtain German support. The Finnish army was allotted a very modest role in the directive for Barbarossa which Hitler issued on 18 December 1940. Under the terms of this directive, its task would be to occupy the Soviet naval base at Hanko in southwestern Finland, which constituted a threat to German communications across the Baltic, and to tie down as many Soviet divisions as possible along the Russo-Finnish border by an attack in the direction of Lake Ladoga. The main objectives in the Finnish theater—the seizure of the base at Murmansk, and the interruption of the Murmansk railway and the canal linking the Gulf of Finland and the White Sea—were to be the responsibility of the German army in Norway. It was thought that the Finns were primarily needed in northern Finland to cover the concentration of German forces and to protect their flank.

In December 1940 the German army in Norway was ordered to dispatch the next summer two to three divisions to northern Finland from Norway over the Swedish rail and road network. A plan was also to be drawn up for using these divisions, once they had reached Finland, for an attack on the Murmansk railway and then on Murmansk, in conjunction with the alpine army corps which would operate from Petsamo, and southward along the Murmansk railway. The plan for carrying out these attacks, called Operation Silberfuchs, was prepared, but it was clear that its execution would depend on Swedish consent to the passage of complete divisions and their supplies across Swedish territory. Hitler thought that Swedish agreement would be forthcoming once the attack had begun. The German army in Norway was asked to draw up alternative plans for these operations for the two eventualities (a) that passage across Sweden would be granted or (b) that it would not, so that most of the troops would have to pass into Finland through northern Norway; the reply stated that no kind of attack eastward from northern Finland was possible unless the Swedish road system could be used and that, even in that case, the objective of the operation should be restricted to cutting the Murmansk railway and assaulting Murmansk itself from the south and west. The attack southward along the Murmansk railway ought to be abandoned, at least until a new supply base had been established on the coast of the White Sea.

The successful raid carried out by the British at Svolvær in the Lofotens on 4 March 1941 had a considerable influence on the strategic situation in the North. It persuaded Hitler to strengthen the German position in Norway, and this in its turn further curtailed the opportunities of the German army in Norway for planning operations in connection with Barbarossa, since its primary purpose was the defense of Norway.

The reports the Germans received from Sweden in February and March 1941 indicated that the Swedish government would be unresponsive to further German demands for transit facilities. This negative Swedish attitude was reinforced by the, perhaps only apparent, growth in British strength manifested in the raid at Svolvær. The Swedish government pointed out that Britain would at the very least retaliate economically if Sweden allowed the number of German troops passing northward across Swedish territory to exceed the normal levels at a time when German-Soviet relations were still formally good, so that such a concession to Germany could be construed as directed against Britain.

In the middle of March 1941 Germany sounded Stockholm about letting 76,000 "soldiers on leave" travel to Norway across Sweden. The Swedish government reacted quickly by ordering on 14 March the mobilization of another 80,000 men, and additional troops were called up later. By the end of the month this strengthening of Sweden's defenses was complete, and five-sevenths of the Swedish army had been concentrated in the south of the country. On 15 March the German legation in Stockholm informed the Swedish government that 76,000 had been an error for 16,000. Although Sweden adopted a negative attitude toward the German feeler concerning the use of the Swedish railways by the German armed forces, the Swedish government was anxious to avoid a deterioration in the relations between the two countries and already on 14 March it suggested that the Germans should transport troops by sea and indicated that they would in this connection be able to use Swedish territorial waters.

The Germans had originally intended to send two divisions across Sweden to participate in the attack in the east. The German army in Norway did not believe that these two divisions, operating far from their supply base and in difficult terrain, were capable of a successful attack, but Hitler insisted that Murmansk should be captured. After abandoning the idea of using the whole of the alpine corps in the campaign against Russia, since part of it had been assigned to the defense of Norway, the Germans began to count increasingly on obtaining the help of Finnish troops in their advance from northern Finland, even if they were still designated as supporting forces. Moreover, the Germans assumed they would be able to send one division from Germany to northern Finland by sea at the outbreak of hostilities with the Soviet Union.

British military activity in the Lofotens and the limitations of the Swedish interpretation of neutrality thus combined to reduce the size of German troop concentrations in northern Finland to one-half of the total originally planned.

The Problems of Finnish and Swedish Security, 1940-41

There was no external change in the positions of Finland and Sweden during the period between the summer of 1940 and June 1941 in which Operation Barbarossa was being prepared. The foreign policies of these two countries were quite different. The Swedish government was conscious of the proximity of German might but at the same time was anxious about Soviet intentions. It considered it wisest— and this was also the only course that could obtain the support of the whole government—to pursue an extremely cautious foreign policy without entering into any commitments toward either the great powers or Finland. Finland, however, sought repeatedly to obtain from Germany or Sweden some kind of guarantee of assistance against a possible Soviet attack.

In September 1940 the Finns began trying to interest Stockholm in affording a guarantee to Finland, on the grounds that in August Germany had, by allowing secret deliveries of armaments, demonstrated a certain interest in the maintenance of Finland's independence. It was now thought that Germany would not oppose such a Swedish guarantee. Since the Soviet Union had in a threatening manner vetoed plans for a Nordic defensive alliance in the spring of 1940, the Fenno-Swedish contacts in the autumn revolved instead around the idea of a political union between the two countries, a union which would involve Finland's renunciation of all revanchist ideas concerning the territories ceded by the Treaty of Moscow. It was thought that the union would, at least to begin with, be limited to a joint foreign policy (with the foreign minister in Stockholm) and a common defense. Risto Ryti, the Finnish prime minister (who became president in December 1940), and Field Marshal Gustav Mannerheim, the Finnish commander-in-chief, tried to obtain Germany's blessing for the plans for a union with Sweden by sending a secret emissary, General Paavo Talvela, to *Reichsmarschall* Göring, who had played a role in establishing a measure of German support for Finland in August. However, it became clear to Finland and Sweden in December 1940 that both Germany and the Soviet Union were strongly opposed to these plans, since cooperation between Finland and Sweden would increase the ability of these two countries to resist demands from either of their great-power neighbors.

At the same time that the idea of a political union encountered difficulties and Sweden consequently became less willing to make binding commitments to Finland, Germany gave repeated indications of its growing interest in the North. In November and December 1940 Hitler caused rumors to be circulated in Sweden and Finland to the effect that during Molotov's visit in Berlin he had placed Finland under his protection and had refused to discuss Molotov's demands concerning that country. However, in their official diplomatic contacts

Risto Ryti (left foreground), Finnish prime minister (1939-40) and president (1940-44), and Marshal Mannerheim (right foreground), commander-in-chief (1939-45) and president (1944-46); between them, J. W. Rangell, prime minister (1941-43). (Yhtyneiden Kuvalehtien kuva-arkisto, Helsinki)

with Finland the Germans still avoided giving promises of support or guarantees, since they did not wish to cause premature strains in their relations with the Soviet Union.

Hitler had ordered that strict secrecy should be maintained concerning the preparations for Operation Barbarossa, and the German military authorities were therefore unable to conduct negotiations with the Finnish military leadership about the role that was envisaged for Finland in German plans. However, the Germans solved this problem by secretly presenting the Finns with a number of inquiries about their military resources and plans. It was explained that these questions were being posed because plans were being drawn up in case the Soviet Union attacked Finland or even Germany. In connection with these inquiries, concrete discussions about operational matters and supply problems were also held. The terrain in northern Finland was also reconnoitered from northern Norway under cover of the German transports through Finland. In response to requests made by the German army in Norway in October 1940, requests made in order to facilitate the execution of Operation Renntier, the Finns began in the spring of 1941 to improve the road links between the northernmost parts of Finland and Norway, since they thought that in view of their inability to defend northern Finland with their own resources it would be better that the area fell into German rather than Russian hands. Moreover, the Germans were more likely than the Russians to withdraw from northern Finland after the war.

General Franz Halder, the chief of staff of the German army, made contact with the Finns in December 1940 at general-staff level by posing a number of questions about Finland's operational preparedness through General Talvela, who had presented Finnish views in Germany. General Erik Heinrichs, the chief of the Finnish general staff, visited Berlin at the end of January 1941 in order to answer Halder's inquiries. In this connection Halder and Heinrichs discussed the Finnish operational ideas in the event of a Russo-German war. No agreements were reached and Heinrichs did not learn more than that the Germans were drawing up plans for an attack on Russia, but these contacts provided the Finns with some guidance for their own planning.

Fenno-Soviet relations deteriorated between January and March 1941 after the Soviet Union had in threatening tones demanded effective control of the nickel mines at Petsamo. Confident of German support, the Finnish government rejected this demand, since it believed that agreement would gravely undermine Finland's capacity for defense: with Petsamo under Soviet control, the Russians would more easily be able to cut off Finland's land communications with Sweden, and Germany would have little reason to be interested in Finland.

The crisis over the nickel deposits at Petsamo, Finland's increasing economic dependence on Germany (particularly for its food supplies), and ever more frequent indications of German interest in the Russian areas behind Finland's eastern frontier combined to impel Finland into a growing pro-German orientation. However, the Finns still maintained a formal neutrality. They tried to persuade Britain to keep Finland's maritime communications open, and in this connection they even allowed British observers to follow the movement of German troops through Lappland. In March and April 1941 a confidential agreement was made between the Germans and some private Finnish circles, with the knowledge of the inner circle of the Finnish government, for a Finnish volunteer battalion to be formed in Germany. This agreement was seen by the ever-growing group of Finns who were aware of recent developments in Fenno-German relations as a concrete sign that Finland now belonged to Germany's sphere of influence instead of Russia's. Revanchist thinking, which the Finnish authorities had discouraged during the unsuccessful attempts to establish a union with Sweden, became more widespread and the extent of Finland's German orientation was widely discussed around the world.

The Finns still tried to persuade Sweden to manifest solidarity with Finland in its diplomatic activities, so that Finland would not lean exclusively on German political support. In particular, Helsinki attempted to interest the Swedes in the defense of the Ålands, a question that had already concerned Stockholm in the 1930s. These Finnish efforts were encouraged by diplomatic reports which the Germans put out at the beginning of May 1941, in order to mislead the Russians, to the effect that there would be no war between Germany and the Soviet Union in 1941. However, the internal disagreements within the Swedish government over policy toward Finland prevented it from reaching any decision, and as the summer approached the hope that both Sweden and Finland could remain outside the world conflict through close cooperation increasingly lost its credibility in both countries.

The Deterioration in German-Soviet Relations

The earliest sign of the preparations for Operation Barbarossa was the concentration of troops along the German border with the Soviet Union. Already in March detailed but unconfirmed reports about German intentions to attack Russia reached both the Western powers and the Soviet Union. These two developments probably influenced the Kremlin's decisions in March and April to increase preparedness within the Red Army and to move it closer to the western frontier.

Departing from his earlier plans, Hitler was in April 1941 drawn into a campaign in the Balkans, a move which caused a serious clash between German and Soviet interests. It also obliged Hitler to delay the initiation of Operation Barbarossa by over one month, until 22 June.

Hitler had ordered that military consultations with countries regarded as presumptive allies should be deferred to as late a date as possible. Accordingly, negotiations with Finland first began on 20 May, when the German diplomat Karl Schnurre arrived in Helsinki. He invited a delegation of Finnish officers to visit Germany to discuss the coordination of military measures between Finland and Germany in the event of Russo-German hostilities. However, the Germans also informed the Finns that Moscow and Berlin were negotiating in the hope of finding a peaceful solution to their differences. On 25 and 26 May German plans and wishes in relation to Finland were explained to the Finnish delegation in Salzburg and Berlin. However, the delegation had no authority to enter into negotiations and was therefore unable to respond officially to the "ideas" presented by the Germans.

In Sweden the rumors of an impending Russo-German conflict gave rise to speculation concerning the Swedish attitude if Finland were drawn into the struggle. The government was agreed that Sweden should be prepared to resist attack from any quarter, but it was clear that the government was unable to reach a decision on the degree of Swedish military assistance that would be given to Finland if the latter became involved in a Russo-German war. Swedish help to Finland would have gained greater support if Finland alone had been the victim of a Soviet attack. On the basis of a number of quite open hints by representatives of the German military authorities, the Swedes also considered whether they would allow the Germans to send troops and material across Sweden to assist Finland if the latter were at war. The Swedish government was reluctant to place its own internal cohesion at risk by discussing this question while it remained hypothetical, but it is known that King Gustav was preparing to throw his prestige into the scales to persuade the government to accept far-reaching German demands aimed at assisting Finland.

The inner circle within the Finnish government and Commander-in-Chief Mannerheim worked out a reply to the Germans in the last days of May and early June. The guiding idea behind this reply was that Finland was willing to increase its military preparedness on a scale which had been suggested by the German military headquarters, and to allow German troops to pass through northern Finland in large numbers (the objective in this latter case was to concentrate in Lappland the German forces that were to attack Kantalahti on the White Sea). However, Finland would under no circumstances initiate hostilities or allow the Germans to do so from Finnish territory before the Soviet Union began military operations against Finland. Since the increase in Finnish military preparedness might compromise Finland if war between Germany and the Soviet Union did not break out, Finland wished to make certain requests of Germany designed to strengthen its position in the negotiations that would be conducted with the Soviet Union in that event. The most important of these requests were that Finland's independence and food supplies should be guaranteed and the frontiers of 1939 restored. On 31 May the Finnish minister in Berlin, Toivo Mikael Kivimäki, conveyed these requests to the *Auswärtiges Amt,* and a positive but unofficial response was obtained from Ribbentrop on 10 June.

Very detailed plans were drawn up during the Fenno-German military consultations that were held in Helsinki between 3 and 6 June. A timetable for Finnish mobilization was established, and it was agreed that the third army corps in northern Finland would, once it had been called up, be placed under the command of the German army in Norway. The precondition for the execution of all these measures was the decision mentioned above: that Finland would not itself begin hostilities if the Soviet Union did not do so. However, it was assumed that Soviet aggression against Finland would occur in the event of a Russo-German conflict.

At the beginning of June the Finnish authorities had accepted without argument the "transit" of large bodies of German troops across Finland and an increase in Finnish military preparedness. It was thought that the alternative was a clash between the Germans and the Russians on Finnish territory, with the Finns themselves being unable to exercise any influence at all over events. Moreover, Russia was seen as the greater threat in Finland. The German occupation of Denmark and Norway had very little effect at that time on Finnish opinion, which wished to regard it — and therefore did regard it — as temporary. It is noteworthy that President Ryti believed that the world war would end in a victory for the Anglo-Saxon powers or at any rate in a compromise peace and that a Russo-German conflict which exhausted both contestants would save Finland's position until a general peace was concluded.

By the middle of June the assembly of German troops in Finland was in full progress (altogether 75,000 German soldiers reached Finland in June), and Finnish mobilization had also begun, but no signs of growing tension in Russo-German relations were discernible to the public. On the contrary, the Soviet news bureau even denied reports that negotiations were being held between the two countries. On 14 June the inner circle of the Finnish government decided, despite some hesitation, to proceed further with the planned mobilization of the Finnish armed forces. On the previous day the foreign affairs committee of parliament had approved the measures that had already been taken. Moreover, when Britain refused to allow any further vessels to call at Petsamo, Finland's only link with the West, thereby closing this route to the outside world, the Finnish authorities were compelled to stick to the understanding reached with Germany.

However, once the decision had been made, the Finnish authorities began to have second thoughts about it, and they delayed the start of general mobilization by just over twenty-four hours. The most important reason for this delay was that the Finns feared the Germans would provoke the Finnish army into attacking on 28 June, even though Helsinki had learned that the German advance against Kantalahti would, according to plan, first begin on 1 July, that is, after the Finns had attacked. By delaying mobilization the Finns wished to prevent such a possibility. However, every indication suggested that Germany did in fact intend to invade Russia, and after Field Marshal Wilhelm Keitel, chief of OKW (German Armed Forces), had told the Finns on 15 June that war was at last imminent and that, if it did not break out, Germany would guarantee the fulfillment of the Finnish requests conveyed by Kivimäki, the general mobilization of the Finnish army was ordered two days later. On 21 June the Finnish military authorities were at last informed that Operation Barbarossa would begin the following morning.

The Outbreak of the Continuation War between Finland and the Soviet Union

In the order of the day issued after the outbreak of hostilities on 22 June 1941, Hitler used the term *im Bunde* to describe the nature of Fenno-German cooperation. This phrase could mean "in alliance" or "together." In the West it was interpreted as meaning "in alliance," and it was therefore assumed that Finland was a participant in the German attack. However, the Finnish government protested its neutrality, and the term was translated into Finnish as "side by side."

A state of war did not immediately arise between Finland and the Soviet Union, despite the open attempt in Hitler's order of the day to bind Finland irrevocably to the war. Both Finland and the Soviet Union avoided provocative measures. Finland had military as well as political reasons for seeking to prolong its neutrality: a Russian attack before mobilization was complete would have caused chaos. The Soviet Union also wished to wait until the situation had become clearer. The People's Commissar for Defense issued an order on the morning of 22 June to the effect that air operations should not be extended to Finnish territory without special instructions. The troops on the frontier with Finland were also ordered to refrain from opening fire. On the same day the Soviet government assured Helsinki that it intended to observe neutrality toward Finland, although it warned the Finns that it would take retaliatory measures if they allowed German military operations from their territory.

During the very first hours of the German attack on Russia a number of clashes occurred along the Fenno-Soviet frontier, owing to the fact that the local military commanders were unaware of the orders issued by the central authorities. Russian planes attacked Finnish as well as German ships and bombed a Finnish coastal fort. However, Soviet aircraft violated Finnish airspace on only a few occasions after the order to refrain from action against Finland was issued.

On the morning of 22 June, only one hour after the Soviet air attack on shipping and the coastal fort, the Finnish navy engaged in unneutral action when some of its submarines began to lay a minefield along the Russian coast. This measure was part of the plan prepared for the eventuality of war with the Soviet Union, and it was carried out despite the persistent orders issued by headquarters to refrain for the time being from laying mines outside Finnish territorial waters; the submarines had been instructed to observe radio silence and consequently could not be contacted. However, the minefield laid by the submarines remained unknown to the Russians. The Finnish headquarters also refused to allow the Germans to carry out the intended reconnaissance and other air activity over Russian territory from Finland.

However, the German bombers that were operating from East Prussia made use of Finland as early as 22 June. They approached their targets in the Leningrad area over the Gulf of Finland, and they stopped at Finnish airfields on their return flights. This was an important advantage for them, since Leningrad lay outside their operational range. It has, however, been suggested that German use of Finnish airfields had the deliberate purpose of creating the impression that the Leningrad area was being bombed from Finnish territory, so as to provoke Finland's immediate involvement in the war, but there is no evidence to support the view that this idea was present in German minds. German naval vessels operating from Finnish waters laid minefields at the mouth of the Gulf of Finland on the night of 21-22 June.

It was not long before the Russians took retaliatory action. On 25 June Soviet air units attacked en masse with the purpose of destroying the Finnish airfields. However, the greater part of these sorties struck at centers of population, which could be successfully bombed without time-consuming preliminary reconnaissance. This deliberate onslaught, directed at fifteen separate targets, could not be interpreted as being due to the ignorance of local Soviet commanders.

The Finnish prime minister, Johan Wilhelm Rangell, was due to present a statement to parliament that very day concerning the measures taken by the government to increase the country's defense preparedness. Although the Germans had in various ways made clear their astonishment over Finland's neutral attitude, it was the government's intention that Rangell should emphasize Finland's desire to remain neutral. However, the Soviet air attacks acted as a catalyst. In his address to parliament on the evening of 25 June Rangell stated that Finland was at war. It was now possible to enunciate the official Finnish standpoint along the lines that had been anticipated: since the Soviet Union had once again resorted to force, Finland would defend itself as it had done during the Winter War. In accordance with German wishes, Rangell also mentioned in his statement to parliament that Finland was fighting Bolshevism.

When the German invasion of Russia began on the night of 21-22 June, the Finnish government had not formally bound itself to participate in the conflict, but planning for Fenno-German military cooperation had proceeded so far that it would have been quite difficult for Finland to remain completely outside the struggle, even if the Soviet air attack had not occurred, and Finland's leaders were aware that their country would be drawn into the war. Finnish historians have written a great deal about the road that led Finland into the Continuation War, earlier research emphasizing the role of the great powers and arguing that developments in world politics drove Finland into the war without giving the Finns any opportunity for avoiding this outcome (this is the so-called drifting log theory). However, scholars have recently tended to stress that the Finnish leadership made conscious decisions even if it did not have many alternatives to choose between.

Once war had broken out in the manner envisaged by the Finnish authorities, through Soviet air attacks on Finland, it was not difficult for the Finnish people as a whole to accept the idea that the conflict had been unavoidable. It was generally believed that the struggle was a continuation of the Winter War and that its objective was to obtain recompense for this earlier conflict. During the first phase of the war there were few, apart from Communists and other members of the extreme left, who criticized Finland's participation in the struggle and the fact that the country was fighting by the side of Nazi Germany.

In accordance with the guidelines formulated before the outbreak of the Continuation War, the Finns avoided from the very start anything that might have given the impression that they were allied with Germany. They took care not to identify Finland's objectives with Germany's war aims and tried to maintain good relations with the Western powers. Resolute denials were put to Germans to prevent any attempts to interfere in internal Finnish affairs. No treaty of alliance was concluded between the two countries; the Finns declared that they were fighting a separate war; and they used the term "comrades-in-arms" to describe the Germans.

The outbreak of the Continuation War did not at the outset influence Fenno-Norwegian relations. Finland did not recognize the government the Germans had set up in Norway, and the Norwegian government-in-exile did not at first allow relations to be affected by the fact that Finland had become Germany's co-belligerent.

The Swedes now adopted a completely different attitude toward Finland's struggle than they had done during the Winter War. Now, assisting Finland was the same as helping Germany in its war of aggression, a circumstance which caused widespread doubts in Sweden. The Swedish government allowed volunteers for the Finnish army to be recruited in Sweden, but in order to avoid divisions in its own ranks forbade them to be equipped with clothing and arms by the Swedish state. During the Continuation War fewer than one thousand volunteers were raised in Sweden.

The Germans' plans in relation to Sweden had been quite drastically curtailed because of Sweden's cautious but unyielding policy: already in March the Germans had abandoned all thought of Swedish participation in the war. However, on the morning of 22 June, immediately after the outbreak of hostilities with Russia, they presented a number of demands to the Swedish Foreign Ministry. They wanted the Swedish government to grant rail passage to one division (the 163rd infantry division, which was known as the Engelbrecht division after the name of its commander) as it traveled from the Oslo district to Finland. The Germans also wanted to transport material through Sweden to Finland; to be entitled to use Swedish shipping and the Swedish telegraph system; to have authority for individual German planes to fly over Sweden and to land in that country in an emergency; to have a number of minefields laid jointly by Swedes and Germans; to have the use of Swedish territorial waters for their ships and as a place of refuge for their warships; and a number of concessions of lesser importance. The chief German negotiator, the diplomat Schnurre, emphasized that Sweden now had to make its position clear, and added that the Germans greatly hoped that Sweden would interpret its neutrality in a manner favorable to Germany.

The Swedish Foreign Ministry examined the German requirements and concluded that the passage of troops and the demand that planes which had made emergency landings in Sweden should not be interned were particularly inconsistent with a policy of neutrality. The Swedish government discussed the German *démarche* on 22, 23, and 24 June. King Gustav was especially insistent that the German demands be accepted. Swedish scholars have long debated whether the king went so far as to threaten abdication if the government did not adopt his attitude, and it is at least certain that he had previously expressed the view that this issue might lead to his abdication. Foreign Minister Christian Günther recommended acceptance of the German requirements, and on 24 June the government decided that the passage of the Engelbrecht division should be allowed, though with the proviso that this was a once-and-for-all concession which was not to serve as a precedent. With regard to the other German demands, the Swedish reply stated that they would have to be the subject of later discussions, which in practice meant acceptance of them: those ministers who had at first resisted the German demands ultimately acquiesced, since they did not wish to cause a governmental crisis in the unexpected situation that had arisen.

As far as Sweden was concerned, the situation soon became calmer. The Germans transported 15,000 men through the country, but the Swedes refused to allow further detachments of troops to use their railways, apart from the passage of soldiers on leave to and from Norway, which continued as before. As tension declined, the number of troops under arms in Sweden was reduced, and by late summer only 175,000 men were still mobilized.

Denmark also succeeded in preserving its position as a nonbelligerent state, although as an occupied country it had to accede to certain German demands designed to serve propaganda purposes. Immediately after the German invasion of the Soviet Union the Danish police arrested 300 Communists, but most of them were later released, only just over one hundred being detained in internment camps. Later, in August 1941, the Danish parliament passed a law banning the Communist party on the grounds that it used violent methods (sabotage, etc.), even though this law was generally viewed in Denmark as a violation of the rights guaranteed to citizens by the constitution.

Denmark also broke off diplomatic relations with the Soviet Union. The Danish foreign minister, Erik Scavenius, publicly defined Denmark's position in the following way in a speech delivered at the time of the outbreak of Russo-German hostilities: he declared that Denmark felt a sense of solidarity with Germany and Finland, two countries which had taken up arms against the Soviet threat and stated that the Danes were by no means indifferent to the outcome of the struggle, even though Denmark itself was not a participant in the conflict.

The War on the Finnish Front in 1941

At the end of June ten of the sixteen divisions that constituted the Finnish army were stationed along the southeastern front and two (the 3rd army corps) were placed in northern Finland along with three German divisions. The plans drawn up earlier envisaged that the center of Finnish strength in the south would be located opposite the northwestern corner of Lake Ladoga. A rapid blow was to be delivered in this direction with the aid of the commander-in-chief's reserve of three divisions with the object of reaching the shore of Lake Ladoga, so as to cut the Russian front in two; and then, according to the development of the situation and German wishes, to continue the attack either eastward north of Ladoga (first to the frontier of 1939 and finally into East Karelia toward the river Svir) or southward into the Karelian isthmus. Another Finnish division was to lay siege to Hanko. At the end of June and the beginning of July the center of the Finnish army's strength was moved to the northern part of the

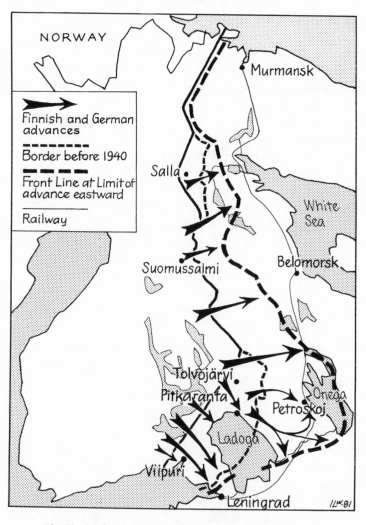

The Finnish front, 1941-44. (Cartographer: Ingrid Lowzow)

southeastern front, a special Karelian army of seven divisions under General Heinrichs being established in this sector. This development clearly favored the eastern offensive in relation to the operation on the isthmus, even in the planning stage.

It was intended that the German Engelbrecht division, which was on its way to Finland through Sweden, should take Hanko, once the requisite material had been released from other German fronts. However, when this division arrived in Finland it was placed in the commander-in-chief's reserve, and on 17 July the Finnish division that was to assault Hanko was also ordered to move to Karelia. Responsibility for the encirclement of Hanko now passed to a rather weak force, and in a surprise move on 3 December 1941 the Russians successfully evacuated their troops from Hanko to Leningrad.

Military cooperation between Finland and Germany was maintained through liaison officers and a sporadic correspondence between Keitel and Mannerheim. The latter was at no stage placed under German command, but the German *Armee Oberkommando Norwegen* in Lappland, to which the 3rd Finnish army corps had been subordinated, received its orders directly from OKW.

The Russian troops on the Finnish front belonged to the Northwest army group commanded by Marshal Klimenti Voroshilov. The 23rd army was stationed on the isthmus, the 7th army north of Ladoga, and the 14th army in East Karelia. These three armies contained twenty divisions, but troops were withdrawn from the initially quiet Finnish front to meet the German attack farther south, so that by the second half of July only thirteen divisions were left and some of these were reduced to the strength of an infantry brigade, even the officer corps being withdrawn to serve against the Germans and replaced by less competent personnel. In July just over 150,000 Russians faced about 230,000 Finns on the isthmus and north of Ladoga, and at times the Finns outnumbered the Russians by more than three to one in the sector of the front where their strength was concentrated. Although the Finnish armed forces were still motorized only to a limited degree and had almost no tanks, the balance of strength had changed decisively since the days of the Winter War.

On 10 July, the same day that the German *Heeresgruppe Nord* initiated the second stage of its assault on Leningrad from the Pskov area, the Karelian army began its attack at German request. After heavy fighting it broke through east of Jänisjärvi and at the same time attacked in the direction of Sortavala west of Jänisjärvi. On 24

July Mannerheim halted the rapid advance in the east, roughly along the line of the 1939 frontier, and the offensive north of Ladoga also came to a stop shortly thereafter. The Germans had asked the Finns to continue all the way to the Svir, but in view of domestic Finnish opinion Mannerheim did not wish to proceed farther into East Karelia until the Karelian isthmus had been reconquered.

The Finnish attack on the Karelian isthmus began already on 31 July and was initially concentrated in the eastern sector. Within a week the shore of Ladoga had been reached, and land communications south of the Russian 7th army, which was fighting to the north of the lake, had been interrupted. Three Russian divisions were thus isolated along the shore of Ladoga, but most of the troops were able to escape by boat, since the Finnish air force lacked the striking power to prevent the evacuation and the air support promised by the Germans failed to materialize. However, another Soviet division, which had only very recently been sent to this front, was almost totally destroyed.

The Finnish attack, which continued southward through the eastern part of the isthmus, also obliged the Soviet troops stationed to the west and north of Viipuri to withdraw. The right wing of the Finnish army pursued these retreating Russian forces and cut off the line of communications from Viipuri to the south through a double enveloping movement. Three Soviet divisions were isolated, but once again, although one of them was destroyed, the remaining two succeeded in breaking out to the south through the forests. The town of Viipuri fell into Finnish hands on 29 August. After the Finnish forces had been reorganized, they continued their advance toward the 1939 frontier, which they reached between 31 August and 2 September.

The German advance to the south of the Gulf of Finland was slow, and this fact caused irritation within the Finnish high command. The Finns were only prepared for a war of two months' duration, and Mannerheim inquired when the Germans thought they would really reach the Svir, since it had been envisaged that the Germans and the Finns would arrive on the banks of that river simultaneously. In response, OKW found it necessary to request that the largest possible Finnish forces should participate in the siege of Leningrad. OKW wanted the attack from the eastern part of the isthmus to approach Leningrad from the east, and also that the Finns should establish a bridgehead beyond the Svir and then push southward toward the

German forces that were approaching from the opposite direction. The idea of "the handshake on the Svir" had thus been abandoned, and the Finns were being asked to play a much larger role than had previously been envisaged.

Mannerheim adopted a negative attitude toward the German request, an attitude which was reinforced by his discussions with the Finnish political leadership. He told the Germans that there could be no question of an advance on the isthmus, since the Russians had prepared strong positions there to protect the border and since the Finnish government would not agree to crossing the old frontier. As for an advance beyond the Svir, there was no need to discuss the question at this early stage. As a minor concession or rather for tactical reasons, the Finns moved a little farther south of the frontier in certain places on the isthmus at the beginning of September in order to obtain more advantageous defensive positions. After this advance the isthmus remained static for almost three years.

Finland had clear reasons not to attack Leningrad: participating in a major and desperate battle for the city would have cost more men than Finland could afford; the defense of Leningrad had for centuries been a sore point to Russia ("the Russians would never forget," said Marshal Mannerheim); and the Finns were not willing to take moral responsibility for leveling Leningrad, a feat well known to be the aim of Hitler (President Ryti, making an analogy to Roman history, said that "such ruins of Carthago" shall not remain in history as a deed of the Finns).

The German *Heeresgruppe Nord* was now told that the prestige of Greater Germany, regardless of operational considerations, required that it make contact with the Finns in the vicinity of the Svir as soon as possible. On 8 September the army group succeeded in reaching Ladoga, thus interrupting Leningrad's land communications to the east, but it was unable to advance farther. When it was also obliged to divert some of its forces to the operations aimed at capturing Moscow, it hoped that the Finns might tie down some Soviet troops by attacking on the isthmus, but OKW's sense of pride prevented a renewed request to this effect.

By the beginning of September the Finnish Karelian army had pushed forward to more favorable positions in a number of places, and on 4 September it began a new offensive southeast of Ladoga. The so-called Olonets group which the Russians had set up was soon defeated, and the Karelian army reached its objective, the Svir, on

7 September and the road junction at Prääsa on the following day. The Finns also obtained a bridgehead on the opposite bank of the Svir. The Russians could now no longer use the Murmansk railway, but they had recently built a secondary track which made it possible for rail traffic to pass from Murmansk to the Russian interior via Archangel. After the Karelian army had been reinforced, its advance was resumed on 16 September and on 1 October it reached the town of Petrozavodsk on the shores of Lake Onega. The Finns soon began to use the Finnish name for this town: Äänislinna.

In November, as the great German offensive against Moscow gathered momentum, *Heeresgruppe Nord* was also able to advance a little farther toward the Svir. However, this attempt was halted at Tihvin during the first half of November by Soviet forces and the autumn rains. At the beginning of December the Germans were obliged to retreat and to abandon the hope of reaching the Svir that year. In fact, they never reached the Svir.

After the front on the Karelian isthmus had been shortened and stabilized at the beginning of September, the Soviet Union reduced the size of its forces in this sector by three divisions so that the troops could be used against the Germans farther south. The Finns also moved some of their forces on the isthmus to Olonets, so that the advance in the latter area could be resumed with fresh troops. In November the Finns attacked northward from Äänislinna, and on 5 December they reached Karhumäki on the northern shores of Onega. Already on 6 November Mannerheim had ordered his troops to consolidate their position at this point and to proceed no farther. Once the Finns had achieved their strategic objectives in both the areas in which they had attacked, the Finnish army prepared itself for static warfare, notwithstanding the fact that at the end of December the German military leadership was obliged to request a Finnish diversionary assault on the isthmus, since its own forces on the Leningrad front had been weakened by Soviet attack and the cold. This request, too, was made in vain.

On 28 June the German *AOK Norwegen* began its attack in Lappland against the Kola peninsula, but as early as 1 July the advance in the Petsamo area had been halted—permanently as it turned out—along the Litsa River. Salla was taken on 8 July, but twenty days later the Germans went over to the defensive in the Kantalahti sector as well. The Finnish 3rd army corps, which attacked on the right wing of the German forces, reached Kiestinki on 8 July. The main thrust of the offensive was now entrusted to the Finns in this sector, even though the Germans had originally anticipated that the Finns would only cover the flank of the German attack. However, Soviet resistance in the Kiestinki sector was tough, and the main thrust of the offensive was changed once again, with the German-Finnish forces beginning a new attack in the direction of Kantalahti on 19 August and continuing the advance for one month.

One of the greatest problems for *AOK Norwegen's* attack was the fact that there were few roads running east to west in Lappland and no north-south roads linking such roads as there were. This made it difficult to shift the main thrust of the attack during the course of the offensive, as the Germans attempted to do. The Germans were accustomed to the tactics of *Blitzkrieg* and found it hard to adjust to the wilderness of Lappland with its paucity of roads and abundance of forests and marshes. In this terrain, motorization lost its importance, and the use of massed tank formations was not crowned by success. Inexperience of warfare in the northern wilderness induced the Germans to attack in areas where there were roads. They were further handicapped because only the Kemijärvi-Salla railway, once it had been completed, provided a good supply line, which could also be used on the Russian side of the border. The Soviet troops, on the other hand, could use the Murmansk railway, which ran parallel to the front and which could be employed to move reserves from one sector to another.

The Germans believed that, if they were to be sure of taking Murmansk before the onset of winter, they would need at least one more alpine division not later than the second half of August. In practice, this proved impossible. On 31 July the Germans asked the Swedes whether an alpine division that was traveling northward from Greece could use the Swedish rail network, as the Engelbrecht division had done, but the Swedes refused this request "so that the credibility of (Swedish) neutrality should not be impaired," in accordance with their warning that the earlier concession was not to serve as a precedent. OKW accordingly decided that the division should be transported to Norway by sea and then by the northern route, once again by ship, to the front. However, after the British had attacked a number of German transports on that route, OKW felt obliged to send the division across the Baltic instead. As a result, the division did not reach Finland before the middle of October, two months later than planned. The alpine division also experienced difficulties in adjusting to its new climatic environment: for example, the pack mules and Bosnian horses it had brought with it from Greece died from the cold.

Interest was now concentrated on the coming winter, when the importance of Murmansk would be enhanced, since the port of Archangel would then become ice-bound for some time, whereas Murmansk would remain open and would constitute the Soviet Union's only northern link with the outside world. Deliveries of material from the Western powers could only reach the Soviet Union via the long and difficult land routes through Siberia or Persia or by sea via Iceland and across the Arctic to Murmansk and Archangel. The sea route took eight to ten days, whereas the route through the Persian Gulf took a couple of months. The sea route was thus the quickest way of sending supplies to the Soviet Union, even though it was also the most dangerous, since for much of its length Allied shipping lay within operational range of the German navy and air force.

When Mannerheim refused to continue the Finnish advances beyond the Svir and on the Karelian isthmus toward Leningrad, he informed the Germans on 25 September, as a sort of compensation, that once Leningrad had fallen some of the Finnish forces on the isthmus could be released for an attack northward from Karhumäki toward Sorokka and Kemi in East Karelia. The capture of these two places would cut Murmansk off from contact with the Russian interior, even along the newly built secondary track of the Murmansk railway. The Finnish 3rd army corps and the German troops in Lappland would participate in this offensive, attacking toward Louhi and Kantalahti respectively.

On 10 October Hitler ordered General Nikolaus von Falkenhorst, the commander-in-chief of *AOK Norwegen,* to initiate preparations for the execution, late in the winter, of the offensive suggested by Mannerheim, the dispatch of more troops from Germany being promised. Once it had received this order from Hitler, *AOK Norwegen* decided to refrain from all further attacks for the remainder of the year, but the Finnish 3rd army corps, which was thought to enjoy the best opportunities for an advance, was instructed to seize positions that would be advantageous for an offensive in the spring. At the beginning of November the 3rd army corps began an attack and even achieved a breakthrough. However, the Finns themselves halted their advance, partly because they did not have sufficient forces to interrupt the Murmansk railway permanently (this was the reason Mannerheim gave to the Germans) and partly because it was not in Finnish interests to continue the advance to the Murmansk railway (this was a reason that Mannerheim mentioned only in a secret directive to the Finnish general in charge of the operation). This second motive for discontinuing the attack was prompted by British and American diplomatic pressure, which had caused President Ryti to express anxiety that the attack might occur "at an inopportune moment for the country's foreign policy."

By the turn of the year the situation on the eastern front was becoming increasingly unfavorable for Germany, and Mannerheim did not wish to engage in any new military enterprise before the position in the main theater of war had stabilized and Leningrad had fallen into German hands. In March 1942 Mannerheim regarded the Sorokka operation as militarily sound, and preparations were made so that it could, if necessary, be carried out, but Ryti believed that the attack might cause the United States to declare war on Finland, and so the preparations were discontinued.

Finland's War Aims and Foreign Policy during the First Year of the Continuation War

Even after war with Russia had broken out, Finland, as a small country, pursued a cautious policy in order to maintain as good relations with the Western powers as circumstances permitted and in order to preserve internal unity. It was for these reasons that official pronouncements concerning Finnish war aims were avoided.

From the very start of the Continuation War, virtually the whole Finnish parliament supported the recovery of the parts of Karelia that had been lost as a result of the Winter War, even if this attitude was not expressed in an official declaration. Among the nonsocialist parties, the Agrarians, the Conservatives, and the small IKL cast glances beyond the former frontier to White Sea Karelia (Viena) and Olonets (Aunus), the two regions known as East Karelia. The idea that East Karelia was a part of Finland was supported by a long tradition, had been revived at the beginning of the twentieth century when Karelianism had flourished in Finnish cultural life, and had since the war of independence been entertained in the dreams of the academic youth. Not even the Finnish government discussed the frontier question officially, but it is known that the issue aroused disagreement among ministers. This disagreement was given concrete expression during the discussions on the advance of the Finnish army. When the Karelian army began its attack on 10 July, Mannerheim issued an order of the day in which he openly alluded to the liberation of East Karelia. Mannerheim's purpose was to inspire the troops and he claimed that the order of the day lacked any larger political objective, but it did nonetheless threaten to cause a split within the government. In public, the representatives of each view spoke or wrote about the order of the day with enthusiasm or restraint depending on their general outlook. However, it was clear that if the publication of the order of the day had been prevented or if it had been repudiated, this would certainly have led to the resignation of the commander-in-chief, who was known for his touchiness, and the government did not feel that it could afford to be the cause of Mannerheim's departure from the scene. In August the Social Democratic ministers opposed the Finnish advance beyond the 1939 frontiers, but this issue too did not lead to a crisis within the government.

Since the campaign against Russia seemed to suggest that Germany was on the way to achieving the leading position in eastern Europe, voices were soon raised within Finland demanding that the country reserve to itself the "Finnish" areas of a Soviet Union that appeared to be disintegrating. Through the acquisition of these areas Finland would gain in economic strength after the war, and the manpower lost during the conflict could to some degree be replaced. The Greater Finland that would be created by such territorial expansion would be able to enjoy a more stable and independent position within the New Europe which it seemed was being created.

The Finns were already prepared in May 1941 to tell the Germans which parts of Soviet territory had previously been Finnish and were most closely tied to Finland. The claims the Finns put forward in connection with the Russo-German negotiations which they had been led to believe might occur related to the recovery of the parts of Karelia ceded by the Treaty of Moscow of 1940 and, as compensation for the areas that the Kremlin would not be willing to return in view of Leningrad's security needs, the acquisition of the areas in East Karelia that the Soviet Union had assigned to the so-called Kuusinen government in December 1939. At the same time President Ryti asked a number of Finnish scholars to demonstrate, while acting as "private individuals," what Soviet areas might on historical and ethnological grounds be attached to Finland. As a result, a number of works were published in the autumn of 1941 which concluded that Finland ought to obtain East Karelia and the Kola peninsula (with the frontier running from Ladoga to the White Sea) and that the remaining Finnish-speaking population of the Soviet Union should be moved to this enlarged Finland, whereas peoples of non-Finnish origin in the newly acquired territories should be moved to other parts of Russia.

Once the Finns had gone beyond the 1939 frontier, Ryti thought it appropriate to inform the Germans unofficially of his attitude. He told them on 11 September that Finland had to have a short frontier stretching from the White Sea along the Svir, Lake Ladoga, and the Neva to the Gulf of Finland. The annexation outlined by Ryti thus included the Kola peninsula, an area which had not been mentioned in the Finnish requirements put forward in May. When the Germans later expressed surprise at this new demand, Ryti explained that further examination of the matter from the military and ethnological points of view had led to the conclusion that the Kola peninsula was Finnish. Ryti's calculations were based on the assumption that the Soviet Union would be permanently destroyed as a great power (he knew that this was Germany's aim) and that a zone dependent on Germany would be created between Finland and Russia.

However, while the outcome of the Russo-German conflict remained uncertain, the Finnish government maintained its official caution and bore in mind the possibility that Russia would remain Finland's neighbor in the future. The influential Social Democratic party also emphasized through its leader, Väinö Tanner, that the Finnish people and economy would be unable to sustain a long period of active warfare or to support permanently the sparsely populated and underdeveloped region of East Karelia. All measures that tended toward the territorial expansion of Finland beyond the frontiers of 1939 would impair Finland's relations with Sweden and the great powers of the West, and it was thought that the latter would provide support and a guarantee for the maintenance of Finnish independence and democracy at and after any peace conference that was held. The contraction of Finland's economic resources, the prolongation of the war, and the growing diplomatic pressure exerted by the Western powers combined to strengthen the position of this cautious body of opinion, which demanded the cessation of Finland's advance into Russia. A compromise gradually emerged: it was agreed that the Finns should speak only of securing advantageous defensive positions during wartime; since the autumn of 1941 less and less was heard about acquiring a militarily secure and ethnologically sound frontier-line.

The Germans maintained an attitude of condescending benevolence toward the expansionist aspirations that the Finns had unofficially expressed. From the very beginning, that is to say from the summer of 1940, Hitler had assumed that Finnish territory would be enlarged. In July 1941, when his belief that victory was certain was at its strongest, Hitler contemplated giving Leningrad, after it had been totally destroyed, to Finland. However, the Finns do not seem at any stage to have expressed a desire to acquire the Leningrad area, even though the province of Ingria, which surrounded the former Russian capital, still contained people of Finnish blood and tongue. Hitler adopted a positive, a "generous," attitude toward the objectives that Ryti unofficially put forward in September, since it was advantageous to Germany that Finnish desires now extended beyond Finland's former frontiers. However, the question of the Kola peninsula, which Hitler had in July described as a future part of the *Reich* which would be colonized by Germans, should be left open. In November Hitler told the Finnish foreign minister, with the aim of encouraging the Finns to send more troops to the Salla front, that it was right and reasonable for Finland to request and reserve to itself the Kola peninsula. In Hitler's thinking, an enlargement of Finland's territories went hand in hand with closer ties with Germany. On 16 July the *Führer* told his closest associates that the ground should cautiously be prepared for Finland's adherence to the Greater Germanic *Reich* as a *Bundesstaat* (allied state or state of union).

Although the Germans often declared that they had no intention of interfering in Finland's internal affairs, the possibility that Germany would try to turn Finland into a protectorate and a one-party state remained a constant anxiety for Finnish politicians. In particular, the Social Democrats, who of course remembered the fate of their German comrades, were apprehensive about their position if the war should end with a complete German victory.

The Finnish government's restraint in foreign policy questions was influenced by its desire to retain the sympathy of the Western powers. Even after it became involved in the war against Russia, Finland stated that it was still neutral in the war between Germany and Britain. The Finns wished to maintain normal relations with the West, but Germany soon expressed a desire that Finland should break off diplomatic relations with Britain, partly because the British legation in Helsinki was passing military information to the Soviet Union. President Ryti and the Finnish government resisted the request, but it was reiterated on 19 July in a personal letter from Hitler to Ryti. The Finnish government now drew up for Rolf Witting, the Finnish foreign minister, new instructions which gave him some scope for breaking off relations with Britain. On 30 July airplanes attached to the British navy bombed Finnish territory as an indication of sympathy with the Soviet Union. (This was the only military operation that Britain carried out against Finnish territory throughout the Second World War). At the same time Witting presented a communication to the British government breaking off diplomatic relations on 1 August. On the following day Britain declared that Finland was an area under enemy occupation, a measure which in practice put an end to all commercial transactions between the two countries and included blockade of Finnish trade. Despite the rupture of diplomatic relations, there was still some understanding in Britain for Finland's desire to regain the territories lost during the Winter War. However, Mannerheim's order of the day concerning East Karelia had strengthened the case of those who argued that Finland had begun a war of conquest.

In September and again in October the Soviet Union asked Britain to declare war on Finland, but London replied that such a step would only throw Finland irrevocably into the arms of Germany. Sweden and the United States, two countries which regarded Finland with great goodwill, also advised Britain to refrain from a declaration of war. The British government contented itself with warning the Finns in September that they should halt their advance and retire to the 1939 frontier. The United States also presented a note supporting these demands. However, the Finnish government took the view that it would be too dangerous to desist from military operations, since it placed no faith in the Soviet Union. The advance in East Karelia therefore continued, and the British government began to consider seriously the possibility of declaring war on Finland, because it felt that Britain ought in some way to manifest its support for the Soviet Union at a time when the Germans were rapidly drawing closer to Moscow. Among the Dominions only Australia was in favor of a declaration of war whereas New Zealand, South Africa, and

Canada were clearly opposed to such a step. In spite of the views of a majority of the Dominions, Churchill issued an ultimatum on 21 November, which stated that Britain would declare war if Finland did not cease hostilities within two weeks. The Soviet Union had indicated that it would be content with a *de facto* end to the war and would not at that stage demand a formal treaty.

During the first successful phase of the war the German leadership does not seem to have been troubled by the idea that Finland might end its separate war by concluding a separate peace. On the contrary, Ribbentrop saw no reason for trying to force Finland into the three-power pact of Germany, Italy, and Japan against its will, since he thought the community of interest between Finland and Germany was already sufficiently great so long as it seemed that Russia would be crushed. Moreover, Finland was dependent on Germany for its grain supplies.

In November 1941 the time had arrived to renew the Anti-Comintern Pact, a treaty which had an ideological basis and which had originally been concluded between Germany and Japan. The Germans tried to make the renewal of the pact as solemn an occasion as possible, and also to acquire new signatories for this treaty directed against the spread of communism. The Finnish foreign minister, however, pointed out that Finland's accession to the pact might undermine Finland's position in the eyes of the American public, and he proposed that Finland should adhere to the pact not on this solemn and demonstrative occasion but "at some more opportune moment." Nonetheless, the Germans applied strong pressure on Finland, arguing that membership in the Anti-Comintern Pact would in no way change the distinct nature of Finland's separate war. With a view to reducing the effects of adherence to the pact, President Ryti urged that it would be of great importance to Finland if Denmark and Norway joined. Norway's legal status created a difficult problem for Germany, but the *Auswärtiges Amt* immediately began negotiations aimed at securing Danish adherence to the pact. The Germans conducted the negotiations very firmly and the Danish government agreed to join, though it was anxious to emphasize that Denmark was still a nonbelligerent country. The result was street demonstrations in Denmark against the government's compliant policy and Scavenius.

When the Anti-Comintern Pact was renewed on 25 November 1941 Finland and Denmark were thus numbered among the new signatories (the others were Romania, Bulgaria, Slovakia, Croatia, and Nanking China). Membership in the pact had no immediate effect on Danish and Finnish relations with Germany, but was certainly of political importance in the eyes of the Western powers. As compensation for complying with German wishes, Finland received an assurance from Germany of sufficient grain supplies to survive until the next harvest, but in practice the severe ice conditions in the Baltic hindered the shipping of food supplies to Finland that winter.

The Finnish government and military authorities discussed the British threat of a declaration of war, along with other important questions connected with the limits of the advance, at the end of November. The army had now virtually achieved the strategic objectives it had been set: to capture Russian areas from which in the Finnish view the Soviet Union had been preparing an attack on Finland, that is to say, to occupy a great part of East Karelia. There was general agreement that what had been achieved was enough.

On 6 December the territories that had been lost by the Peace of Moscow and now reconquered were declared to be rejoined to the republic, but the Finnish authorities did not feel that they could act as directly over East Karelia, nor was it thought desirable that Finnish publications should contain demands for its incorporation. The Finnish government realized that the area could be used as a bargaining counter in the peace negotiations. Consequently, East Karelia was placed under military administration in accordance with international regulations.

Since the attack against Karhumäki was still in progress at the beginning of December, the Finnish government felt obliged to reply to Britain that Finland had not yet quite reached strategically favorable defensive positions. Accordingly, Britain declared war on 6 December, Finnish Independence Day. Its example was followed by Canada, Australia, New Zealand, and India. One day before the British declaration of war the Finnish army reached its objectives and halted its advance. These declarations of war did not mean at any stage of the Second World War that Finland had become involved in real hostilities with the Western allies. The United States, which was also drawn into the great conflict in December, did not declare war on Finland nor even break off diplomatic relations. Norway, on the other hand, broke off diplomatic relations on 7 December.

Although the Finnish government informed Britain that its aim was to guarantee Finland's security by acquiring control of the bases that would be used in a Soviet attack, it made no official statement about Finland's territorial objectives in the longer term. However, the requirements that Ryti had unofficially conveyed to the Germans and which had also been mentioned in certain Finnish publications, gradually became known to a wider circle. Finns became accustomed to the idea, and in August 1942, after a year of war, Ryti optimistically suggested that the younger generation that had borne arms and the right wing of the Social Democratic party agreed with it. However, it is quite impossible to estimate the degree of support the concept of Greater Finland enjoyed at the time of its greatest popularity. Once the fortunes of war had turned, the hopes of those who had most zealously upheld the idea were disappointed. Less and less was heard of the frontier Ryti had mentioned to the Germans and Finnish public opinion, like official thinking, increasingly came to see East Karelia as a negotiating counter in future peace negotiations.

Static Warfare

By the autumn of 1941 Finland's material and spiritual resources were under extreme strain. The Finnish military authorities were able to refuse German demands for greater military efforts by pointing to Finland's exiguous resources, and this explanation was given further credibility by the fact that Hitler had acknowledged, even before the campaign against Russia began, that Finland had been bled white during the Winter War. In 1941 Finland lost 25,500 men killed in combat, a figure that represented about 80% of conscripts born in a given year and which exceeded by 2,500 the casualties in the Winter War. Even before the Finns had reached their military objectives, Mannerheim had decided on 15 November 1941 that the armed forces would be sent home in stages. It was, of course, the oldest conscripts (those born between 1897 and 1908) who were released first. By the beginning of March 1942 about 70,000 men had been sent home, and the figure had risen to 180,000 men by the end of June. However, there were still 450,000 men under arms.

The shortage of food severely tested Finnish morale. Finnish agriculture experienced great problems, since it became more difficult to import fertilizer and fodder. Agriculture also suffered from a shortage of labor: 16% of the population had been called up into the army, a conscription rate which is said to have been one of the highest in the world. As a result of these factors, the volume of agricultural production in 1941 was only 73% of that in 1938. Finland had been 80-90% self-sufficient in agricultural produce before the war, but now became increasingly dependent on grain from Germany. Moreover, in 1942 the volume of agricultural production fell to only 68% of the figure in 1938, even though a sizable number of soldiers had been released from the army and added to the labor pool, and a large part of the farmland in the reconquered areas of Karelia had been brought under cultivation. It has been suggested that the causes of this continuing decline in production were the reduction in the amount of autumn plowing undertaken and the ever more apparent effects of the shortage of artificial fertilizers. In the spring of 1942 the Finnish urban population at least was put on a low-calorie diet.

The morale of the Finnish people was sustained by the state information services, discreet censorship, and exhortations to participate in voluntary group labor (the so-called *talkoo*-spirit). The activities of the information service were facilitated by the fact that its personnel represented a wide range of political opinions. Censorship was applied only to material concerning military secrets and relations with Germany and the Western powers. The Finnish public was almost as well informed of the course of the war as the Swedish people.

Once the front had been pushed farther away from the country's frontiers, Finland's security seemed greater, especially since the German attacks in the south had almost entirely directed Soviet attention away from Finland. Nonetheless, operations did not come to a complete stop on the Finnish front, even though the Finns had taken up defensive positions at the beginning of December 1941.

Half a year after the beginning of the German attack the Soviet Union had begun to organize its enormous resources of manpower effectively. New units were hastily assembled and quickly trained. In some cases, seamen taken from the navy were used to form the core of the new units. Thirteen infantry brigades of marines arrived on the Finnish front around the end of 1941 or the beginning of 1942. The Soviet Union intended to launch a counterattack with the assistance of these reinforcements. In December 1941 Stalin in vain asked the British to participate in an assault on Petsamo in February, the object of the operation being to defeat the Fenno-German forces that threatened the port of Murmansk and the Murmansk railway and to destroy the bridgehead the Finns had established south of the Svir, which threatened Leningrad. Once the

Russians became aware that the Finns were not attempting to advance further, they were able to reduce their forces in some sectors of the front in order to strengthen their resources in the areas where they intended to attack.

The Soviet assaults on the Finnish front began in January 1942 and lasted until late April and early May, when the thaw seriously impeded operations. The biggest attacks were launched in April along the Svir, where six divisions and six brigades began their offensive on 11 April, and in the Kiestinki area, where three divisions and three brigades initiated their operations almost a fortnight later. The Finns were able to halt all these assaults, and these operations demonstrated that long lines of communication, which became longer as the attack developed, impeded any Russian or Finnish advance.

After the failure of the Soviet spring offensive against Finland, the Russians in the course of the summer and autumn moved at least two divisions and three brigades away from the Finnish front, some to the southeast of Leningrad and some to the Stalingrad area. Nonetheless, Soviet troops remaining on the Finnish front were ordered to intensify their activities there so as to tie down enemy forces, and a specially trained guerrilla brigade, for example, carried out an incursion far behind the Finnish lines.

At the turn of the year 1941-42 the Germans changed their commanders in Lappland: Falkenhorst was sent back to Norway to take charge of the defenses of that country, and a new army which was not under Falkenhorst's command, *AOK Lappland,* was established under "the hero of Narvik," General Edouard Dietl. The whole force of the great German summer offensive of 1942 was directed against southern Russia, but since this advance seemed to go well, Hitler's appetite grew and he began to make plans for an attack in the north as well, in the Leningrad area and in Finland.

On Dietl's initiative, the Germans proposed to the Finns in July and August that an attack should be carried out in the late autumn against the Murmansk railway along the lines planned the previous autumn: the Germans would advance toward Kantalahti and the Finns against Sorokka and Kemi. Mannerheim's reply, however, also resembled the one he had given the previous year: the prerequisite for Finnish participation was that the Germans should take Leningrad and press forward to the southern shores of Lake Onega, thus releasing Finnish troops for the offensive, and that they should provide powerful air support in the Sorokka area. The Finns calculated that, if the Germans won a great success in the Ladoga region, a Finnish attack against the Murmansk railway (and thus also against Anglo-American deliveries of material to the Soviet Union) would not decisively impair Finland's relations with the United States.

The most important of the preconditions for the Sorokka offensive remained unfulfilled. At the end of August Soviet troops attacked in an effort to break the ring of besieging forces around Leningrad, and the Germans were obliged to use the reserves intended for the capture of this city to repel the attack. By the beginning of September the German military authorities had abandoned the idea of an operation against the Murmansk railway, and in October the attempt to take Leningrad was also postponed indefinitely.

A Landing in Norway?

With the German invasion of Russia, Britain, which had been close to war with the Soviet Union during the Winter War, achieved the objective that its diplomacy had pursued since the summer of 1940: Russia had been transformed from Germany's associate into Germany's enemy. Sharing the experience of German pressure, Britain and the Soviet Union rapidly drew closer to each other, despite their mutual ideological mistrust, and on 12 July 1941 they agreed in principle to conclude an alliance for the duration of the war. The United States, which was still not involved in the war, also changed the regulations governing its foreign trade to the advantage of the Soviet Union.

Moscow hoped that Britain would undertake military operations against Germany that obliged the latter to reduce the force of its attack in the east. In this connection, three alternatives were available: the bombing of Germany (which indeed occurred); a landing in France or northern Norway; and naval operations off Petsamo and Murmansk. Stalin was most attracted by the idea of attacks against northern Norway and Petsamo. Churchill became interested in the idea, and the British military experts had their hands full in trying to convince the prime minister that a landing in Norway would be crushed by the Germans at an early stage. Since the British had transport ships for only 5-6,000 men and since they thought Russia would be defeated in the course of the summer, they wished to retain these ships and the troops they could carry for the occupation of the Spanish and Portuguese Atlantic islands, because they expected

Hitler to try to gain control of the Iberian peninsula after his campaign in the east.

Stalin suggested that the light division raised from Norwegian volunteers could be used for the landing in northern Norway, but Churchill was obliged to reply that such a division had not yet been formed. Refugees from Norway had in the first instance volunteered for the Norwegian naval and air force units that were being trained in Britain and Canada. Moreover, manpower was required for the Norwegian merchant marine, which was largely in Allied service. It would therefore be some time before men could be found for the Norwegian army that was being built up, though the Norwegians were subject to conscription by the government-in-exile.

British military operations in the North were initially restricted to an air attack carried out from an aircraft carrier on Petsamo in Finland and Kirkenes in Norway on 30 July. This attack, which was of some political but little military significance, resulted in a number of Finnish civilians being injured.

After his suggestion that a second front be formed had been turned down, Stalin proposed in the autumn of 1941 that Britain send twenty-five to thirty divisions to the Archangel area in northern Russia or through Iran to southern Russia. These troops would then fight side by side with Soviet forces. This proposal was also rejected by Britain, since it was unable to transport and supply such a large number of troops. However, the British did consider the possibility of carrying out a landing in the spring of 1942, for example on the northern or southern section of the Russian front.

It was hoped that a landing in Norway would at least provoke a large-scale uprising in that country and might also bring Sweden into the war on the Allied side. If the attempt succeeded, it might prove possible to begin to push back Hitler's "fortress Europe" from the north. However, Britain feared that if such an operation were carried out in conjunction with Russian troops, Sweden might become apprehensive about its territorial integrity and become irrevocably committed to Finland and thus also to Germany. The Norwegian government-in-exile was also skeptical and thought that the enterprise was doomed to failure, since it would be both premature and backed by too few troops. To unleash a popular uprising among the Norwegians at that stage would merely lead to unnecessary bloodshed among the civilian population.

As early as the summer of 1941 Hitler regarded Norway as one of the most probable places where the Western powers would attempt to create a second front, but he thought the danger would only become actual after the United States had entered the war. In his view, troops suitable for mobile operations (one to two panzer divisions) should be stationed in Norway as soon as the state of German resources permitted. Hitler expected an attack on Norway immediately after the winter of 1941-42, and thought that British troops (or their Norwegian or Canadian allies) might carry out a landing on the Murman coast even earlier. As we have seen, Stalin had indeed proposed such a landing. In November 1941, while the great battle around Moscow was still undecided, Hitler regarded the Far North as the most dangerous area in the European theater of war, not only for purely military reasons but also because the nickel deposits at Petsamo were threatened.

In December 1941 the United States entered the war and British naval units attacked the Lofotens. These developments increased Hitler's fears: he believed the risk of an assault on Norway had become greater, and he is reported to have said that "the outcome of the war will be decided in Norway." He ordered all available battleships and cruisers to be sent to strengthen the defenses of Norway. The first of them was dispatched in November, and the largest German battleship, the *Tirpitz*, was sent to Trondheim in January 1942. Moreover, the Germans reinforced the coast artillery units in Norway and, in order to increase the mobility of the defending German forces, intensified the work of improving the Norwegian road network, which had been begun in 1940 with the aim of linking the northern part of *Neuropa* more closely to Germany.

At the beginning of 1942 Stalin added his signature to the British-American Atlantic declaration, and in this connection he demanded that Britain immediately establish a second front. In May 1942 Molotov obtained a promise from Roosevelt that the Western powers would both open a second front and deliver material to the Soviet Union. However, Churchill would not agree to a landing on the European mainland at the beginning of 1943, which he thought was too early, and in the summer of 1942 he told Stalin that the operation had been postponed.

The passage of convoys across the Arctic increased German anxieties about a landing in Norway, for there was no guarantee that these convoys did not carry an invading force. So that the large battleships and new submarines and aircraft that had been sent to

Norway in the winter of 1942 to prevent an Allied landing might serve more than a purely defensive purpose, the German naval authorities requested that these resources might be used against the convoys. This request was acceded to, and as a result the Western powers sent only one convoy across the Arctic between June 1942 and January 1943. The Germans were thus successful during this period in almost entirely interrupting the northern supply route to Russia. However, in the autumn of 1942 the Western powers carried out a landing in North Africa, a theater of war remote from the North and Germany.

Since June 1941 Sweden had been almost entirely surrounded by the German armed forces, even in the Baltic, and it is not surprising in these circumstances that rumors of an impending German attack on Sweden were already circulating in the autumn of 1941. In February 1942 the Swedish intelligence service received a warning, which proved to be false, of a German invasion of Sweden, and the number of men under arms in Sweden was increased to 300,000. Although the Germans did not, as far as we know, have any plans for attacking Sweden at this stage, it is clear that the strategic situation in Scandinavia was becoming more tense and that the mobilization of the Swedish armed forces increased Hitler's apprehensions. He feared that Sweden would join the Allies if the latter landed successfully in Norway, and the Germans accordingly increased their preparedness in the North. The Finns indeed told the Germans, in response to an explicit Swedish request, that the risk of an Allied landing was very slight. In Mannerheim's view, the British had had enough of the problems of the terrain in the Murmansk area in 1918 and would not want to repeat the experience, while President Ryti assured the Germans that the Swedes would resist an Allied incursion in the North, just as they would resist all other violations of their territory. Ryti advised the Germans to refrain from putting pressure on Sweden, which might lead them quite unintentionally into war with that country.

Fenno-Swedish relations deteriorated to some extent after Finland entered the war. Disappointment about the limited scale of the help they received from Sweden led the Finns to think unkindly of "those who hide themselves behind us," and the concept of Greater Finland was also directed in part against Sweden. Some Swedish ministers even seem to have suspected that the Finns would not have objected if the Germans had used force to coerce Sweden into closer cooperation, even if this force were applied from Finnish territory. However, this was a mistaken view. Despite the disappointments Swedish attitudes had occasioned, the Finnish government still regarded Sweden as its only certain, albeit weak support in the hurly-burly of the great-power war. At the end of 1941 and the beginning of 1942 Ryti, for example, believed that Sweden ought for this reason "to be kept warm"; Finland might after all be able to withdraw from the war with Swedish help if the military situation deteriorated.

With the coming of summer in 1942 the German intelligence service concluded that the risk of an attack on Norway had declined, but Hitler's anxieties were again aroused in October and November. He immediately moved a number of small units to Norway from Finland and the Baltic states and interrupted the transportation of troops to the eastern front, since he considered the absolute security of the northern theater to be of greater importance than an extension of the offensive in the east deeper into the Russian interior. Moreover, early in the autumn a panzer division was formed in Norway, as had long been planned. The strategic situation in the North, that is to say Hitler's fear that the Allies would establish a second front in that region, thus influenced the outcome of the battle of Stalingrad, one of the turning points of the Second World War.

Nordic Volunteers in German Service

The 13-15,000 men from the Scandinavian countries who joined the German armed forces during the Second World War played a direct part in the struggle begun by Barbarossa. Non-German volunteers who were prepared to espouse the concept of a Germanic Europe were enrolled in the military wing of the SS, the so-called protective corps of the Nazi party, the *Waffen-SS*, which was established in 1940 and which was regarded as the rival to the *Wehrmacht*. The Scandinavian peoples were perhaps the purest representatives of the Germanic type, fair and blue-eyed, and the head of the SS, Heinrich Himmler, thought it especially desirable that Scandinavians should be recruited for his army.

During the spring and summer of 1940 Germany's military position was so stable that the additional manpower such volunteers could provide was not regarded as decisive. However, they were seen as important from a political and racial point of view in connection with the idea of a New Europe. In April 1940 the SS regiment *Nordland* was founded and a number of recruitment bureaus were discreetly opened in Copenhagen. About 300 Danes were enrolled in the summer of 1940, and Norwegians soon began to join the regiment as well. A former officer in the Danish royal guards, Count C. F. Schalburg, was placed in command of the Danish volunteers. The regiment was not organized along national lines; indeed all special national emblems were forbidden.

A great number of the Danes who arrived at SS training centers in 1940 thought that they would return home after a short period of training to participate in the *Machtübernahme* in Denmark. When it became clear to them that they were instead to serve in the German armed forces, they withdrew. Moreover, in 1940 the SS applied very strict standards when deciding whether to accept new recruits, and many were excluded because of their racial, physical, or other characteristics or because of their bad reputations. At that time 80% of the Danes who reached the training centers changed their minds or were rejected. The disappointment felt by those who returned home led to a virtual stoppage of enrollment in Denmark. It was in the spring of 1941 that the SS first sought the assistance of the strongest Danish Nazi organization in disseminating propaganda on behalf of the *Waffen-SS*. This step and a reduction in the standards for acceptance, including the raising of the upper age limit, increased recruitment; between March and June about 800 men in Denmark joined the *Waffen-SS*. Recruitment also increased in Norway after a public announcement on the subject was made in January 1941. A total of about 800 Norwegians joined the SS regiment *Nordland*. The older volunteers were placed in the new SS regiment *Nordwest*.

Although Finns were not regarded in Germany as a Germanic race, Hitler agreed in February 1941 that they might also be recruited. The inner circle of the Finnish government discussed the question on 11 March and decided to adopt a positive attitude toward the enrollment of Finns in the *Waffen-SS*. It saw this decision as a demonstration of Finnish goodwill toward Germany, and in its way a guarantee that Finland belonged to the German and not the Soviet sphere of influence. The inner circle was none too happy that Finns would have to serve along with the citizens of occupied countries (Norway, Denmark, and Holland) and in the *Waffen-SS*. The Finns therefore suggested that Finnish volunteers might serve in the *Wehrmacht*, which was rejected, and that they might form a battalion of their own, which the Germans could accept. On 28 April the Germans and Finns agreed to the formation of a Finnish SS battalion. Since the Finnish government did not wish to be directly involved with this battalion, a committee was set up with the task of secretly handling recruitment and of ensuring that no Communists and only a limited number of right-wing extremists were included. As a result, those Finns who joined the SS, unlike a large proportion of their Danish and Norwegian counterparts who were fired by the idea of creating a new national socialist order, were not motivated by the idea of changing Finland's internal political system. About 1,200 Finns were enrolled in the *Waffen-SS* in May 1941. Just over 400 of them were, despite protests, dispersed among the *Nordland* and *Westland* regiments. The remaining 800 or so formed the SS volunteer battalion *Nordost*. In the autumn of 1941 its name was changed to the *Waffen-SS* Finnish volunteer battalion.

After the invasion of the Soviet Union, a crusade against Bolshevism was proclaimed in all the countries that were under German control, and volunteers were recruited in all of them for formation into "legions," which were allowed to remain national groupings. The legions raised in the North came under the control of the *Waffen-SS*. In Denmark men began to be enrolled into a *Freikorps Dänemark* on 28 June. Recruitment now occurred openly, and Scavenius publicly announced that it was taking place. Now that Communism was described as the enemy, many more volunteers came forward than the Danish government had expected when it allowed recruitment. By August 800 Danes had volunteered, and the figure had risen to almost 1,400 in December. Another 130 Danes were provided by the regiment *Nordwest*, which was disbanded. In Norway the *Norske Legion* was established on 29 June. It was publicly supported by Knut Hamsun, a winner of the Nobel Prize for literature, and by twenty-seven parish priests. The legion used the cross of St. Olav and two swords as its emblem, and 1,100-1,500 men joined it in the course of the summer.

A number of the Danish and Norwegian "legionnaires" volunteered for or were directed to the SS in an attempt to reach the Finnish front. In Denmark, efforts had been made immediately after the beginning of the Russian campaign to establish a volunteer corps for Finland. The *Auswärtiges Amt* informed the Finns that it would take care of these volunteers, and proceeded to refuse them permission to travel to Finland. However, the ban was not absolute, since a number of Danes were able to go to Finland with the help of the Finnish legation in Copenhagen. When the Germans began to complain that individual Danes were making use of such assistance in order to reach Stockholm and make contact with the British intelligence service, the Finnish government agreed in September to announce that it would only accept groups. At the beginning of 1942 a group of about 120 Danes tried to travel to Finland, but the SS was anxious lest Finland might become its rival for the affections of Scandinavian volunteers, and the journey was forbidden.

The Norwegian legionnaires protested when they were obliged to swear an oath of loyalty to Hitler, and suggested, without result, that their oath should be sworn to the Finnish armed forces instead.

The *Nordland* and *Westland* regiments, and the Finnish SS battalion, were used on the eastern front as parts of the SS *Wiking* division. In 1941 this division fought in Galicia and the Ukraine, participating in the capture of Rostov, and in 1942 it took part in the conquest of the Caucasus. The *Norske Legion* and the *Freikorps Dänemark* were both sent to the front at the beginning of 1942, and they were used in the SS *Totenkopf* division in the Leningrad sector throughout the year. In the spring of 1943 the remnants of the Nordic SS troops at the front were withdrawn for rest. The *Nordland* regiment and the Danish and Norwegian legions were amalgamated to form the basis of the new SS *Nordland* division. About 650 Danes came to belong to the Danish grenadier regiment of the division, and 600-700 Norwegians to its Norwegian grenadier regiment. The division was stationed in Croatia from May to November, fighting Tito's partisans. It was moved to the Baltic states at the end of 1943, and was evacuated to Germany at the end of 1944. The division continued to fight in Germany, at the end in Berlin, until the German capitulation at the beginning of May 1945.

Sweden was the only Nordic country in which troops were not recruited for the SS. At the beginning of July 1941 Schnurre had proposed to Günther that Swedes should be given the opportunity to volunteer for the German armed forces, and the question was also raised with the Swedish military authorities. The Swedish reply, however, was a negative one and stated that Swedes might volunteer for the Finnish army but for no other foreign force. The Swedish attitude concerning Swedish enrollment in foreign, that is to say Allied as well as German, armies was made public at the beginning of September; nonetheless a few hundred Swedes did join the SS forces, though no special military unit was formed for them.

After the outbreak of Russo-German hostilities the Germans also tried to acquire additional troops for the *Waffen-SS* from Finland, but the Finnish government was now able to point to its own requirements of manpower and resisted these attempts. However, in the spring of 1942, 200 Finns were enrolled as replacements for the SS battalion, but the Finnish government refused to allow a further contingent of this kind to be recruited. When the SS battalion in the summer of 1943 arrived in Finland on leave, the Finnish government succeeded in having it disbanded and its personnel was placed in the Finnish army.

In Denmark and Norway, on the other hand, the recruitment of volunteers for the *Waffen-SS* continued. In 1942 and the first half of 1943, 300 new volunteers were recruited in Denmark for service in the German armed forces, and the *Korps Schalburg,* which was of battalion strength, was formed in Denmark itself, although to be sure most of its manpower was provided by volunteers who had returned home. The corps was later formed into the SS training battalion *Sjælland* and later still into a guard battalion. There were brawls and other clashes in Denmark between Danish members of the SS who were serving in Denmark or on leave and other members of the Danish population. Danish members of the SS were seen by their countrymen as traitors who had made common cause with the occupying power and who often behaved in a brutal manner. SS training did not fit in well in a democratic environment.

In August 1942 an SS battalion of ski troops was established in Norway for service on the Finnish front. The battalion gradually grew in strength so that a first contingent could be sent to Finland in the spring of 1943 and the rest of the battalion in the following autumn. In the spring of 1944 the battalion was responsible for a section of the front in Lappland, but it was evacuated to Norway at the end of the year after Finland had withdrawn from the war.

It is very difficult to estimate the number of Nordic citizens who served in the *Waffen-SS,* since it is hard in the case of Norwegians to distinguish between those who belonged to the *Waffen-SS* and those who were active in the Norwegian *Hird,* the militant guards of Quisling. However, it can be said that 1,400 Finns, 6-7,000 Danes, 5-6,000 Norwegians, and at the most a few hundred Swedes served in the *Waffen-SS,* that is to say about 15,000 men altogether or 0.5% of the approximately 670,000 non-Germans who belonged to the *Waffen-SS.*

The Nordic Countries during the First Year
of the Russian Campaign

Because of the importance of the strategic position of the Nordic countries on the northern flank of Europe and of their natural resources, they had been brought under German control before or at the beginning of the invasion of Russia. The two occupied countries, Denmark and Norway, did not play an active role at this stage of the war, although they did tie down German troops. Finland, on the other hand, provided the Germans with an opportunity for attacking the Soviet Union through Lappland and participated directly in the Russian campaign. Sweden, which was completely isolated with the arrival of German troops in Lappland and the German conquest of the whole south coast of the Baltic, was obliged to support the German war effort through various concessions. However, Sweden and Finland both reached the limit of their concessions to Germany within a short time of the initiation of Operation Barbarossa, and were able to resist further German demands. After August 1941 Sweden refused to allow German troops bearing arms to use its territory, and in the same month Finland refused to increase its military efforts to interfere with the deliveries from the Western powers to the Soviet Union, or to attack Leningrad. However, at the end of 1941, it was still only Germany's involvement in the world war which prevented it from subjecting the Nordic states to its complete control.

The Beginnings of
the Resistance Movement

by Ole Kristian Grimnes

Resistance is here defined as a type of political opposition that unfolds in the face of an established regime which illegalizes and persecutes that opposition. In a way, then, it is the regime which determines what is resistance, i.e., what opposition it illegalizes and turns into resistance. On the other hand, of course, it is the resisters who determine this since they decide whether they will persist in an activity that exposes them to persecution and punishment. To illegalize is to criminalize. From the point of view of the regime, resistance is always a criminal activity, directed against the very regime that illegalizes it. From the point of view of the resisters, their activity may be illegal. In fact, the most common word for organized resistance in both Danish and Norwegian during the war is translated as "illegal work." But such resistance certainly is not considered illegitimate or criminal.

At its very core resistance is political. It may assume other forms not the least of which may be military. Still it is political since its main objective always is the disestablishment of the regime it resists and the setting up of some other political order, in the case of Denmark and Norway during World War II the traditional prewar order. Political opposition turns into resistance when there is no legal political channel for that opposition; thus resistance must continue under circumstances of illegality. It is its political essence which distinguishes resistance from ordinary criminal activity which is not political but which has some personal or group gain as its main objective. Ordinary criminal activity does not question the order within which it occurs. It takes it for granted and violates it. Thus resistance is always bound up with the issue of political legitimacy, the issue of whose job it is to run the country and how it is to be done. This holds true even when there is a legitimate government, as there was in Denmark during the first part of the war, so long as there is also an illegitimate regime, the German one, behind that government.

During the Second World War, resistance in Scandinavia was confined to Norway and Denmark because they were the only countries to be invaded and occupied, and thus to have illegitimate occupation regimes on their soil. In Sweden there were German soldiers passing through Swedish territory, and in Finland German troops were invited in to fight the Soviet Union. But these countries were not occupied against their will as were Denmark and Norway. In the non-occupied countries ordinary government continued to work in a more or less normal manner. Political opposition, except for the Communists in Finland, was not illegalized and did not have to turn into resistance. Nor was there any alien regime to resist. But interestingly, some of the Finnish Communists whose party was illegal attempted to carry out acts of sabotage against their country when it was at war with the Soviet Union. This was resistance, but it was a marginal phenomenon. In Sweden there was nothing like this kind of activity. Sweden assisted the resistance movement in Norway and Denmark. In the beginning this was done mostly by private individuals because Swedish neutrality was slanted toward the Germans at that time and thus incompatible with giving assistance to any anti-German movement. The Swedish individuals who engaged in such assistance even ran the risk of being persecuted and jailed, so that their activity took on some aspects of resistance. But their actions did not represent resistance per se, because there was no regime on Swedish soil which they wished to disestablish.

Resistance as a general phenomenon need not be national in the sense of being triggered by a threat to a nation's identity, fundamental values, self-image, or sovereignty. For example, when a domestic resistance movement fights a domestic regime and there is no foreign presence or intervention involved, the resistance is not truly national, even though it might be conducted on a nationwide scale. But in the two Nordic countries during the war resistance was thoroughly national because it was directed against a foreigner and his collaborationists. The only difficult case to determine is that of the Communists. They did not resist only because their country had been occupied. They also resisted because the Soviet Union had been invaded. They took up resistance wholeheartedly only after and because the Socialist Fatherland was in mortal danger. Was their resistance then national? Perhaps it is best to distinguish between original motives and later development. The Communists' original motives for joining or starting the resistance movement were at best only partly national. But once they became involved they were certainly part of a national movement, and even more so when they gave up their policy of revolution and became reformist during the war, dedicated to the restoration of the traditional political democracy which was the general platform of the whole resistance movement.

Resistance was a national activity, but not all national activity was resistance. There was always another national option: the "policy of negotiation," to use the term coined by the Danes. It meant conducting regular negotiations with the German authorities and trying to further national interests through negotiations. Such negotiations were conducted on the Danish or Norwegian side by legitimate national representatives who were acknowledged as such by the Germans. Resisters they were not because they did not engage in any illegalized activity. But national they were, both in their background and in the way they tried to protect national interests during the negotiations. National interests were thought to be best defended through negotiations, not through a rupture in the relationship with the Germans which was always the prerequisite for resistance. If resistance was the response of war (though not necessarily war in its military form), the "policy of negotiation" was the response of forced adjustment. It meant "cooperation" with the Germans, though not "collaboration," which entailed much more of a positive acceptance of the German presence or an active exploitation of it to further one's own political, economic, or social interest.

In Norway the heyday of the "policy of negotiation" lasted from the summer of 1940 until 25 September, in Denmark from the beginning of the occupation until 29 August 1943. After those dates the traditional politicians no longer haggled with the Germans over conditions in the occupied country. The last vestige of political normalcy was thereby gone and the stage set for resistance. Still, this did not mean the end of the "policy of negotiation." It meant only that the legitimate political representatives, the men of the traditional political organs, stopped conducting negotiations directly with the Germans. The legitimacy of the traditional political system was then no longer behind the German presence as it had always been to some degree when the politicians agreed to negotiate with the Germans. But even without such political legitimacy the "policy of negotiation" continued at an administrative "nonpolitical" level. Norwegian and Danish civil servants went on with their jobs in a working relationship with their German or Nazi counterparts. These societies could not be run otherwise. If it were a national interest to wage a war of resistance against the Germans and Nazis, it was also a national interest to keep the country functioning by negotiating with the Germans. In every relationship between an occupier and the occupied, even though the occupier is in a position of power, there is some degree of negotiation which can be exploited by the occupied in the national interest, if only because the occupier does not know the country well enough to give orders offhand and has to enter into some sort of negotiation. There was a natural development from negotiation to resistance without the latter ever superseding the former. Both coexisted as two different national lines of policy and conduct. They might conflict, the one trying to resist the occupying power, the other trying to run the country alongside that power. But there might also be a symbiotic relationship between them, as when civil servants in the Ministry of Supply argued (i.e., negotiated) with the Germans over the flow of supplies, then channeled a portion of those supplies to resistance organizations illegally.

As an organized activity resistance was by its very nature secret. Otherwise it would be erased through police action. Resistance members were concealed behind the facade of normal society or—as military resistance groups were in Norway in 1944-45—at hiding places in uninhabited areas. Their whereabouts should not be known to the police or the general public. Some resistance "products" were visible, such as acts of sabotage, collective action brought forth by underground directives, and clandestine newspapers (even though they were to be read in secret); others were invisible to the public at large and the police, and included intelligence material and the transportation of refugees across the border. The men and women behind the "products" were always invisible. But resistance was by no means only an organized activity or collective action elicited by organized activists. It was also spontaneous mass action which had not been stirred by the organized underground and which that underground was hard put to direct or control. It was then thoroughly "overground," with the resisters and their "product" being eminently visible.

In the course of the war resistance became political, ideological, economic, and military. It was political in a basic way, as has been indicated, and it was political in a more special sense when it attempted to avert particular German or Nazi drives to gain political legitimacy or politically significant positions. It was ideological in its fight against nazism as an ideological system. Economically its objective was to impede or block the German exploitation of key resources. And it was military when it gathered intelligence to be transmitted abroad or organized armed groups to engage in current or future action.

The Norwegian Resistance Movement

The Nazi Offensive

The nature of the German occupation regime determined the way in which the resistance movement developed, and since the occupation assumed very different forms in Norway and Denmark, the character of resistance in the two countries was also very different. In Norway 25 September 1940, the day that Terboven installed the Norwegian Nazis in a position of power, constituted a watershed. It is hardly possible to speak of "resistance" in Norway before that date, since national activity had not yet acquired that stamp of illegality which was typical of resistance. Before 25 September the two methods of opposing the Germans that were pursued were open warfare and, in the occupied parts of the country, negotiation. After the end of the war on Norwegian territory in 1940, "the policy of negotiation" was dominant, but the events of 25 September brought it to an end above the administrative level. The Germans no longer recognized any political representatives of the Norwegian population other than those who belonged to the Norwegian Nazi party, all political activity outside this party and all opposition to it being forbidden. Exactly what constituted political activity or opposition to the new adminstration in the country remained to be more closely defined. It was not certain that all forms would be suppressed and punished, but in principle anyone who manifested an aversion to the new regime in one way or another faced the prospect of punishment. Norwegians were given a speedy reminder of this when a former republican, who made a speech expressing loyalty to the king at a students' union meeting in Oslo 21 September, was arrested 26 September along with the chairman of the students' union. Still, not all opposition to the Norwegian Nazis or Germans was actually punished after 25 September, and much civilian opposition in the winter of 1940/41 and in the spring of 1941 was even deliberately shaped as if it were perfectly legal. But more and more the German or Norwegian Nazi reactions to it showed that it was not legal, that it was punishable, that it was really resistance, not just opposition.

When the Germans established a new regime in Norway on 25 September, representatives of the Norwegian Nazi party, *Nasjonal Samling* (NS), received positions in the government. The party had not taken over the government completely, but the overwhelming majority of the heads of ministries whom Terboven appointed belonged to the NS and wanted to carry out its platform. Moreover, their activities were to some extent coordinated by the party, even though formally they were responsible to Terboven only on an individual basis. Terboven had given NS his public support, and it seems that

Reichskommissar Joseph Terboven (left), the supreme civil authority in German-occupied Norway, and Vidkun Quisling, the leader of the Norwegian Nazi party, at the installation of Quisling as "Minister-President" in February 1942. (Norges Hjemmefrontmuseum, Oslo)

the prospect of greater power at a later stage had also been held out to the party. For the moment, the party was too small and had too little popular backing, but it was reasonable to hope that it could extend its position and acquire a broader basis through its control of the central administration under German supremacy and through German support. True, German support could not always be taken for granted. NS had to some degree been forced on Terboven, and he was skeptical about the party and its leader, Vidkun Quisling. The German institution that gave the most solid backing to NS was the navy, which intrigued against Terboven partly because he did not support NS actively enough. However, even Terboven seems to have wanted to give NS a chance to show what it was capable of. At any rate, after 25 September he was obliged to let the party have that chance. The NS leadership even got the impression that it had received a firm guarantee from the Germans that it could assume full power eventually, if only it could show that it deserved it, i.e., could show that it enjoyed a modicum of popular support and was capable of governing. It is, of course, clear that the Germans and NS might arrive at differing opinions as to when the party had shown this, but both seem to have agreed that NS now had a chance and had to try to exploit it.

This is the background to the political and ideological offensive that NS launched against Norwegian society after 25 September and which determined the nature of Norwegian resistance in its first phase. It seems that the offensive did not follow a broad strategic plan but rather was the result of a series of scattered and not always coordinated initiatives. The offensive continued during the remainder of 1940 and the whole of 1941, and reached an especially concentrated phase in 1942, when on 1 February Quisling was formally appointed minister-president of a "national government" composed exclusively of representatives of NS. The German motives behind this change in the form of government are obscure, but it is clear that it led to very little actual change. As before, real power remained with Terboven as *Reichskommissar.* However, NS itself ascribed importance to the change, and it seems that the new "government" was initially allowed a certain latitude. At any rate, it undertook new and important initiatives which led to a climax in the resistance in 1942.

The Nazi offensive of the years 1940-42 was launched over a wide and complex front. The various individual measures taken will be discussed here only if they served to provoke resistance, and far from all of them did so. The offensive was in part a propaganda campaign on behalf of "the new age," and the party was able to conduct this campaign through the controlled press, political meetings, Nazi processions on the streets, exhibitions, posters, and leaflets. Now that NS controlled the resources of the state, there were fewer practical difficulties standing in the way of such a campaign than before. The campaign included propaganda for the party and Nazi ideology, against "Bolshevism" and the Western "plutocracies," and in favor of enlistment in the *Nordland* regiment, the Norwegian legion, and other units that were set up as time went by for employment at the front. However, the Nazi offensive also took the form of more concrete initiatives aimed at gaining control of institutions and organizations so that NS might at least appear to enjoy mass support for its politics and ideology. Occupational, economic, and cultural organizations were not the least important objective in this connection, since NS was strongly attracted by the corporatist element in fascism, that is, by the state's use of such organizations for its own purposes. Especially after the appointment of "the national government" on 1 February 1942, NS became engaged in efforts to set up a so-called *Riksting* (National parliament) which was to consist of representatives of the organizations, replace the *Storting*, and provide "the national government" with a seemingly firmer legitimacy and a broader base. The new regime also took an interest in the legal apparatus (whose independence it tried to attack), local self-rule (which it wished to curtail), the central and local administration, cultural life, and not least the education system. In most fields, the Nazi offensive was conducted by two means: (1) through public decrees or laws which NS could now, given Terboven's approval, issue freely and back with the authority and resources of the state; and (2) through attempts to place or favor party members or sympathizers within organizations or institutions. NS thus tried during its offensive to determine both the content of policy and the composition of organizations and institutions.

On the whole, the Germans allowed NS a free hand with its campaign against Norwegian society. They supported the same ideology as NS, but largely left it to NS to conduct the campaign for this ideology. However, there was always a German presence in the background. It was the Germans who in the last resort approved all measures, and some of their own special measures were sometimes included among those taken by the Norwegian Nazis. The Germans were always able to intervene, and they did so especially when NS's offensive had been brought to a standstill by substantial resistance. A show of strength was then needed, and the Germans took the requisite action.

The Nazi offensive was far from ineffective, especially during its initial phase when the resistance front had not yet become well established. NS enjoyed some success in its attempt to recruit new members. The total membership grew rapidly during the autumn of 1940, rising from about 4,200 at the end of August to about 25,200 on 10 January 1941, and continued to increase until November 1943, when it reached a peak of 43,400. The party was particularly successful in recruiting policemen, so that the police became the most Nazified of all the public services during the occupation. Five to six thousand men also served as volunteers at the front, as was described in the previous chapter.

The most striking success enjoyed by NS was perhaps the ease with which the nazification of local government was achieved. Elected local councils had been introduced in 1837 and were regarded as a cornerstone of Norwegian democracy. Yet they fell under NS control almost without lifting a finger in self-defense when the NS moved against them in December 1940. At that time the Nazi authorities demanded that new chairmen of all local councils be nominated at the beginning of the new year. The new chairmen were not to be elected, and they alone were to make all decisions on local affairs, in accordance with the Nazi leader-principle whereby appointed leaders from above, not elected assemblies from below, should direct policy. The only restriction on them was that they were to be obliged to consult with a circle of advisers who were also to be appointed. The appointments of chairmen and advisers were made by the newly established Ministry of the Interior in accordance with proposals made by the county governors, who were to confer with the county leaders of NS on the matter. In other words, the county governors actually cooperated in the nazification of local government, for it was largely Nazis who were appointed as the new chairmen and to some extent as advisers. When existing, elected chairmen or members of the local councils were reappointed, this often happened quite simply because there were no qualified NS members that could be appointed, and they were later replaced by Nazis if competent NS members appeared on the scene. Under the new arrangements, the county governors were also to administer the counties in accordance with the new principles. The county governors were civil servants who had been appointed, not elected, to their posts, and no attempt was made to replace them at first. However, the county assemblies, which consisted formerly of the elected chairmen of the local councils, were now deprived of all authority, and all decisions were placed in the hands of the county governors themselves, while the chairmen played only an advisory role. In all this the county governors followed a "policy of negotiation." Their sentiments were overwhelmingly national, even though they actually participated in the nazification of local government. Their argument was that it was better to try to influence the selection of the new chairmen, which might perhaps secure the appointment of patriotic individuals, than to leave the whole business to NS and perhaps as a result see the worst Nazis appointed to every position. Influence exercised in the course of negotiations would serve the population's interests better than an open breach, which would destroy all possibility of exercising influence over the authorities. The "fault" from the point of view of resistance was that this policy contributed to papering over disagreements that ought to have been made explicit and to legitimizing a violation of democracy which ought not to have been endorsed. Despite their cooperation, the county governors were soon replaced by Nazis or NS sympathizers.

Resistance as a Reaction

The offensive that NS launched against Norwegian society was both political and ideological. The resistance was, in its initial phase, above all a reaction, a reply to this offensive. The fundamental objective of the resistance at this stage was to prevent NS from achieving broadly based popular support and from carrying through the conversion of the population to Nazi ideology. Thus, during its initial phase the Norwegian resistance was not directed against the German military forces that had occupied the country or against German decrees or German military and economic interests. True, the *Wehrmacht* might for military reasons become anxious about the unrest resistance created among the population, unrest that might cause complications if the feared Allied invasion should occur. However, the resistance itself was primarily directed against the initiatives taken by NS that aimed at nazifying Norwegian life, against the decrees and laws that were issued in the name of Norwegian NS ministers or the Quisling government, and against the occupation by

Nazis of important posts within the structure of Norwegian society. It was above all these initiatives which disturbed Norwegians and most immediately provoked preventive action, and which therefore determined the nature of Norwegian resistance in its first phase. Norwegians reacted most directly against those of their compatriots who were seen as traitors and who represented values that were thought to be alien and a threat to Norway's national integrity. Norwegians did not react as directly against the foreign occupying power that stood behind NS, which represented the same ideology, and which made the threat to Norway's national integrity possible.

Various manifestations of resistance began early in the occupation. At one moment, resistance came from those engaged in a leisure activity; at the next, from an established group within the traditional legal apparatus; then from a religious institution and next from some of the great secular organizations; and often as a more or less spontaneous grass-roots reaction that developed independently of established organizations. There were certainly important contacts as early as the winter of 1940-41 between many of the groups involved, and they influenced each other; there was even an attempt at that time to establish a nationwide organization and leadership for the resistance. However, on the whole, resistance was characterized during its first phase, not by unified leadership and coordination, but by many scattered acts of defiance in different areas.

One of the first mass reactions to the Nazi challenge was the so-called sports strike, which began in the autumn of 1940 and lasted until the end of the war. The newly established Nazi Ministry of Labor and Sport tried to interfere in free sporting activities and set up a state-controlled Sports Union (*Idrettsforbund*), to which all sports teams would belong. As a result, all sports organizations discontinued their activities and no further sporting events were arranged publicly except by the new Nazi sports leaders; henceforth Nazis were virtually the only participants in the events, and there were few spectators. However, national sporting events were secretly arranged for the old teams that had officially ceased to function, and they attracted far more spectators.

In December 1940 the Supreme Court resigned in protest against the attacks on the independence of the courts that had occurred since 25 September. First, the new Nazi head of the Ministry of Justice had usurped the right of appointing and dismissing jurors, magistrates, court officials, and so on. Then the age of retirement for public servants had been lowered, so that the Minister of Justice could remove some of the older members of the Supreme Court and replace them with men who were loyal to the new regime. Terboven declared that the Supreme Court did not have the right to examine the validity of the decrees that he or the Nazi ministers responsible to him issued. Moreover, on 30 September one of the Supreme Court judges was arrested and accused of engaging in oppositional activity. The Supreme Court protested several times against these infringements of its authority, the last occasion being on 12 December, when it stated that Norwegian courts were in duty bound to examine the validity of laws and decrees, and also claimed the right to judge whether the decrees issued by the occupying power were valid under international law. Since this was no longer possible, the Supreme Court judges felt obliged to relinquish their posts. The Nazi Supreme Court that was set up as a replacement did not come to play much of a role in the state. The attitude taken by the Supreme Court made a strong impression on many Norwegians, given the fact that the constitution had made it the third organ of the state. The first, the king and the cabinet, had rejected the new regime by going abroad and participating in the Allied war effort. The second, parliament, had been removed from the scene by the occupying power. The third had now ceased to function on occupied soil, and by doing so had clearly shown its will to defend an important element in the traditional democratic system, the idea of a state subordinate to the law and of the independence of the courts from the state.

In the face of the new situation, the various elements within the Church drew closer together in the autumn of 1940. A meeting of prominent clergymen and leaders of the major Christian organizations was held at the official residence of the Bishop of Oslo on 25 October. The purpose of the meeting was to create a united Christian front against Nazism by overcoming the old division between "high church" and liberal theologians on the one hand and the orthodox lay movement on the other. An informal Christian Council (*Kristent Samråd*), representing the most important Christian groups, was formed and served as the basis for the church leadership for the remainder of the occupation. On 15 January 1941 the Norwegian bishops sent a letter of protest to the Minister of Church Affairs. The letter pointed out that it was difficult for the Church to maintain the traditionally intimate relationship between the state and Church when the state had ceased to respect the law. The Church now seemed to face a state that was alien to it; the letter mentioned as examples the violent behavior of the Nazi *Hird* (youth organization), the resignation of the Supreme Court, and the attempts made to encroach upon the duty of priests to respect confidences. The Church tried to argue on a theological basis as much as possible, but posed the problem of the new Nazi state in a general way and took many of its examples from secular society. By doing so it came to defend the same democratic values as the resistance as a whole and thus became an important part of the resistance movement that was evolving. When no reply to the letter was received, one of the bishops called on the minister of church affairs and handed him an even sharper protest. The authorities now produced a reply, but the bishops did not find it satisfactory and they had the whole of the correspondence published (with an introduction) in February 1941. This publication, of which 50,000 copies were printed, was the well-known Pastoral Letter, which obtained the support of a number of national Christian organizations and other religious bodies. The police seized about 20,000 of the printed copies, but the remainder were distributed over the entire country; additional copies were duplicated; and failing intervention by the police, clergymen read the Pastoral Letter from the pulpit.

There was also considerable spontaneous resistance at the grass-roots level. Many Norwegians demonstrated their opposition to the regime in small ways and consequently ran the risk of being assaulted by the *Hird* or arrested by the police. The aggressive behavior of the *Hird* also caused disturbances and street fights in some places. Attempts by Nazis to deliver speeches led to heckling or other difficulties. During the first six months of 1941, the most important development in the resistance movement was the sending of three great letters of protest to Terboven. The first letter, which was dated 3 April, sharply rejected the political values that had now been made the basis for employment in the public sector at both national and local levels. The letter thus sought to defend the democratic principle that public service should be neutral in relation to the political parties which struggled for the right to govern society. The letter was signed by prominent representatives of twenty-two organizations, especially associations of public servants which were affected by the new policy toward employment in the public sector. The largest organization involved was the national federation of trade unions, LO (*Landsorganisasjonen*), which had been in a difficult position since the beginning of the occupation, as was the labor movement as a whole. Some of the most important labor leaders were members of the government-in-exile, and certain others who had remained at home had been forbidden to resume their positions within the movement. The Labor party, along with the other parties, had been banned on 25 September 1940 and retained only a secret central executive committee, which followed a cautious policy. LO was allowed to continue, but on 28 September the Germans forced it to accept a number of more compliant people, including individuals who were under Communist influence, in senior positions within the organization. However, the chairman and vice-chairman who had been dismissed set up a clandestine committee, which worked closely with the secret committee of the Labor party. Together, these two bodies constituted a center of resistance which tried to induce LO to pursue a tougher policy toward the occupation regime. A sign that they had at least some success in this connection is that LO's new vice-chairman was one of the signatories to the letter of 3 April.

On 15 May 1941 a second letter was sent to Terboven, which in more general terms attacked the policy that NS was pursuing from its dominant position in the Norwegian administration. The Nazi ministers had "on a number of occasions issued decrees and made decisions which were openly contrary to international law, Norwegian law and the Norwegian sense of justice." This letter was signed by representatives of forty-three organizations, most of which were professional bodies though there were also a few economic organizations. LO was once again the most important signatory. The third letter, which was dated 30 June 1941 and came from LO alone, complained about LO's present lack of influence on wage questions and of its subjection to such close control that it could hardly function any longer as the protector of its members' interests. If the authorities would not allow the trade union movement "satisfactory working conditions," the LO leaders would be unable to continue in their posts. During the spring of 1941 an important part of the incipient resistance movement thus manifested itself through a lower stratum of the traditional political system, that is to say through some of the country's professional and economic organizations. Since the highest organs within the traditional system were either in exile, like the king and cabinet, or had ceased to function, like parliament, the democratic parties, and the Supreme Court, the lower stratum which was still intact, "the organization society," assumed a central role within the resistance.

The occupation regime's reply to the first and second letters was a counterattack aimed at bringing those organizations that had protested under its control or eliminating them and which declared that such protesting was not legal oppositional activity but illegal resistance subject to punishment. On 12 June Terboven had the leaders of three of these organizations arrested. On 18 June another six were arrested, eleven of the forty-three organizations that had subscribed to the protest on 15 May were dissolved, and the rest, except for LO, had Nazi or pro-Nazi commissioners imposed on them as leaders. Several of the leaders of the organizations involved in the protest who were state employees also lost their posts. The regime moved against the trade union movement next, in September 1941. A series of strikes in the capital led the Germans to declare a state of emergency in the Oslo area, under which two trade union leaders were executed (these were the first political executions in Norway during the occupation) and most of the LO leaders were arrested and replaced by Nazis or pro-Nazis. At the same time, two organizations that had not participated in the protests, the Employers' Federation and the Craftsmen's Association, were placed under the control of commissioners. The Shipowners' Association had been under Nazi control for some time, and the Nazis had gradually infiltrated the Farmers' Association until they gained full control of it and also of the Association of Farmers and Smallholders later in the autumn. However, it was some time before certain other organizations, including the Association of Industries, were brought under Nazi leadership.

There were two types of reactions to these developments. First, most members of many of the organizations that had come under Nazi control resigned, and their delegates and officials discontinued their work. Those delegates, officials, and members who remained within the organizations ceased to participate in their activities or did so only to a limited degree. In this way, many organizations either ceased to function completely or became a shadow of their former selves, so NS obtained little political advantage from its move against them. Second, clandestine action committees and clandestine networks of delegates developed at varying speeds within a number of the occupations and branches of the economy whose legal representative organizations had been nazified. As early as the autumn of

1941 some of these clandestine bodies sought contact with each other and thus became an important basis for the civilian resistance leadership that was emerging in the capital.

New acts of resistance followed in 1942, which was the "great year" of the civilian resistance movement and a high point in the evolution of a nationwide resistance movement. These manifestations of resistance were provoked above all by the intensified offensive launched by the new Quisling government, which took office on 1 February 1942. The teaching profession was the first to react. The teachers protested when the new government passed as early as 5 February a law that obliged all girls and boys between ten and eighteen years of age to participate in "national" youth service and another law that compelled all teachers to join a Nazi professional organization. Thousands of teachers sent in written declarations that they could neither cooperate in the education of young people according to the principles behind the Nazi youth service nor join the Nazi teachers' organization. Supporting the teachers in this cause were thousands of parents, whose individual protests against the proposed youth service streamed into the Ministry of Education at the beginning of March. The authorities threatened the teachers with dismissal, and when they still stood firm, the Germans intervened. On 20 March about 1,100 teachers in different parts of the country were arrested, and a short time later another couple of hundred were detained by the authorities. The teachers were interned in camps and treated harshly. In the second half of April about 500 of them were crammed onto a small steamboat that had room for 150 people and sent to the northernmost part of Norway, where they were forced to perform hard labor. They were not allowed to return home until well into the autumn.

The Church joined the teachers in their struggle against the authorities. On 14 February 1942 the bishops protested against the proposed youth service in a letter to the Ministry of Education, and they were supported by the major religious organizations. When a dean was dismissed because he had held a service in competition with a clergyman whom the authorities had told to officiate, all the bishops resigned their official posts in protest. Their letter of protest was read from most pulpits on 1 March, and the pastors declared their solidarity with their bishops, who were at first placed under police surveillance and later formally arrested. A number of pastors were also dismissed, and the leading figure in the Norwegian church,

Bishop Eivind Berggrav, was interned. During the Easter services at the beginning of April, nearly all the pastors followed in the footsteps of the bishops by resigning their posts at the same time that they read to their congregations a declaration that was to be important in the history of both the Church and the resistance. By this step, the clergy had renounced the traditional contract between Church and State. For the remainder of the war the Church functioned as a self-administering entity, since the bishops and pastors had only resigned their official positions and still performed their pastoral work and held services insofar as this was possible.

This mass demonstration by teachers, parents, and the clergy against the occupation regime in the spring of 1942 was accompanied by other acts of resistance. The youth clubs, which had tens of thousands of members around the country, ceased to function, in protest against the nazification of their national committee. Several small professional groups like the shipowners and lawyers were also active in various ways at this time. In addition, the different acts of resistance that took place attracted much public attention, which roused other groups to manifest their support by such methods as collecting money for resistance purposes, and which created a more actively anti-Nazi attitude throughout the country. A new wave of resistance, which was briefer and left a smaller mark, occurred in September 1942 and involved the trade unions and economic organizations. It was clear that the Quisling government now wished to set up the corporatist *Riksting* to replace the old *Storting*. Many workers protested against this idea by formally resigning from their nazified trade unions, and most of the members of a number of economic organizations, including the Association of Industries and the two large banking associations, also resigned or threatened to do so. However, when the Germans rapidly intervened to threaten drastic reprisals, the resignations or threats of resignation were withdrawn. The resisters yielded when confronted with bayonets, but they had succeeded in registering a massive protest against the Quisling regime.

During the two waves of resistance in the spring and autumn of 1942, a power base for the civilian resistance, a civilian home front leadership, evolved in Oslo. It was divided into two parts. One was the so-called Coordination Committee, which had its origins in the protest letters drawn up by the organizations and in the events of the autumn of 1941; this committee began to function in earnest from late 1941 or early 1942. It was a representative body, which acquired members from a number of academic professions, the trade union movement, the business world, and agriculture. It had a nation-wide network of representatives and actively participated in shaping resistance slogans for greater or smaller parts of the population. The second part of the civilian home front leadership was the so-called Circle (*Kretsen*). It handled contacts with the government-in-exile, served as the spokesman of the civilian home front in relation to the government-in-exile, distributed the money the latter sent to Norway to support the home front, and also exercised a strong influence on the main principles and central slogans that the civilian leadership as a whole tried to apply to the civilian resistance struggle. Its members, who generally had a higher political and social status than the representatives of the Coordination Committee, were drawn from the Supreme Court, civil service, business community, and labor movement. As a whole the civilian resistance leadership had strong roots in the traditional order of Norwegian society. The structure of the civilian resistance movement was not definitely established in 1942, but its fundamental characteristics had already emerged.

The winter of 1942-43, during which the situation quieted after the great manifestations of resistance earlier in 1942, marks the end of an important stage in the development of the Norwegian resistance movement. The movement would follow new directions in the following years. It would come to be less ideological and political than in the 1940-42 period and to direct its activities more against the exploitation by the occupation regime of Norway's physical and economic resources. It would also come to adopt to some extent the use of violence in the form of sabotage and assassination and to have a more strongly military character than in the firmly civilian, nonviolent period of 1940-42. These developments will be discussed in later chapters.

The Military Resistance Movement

It was emphasized earlier in this chapter that the first years of the Norwegian resistance movement should be seen above all as a reaction against the efforts of a domestic Nazi party that had gained control of the government to disseminate Nazi ideology and secure more widespread popular support for its policies. However, the first phase of the resistance movement cannot be viewed exclusively in this light. The movement was too protean and heterogeneous for that. Scattered attempts to set up some kind of military organization within the movement also occurred at this time. Officers and soldiers who had fought in the campaign of 1940 could not forget the shared experiences and comradeship of the campaign, were bitter over the defeat, and hoped for a new opportunity of taking up arms against the invader. They set up military groups around the country as early as the autumn of 1940 and the winter of 1940-41, but there were no firm guidelines for the activities of these groups. Some groups organized physical training and exercises in the countryside and concealed arms they had acquired during the campaign. Others began to gather information about the German forces in Norway and to think about conveying this intelligence to the British and Norwegian authorities abroad who might be able to use it. Everything was still very ineffective: the tasks performed by different groups were not clearly defined and often overlapped both with each other and with the work of civilian groups. In the winter of 1940-41 leading officers of unquestioned patriotism still deprecated the establishment of regular organizations on a large scale.

However, two extensive military organizations did gradually evolve from this incipient military resistance movement, and their activities still spilled over at times into civilian and political resistance. One was a military intelligence organization, called XU, which together with other individual intelligence groups gathered information about the German forces in Norway and transmitted it to the military office at the Norwegian legation in Stockholm. The information was then conveyed to the Norwegian military authorities in London. This intelligence was not of immediate importance for operations in progress, but was significant for a general assessment of the German forces in Norway or for planning an Allied landing in that country. The British Secret Intelligence Service (SIS), which had an operational section, always worked alongside XU and landed Norwegian agents with their own radio transmitters along the Norwegian coast. Their task was to send reports on the weather and the movements of German ships, reports which often led to British attacks on German shipping. The Russians also sent in some Norwegian agents who reported by radio to the Soviet Union, particularly in the northernmost part of Norway.

The second organization that grew out of the first military resistance groups was *Milorg*, the Norwegian underground army that was gradually established on occupied soil. The leadership of *Milorg* was first set up in Oslo in the spring of 1941, with the aim of contacting

all military resistance groups in southern Norway and forming a
military organization that covered the whole of that region. But the
task of making contact with and obtaining recognition from the various military groups around the country and of integrating them into
one military organization proved a difficult and protracted process.
It was constantly interrupted by the arrest or flight of members of
the groups involved, which meant that repeatedly the work of setting
up these groups had to begin again at the local level and the *Milorg*
leadership in the capital had to reestablish contact with these groups.
However, the leadership gradually succeeded in making contact with
all parts of the country, except for the northernmost county of Finnmark, where *Milorg* groups were never set up.

Purely organizational problems were only one side of the difficulties faced by the *Milorg* leadership. Problems of at least equal gravity
were raised by the political side of its activity, that is to say by the
task of drawing up guidelines for the activities of the military resistance and getting these guidelines legitimized. First, there was some
doubt whether a secret military organization should be created in
Norway at all. Many of those who were most eager to make a military contribution to the struggle against Germany did not intend to
remain in Norway but instead tried to leave the country in order to
join the Allied armed forces. Some of them succeeded in reaching
Britain and served as airmen or sailors or became soldiers in the
Norwegian brigade that was built up in Scotland, though others
returned to Norway after training in Britain as intelligence agents,
instructors, or radio operators. Second, it was clear that the problems
raised by resistance policy were far more troublesome on the military
than on the civilian level. Military operations were more dangerous
and provoked more severe reprisals than did acts of civilian resistance,
whether such reprisals were directed against the resistance movement
itself or against innocent members of the population. This point was
brought home forcefully in the spring of 1942, when eighteen
Norwegians were executed after two Germans had been killed during
an exchange of fire with agents sent in from Britain, and again in
October, when a state of emergency was declared in Trøndelag and
thirty-four persons faced German firing squads after an act of sabotage had been committed. Under such conditions, a strong and
authoritative leadership was required to say what principles should
be the basis for military resistance activity. The *Milorg* leadership did
not believe that it was strong and authoritative enough to do this,

and from the very start it sought some responsible body distinct from itself which could legitimize its activities and take ultimate responsibility for the principles it followed, and above all which could order *Milorg* into action, a decision that might be expected to lead to drastic German countermeasures. At first, the *Milorg* leadership had thought that it might be subordinate to some civilian body in Norway which would be recognized by the king. However, it was unable to find such a body within Norway, and as early as the late summer of 1941 it accordingly sought to be placed directly under the Norwegian authorities in London. After various complications the *Milorg* leadership was formally recognized by the government-in-exile on 20 November 1941 and placed under the authority of the Norwegian high command.

Milorg would prepare for action to be taken exclusively during the final liberation of the country. In 1942 it was thought that this liberation would take the form of an Allied invasion, when *Milorg* would contribute to the reconquest of Norway by sabotage and guerrilla warfare carried out by small units behind the enemy's lines. Before the liberation phase, *Milorg* would not take part in any action whatsoever against the occupying power. The *Milorg* leadership did not want to receive arms from abroad except for training purposes before the liberation phase, and thought that significant quantities of arms ought to be dropped by plane no sooner than immediately before the operations were due to begin. It believed that it would be too dangerous to possess a large supply of arms before that time.

Despite agreement on broad principles, there were several reasons why the *Milorg* leadership and the high command failed to establish really intimate relations until the spring of 1943. One was the constant turnover of personnel within the leadership at home and the reorganizations of the high command that were undertaken in London. However, the most important reason for this failure was that SOE (Special Operations Executive), the British organization charged with supporting and building up military resistance groups in occupied countries, came to regard *Milorg* and its leadership with skepticism. SOE doubted whether it was correct to establish a nationwide organization that could easily be destroyed if the Germans captured its central body. SOE thought that it was better to set up mutually independent military groups, which were built up by Norwegian instructors and radio operators sent in from Britain who were directly under London's authority and who could receive their orders directly from London by radio. SOE also did not agree with the *Milorg* leadership's cautious policy of not wanting arms in large quantity before the liberation phase and of refraining from all acts of sabotage. Especially at the end of 1941 and in the first six months of 1942 SOE sent a considerable quantity of arms and equipment, a number of Norwegian instructors and radio operators, and some sabotage parties into Norway without the knowledge of the *Milorg* leadership. In fact, the SOE agents were ordered to avoid contact with the *Milorg* leadership in Oslo and to organize military groups or carry out acts of sabotage on their own. This high level of British activity was closely connected with the fact that an Allied landing in Norway had not been ruled out at that time. It was still not settled that the Allies would land in North Africa, as they eventually did in the autumn of 1942, and not somewhere in northern Europe. SOE worked intensively in Norway until the summer of 1942 with the aim of building up a position from which it could support an Allied invasion from inside the country. However, in September 1942 SOE was obliged to change its policy and began to cooperate with *Milorg*. It placed its agents and its equipment at the disposal of *Milorg* insofar as there were local *Milorg* groups around the country, which was far from the case in all districts. Nonetheless, for various reasons another six months were to pass before all problems had been cleared up and the relationship between the leadership at home and abroad had become wholly smooth. These difficulties, and especially the many executions and arrests that followed in the wake of military activity on occupied soil, made 1942 a black year for *Milorg*, a circumstance that contrasted strongly with the many successes won by the civilian resistance that year. However, with the change in British policy the shape of the pattern that was established in 1943 was already apparent in late 1942: The *Milorg* leadership at home cooperated intimately with the Norwegian high command in London, and the latter in its turn had a close relationship with SOE. The Norwegian high command and SOE placed instructors, radio operators, and equipment at the disposal of local *Milorg* groups. The agents of the Norwegian high command and SOE organized military groups in areas where *Milorg* had not established any, but these groups made contact sooner or later with the *Milorg* leadership in Oslo. In the event of invasion all military groups would take their orders from London by radio, but if the liberation occurred in some other way, both London and the *Milorg* leadership in Oslo would be entitled to issue orders. The Norwegian high command and SOE also sent sabotage parties of their own into Norway. These parties operated independently of *Milorg* and usually left the country after they had carried out their acts of sabotage. *Milorg* itself did not engage in sabotage, but continued its preparations for action during the liberation phase.

Other Forms of Resistance

The illegal press was a distinct area of resistance. Contact was gradually established between the civilian home front leadership and the clandestine newspapers, which it helped with money, technical equipment, and information, and presumably also in the distribution of the papers around the country. In return, the illegal press publicized the directives of the home front leadership. However, the publication of the many hundreds of small and large newspapers which gradually emerged must be seen above all as a spontaneous and largely independent form of resistance. During the first phase of the occupation, the illegal press often consciously tried to influence public opinion and to create an anti-Nazi movement among the population, but it soon became primarily a transmitter of news about the war, especially after the autumn of 1941 when private radios in Norway were confiscated. Many of the papers came to contain mainly the news that was read out in broadcasts from London, and this fact was reflected in some of their names: *London-Nytt* (News from London), *London-Radio, Radio-Nytt* (Radio News) and *Krigens Gang* (The Course of the War). Nevertheless, the illegal press as a whole also carried uncensored domestic news about the deterioration in the food situation, the arbitrariness of the Nazi authorities, the various foolish acts committed by the Nazis, and the like. There was some debate on the transition from war to peace toward the end of the war, but it is striking how little discussion of policy there was in the Norwegian illegal press as compared with its Danish counterpart. The primary task of the illegal press in Norway was to meet the enormous need for the kind of information about conditions at home and abroad that censorship either suppressed or greatly distorted.

The establishment of escape routes by which Norwegians could flee the country was also a response to an immediate need, in this case the need to move people illegally out of the country either because they were no longer safe at home or, as occurred during the first years of the occupation, because they wished to join the armed forces abroad. Like the illegal press, the transportation of individuals out of Norway must largely be seen as a distinct and independent area of resistance, although in eastern Norway at any rate, such activities to a greater extent came to be linked with or were developed by the leading resistance groups. Both *Milorg* and XU evolved their own transportation systems which assisted members of these organizations exclusively, whereas the civilian system, which was associated with the civilian resistance leadership, helped all kinds of Norwegians. The major escape routes were built up only gradually. There were also many among those who left the country—indeed they may have been a majority—who did so without resorting to the organized escape routes but quite simply by walking through the forests and crossing into Sweden where the border was not well patrolled. A large majority of those who left the country did so by entering Sweden—a total of about 50,000 people in the course of the war. During the first years of the occupation there was also another route out of the country, that across the North Sea, and just over 3,600 Norwegians crossed to Britain in fishing vessels or other small boats. However, German patrolling eventually became so effective that the use of this route virtually ceased.

The Communists constituted a distinct element within the resistance movement with their own leadership and their own organization. Initially they were hampered by the existence of the Nazi-Soviet Pact, and it was only at the end of 1941 that the party as a whole changed course and adopted a radical resistance policy. From this time on the Communists in principle argued that the resistance ought to employ sabotage and guerrilla warfare, and while its leadership withdrew to the forests and the mountains, the party founded its own illegal press, attempted to recruit people to work for these newspapers, and set up its own sabotage and military groups and its own escape routes. Little is known about the extent to which the Communists themselves in accordance with their new policy tried to carry out sabotage and succeeded in doing so. A bomb attack on the headquarters of the Nazi police in Oslo in August 1942, which caused the death of a Nazi policeman, was carried out by a Communist group and aroused some popular attention and strong reactions from the civilian home front leadership, which supported a policy of nonviolence at this time. However, there is little to suggest that by 1942 the Communists had got especially far in their resistance work

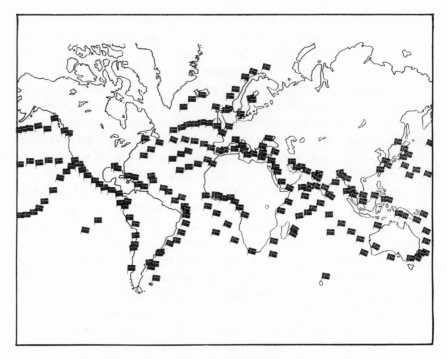

Norway's most important contribution to the Allied war effort: the merchant
marine. The flags represent a total of 1,024 Norwegian ships and their positions
at the time of the German attack on Norway on 9 April 1940. (Norges Hjemmefrontmuseum, Oslo)

or had met with much of a response from the population or had
begun to carry out acts of sabotage on any great scale. It is indicative
that there was for the time being little agitation for sabotage or
partisan warfare in the illegal Communist press. Like the *Milorg*
leadership, the party was in its way obliged to tread carefully with a
population that was still reluctant to espouse violent methods in the
resistance struggle.

The fact that the legal state authorities of Norway, the king and
the cabinet, were in exile during the occupation had an impact on
the resistance movement. They maintained Norway's existence as a
free state; the king especially was an inspiration and symbol for all
Norwegian endeavors in the cause of freedom during the first years
of the occupation; and the government gradually strengthened its
position with the Norwegian people. It was essentially a Labor
ministry, but it contained enough nonsocialist members to be able

to serve as a government of national unity. It consciously sought to follow a national policy that transcended party politics. Its most important asset was the large Norwegian merchant marine, which the British needed to use, especially during the first years of the war, and which provided revenue that made the government financially independent. Because of this revenue, the government was able to finance the resistance movement at home, mainly by smuggling money into Norway through Sweden; substantial amounts eventually reached the resistance movement from abroad in this way. Members of the Norwegian radio service who were in London participated in the preparation of the BBC's Norwegian broadcasts, which shaped public opinion in Norway. The Norwegian government sought to contribute to the Allied military effort by having its air and naval forces take

Resistance in a symbol: "H7" (for King Haakon VII) marked in the snow. (Norges Hjemmefrontmuseum, Oslo)

part actively in operations and by establishing a brigade of soldiers earmarked for use in the final liberation of Norway. The total strength of the Norwegian armed forces abroad reached just under 15,000 men, of whom about 1,100 lost their lives in the course of the war. There were also another 13,000 men in the Norwegian police corps that was set up in Sweden from 1943 on. The Norwegian military authorities in London also helped to organize and direct secret operations in Norway. However, it was the Norwegian merchant marine that was of the greatest importance to the Allied war effort; about 3,000 of the 25,000 men who served in this branch of the service lost their lives in military operations conducted during the war. In its foreign policy, the government attempted above all to maintain the closest possible relations with Britain. During its first years in exile it tried to promote the idea that initiatives should be taken while the war was still in progress to establish political and military cooperation between the countries of the North Atlantic in the postwar period. The Norwegian foreign minister, Trygve Lie, even went so far as privately to offer the British military bases in Norway after the war. This Atlantic idea later lost much of its importance.

The Danish Resistance Movement

The Norwegian and Danish situations during the occupation were very different, the only striking similarity being each country's relations with Sweden. Both Norwegians and eventually Danes fled to Sweden. Both Norwegian and Danish police corps were set up in Sweden. Sweden became the geographical link between Norwegians and Danes on occupied territory and their compatriots in the free world. There was both a Norwegian and a Danish legation in Stockholm to serve as a nucleus for the extensive Norwegian and Danish administrative agencies which gradually emerged in Sweden; these dealt with refugees and the training of the two police corps in cooperation with the Swedish authorities, and were responsible for secret contacts with occupied Norway and Denmark.

The Danish constitutional authorities did not go into exile but remained at home. The king stayed in the country and the cabinet, parliament, and the political parties continued to function there. The policy of negotiation was the generally accepted Danish method of opposing German demands and German pressure. This was of cardinal importance for the early development of the Danish resistance, since it meant that the first members of the resistance in Denmark, who wanted to use one form or another of direct warfare against the occupying power, had to oppose not only the latter but also a national government and its policy, which enjoyed solid popular support. Those who wanted to break with the policy of negotiation therefore worked against overwhelming political odds initially. They could justifiably be described as "national extremists" during the first phase, so few were their numbers and so repugnant were their activities to the public at large. The established Danish authorities took the most direct action against the first pioneers of resistance, who were mainly arrested by Danish police and tried by Danish courts. This attitude of the authorities was a significant part of the policy of negotiation, since one of the latter's most important objectives was to ensure that the Danes retained full sovereignty on their own territory. In order to achieve this aim, Danish institutions had to deal with and punish those who in word or deed attacked the occupying power and endangered the policy of negotiation, because if the Danish authorities did not do so, the Germans would.

The Danish Nazis, unlike their Norwegian counterparts, never became the only legal political party and were never given an opportunity to carry out an ideological and political offensive from a position of strength within the state apparatus. As a result, the great ideological and political resistance campaign that was typical of the first phase of the Norwegian resistance never occurred in Denmark. There was, however, in Denmark too a national awakening and national unity on the basis of democratic principles. The *Dansk Ungdomsamvirke* (Danish Youth League) was not the least significant expression of this trend. This body was a joint organization for the youth sections of the Danish political parties and for several national nonpolitical youth associations. It worked for national solidarity and made democratic ideas and a democratic outlook the general political basis for this sense of solidarity. Its activities were directed against national socialism and certain antiparliamentary trends that emerged in Denmark, especially during the first year of the occupation. Thus the Danes believed, as the Norwegians did, that a fundamental ideological danger threatened their national integrity; there was a national closing of ranks in response to this danger, and in both countries during the first phase of the occupation a national movement developed which in principle pursued the same aims.

However, it was only in Norway that this movement as a whole assumed the form of "resistance." In Denmark national unity functioned primarily as support for the democratic system that was intact and for the policy of negotiation that had evolved within this system. The latter expressed precisely the values that the national movement wished to defend. In consequence, the national movement was a source of strength for the government and its policy of negotiation, and the government largely regarded this movement with goodwill and encouraged it, even though sections of it, like *Dansk Ungdomsamvirke*, sometimes criticized the government. In Norway, the national movement functioned in the same way as support above all for the king but ultimately also for the government as an important part of the traditional democratic system. The Norwegian situation was complicated by the fact that the cabinet was criticized for its foreign and defense policies before the war and for the military defeat of 1940, while parliament was exposed to even more severe criticism, since many believed that it had failed the nation in 1940. However, this did not prevent the Norwegians from supporting in principle the main institutions of the traditional system, in the same way that the Danes did. The essential difference between Norway and Denmark was that the Norwegian king and government were in exile and that the Norwegians were forbidden to support them and that those who controlled the government in Norway were Nazis who actively sought to disseminate an antidemocratic ideology and to secure backing for their own antidemocratic party at the same time that the police took action against those who openly sustained democratic values. As a result, the national movement in Norway was "resistance," while in Denmark it was not. Instead, the Danish movement was channeled into support for the policy of negotiation. Thus during the first half of the occupation, resistance in Denmark was a question of going against national unity, of asserting a different national line from that of the majority. The Danish resistance did not oppose the ideological foundation of national unity, since democracy was the objective both for the adherents of the policy of negotiation and for those who wished to break with this policy. However, the pioneers of the Danish resistance opposed the policy toward the occupying power which was sustained by national unity, aiming instead at national unity behind a different policy, namely, making a break with the Germans and engaging in direct warfare against the occupying power.

All this meant that the Danish resistance movement began later and was initially more modest than its Norwegian counterpart and remained a marginal phenomenon in the overall political scene during the years 1940-42. Whereas the Norwegian resistance was largely set in motion by especially provocative measures taken by Norwegian Nazis, that is, concrete and immediate initiatives against which Norwegians felt a need to defend themselves, the driving force behind the Danish resistance was more general and abstract, namely, a desire to contribute to the Allied war effort against Hitler and to place Denmark in the Allied camp. This motive became ever more dominant as the fortunes of war began to turn and it became clearer that the Allies were going to win. It was a question of demonstrating that Denmark really was on the right side of the war or, at the very least, of expressing the growing Danish dislike of the occupation as the Allies won greater successes on the battlefield. The Danish re-sistance movement that ultimately emerged therefore evinced an impatience, a sense of anger, and a lack of restraint that far exceeded anything in the actions of its Norwegian counterpart, which de-veloped more gradually and followed a more cautious path. The Nor-wegian resistance movement, of course, never needed to demonstrate that it belonged to the Allied camp, since it did so simply by sup-porting a king and government that were already in that camp. In the case of the Danes, this need ultimately became acute, but down to 1942 was not considered to be pressing.

Espionage, Communists, and Illegal Newspapers

The very first pioneers of the Danish resistance were a small group of Danish intelligence officers. The terms of the capitulation in 1940 allowed the Danish army, including its intelligence section, to remain in operation to some extent. The intelligence section was in a very favorable position to gather information about the German forces in Denmark, the movement of German troops through Denmark to such destinations as Norway and Finland, and the movement of German ships in Danish waters. As early as the summer of 1940 the Danish newspaper editor Ebbe Munch, who had good contacts with the British, held discussions with the Danish intelligence officers about how information could be transmitted to the British. As a result of these discussions, Munch established himself in Stockholm as the correspondent of a Copenhagen newspaper; the officers would send him information on microfilm, which could relatively easily be taken to Stockholm by couriers who were going there on legal business, and he would then convey it to the British legation there. The first intelligence report was dispatched in October 1940, and a regular stream of information was sent to the British from that time on. Contact became especially good after SOE had placed its own agent in Stockholm, who in close consultation with Munch corresponded with the officers in Denmark. Cooperation became so intimate that in the spring of 1942 the British agreed to refrain entirely from attempting to set up an intelligence network of their own in Denmark. SIS had sent an agent to Denmark in the autumn of 1941, whose attempt to establish a network had failed, and intelligence was now placed instead entirely in the hands of the Danish officers. This development contrasts sharply with the situation in Norway where, as we have seen, SIS developed its own network of intelligence agents equipped with radios, who operated along the coast in particular and who kept London informed of the movements of German ships. Espionage was a very special form of resistance, which was to a great degree technical in nature and which required special skills; in Denmark it was carried out by professional soldiers who made careers of intelligence. It had little connection with resistance as a political phenomenon which depended on the nonprofessional attitudes of the population; being a secret, "quiet" activity, it had no effect on public opinion. The interaction between acts of resistance and the development of opinion, with acts of resistance influencing opinion and vice versa, was often discernible in other contexts but was absent in the case of espionage.

If the Danish intelligence officers were the first albeit highly isolated pioneers of the resistance, then the Communists were the second group to become involved in such activities. The Danish Communist party, like its Norwegian counterpart, was small and had declined because of the Russo-Finnish Winter War of 1939-40. It had also taken no part in resistance before the Germans attacked the Soviet Union on 22 June 1941. It was then immediately forced underground, for the Danish police, in response to insistent German demands, arrested a number of Communists, and the party was banned shortly afterward. The Communists had at their disposal a network of small but industrious party groups in Copenhagen and other towns around the country; there are, of course, no statistics for the membership of an illegal party, but its active nucleus cannot have been much larger than one thousand. The heart of the organization was the members of the central committee in Copenhagen, three or four traveling party secretaries in Jutland and on Fyn, and a few full-time officials in the most important towns. This was not a sizable number, because it was costly for a poor party to maintain a large number of people underground. The primary activity of the local party sections was political work. Their main task, aside from the goal of survival, was to agitate for the party's policies; the Communists did not restrict themselves to resisting the Germans but devoted equal attention to the problems of domestic policy. As the party agreed after the election of March 1943, it was impossible to oppose Scavenius's foreign policy while supporting the government's domestic policies, since the latter created the preconditions for the former, and since the struggle to maintain the living standards of the working class was identical with the fight against the Germans. The tough and unrelenting fight with the Social Democrats for the support of the working class was of central importance to the Communists until the dissolution of the Comintern in June 1943, when the struggle was suddenly discontinued and replaced by appeals for cooperation, appeals that were categorically rejected. The propaganda weapons of the Communists were study circles, verbal agitation on the shop floor, and above all their illegal press. As soon as it was banned the party seized every opportunity to issue leaflets and pamphlets, a method which it continued to employ throughout the war, but the nationwide monthly *Land og Folk* (Country and People), which appeared from October 1941 on, was of more importance. The widest possible distribution of this paper was at all times and under all circumstances the primary task of the local party sections. At first, they received packages containing the paper for distribution, but later they were merely sent a manuscript which they then stenciled themselves. If they were capable of doing more, they also issued their own local papers, as they were instructed to do in the autumn of 1942.

Early in 1942 the Communists adopted sabotage as a weapon in their struggle, fixing upon 9 April 1942 as the starting point for their sabotage campaign. This campaign was initially modest in scale and highly unsuccessful. Indeed, it was not mentioned in the illegal Communist press before the spring of 1943, a clear indication that there was believed to be little sympathy for sabotage among the broad mass of the population. The party set up a sabotage organization in Copenhagen called Kopa, later renamed Bopa, and sabotage groups were also established eventually in the larger provincial towns, sometimes with great difficulty. The first acts of sabotage often had a political purpose. Their primary objective was not to damage the occupying power, but to attract attention, to show the Danish population that there was an active resistance movement, and to incite the populace itself to adopt an attitude of resistance. For this reason, several acts of sabotage were often carried out on the same day, so that the effect on public opinion might be as great as possible. The Communists were thus the first organized group to adopt what was to become the main weapon of the Danish resistance movement, namely sabotage. There had certainly been occasional acts of sabotage before the party started to use this weapon, but they had been comparatively harmless and the perpetrators largely remain unknown, a circumstance which strongly suggests that they were private individuals and not groups consciously following a definite resistance policy.

Until the winter of 1942-43 the overwhelming majority of the Danish people opposed sabotage. In a radio broadcast on 2 September 1942 the prime minister publicly expressed opposition to sabotage and even in effect urged the population to report saboteurs to the police. The disapproval of government and people was not the only problem saboteurs faced. Sabotage is an activity that requires some technical knowledge and demands both supplies of explosives and skill in their use, both of which take some time to acquire. The first saboteurs had only such materials as they had happened to be able to get hold of, oil, gasoline, phosphorus, and the like; they were not even able to obtain black gunpowder at first. They bought supplies with their own money or stole the chemicals they needed to produce homemade incendiary devices and other instruments of destruction. It was only in December 1942 that Kopa was able to pull off a real coup by smuggling ten to fifteen kilos of aerolite out of a limestone quarry, a coup that led to the arrest of four men.

The status of the Communists as pioneers came to be of considerable importance for their later position in the broader Danish resistance movement. In Norway, they always suffered from the disadvantage that they were not the first to become involved in resistance activity, which always gave other people an excuse for questioning their patriotic motives. In Denmark, on the other hand, the Communists enjoyed the prestige that came from having been the first organized group to issue a large illegal newspaper and initiate sabotage. As a result, they came to be more integrated into the wider resistance movement in Denmark than they were in Norway, where they were always excluded from the leading organs of the resistance. Moreover, there was another factor that made the Norwegian Communists, far more than their Danish counterparts, an opposition faction within the resistance movement. There were always some representatives of the traditional social democratic labor movement, the old political enemy of the Communists, in the leading organs of the Norwegian resistance, which helped maintain the distance between the home front leadership and the Communists. In Denmark, on the other hand, it was only the extremist parties, including the Communist party, that were represented in the resistance movement or its leading organs since the major parties, including the Social Democrats, were too closely tied to the policy of negotiation for such representation. Consequently the Danish Communists had less trouble within the resistance movement from their traditional opponents in the labor movement.

The first large noncommunist newspapers of the underground appeared in the winter of 1941-42. *De Frie Danske* (The Free Danes) and *Frihedsstøtten* (The Pillar of Liberty) began publication in December 1941. *De Frie Danske* was published by a group that had formed as early as 1940 under the name *Vædderen* (The Ram). Its members tried to incite disorder at Nazi meetings, became involved in fights during Nazi demonstrations, painted slogans on the windows of Nazis, and produced leaflets. Later they acquired stencils and a duplicator; a young man carved the title *De Frie Danske* into a piece of linoleum; and they began to issue their newspaper. *Frihedsstøtten,* which was the third illegal newspaper that was of any national, as opposed to local, importance, was issued once a month by a circle of young academics. They focused on objective reporting, especially on foreign policy questions, and only 300 copies of each issue were printed at first, though the number of copies was to increase greatly over time. Discussions about the establishment of what was to become the largest and most important of Denmark's illegal newspapers during the occupation, *Frit Danmark* (Free Denmark), also began in late 1941 and early 1942. The original intention was to publish it as a legal though strongly anti-Nazi journal, but this plan was rapidly abandoned. It seemed clear that if the paper was to have a sufficiently sharp tone, it would be too offensive toward the policy of negotiation and would soon be banned, so it would be better to organize it from the start as a secret newspaper whose editors, printers, and distributors would remain unknown. Both Conservative and Communist circles were involved in the discussions about starting this newspaper, which accordingly came to symbolize a wider inter-party and national unity behind the policy of resistance. Those who collaborated in issuing *Frit Danmark* had good contacts with SOE's Danish agents, the Danish intelligence service, and political circles, and the newspaper was therefore a more authoritative and well-informed organ than most of the illegal press. Moreover, it adopted a sober tone, which made a good impression on the public. The first issue appeared on 9 April 1942 in stenciled form, but the paper was later printed and expanded to eventually 150,000 copies per issue. From the start *Frit Danmark* adopted the line that Denmark had to contribute actively to the war against Nazism and desist from con-cessions to and compliance toward the Germans. It did not insist on an immediate break with the policy of negotiation, and it even supported the government and parliament insofar as they were able to resist German demands. However, it believed that the struggle against Nazism was the overriding aim and that if the authorities did not succeed in standing up to German demands, the breakdown of the policy of negotiation was the best alternative. *Frit Danmark* also called for passive sabotage, that is to say it urged Danes not to work for the Germans and to stop or delay deliveries to them. However, the paper did not agitate for active, violent sabotage before October 1942, when it responded positively to an appeal for sabotage made over the BBC by the Danish politician Christmas Møller, who had played a role in starting the newspaper but who had later gone to Britain. Even so, *Frit Danmark* was moving more rapidly than public opinion, which did not seriously begin to swing in the direc-tion of accepting sabotage until the following winter.

SOE and Other Resistance Activity

The British SOE set to work at a later stage in Denmark than in Norway, and its activities were also less extensive in Denmark. An important reason for this state of affairs was that in the years 1941 and 1942 Norway had a much higher place than Denmark on the Allied list of priorities as a possible theater for Allied invasion. Another reason was that the climate of opinion in Denmark was less favorable to resistance, both because Denmark had not taken up arms in self-defense in 1940 and because the government's policy of negotiation did not encourage any form of direct resistance. A third reason was probably that SOE had a smaller pool of manpower from which to recruit its agents in the case of Denmark. The number of young fit men willing to make a personal contribution to the war who reached Britain from Denmark during the first years of the occupation was less than that from Norway. A fourth reason was perhaps that the intelligence service for a long time tried to prevent attempts to carry out sabotage and create unrest in Denmark, since it always functioned best when there was a calm atmosphere and little German police activity. Attempts by intelligence organizations to dampen enthusiasm for sabotage and other forms of active resistance are not unknown in the case of Norway either, and were a cause of friction between SOE and SIS in relation to that country. However, it is possible that the Danish intelligence officers had greater influence in this area than did their Norwegian counterparts.

The first expedition that SOE sent to Denmark was dropped by parachute at the end of December 1941. It consisted of two men. One of them, the leader, was killed in the parachute jump, and only the radio operator survived; he made contact with Danish resistance circles, including the people behind the newspaper *De Frie Danske,* but apart from this experienced difficulty in building up an SOE group of his own. However, this solitary SOE agent did get in touch with an engineer, and together they were able to make radio contact with London, which had thus been established by the time that arrangements were made to receive a new expedition from Britain. Three men were dropped by parachute in April 1942, and once again there were problems, one man landing in a tree, another being knocked unconscious by the jump and only able to join the others later by taking the train alone to Copenhagen. Another three-man expedition arrived in August. The first task of the SOE agents was to make contact with Danish resistance circles and to organize and build up sabotage groups. However, they were not to carry out acts of sabotage for the time being, since the situation was not yet regarded as ripe for that. By the summer of 1942 the work of setting up sabotage groups had begun, with personnel recruited from *Dansk Samling,* a small and originally antiparliamentary party on the extreme right of the Danish political spectrum. It was, however, very anti-German and anti-Nazi, had actively participated in the national movement, and was such a strong opponent of concessions to the Germans that it had, in contrast to *Dansk Ungdomsamvirke,* dissociated itself from the policy of negotiation, an attitude which it expressed so vigorously in several publications that their authors received prison sentences. When members of the party then began to cooperate with SOE agents, it came even closer to having one foot in the camp of the legal parties and the other in that of the illegal resistance movement. To the extent that the early members of the Danish resistance were associated with the political parties, they were thus drawn mainly from the extremist parties, the Communists and *Dansk Samling,* which were not involved in that broad cooperation between the parties at the center of the political spectrum which supported the government and its policy of negotiation. The SOE agents encountered new difficulties in the autumn of 1942. One of them took poison when he was arrested; their new leader was shot during an encounter with the Danish police; and another of them was arrested in December. There were only two men left by the end of the year, so it was only after more agents were dropped by parachute into Denmark in February and March 1943 that serious work on organizing sabotage groups was resumed.

The winter of 1941-42 was in a way a watershed in the early history of the national movement in Denmark during the occupation, for during this time organized resistance began to emerge as a distinct tendency within the broader national movement. To be sure, the Communists in particular had begun their illegal activity before this time. However, the decision of the Communists early in 1942 to engage in active sabotage did represent something new in the underground work they were already involved in. At the same time, several illegal newspapers began to appear and preparations for another, *Frit Danmark,* were begun. Finally, the first SOE agents arrived and initiated SOE activity in Denmark, although the results of their work were very modest to begin with. Around this time, another form of resistance also manifested itself, namely, popular mass actions of a more or less spontaneous character. The anti-German atmosphere in the country first led to open demonstrations in Copenhagen in connection with Denmark's joining of the Anti-Comintern Pact on 25 November 1941, these demonstrations being aimed directly at the government's policies. It was the students who set events in motion. A poster was put up at the university calling on them to gather for a demonstration, and although the rector of the university had the poster taken down and the student council tried to quiet the atmosphere, a procession of several hundred students, singing and shouting "Down with Scavenius!" started off from the university.

Many persons joined the march, and in the evening the demonstrations became larger and began to assume the character of riots. The police intervened and arrested a number of people, and the Germans immediately demanded severe penalties. The authorities of the university and other educational institutions urged the students not to take part in further disturbances, and the rector of the university even used the threat of expulsion. The demonstrations died down after a couple of days, but this first eruption of unrest was followed by similar demonstrations when the Danish section of the *Waffen-SS* returned home on leave and paraded through the streets, an act that had an especially provocative effect.

One characteristic of the first phase of the Danish resistance was that a number of individuals took a strong personal stand against the policy of negotiation and the Germans. Their names and their acts of defiance became publicly known, so that the latter influenced public opinion. As the resistance movement gained ground, however, it became common practice for those involved to hide behind the mask of anonymity. In Norway anonymity began immediately after 25 September 1940, and public acts of resistance by named individuals consequently played a small role there, whereas in Denmark certain individual names are known to posterity precisely because they were also known to contemporaries. One such name is that of Christmas Møller. He was the chairman of the Conservative party and had joined the national government in April 1940, but proved so uncompromising in his attitude to the Germans that he left the government in October in order to forestall a German demand for his removal from office. In January 1941 he also resigned his parliamentary seat and all his political posts within the Conservative leadership under German pressure. After these events his name was an inspiration for those who wanted the government to pursue a far tougher line toward the Germans and who were willing to accept a break with Germany and "Norwegian conditions," if this was the result of such an uncompromising policy. Møller was a central figure in the discussions that led to the appearance of *Frit Danmark,* and he wrote the article setting out the newspaper's editorial policy in its first issue. By that time (August 1941) he had already accepted an invitation from SOE to come to Britain. However, his departure was delayed, and in the meantime he was on hand to welcome the first SOE agents in Denmark. He did not actually leave until about the end of April 1942, and he spoke to his countrymen over the BBC for the first time on 14 May. The news of his dramatic flight spread rapidly around the country. Those who had helped him escape were tracked down and arrested by the Danish police, and the government issued an official communication regretting Møller's departure and stating that a criminal charge would be brought against him, a statement which received the unanimous support of the Conservative party.

Another name on the lips of many people was that of the historian Vilhelm la Cour. He deliberately acted in a way that exposed him to the risk of punishment by the authorities. In the first half of 1941 la Cour issued a number of publications, which he had printed at his own expense, attacking the Germans. As a result, he was sentenced to eighty days in prison, but he continued to publish his views. At meetings he attacked the Germans in such strong terms that the German military court took an interest in the case and two Gestapo men were sent to his home to arrest him. However, he was not at home, and he was later arrested by the Danish police instead. The Germans nonetheless demanded that he be transferred to a German prison, and this was eventually done. He then appeared before a German military court, but the case was dropped and he was returned to a Danish prison. However, by this time the indignation of the Germans had reached such heights that the government realized that great difficulties would be created if the sentence were too mild. Accordingly, when la Cour was sentenced to only four months by the municipal court, the authorities appealed to the Supreme Court. The latter heard the case in private and announced in July 1942 that it had increased the sentence to seven months. Just before this announcement, la Cour had been dismissed from his post at a secondary school. Precisely what la Cour had been convicted of was not disclosed, and this secrecy served to enhance his popularity and damage the government.

Scandinavia and
the Turn of the Tide

by Aage Trommer

It is generally accepted that during the period around the end of 1942 and the beginning of 1943 there was a turn of the tide in World War II and that the battle of El-Alamein, the Anglo-American landings in French North Africa, and the battle of Stalingrad constituted a decisive turning point. After these events the fortunes of war were against the Germans right until the bitter end in the battle of Berlin. This view is not entirely mistaken; but it is not entirely correct either. The course of the war was not as simple and uncomplicated as it suggests. The Allied military successes at the end of 1942 and the beginning of 1943 did not deprive the Germans of the strategic initiative once and for all. The operational intentions behind the landings in North Africa were only partially realized, so that the Germans got the opportunity to occupy Tunis. On the eastern front, the German 6th army was defeated at Stalingrad, but the grandiose Russian plan of annihilating all the German forces in the Ukraine failed, and it was not until the tank battle at Kursk in July 1943 that the Russians seized the initiative from the Germans. The battle of the Atlantic first turned in favor of the Allies in the course of the spring of 1943.

The decisive question for our purposes is whether El-Alamein, the North African landings, and Stalingrad were regarded *at the time* as a definitive turning point in the war, and it can hardly be said that they were. Contemporaries had witnessed many fluctuations in the fortunes of war in the deserts of Libya and Egypt. How could they foresee that the wheel of fortune had now turned for the last time?

They had seen that the Germans had reacted to the landings in North Africa with their customary speed by occupying Vichy France and Tunis. They could observe the encirclement of the German forces in Stalingrad and the German withdrawal from the Caucasus, but the Germans had also experienced setbacks the previous winter, and this had not prevented them from launching a major offensive the following summer. It was possible in December 1942 and January 1943 to hope for the best and even, perhaps, for miracles, but a more sober attitude held sway between January and March 1943. During the summer of 1943, it first became clear to the Allies that events were moving in the right direction. The eviction of the Germans from Tunis in May; the collapse of the German summer offensive on the eastern front in July and the Russian counteroffensive in August; the Anglo-American landing in Sicily in July and Mussolini's fall later the same month; and, finally, the intensification of the bombing campaign of the Western Allies against Germany with heavy attacks on a number of large cities, above all Hamburg, were all milestones in this course of development. With this rapid succession of events, it became apparent to all parties that it was the Germans who were going to lose the war, and the atmosphere, attitudes, and actions in all the Nordic countries came to be shaped by this realization. However, the individual Nordic countries did not respond at the same tempo, and it is the varying pace of their reactions that is striking.

Denmark: The August Uprising, Its Background and Consequences

The Danish response to the turn of the tide was strong and violent when it came in the summer of 1943. However, even the most activist circles had not dared during the preceding winter months to count on an early German defeat, as can be seen from their behavior during the parliamentary election that was held in March 1943. If the activist groups of the resistance movement had been confident that the climate of opinion among the voters was what they thought it ought to be, they would have called for a boycott of the election so that it might be clear to the whole world that collaboration did not have a chance in Denmark. However, this did not happen, and the activists' uncertainty about how to handle the situation led them to adopt a number of conflicting attitudes. The Communists and the Free Denmark (*Frit Danmark*) groups called on voters to return blank ballots; Danish Unity (*Dansk Samling*) urged them to vote for itself; and Christmas Møller advised them through the BBC from London to vote for one of "the democratic parties." This last cautious course proved to be wisest, since the other two met with disaster. *Dansk Samling* received as few votes as did the Danish Nazi party, and the number of blank ballots was the same as the number of votes cast for the other collaborationist party, *Bondepartiet* (The Farmers' party). The election, which was in no way manipulated or marked by irregularities, also delivered a clear verdict on the Danish Nazis, who were definitely eliminated as a potential force in Danish politics.

A total of 60-70,000 votes were cast for the two extreme wings of the political spectrum. The remainder of the approxmately two million votes cast were divided among the so-called old parties which supported the policy of negotiation with the Germans. These parties had also faced the election with considerable uncertainty, as is clear from the fact that they did not dare to seek a renewed mandate for the policy of negotiation. Instead, they called on voters to manifest their support for democracy as such by participating in the election. However, the fears of the old parties that they would be rejected by the electorate proved quite unfounded. The turnout at 89.5% set a new record, and the electorate expressed its national sentiment and dislike of the Germans only insofar as it gave more support to the Conservatives and less support to the Radical Liberals,

Danish Parliamentary Elections of 1939 and 1943

Party	1939		1943	
	No. of Votes	% of Total Votes	No. of Votes	% of Total Votes
Social Democrats	730,000	42.9%	895,000	44.0%
Radical Liberals	162,000	9.5	175,000	8.6
Conservatives	302,000	17.8	422,000	20.7
Liberals	309,000	18.2	377,000	18.5
Justice party	34,000	2.0	31,000	1.5
Farmers' party	51,000	3.0	25,000	1.2
Nazis	31,000	1.8	43,000	2.1
Danish Unity	9,000	0.5	43,000	2.1
Communists	41,000	2.4	. . .	. . .
German minority	15,000	0.9	. . .	. . .
Others	17,000	1.0	. . .	. . .
Blank ballot papers	4,000	. . .	24,000	1.2
TOTAL	1,705,000		2,035,000	

N.B. Representatives of the German minority in north Schleswig did not contest the election of 1943.

who had traditionally stood for disarmament and who were especially identified with the policy that had collapsed on 9 April 1940.

Regarding German policy toward Denmark, the outcome of the election was highly satisfactory, not only because the activists received so little support but also because the number of votes cast for the Danish Nazis was so insignificant. In this case, German policy means the policy of Werner Best. In November 1942, Best arrived in Copenhagen as the plenipotentiary of the German *Reich*. Best was a lawyer who had made a career in the security police. From 1940 to 1942 he had occupied a senior position within the German military administration in occupied France. Then, after a short period in Berlin, he had been sent to Denmark. His arrival was viewed with misgivings in that country: in the illegal press, he was called "the expert in terror" and "the bloodhound from Paris." However, Best was neither an expert in terror nor a bloodhound. He had certainly begun his career in the SS, but he acted in Denmark as the representative of the German Foreign Ministry and worked quite deliberately on the German side to strengthen the policy of negotiation. His ability to do this effectively depended in no small measure on the contacts he had maintained with Heinrich Himmler and the leadership of the SS. There was no place for the Danish Nazis in Best's policies. In direct opposition to the directives he had received in Berlin before his departure, he cooperated, after the telegram crisis, in the establishment of a new Danish government that did not contain Nazi ministers. On this occasion, he was prepared to accept as prime minister the director of the Danish national bank, who was a Social Democrat, but when the latter declined to respond to the urgings of the parties that he occupy this post, Best was insistent that the new prime minister should be the man who for more than two years had served as the Danish guarantor of the policy of negotiation, the foreign minister, Erik Scavenius. The Danish politicians were not enthusiastic at the prospect of Scavenius, but accepted him as the lesser evil. Scavenius, by the way, retained his post as foreign minister.

Best saw the relationship between Denmark and Germany as a marriage of convenience. This was the phrase he himself used during a meeting with the new government in the middle of November 1942. In accordance with the terms of this marriage of convenience, the new government issued a declaration in which it, like its predecessors, stated that it intended to strengthen "the good and neighborly relations between Denmark and Germany," that it would not tolerate sabotage, and that Communist activity was illegal; while Best ensured that parliamentary elections could be held in Denmark when they next fell due in March 1943—something that was absolutely unique in German-occupied Europe.

Best's most dangerous opponent was to be found in his own camp: General Hermann von Hanneken, the commander of the German forces in Denmark, who had arrived in Denmark one month before Best. Not only did Hanneken's rough personality make him disposed to solve problems in another way than that favored by his political counterpart, but the two men also had to deal with problems of quite different kinds. Whereas Best had been given the chance of putting into practice the theories he had developed while in France on how occupied countries might most easily and painlessly be administered, Hanneken faced a difficult military problem, the risk of invasion, and was responsible for its solution.

With OKW's directive of 14 December 1941, the Germans adopted a defensive strategy in the West. The directive ordered the reinforcement by troops and fortifications of the most exposed points of what was called a "new West Wall." In this connection, the western coast of Jutland was ascribed, along with the Dutch coast, a low priority, and they were allotted the third place in importance after Norway and the coast of France and Belgium. In accordance with this attitude, until 1942 Denmark was occupied only by two weak divisions, one of which trained reserve troops, while the other was made up of older men. On 1 May 1942, Denmark's military status was changed from being a "home area" to an "operational area," but it was not until the end of October 1942 that Denmark was, in response to the representations of the German navy, militarily reinforced by the allotment of a further division, which was still in the process of being formed. German troops continued to arrive in Denmark throughout 1943, so that the number of divisions in the country grew from three to six, of which five were stationed in Jutland. There were also about forty coastal batteries. From December 1943 on, all the German divisions were stationed in Jutland, while thirteen battalions of convalescent troops were responsible for the occupation of the Danish islands (see map on p. 226). In the spring of 1944 the country contained about 40,000 troops fit for combat. This increase was an expression of the seriousness with which the western coast of Jutland was regarded by the German high

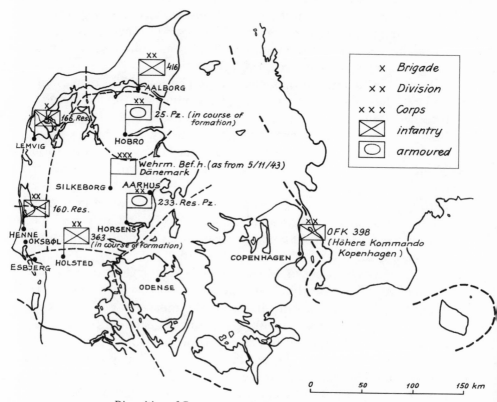

Disposition of German troops in Denmark, 1 June 1944

command as a possible site for the invasion by the Western Allies. This anxiety was explicitly mentioned in the *Führer* directive no. 51 of 3 November 1943, with its supplement of 28 December, which ordered a considerable reinforcement of Denmark's defenses, as of other areas along the West Wall, and forbade the withdrawal of troops and material from the country. However, good intentions were one thing, and harsh realities were another. Both before and after November 1943 divisions were continually being moved from Denmark, owing to pressing needs for their services elsewhere, and replaced by other, less effective divisions. In fact, at no point during the war was a truly effective division stationed in Denmark for any length of time. As soon as a division had become *feldverwendungs-fähig*, it was withdrawn. This was Hanneken's constant problem and insoluble dilemma: his task was to defend Denmark from invasion, but his troops were neither large enough nor skilled enough for him to accomplish it.

Moreover, Hanneken felt that the enemy, or at any rate a potential enemy, was also within his own camp in the form of the remainder of the Danish army. The latter consisted to be sure only of 5-6,000 men, but the permanent officer corps was intact and Hanneken did not therefore dare to regard the army as a *quantité negligeable*. He feared that the Danish army would attack his forces from the rear in the event of an Allied invasion. So immediately after his arrival in Denmark he saw to it that the small Danish garrisons on Jutland were moved to the island of Fyn and that about half the rifles and ammunition in the possession of the Danish army were "lent" to the Germans. Hanneken would have preferred to have secured all the armaments of the Danish army, and he would have liked even more to see it completely disbanded, a subject on which he made several, for the time being fruitless, representations to Berlin. Above all, he would have liked to see Denmark placed under military administration without the encumbrance of a Danish government or a Werner Best. (His relations with Best were troubled by serious differences of opinion.) However, for the time being it was Best who had the upper hand, and it was Best's policy that was carried out.

In his power struggle with Best, Hanneken received assistance from a quarter which he presumably regarded as the least likely to provide it. Although it is highly debatable whether the Danish resistance ever became a military factor to be reckoned with—and at any rate it certainly was not one in the years 1942-43—it is incontestable that it became an important factor in domestic politics and ultimately more important than any other during the spring and summer of 1943. During this period the Communists continued their sabotage activities and gradually organized these activities more effectively. In addition to Bopa, their sabotage organization in Copenhagen, they established sabotage groups in several provincial towns, and in the spring of 1943 they began to publicize acts of sabotage in their illegal newspapers—a clear indication that the hitherto negative attitude of the broad mass of the population toward this form of warfare had begun to change. In May 1943 the sabotage group Holger Danske, which developed into a nonsocialist counterpart of Bopa, initiated its activities. In the first half of 1943, the number of acts of sabotage carried out in Denmark rose to about 300, three times the number for the previous six months, and a further high point was reached in August 1943, when about 200 acts of sabotage were committed. But many of these operations were quite insignificant, so the fact that the use of explosives began to be in evidence from February 1943 on was as important as the numerical increase. The Communists obtained some explosives themselves and others through their contacts with SOE agents from Britain. SOE activity in Denmark had been a long series of mishaps and disasters in 1942, but it became more effective in 1943. The first supplies of sabotage material were dropped by plane in March, and Captain Flemming B. Muus arrived in Denmark the same month. As the SOE's "chief organizer in the field," Muus established contact with both the Communists and right-wing activists, above all the *Dansk Samling* group.

It is difficult, or rather impossible, to establish precisely when the previous stability of public opinion began to dissolve. As we have seen, the outcome of the parliamentary election in March could be interpreted as a victory for parliamentary democracy and was taken as support for the policy of negotiation. However, a change was discernible in the local elections at the beginning of May. In many places, the Communists put up candidates for the local elections while camouflaging their party affiliation, and in several towns their candidates won seats on the town councils, at the expense of the Social Democrats. The Communists obtained their highest level of support in Nakskov, a shipbuilding town of 15,000 inhabitants, where they won 19% of the vote and four seats on the town council. This was a sign of unrest among the working class. The number of local strikes grew during 1943, and this was another sign of unrest. This phenomenon is probably connected with the fact that unemployment was declining. There was not much to be lost by industrial action; indeed, experience suggested that there was often something to be gained. It was not difficult to find alternative employment in 1943, and in the worst event Danish workers did not need to take a job in Germany, but could work on German fortifications on the west coast, where conditions were certainly primitive but wages high.

Both the Danish and German political authorities realized by the summer of 1943 that the situation was no longer quite the same as it had been. Hanneken had plans drawn up for the disarming of the Danish armed forces, the so-called Operation Safari. The Danish politicians were interested in the idea that a government which, in Scavenius's words, was "fully parliamentary" would provide them with the degree of authority among the population needed to continue the policy of negotiation, whose day they certainly did not see as over. Scavenius, who was by no means hungry for office, was not slow to seize on the idea. The threat of resignation had been his trump card ever since 1940, and at a cabinet meeting on 9 August 1943 he raised the question whether a restructuring of the government was not desirable. However, neither the occupying power nor the Danish politicians had anticipated the events that occurred next. The August uprising had begun in Esbjerg by the ninth (see below), and in the course of the following three weeks the street disturbances and strikes developed into a flood that swept away the policy of negotiation. There had certainly been some increase in these phenomena during the preceding spring and summer, but the torrent that suddenly occurred during these hot August days took everyone by surprise.

In Esbjerg, a town of 40,000 inhabitants, the local Communist sabotage group carried out a series of acts of sabotage with British explosives, culminating on the night of 5-6 August with a great fire in the harbor which destroyed 400,000 empty fish crates. As a preventive measure the Germans imposed a curfew between 10:00 P.M. and 5:00 A.M. This was, naturally, seen as a punishment and led to street riots and brawls between German soldiers and young Danes on successive evenings. On Monday morning the smiths and mechanics in a number of workshops went on strike in protest "against the conditions that prevail in the town," that is, against the curfew and German brutality toward demonstrators. The authorities—the trade union leaders, the police, and the German commander in the town—succeeded in having this strike called off the same afternoon, but on Tuesday the men employed on the German fortifications along the west coast came home again, and in the course of the day the men who worked in the town itself went on strike, ostensibly in response to a new German provocation. On Wednesday the strike spread to embrace the whole town, and offices and shops were closed, including the local government bureaus, even the police office, so that all was "as on a Sunday." Only the railway more or less continued to function. On Wednesday evening an offer of a compromise, which had been drawn up in Copenhagen, was presented to a big meeting of strikers, and they agreed to go back to work in return for a lifting of the curfew. On Thursday life was back to normal in Esbjerg.

However, on the island of Fyn life became extremely abnormal. There is not enough space here for a detailed account of the course of events on Fyn, and what happened in Esbjerg can, by and large, be taken as a model of what took place elsewhere. After several evenings of disturbances and brawls on the streets, there was a strike in Odense (101,000 inhabitants) from 18 to 23 August. It was a wild and bloody period; the strikers looted the homes and businesses of Danish Nazis, and shaved the heads of "female collaborators." The unrest spread to the surrounding area, as it had not done in the case of Esbjerg, and strikes occurred in all the market towns on Fyn. However, except in the largest of these towns, Svendborg (21,000 inhabitants), these strikes lasted only one or two days. From Fyn the wave of strikes reached Korsør (10,000 inhabitants) in Zealand in the east and Fredericia (22,000 inhabitants) in Jutland in the west on 24 August. However, at this stage the center of unrest moved to north Jutland. From 23 to 29 August there was a determined and continuous strike in Aalborg (92,000 inhabitants), with subsidiary stoppages in Frederikshavn (16,000 inhabitants), Skagen (6,000 inhabitants), and Sæby (3,000 inhabitants). Finally, the largest provincial town, Aarhus (131,000 inhabitants), joined the strike movement, but only from 26 August on.

A total of seventeen towns were involved in the wave of strikes, but there were rumblings of discontent in other places too. Street riots and attempts to organize strikes occurred in Kolding (26,000 inhabitants) and Randers (44,000 inhabitants), but they came to nothing. Street riots were the only disturbances that occurred in Vejle (32,000 inhabitants), Haderslev (17,000 inhabitants), Horsens (32,000 inhabitants), Hjørring (14,000 inhabitants), and Roskilde (23,000 inhabitants), among other places. It is noteworthy that these events largely bypassed the capital, Copenhagen, the only very big city in Denmark (1,050,000 inhabitants). Although the large exhibition hall, Forum, was blown up on 24 August (this was one of the most famous episodes of the occupation period) and there were lively disturbances on the town hall square, this was a pale reflection of what happened in Odense and Aalborg, and no general strike, let alone strike by the whole city, took place.

The wave of strikes in Denmark during August will receive closer consideration for two reasons. First, it was an event of essential importance in the history of Denmark during the occupation. Second, apart from a few isolated exceptions, the use of the strike weapon as an illegal instrument has been sadly neglected by scholars working on the European resistance. Instead of systematic analysis, one finds either fragmentary references in passing or mere heroics.

What led to the wave of strikes and what were the necessary conditions for it? As we have seen, in Esbjerg it was the German countermeasures against sabotage that set events in motion. In Svendborg, there had been unrest on the streets for many days with mutual provocations by local youths and Danish soldiers on one side and German sailors on shore leave on the other, but neither these disturbances nor an act of sabotage against a ship carrying foodstuffs to Germany triggered a strike. It was only after three drunken German soldiers had wandered round the streets of Svendborg one evening that the activists were able to persuade the local shipyard workers to go on strike, and both a propaganda leaflet and a further act of sabotage were required before a general strike of the whole town occurred on 24 August. Real or supposed German provocations alone were not necessarily enough to produce a strike; yeast in the dough was needed as well.

In Odense, many nights of street disturbances culminated in a foundry worker being stabbed by a German bayonet, and this caused a general strike in the town on the following day. In Aalborg, events were set in motion when Germans discovered members of the resistance transporting material that they had received from the British to the south of the town. One man was shot and another arrested. The funeral of the man who had been killed was the occasion of large demonstrations in Aalborg, even though the authorities had tried to prevent disturbances by holding the funeral at an earlier time than had first been announced. The demonstrations led to clashes with German troops, and a strike was the result. The man who had been arrested came from Aarhus, and when he was condemned to death by a German military court in Aarhus, this unleashed violent disturbances followed by a strike in this town.

There were both street riots and several minor acts of sabotage in

Kolding, but an attempt to bring the town out on strike in sympathy with Odense did not arouse a response among the population. There were street brawls between Danes and Germans in Haderslev, but the irritation against the Germans was dispelled and replaced by enthusiasm for the town's rowing team, when the latter returned from Stockholm with the Nordic championship in rowing.

It is noteworthy that the cause of the strikes was local, and sympathy strikes were rare. In general, a tangible local cause was required to bring a town out on strike. This did not need to be an act of sabotage, as the BBC claimed at the time. Sabotage served as a catalyst in Esbjerg and Svendborg, but in Aalborg it was the funeral of a man shot by the Germans followed by the death of another man at the hands of the Germans; in Aarhus it was the sentencing to death of a member of the resistance, and in Odense it was the stabbing of a worker in the back by a German bayonet. In Fredericia a campaign in the workplaces against women who consorted with the Germans led to street fights with German soldiers who sought to protect these women, and a similar pattern of events occurred in Fåborg, a small town on Fyn.

In line with their origins, all these strikes occurred in support of concrete demands, and in this respect they clearly differ from the many strikes that took place in Denmark the following year as protests or demonstrations (the great strike in Copenhagen at midsummer 1944 was an exception). The strikes of 1943 were of indefinite duration and in support of a series of demands that were similar or identical in many towns: the Germans should be removed from the streets, and the Danish police should be responsible for the maintenance of law and order (this was a demand that usually emerged during the strikes, since the Germans began to patrol the streets at this time). Other demands, which varied according to local conditions, were the return of buildings requisitioned by the Germans; the release of Danes under arrest; the lifting of the curfew; the exclusion from public places of women who consorted with the Germans; and even that the Germans should honor the agreement of 9 April 1940, despite the fact that there was no such agreement. The negotiations aimed at ending the strikes were a search for a middle way, for both sides did not want to lose face any more than was absolutely necessary.

There was no overall strategy or cunning master plan behind the strikes, as the Germans believed at the time: watching as the strikes flared up along the Copenhagen-Esbjerg axis, they tended to see them as a deliberate attempt to disrupt the line of communication between the political center, Copenhagen, and Jutland, the area of greatest military importance. Nor were there agitators and provocateurs who traveled from one town to another rapidly arranging strikes in each, as the authorities and the Social Democrats tended to think. It was the local Communists who sustained the wave of strikes. They did not work in accordance with any overall strategy, but they had their general directives, they were sufficiently well trained to be able to recognize a good opportunity when it offered itself, and they were sufficiently well versed in Communist theory to know what should be done. Sometimes it was the local party leadership in a town which exploited the situation; on other occasions this was done by groups at a lower level in the party organization. Once the strikes had begun, it was the Communists who organized and sought to extend them. They constantly printed leaflets; for several days the illegal Communist paper *Trods Alt* was the only daily paper that appeared in Odense. In Esbjerg, Aalborg, and Aarhus the Communists mobilized the *Frit Danmark* groups in the service of the strikes and the Popular Front policy. It was Communists who set the strikes in motion in many workplaces, and it was they who spoke up at the numerous workers' meetings.

Communist representatives on the shop floor were of decisive importance for the August uprising. It is quite clear that strikes do not break out spontaneously, even if a foundry worker has been stabbed in the back with a bayonet. They do not begin on the streets, regardless of how many brawls occur. Nor do they begin because people decide to stay away from work. Strikes begin when people decide to go home from work, and there had to be someone on the shop floor who came forward to say that it was time to walk out, since the Germans had now gone too far. At Kolding the Communists never succeeded in getting the people at any single workplace to go home, and that is presumably an important part of the reason why the town never passed from the phase of street brawls to that of striking. Control over the largest and most important places of work —that is perhaps the root of the matter.

The strikes involved a peculiar mixture of nationalist emotion, helpful cooperation on an apartment-to-apartment and house-to-house basis—and violent excesses. Very few of them ran their course without illegal actions against pro-German businesses, local Nazis, and "soldiers' tarts." The indignation over the betrayal of national

234 □ AAGE TROMMER

interests was mixed up with an aggressiveness and perversity which found an outlet in breaking windows, destroying the fixtures of shops, and stripping and clipping the hair of the Germans' girls. Equally heavy-handed methods were sometimes used to ensure that all shops closed. In the words of an illegal paper, *Aarhus Ekko*, "All shops closed on Thursday afternoon. Only those shopkeepers who preferred to trade with the Germans remained open, but they were quickly taught by the people on the streets that it was best that they closed their shops." The hesitancy about closing offices and shops indicates that in certain places the middle class had some reservations about the strikes. This is hardly surprising, since under normal circumstances the middle class certainly does not think in terms of striking.

The Social Democrats opposed the strikes at both the political and the trade union level, and in those cases where the local party was inclined to give way before the wave of strikes, it was kept up to the mark by the party leadership in Copenhagen. At first, in Esbjerg and Odense, the party adopted an unequivocally hostile stand toward the strikes, but after this attitude met with stinging rebuffs in these two towns, the party learned to act with greater suppleness, to allow the strikes to run their course, and to try to intervene at the right moment in order to direct the uprising into such channels as would allow the strikes to be settled as rapidly as possible. The Social Democrats thought that the strikes were directed not only at the Germans but also at themselves. They believed that their backs were against the wall under the pressure of this sudden Communist assault, and the political and trade union leadership of the Social Democratic movement wondered anxiously whether they had lost their mass support. Their importance and anger were clearly expressed in the editorials of the Social Democratic press, which spoke of chauvinists and opportunists who had never before had an honest interest in the workers' cause and who were now attempting only to further their own interests. It was a struggle for power and influence not only in the short term but also for the postwar period which might not be far off, since it might be affected by the outcome of the strikes.

It is self-evident that the Danish cabinet did all that it could to combat the uprising. It saw that the whole basis for the policy of negotiation was giving way at a time when neither cabinet nor parliament believed that the advantages this policy could confer were exhausted. Encouraged and supported by Best, the central political and administrative authorities made the most energetic efforts to bring events under control. Danish police forces were sent from the towns that remained quiet to the areas of unrest in order to assist in the maintenance of order. On 21 August the government made a last attempt to restore calm by issuing a proclamation, which stated that no one could take the law into his own hands and that it was the country's legally empowered authorities and responsible leaders who would take the measures necessary for the protection of Danish interests. However, this proclamation had no effect and the strikes continued in full force in north Jutland and other areas.

It was a common view at the time that the Germans systematically provoked the unrest that flared up into strikes, so that they might at the right moment eliminate the Danish government and assume full power themselves. This is what they had done in Austria and Czechoslovakia a few years earlier. However, this view was quite unfounded. On the contrary, the local German commanders were extremely moderate and supple in their attempts to secure a restoration of order and frequently kept their troops in barracks for a few days so that calm might return to the streets and a strike be settled—this also says something about the discipline among the German soldiers. This moderate attitude was not determined by the local commanders, but they agreed with the line adopted by Hanneken. It reflected the fact that the policy of negotiation had created a situation that not only obliged the Danish government to grant one concession after the other but also limited the *Wehrmacht*'s freedom of action. It could not solve the problem of order in Denmark by sending in the troops, taking hostages, or carrying out executions, as had been done, for example, during similar strikes in Holland in 1941 and 1942. Hanneken did not try to solve the problem by sending off-duty soldiers onto the streets, but by appealing to the *Führer's* headquarters for permission to carry out Operation Safari.

In the summer of 1943 Britain certainly wanted to see more illegal activity in Denmark. On 26 June 1943 a Foreign Office official minuted that the British strategy was intended to stretch German resources to the utmost everywhere, and the greatest possible unrest in Denmark was a facet of this strategy. No opportunity, he declared, was too small to be ignored. What London had in mind was "non-detectable sabotage" but not the overthrow of the Danish government. The British were surprised by the actual course of events in

Denmark, and the BBC's news coverage of developments in Denmark was also very slow to report what was happening.

The conclusion to be drawn from all this must be that the August uprising was made in the large provincial towns (if Danish provincial towns can be called large) without the assistance of the inhabitants of Copenhagen or the rural population. It was made by the workers and the excited crowds on the streets. It was made by a number of activists, among whom the Communists were the dominant organizers, and supported by a middle class which in most places willingly played their part and turned a general strike into a town strike. The uprising was opposed by the local and central authorities and, behind them, by the cabinet and parliament. The politicians did not take the opportunity provided by these events to seize the initiative and bring the policy of negotiation to an end.

The Germans, however, did. Because of the strikes and the unrest in Denmark Hanneken was finally able to defeat Best, the convinced adherent of the policy of negotiation, in their struggle to win Hitler's favor. On 24 August Best was summoned to Hitler in order to be taken to task, and he returned to Denmark with an ultimatum to the Danish government, which demanded the introduction of a state of emergency and the death penalty for strikers and saboteurs. All the ministers, with Scavenius at their head, agreed at a cabinet meeting on 28 August that demands of this nature could not be accepted.

Early on the morning of Sunday, 29 August, Hanneken declared martial law in Denmark and assumed executive power in the country. Operation Safari was set in motion against the Danish army and navy. The army, which had been ordered not to resist except in the case of a surprise attack, was disarmed and interned. The navy scuttled itself, except for a few ships which escaped to Sweden. The Danes lost twenty-four dead and fifty wounded, the Germans five dead and fifty-nine wounded. A total of about 10,000 men from the Danish army and navy were interned. The Scavenius government handed in its resignation to the king and ceased to function.

Within a very few days, the Germans decided they wanted to see a new Danish government formed. On 1 September Best received instructions from the *Auswärtiges Amt* that he should secure the establishment of a new government, but the leading Danish politicians, with the Social Democrat Vilhelm Buhl at their head, absolutely refused to cooperate. The dreaded alternative might be that the Germans themselves took over the administration of the country, but this did not happen. Instead, the alternative proved to be government by the permanent heads of the ministries, who since 29 August had been looking after current business as an interim measure. In the course of September an arrangement emerged, with the approval of the political parties and the acquiescence of the Germans, whereby the permanent heads of the ministries were authorized to issue ordinances (which the courts declared they were prepared to enforce) and to dismiss and appoint civil servants. There was no question of collective responsibility. These permanent heads, of whom there were twenty-six, did to be sure hold very frequent joint meetings to discuss such issues and problems as arose, and the director of the Foreign Ministry, Nils Svenningsen, did certainly conduct all negotiations with the Germans through Werner Best, so as to keep the Germans as remote from the Danish administration as possible, but the principle that each permanent head was himself fully responsible for the area of competence of his ministry was nonetheless maintained.

It was thus the permanent heads of ministries who, at a lower level, continued the policy of negotiation, sometimes in cooperation and sometimes in conflict with Werner Best. One of the most important areas in which they could cooperate with Best—against Hanneken—was on the problem of the supply of labor. In November 1943 they averted the threat of the conscription of labor for the fortifications on the west coast by promising that the requisite manpower would be provided through the Danish employment agencies, and as it turned out this could be done without difficulty. By the beginning of 1944 about 50,000 men were working for the Germans in Denmark.

Although the permanent heads of ministries were now responsible for the government of the country, this did not mean that the politicians had lost interest in what was happening within the administration. The ministers who had resigned paid regular unofficial visits to their old ministries, and the permanent heads of ministries also consulted the so-called *Samarbejdsudvalg* (The Cooperation Committee), which consisted of thirteen senior politicians from the parties that had served in the outgoing government. These consultations primarily concerned internal Danish matters which had nothing to do with the Germans, but sometimes also involved questions of a sensitive nature. The director-general of customs wanted advice on whether he should pay extra wages to those who put out a special effort on the job, and was told that he should not do so for the time being. The permanent head of the Ministry of Justice wanted advice on whether senior police officers should negotiate with the German police concerning the suppression of sabotage, and was told that they might. These two examples demonstrate the scope of the consultations that were held. It was only after the people's strike in Copenhagen in June 1944 that the politicians lost interest in the administrative activities of the permanent heads of the ministries and turned their eyes instead to the future.

When Best returned to Denmark on 28 August after having been called to account by Hitler, he felt like a beaten man. His policy was in ruins, and Hanneken was the man of the hour. However, a few days later Best was so to speak restored to favor. He received a telegram from Berlin that he, as the plenipotentiary of the *Reich*, still had political responsibility in Denmark even while the country was under martial law. The fiction that Denmark was a foreign country and as such fell within the area of competence of the German Foreign Ministry was thus maintained—there were not many countries left with which the *Auswärtiges Amt* could conduct diplomatic relations. However, Best never wholly recovered his old influence. Quite apart from such considerations as the fact that from September 1943 the Gestapo acted directly in Denmark against the resistance (the Danish police had dealt with illegal activity until 29 August 1943) and the fact that Himmler sent the SS general Günther Pancke to Denmark in December 1943 to lead the counterterror that was initiated at that time, it could clearly be foreseen that the course of the war was such that first priority would be given to the demands and requests of the military authorities and therefore also of Hanneken. Best was perpetually engaged in a rearguard action.

It is perhaps against this background that one should view Best's initiative at the beginning of September 1943 when he urged the *Auswärtiges Amt* to "take a stand concerning the solution of the question of the Danish Jews and freemasons." Although he stated that the moment was opportune while martial law was still in force in the country, his initiative is nonetheless amazing. If the Germans wanted to have a Danish government again (and at this time they still did) as well as what from the German point of view was a reasonable climate of opinion which gave no more scope to the activists than was absolutely necessary, then the deportation of the Danish Jews was not the wisest course to follow. Best's action has been explained as an attempt to play a trump card in his struggle for power with Hanneken, and this seems plausible when combined with another explanation, namely that Best, as an SS man, must have known that, once a country came under the domination of the Nazi system, the final solution of the Jewish problem would under any circumstances rapidly follow. This had occurred in all other countries in occupied Europe and would also happen in Hungary, which was occupied in the spring of 1944. If Best knew that action would be taken against the Danish Jews, he may well have reasoned that he should try to turn this development to his own advantage. However, these are only hypotheses, and we shall probably never be totally sure about Best's motives. In any event, an order from the *Führer* concerning the deportation of the Danish Jews arrived on 18 September.

Whatever Best's motives, it was with his knowledge and consent that one of his subordinates, Georg Ferdinand Duckwitz, first tried to prevent the action against the Jews by intervening in Berlin and Stockholm, and then sabotaged it by warning Danish politicians and officials of what was about to occur a few days before it was due to begin. As a result, the attempt to arrest the approximately 8,000 Danish Jews, most of them residents of Copenhagen, which began on the night of 1-2 October 1943, was a fiasco. Only about 500 of the Danish Jews were sent to the concentration camp of Theresienstadt in Bohemia, whereas well over 7,000 of them escaped this fate. At first, because of the warnings that were received, they hid with relatives, friends, or other helpful people. Then, throughout October and November, they were secretly transported across the Sound to Sweden, where they were received with great friendliness and were found temporary accommodation by the Swedish state. A precondition for the rescue of the Danish Jews was that many individuals, private organizations, and public bodies in Denmark rose to the challenge and evinced solidarity and selflessness. It is self-evident and hardly surprising that there were also examples of human frailty and greed.

The rescue of the Jews led to an unexpected gain for clandestine circles in Denmark in the form of better contacts with Sweden. Until that time, secret journeys by sea to Sweden had been very difficult and often encountered insuperable problems. The need to transport many Jews over the water and a change in the attitude of the Swedish authorities toward such illegal activities created the basis for the emergence of a number of clandestine refugee organizations, which continued to function after the immediate crisis had passed. These organizations were run by Danes and operated from Swedish ports like Malmö, Helsingborg, and Gothenburg, though they had a well-developed network of contacts in Danish harbors. Fishing and motor boats were used on their "routes." Occasionally, vessels on lawful business were also used, and in such cases boats from Denmark and Sweden met in open sea and exchanged passengers, cargo, and mail. Because of these routes, communication with Sweden became less of a problem. A total of about 20,000 Danish refugees were transported to Sweden in this way. There was also a stream of traffic, above all armaments deliveries from Sweden and Britain, in the opposite direction.

In another respect, too, the action against the Jews had consequences for clandestine activities in Denmark. On 2 October 1943 the Germans announced that "since the Jews . . . have, because of the measures taken by the German authorities, been eliminated from public life and prevented from continuing to poison the atmosphere . . . the release of interned Danish soldiers will begin in the next few days and will occur at a rate to be determined by practical considerations." Few, if any, fell for this action against the Jews as a prerequisite for the release of the officers and the other ranks. But whatever the real reason, the release took place in October and provided the resisters with a valuable addition of men who had more understanding of military matters than most Danes.

At first, that is to say after the release of the army had been announced but before it was completed, the army leadership planned to have the officer corps transported to Sweden so that it might form the nucleus of a force that could be used during the last phase of the war and the occupation by the government which had presented its resignation to the king on 29 August. However, immediately after the ending of the internment of the army, around 1 November 1943, the plan was changed after consultation with Vilhelm Buhl. Only a small group of officers was sent to Sweden to take part in the building up of a Danish "police corps"; the great majority were concentrated in Copenhagen and were assembled in special military groups, the so-called O groups, only a few being stationed in the provinces. The idea behind this concentration in Copenhagen was the same as that behind the original plan of evacuation to Sweden, namely, to establish a force that would be at the disposal of the government.

As had been the case before 29 August, the Danish armed forces were a loyal instrument for the Danish politicians, and this loyalty was in no way undermined in December 1943 when the army leadership ("the little general staff") began to cooperate with the "civilian" resistance movement.

The O groups in Copenhagen were not the only resistance forces the army set about establishing in the autumn of 1943. In Jutland and on Fyn it set up resistance groups that were to be built up around the so-called P organization, which had existed for some time. The P organization, as revised at this time, consisted of ten or so companies of men with previous military training, which it was thought could be mobilized at the appropriate moment. Although little came of the attempt to set up further companies and it was quickly discontinued, the original P organization was maintained until the end of the war.

Other resistance groups were also formed during the autumn of 1943. Although the membership totals should not be overestimated, recruitment for these groups was so successful that the number of people engaged in illegal activity was now many times greater than it had been before 29 August. The Communists supplemented their illegal party branches (which were responsible for the party's local press) and their sabotage groups by establishing military groups and groups to protect factories. *Dansk Samling* began to agitate for the formation of six-man military groups, and the party set about doing so in many places and allowed in other places its perfectly legal open-air sporting activities to undergo a hidden transformation. In Copenhagen the illegal organization *Dannevirke* was formed from conservative circles. It also tried to set up military groups in the provinces, and signs of its activities can be detected, for example, in North Schleswig.

The picture of the military groups formed by the Communists, *Dansk Samling,* the army, and *Dannevirke,* all of which were set up with a view to the invasion which was widely expected to occur in Denmark (hence the name "waiting groups"), is confusing and blurred. However, the full spectrum of illegal groups in Denmark was still more complicated. The Communist and *Frit Danmark* groups were mentioned earlier, but there was a constant increase in the number of groups producing illegal papers, groups which were based on *Dansk Samling* or which were of bourgeois-conservative origin. Moreover, *Ringen,* which recruited its members primarily from bourgeois and Social Democratic circles and which had begun in 1941 in an attempt to strengthen national feeling and disseminate information, was made illegal during this period, and after February 1944 became involved in setting up military groups. Finally, SOE's network of groups ("circuits") formed to receive material from Britain and to carry out sabotage should be mentioned. It was above all the SOE groups that were responsible for the sabotage operations against railways that occurred in Jutland in the autumn of 1943. Apart from such activities, the SOE groups were important mainly because they could acquire weapons and explosives. Although only small quantities were dropped by plane for the time being (over ten tons during 1943), these deliveries were of great practical and psychological significance.

The resistance movement in many European countries was characterized by the emergence of a number of independent "party armies," which in the best case coordinated their activities and cooperated with considerable difficulty, and which in the worst case openly battled with each other while fighting, or instead of fighting, the Germans. France is an example of the former and Yugoslavia and Greece of the latter. In the autumn of 1943 there was also a tendency toward party armies in Denmark, a tendency that was accentuated by the tension that was known to exist between the Communists and the other illegal groupings. Fear of Communist intentions at the end of the war was strong in such quarters as *Dansk Samling* circles and *Dannevirke.* It was also present among Social Democrats, and the measures taken by the army leadership, which as we have seen were decided on in close consultation with the politicians, should be seen in the light of such anxieties. But this polycentric tendency failed to develop any further because of two circumstances—the establishment of *Frihedsrådet* (The Freedom Council) and SOE's guidelines for illegal activity.

Tradition has it that the Freedom Council was founded on 16 September 1943, but attempts had been made as early as the preceding summer to establish a nationwide umbrella organization, which could coordinate and draw up common guidelines for illegal activities. In fact, two such organizations were set up. One disappeared in the maelstrom of the events of August. The other and more representative organization survived to see the light of day. The four large clandestine organizations—the Communists, *Frit Danmark, Dansk Samling,* and *Ringen*—along with SOE were represented on

The Danish Freedom Council, the unofficial government which the people of
Denmark obeyed for almost a year, from July 1944 to May 1945. It was in nearly
every respect different from an ordinary government, because it included a high
proportion of young, highly educated members. (Museet for Danmarks Frihedskamp 1940-45, Copenhagen)

the Freedom Council. The number of members varied, but was
around ten, and continuity and the hard core of resistance policy
were represented by figures like Frode Jakobsen from *Ringen* (a
teacher with a university education, a rank-and-file member of the
Social Democratic Party, thirty-seven years old); Mogens Fog from
Frit Danmark (a professor of medicine, a Communist though not a
party member, thirty-nine years old); Børge Houmann from the
Communists (a writer and party functionary, forty-one years old);
and Arne Sørensen from *Dansk Samling* (a writer, the founder and
chairman of his party, thirty-seven years old). It was a long time
since such young men had sought to rule Denmark. The Council
defined its task in its first proclamation as follows: it would "organize
resistance to the Germans in all fields and by all methods." It would
work for democratic ideals and fight not only the external enemy
but also "Danish Nazis, renegades and defeatists." In November 1943
the Council issued a pamphlet, entitled *Når Danmark atter er frit*
(When Denmark Is Free Again), in which it defined the aims of the

struggle: the immediate reintroduction of democracy; legal proceedings against all who had been guilty of or responsible for violations of democracy and the rule of law or who had derived "personal advantage" from the occupation of the country; and punishment in accordance with the Danish sense of justice without individuals taking the law into their own hands.

The Freedom Council acquired great political prestige and influence as the highest Danish authority within the resistance movement, but not until the middle of 1944. The BBC first mentioned the Council in its Danish broadcasts around 1 November 1943, despite requests that it should do so earlier. The Council first had to be evaluated by a great number of British institutions and found to be sufficiently important. The Council was, however, publicized by the greater part of the illegal press within Denmark. The limited authority the Council initially enjoyed can be seen from the fact that, when it asked the large political parties to appoint representatives to the Council, they refused. The politicians were not interested. They still believed they could disregard the new organization.

In December 1943 Flemming Muus, SOE's chief organizer in the field, returned to Denmark after spending two months in London. He brought with him new directives of far-reaching importance. London regarded the illegal activities carried out until that time in Denmark as "day-to-day sabotage" in military terms, and believed that it was now time for "synchronized operations as part of a general offensive." The resistance struggle should, in other words, be fitted into the general strategy of the Western Allies and play a part, albeit a modest one, in the preparations for the invasion of northwest Europe. To this end, Muus returned to Denmark with a message that sabotage should be discontinued for the time being. During this interval, intensive work should be done to build up military groups in six regions, each with its own leadership. The guidelines that SOE laid down in this and later directives determined the nature of all illegal military activity in the country during the last eighteen months of the war. The military groups that had already been established were linked to the new regional commands, and although new groups could have political labels, militarily they all functioned within the framework of the regions prescribed by SOE and the tasks set by SOE.

The situation at the very end of 1943 and the beginning of 1944 can be summarized as follows. With regard to legal activity, the

permanent heads of ministries, discreetly supervised by the politicians from an unobtrusive position, continued the policy of negotiation as far as possible with Werner Best, the *Reich's* plenipotentiary, whose position had been gravely weakened by the collapse of
his policy in August 1943 and whose room for maneuver was limited
by the military authorities and also, after December 1943, by the
often arbitrary actions taken by the German police. With regard to
illegal activity, the establishment of the Freedom Council as the
supreme political organ of the resistance movement and the subordination of military actions to the direction of SOE impeded all
centrifugal tendencies. The victory won by the resistance movement
in August had enhanced its prestige, while the expectation of an
early invasion made its activity meaningful. Both these factors
contributed to consolidating its position among the population and
were the basis for the enormous growth in its membership during the
last phase of the war.

Norway: Economic Warfare and the Struggle against Nazification

After the year of struggle in 1942, when the civilian resistance enjoyed a number of great triumphs while the military resistance was
severely battered, Norway went through a period marked by ex-
haustion and maintenance of the status quo in 1943 and the beginning
of 1944.

The German military authorities maintained the level of German
military strength in the country. At the beginning of 1943 there were
eleven infantry divisions and one armored division in Norway; at the
end of the year there were twelve infantry divisions. There were also
250 coastal batteries in the country. The size of the German forces
in Norway impressed and surprised their opponents at the time and
the historians of later years, but the German army leadership itself
did not regard it as impressive. As the positions where the troops
were stationed show (see map, p. 247), German strength in Norway
also ensured that Sweden would remain neutral under all circumstances. The only armored division in Norway was stationed in the
Oslo area (so that the Swedes would be discouraged from getting any
ideas about attacking Norway) until it was sent to France in August
1943. To the Germans, Norway was of decisive importance for the
outcome of the war, partly because of its ore deposits, partly because

of the Germans' continuing need to transport nickel from Petsamo along the Norwegian coast, and partly because they knew that possession of the ice-free ports of northern Norway would be to the advantage of the Soviet Union. The Germans did not exclude the possibility of an Allied attack against Trondheim or Oslo, but did not overestimate this risk. However, they felt obliged not only to make these two towns militarily secure but to station a "screen" of divisions along the coast to protect the lively German coastal traffic.

The relationship between the commander of the German troops in Norway, General Nikolaus von Falkenhorst, and the Civilian *Reichskommissar*, Joseph Terboven, was not particularly good, but they both held the same opinion of Quisling. After the latter's fiasco in attempting to set up a corporate *"riksting"* (national parliament), Hitler had also put him on ice in September 1942 and had informed him that he should consult Terboven on all political questions. Immediately after this development, Terboven took action against the Norwegian Jews. However, reports of the preparations that were being made leaked out, and about half of the Norwegian Jews escaped to Sweden. The other half, about 700 people, were arrested and perished in the German death camps. In August 1943, as a preventive measure against the resistance, Terboven had about 1,100 military officers and about 500 policemen arrested. Finally, he took action against Oslo University at the end of November 1943, when an act of sabotage was committed against the great hall of the university; he had about 1,200 male students arrested, and about 700 of them sent to "re-education camps" in Germany. This was the first time that Terboven had acted without directives or backing from Berlin, and Hitler was furious at his tactical ineptitude.

In the political sphere, the most important offensive measure taken by the regime was the national labor law of February 1943, which Quisling issued with Terboven's consent. The background to and the objectives of this initiative have not been the object of detailed research, but its timing suggests that it was closely connected with the general German campaign to mobilize labor throughout Europe during this period. The wording of the law was ambiguous, and this was probably deliberate. It was stated that the Norwegian people should now devote all their energies to the struggle against Bolshevism, but should also increase production to safeguard the economy and supplies in the difficult times ahead. With a view to the conscription of all labor "which is not being fully exploited or which

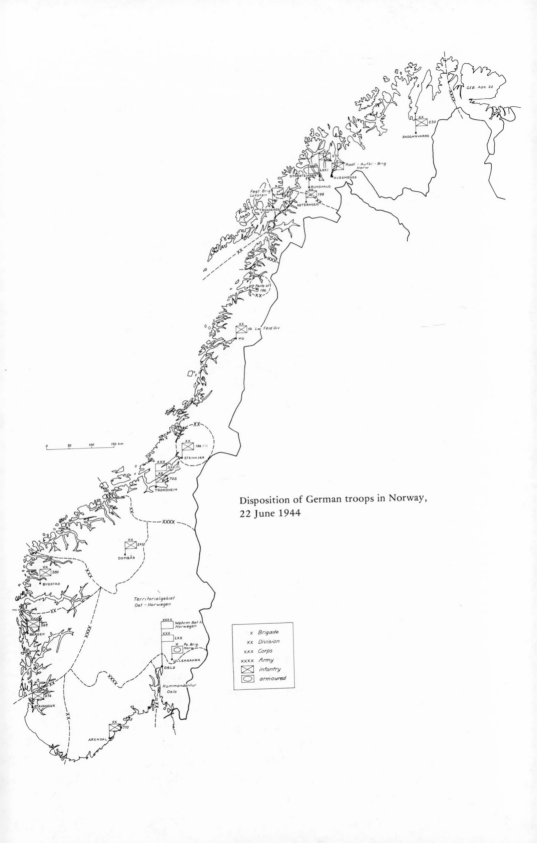

Disposition of German troops in Norway,
22 June 1944

GEB AOK 20

SKOGANVARRE 230

Radf - Aufkl - Brig Norw

STORSTEINNES KVESMENES

RUNDHAUG

Fest Brig Lofoten SETERMOEN 199

TRONDENES

2 Parts of 196

14 Lw Feld Div MO

196 (-) STEINKJER

702 TRONDHEIM

0 50 100 150 km

XXXX

Territorialgebiet Ost - Norwegen

DOMBÅS 295

BYGSTAD 280

BERGEN 269

Wehrm Bef h Norwegen

LXX

Pz Brig Norw

ULLENSAKER

OSLO

Kommandantur Oslo

STAVANGER 274

ARENDAL 710

x	Brigade
xx	Division
xxx	Corps
xxxx	Army
⊠	infantry
⬭	armoured

is being used for work that is not necessary at this time," all men between eighteen and fifty-five years of age and all women between twenty-one and forty years of age would therefore be registered. Those who were in fact conscripted were employed both in "the struggle against Bolshevism" and in increasing Norwegian production. Of the more than 40,000 people who were conscripted in the following six months, just under half were used to work for the Germans and just over half were employed in agriculture and forestry. It is noteworthy that, in contrast to Dutchmen, Belgians, and Frenchmen conscripted during the same period, the Norwegians remained in Norway.

In connection with the national labor law, a *Norges Næringssamband* (Norwegian Economic Union) was established from 1 May 1943 on the grounds that it would facilitate the movement of labor. It consisted of ten "occupational groups," which were occupational organizations that had gradually been brought ideologically into line with the views of the regime. In other words, these bodies represented an attempt to reintroduce the corporatism that had broken down less than a year before and were a by-product of a measure whose primary purpose was presumably, as we have seen, to incorporate Norway into the general German drive to mobilize European labor.

The national labor law was a great challenge to the civilian resistance and proved a difficult one to surmount. As was described in the previous chapter, the civilian resistance leadership—through the Coordination Committee, one of its two direction organs—had in 1941 got a number of occupational groups to support its policy of noncooperation, groups which the Quisling regime had tried to bring under its practical and ideological domination. The policy of the Coordination Committee had been directed not at the Germans but at *Nasjonal Samling*. In August 1942 the leadership of the civilian resistance wrote to the government-in-exile in London that "we have tried to give such a form to our actions that it would be difficult for the Germans to respond by introducing a state of emergency and executions." In July 1942 the provisional leadership of the Norwegian church expressed the same view in the following, more pointed terms: "We are loyal to the occupying power within the framework of international law." The new element in the situation which emerged in the spring of 1943 was that the national labor law applied to all Norwegians. To defy this law, it would take more than a small academic group, all of whose members more or less knew each other; the support of the broad mass of the population was needed. As one of the members of the Coordination Committee wrote after the war, "The question was now whether we should undertake the task of organizing and leading national civilian resistance to the occupying power." However, it would perhaps have been more correct to ask whether they were capable of undertaking this task, whether their slogans would achieve the requisite response from the broad mass of the people. And since the national labor law was supported not only by *Nasjonal Samling* but also by the Germans, one also had to ask how the occupying power would react to an attempt to boycott the law, an attempt that sought to impede the mobilization of Norwegian labor.

After some hesitation and much irresolution, the civilian leadership decided to take up the challenge. In the middle of April 1943 the following proclamation was issued: "No one should appear when summoned to an office, a place of departure or a place of work. No

"Present spades!" The Nazi authorities drafted young Norwegians for the semimilitary Labor Service. (Norges Hjemmefrontmuseum, Oslo)

one should participate any longer in any form of registration."
However, this appeal enjoyed only limited success. In December
1944 the illegal paper *Bulletinen* (The Bulletin), the official organ of
the resistance leadership, contained a retrospective review of this
episode. "Resistance was certainly quite good in Oslo and its en-
virons, but the national labor law was not sabotaged to any significant
degree in the countryside and the small towns." The civilian resistance leadership was thus able during 1943 to establish itself as the
supreme body responsible for guiding the civilian resistance struggle
(something the Danish Freedom Council never attempted beyond
proclaiming two minutes of silence on the anniversary of the occupation), and it had also given a new economic and military aspect to
this struggle. However, it was not yet able to involve the whole of
society in this cause.

It would be a long time before the civilian leadership's efforts to
secure the support of the whole population were crowned by success.
In March 1944 it began a campaign against *Arbeidstjenesten* (The
Labor Service), calling for a boycott of its medical examinations and
work. *Arbeidstjenesten* was an established institution, which had
existed since 1940. The resistance movement decided to challenge it
now only because it had got wind of a memorandum that had been
drawn up by Quisling's minister of justice and which proposed that
75,000 young Norwegians should be mobilized and employed on the
eastern front. Whether this plan would in fact be implemented was
another and highly uncertain matter. At any rate, there was a call for
a boycott, but it was not followed; 70% of those summoned attended—"a normal figure like the year before," as the German security police observed.

The resistance had more success two months later. On 19 May
1944 the Quisling regime summoned those born in 1921-23 to
register with the employment agencies, in accordance with the
national labor law. As usual, the resistance called for a boycott, and
this time its appeal met with a considerable response. Only a few reported for the medical examination, and fewer still turned up when
summoned to a place of work. Many thousands went underground in
the neighborhood where they lived or took to the mountains or
forests. The phrase *"gutta på skaua"* (the boys in the forest) was
coined at this time and is intimately associated with these events,
although only a very small minority remained *"på skaua."* Most
returned home after a week, if they could not find work in the

countryside, or fled to Sweden. At first glance, it seems surprising that an appeal which met with little response in April 1943 and March 1944 should have been successful in May 1944. The course of the great war could hardly have been the determining factor here, although it seems natural to believe it was so in the case of Denmark in August 1943. No great military events occurred at the front in the spring of 1944, and the call for a boycott had already succeeded before the landings in Normandy on 6 June. The time of year undoubtedly played a role: it is quite a different matter to take to the forest in the greenery of May as compared with the snows of March. The fear of being conscripted into the German armed forces on the eastern front may also have played a role, and this must have seemed quite a likely prospect to those concerned when the government summoned young men of the most suitable arms-bearing age. What fear could not achieve, group pressure did: when all others boycotted the summons, the individual felt compelled to do so as well. In this way, responding to the summons, which had not previously been regarded as a clearly unpatriotic act, was now suddenly seen in this light. However, a detailed study of these events has not yet been undertaken. This act of resistance, which occurred in the spring of 1944, was the Norwegian counterpart of what a number of Danish provincial towns had experienced ten months earlier. At the end of May 1944 one of the veterans of the civilian resistance leadership described this turn of the tide in Norway in the following terms: "The mobilization of labor has been wrecked. In my view, this is the greatest victory we have won here at home. The atmosphere is excellent, and we are today one people and one soul."

The military resistance movement was weakened in the course of 1942. The lively expectations of invasion were disappointed, and *Milorg* was instead struck by a series of violent waves of arrests, the last of which occurred at the end of the year, and as a result the organization was crippled at both its higher and lower levels. In the late summer of 1943 the leadership of *Milorg* reported to the government-in-exile in London that there was no military organization in northern Norway, that *Milorg* was weak in Sydlandet, Vestlandet, and Trøndelag, and that "a far greater part of the preparations in these areas must fall on the shoulders of the local leadership." In these weak areas the home leadership was represented by unobtrusive district commanders, while the organization and training of personnel had to be a task for the SOE agents who were sent in from Britain (called the Linge men after the first commander of the unit). There is some similarity here with SOE's "private" circuits in France, which also operated independently of whether or not local groups had already been formed. District commanders were not appointed for Trøndelag till October and for Stavanger and Bergen till November 1943. *Milorg* groups were not set up in Stavanger, a town of about 75,000 inhabitants, in either 1943 or 1944. The Linge men who had been sent in first began to establish military groups and to give instructions in the use of arms in the area around Stavanger in the summer of 1944, but nothing was done in Stavanger itself. There were only selected officers but no armaments in the town. *Milorg* being weak in Sydlandet, Vestlandet, and Trøndelag, only Østlandet and Oslo itself were left for *Milorg* activities. According to a list of *Milorg*'s forces drawn up in the middle of 1944, 75% of its 32,000 men were in eastern Norway. There was always greater activity and a higher level of organization in this area than in the rest of the country despite frequent arrests. Moreover, the figure of 32,000 men is probably an exaggeration.

The *Milorg* groups, like the Danish "waiting groups" which were their exact counterparts, were to be used during the liberation of the country. Until that time arrived, they were to remain in readiness. This was the view of the military leadership both in 1942, when there was a strong expectation of invasion, and in the years 1944-45, when a German withdrawal or capitulation were equally likely. The groups were not to place themselves at risk by going into action in the event of brief commando raids but only if a landing of a permanent nature occurred. Their task in the event of an invasion was to assist the regular forces of the Allies by guerrilla operations (the destruction of lines of communication and of German depots and installations, etc.). The normal tactical unit was to be a group of eight to twelve men.

This policy was established in May 1943, when leaders of *Milorg* met in Stockholm with representatives of the Norwegian high command in London. One of the latter observed after the meeting that

the *Milorg* leadership does not want *Milorg* to be used during the period of waiting or in partisan operations. The question of whether to employ it in acts of sabotage should be considered, but the *Milorg* leadership feels that this too should be avoided. It is a matter of keeping the organization intact until it can be used with advantage.

This was still the prevailing view when a new meeting was held in Stockholm in March 1944. There was agreement that "neither military nor civil considerations for the moment suggest that the organization at home should be employed in guerrilla operations or open acts of sabotage on a large scale . . . nor are the requisite means available at this time for such a policy." However, the words "for the moment" show that the hitherto wholly negative attitude toward sabotage had begun to be undermined. The minutes of the meeting continued, "it may become [necessary] from a military point of view [for the *Milorg*] organizations [to] cooperate in or themselves initiate action against important objectives during the period of waiting." The meeting also sanctioned the possibility of action "in support of the boycott of *Arbeidstjenesten*"—in other words, action that might be called political in support of the civilian leadership in its struggle for popular support. However, it was not until the end of July 1944 that the decisive change occurred in the attitude toward sabotage: London informed the *Milorg* leadership that from now on German gas and oil supplies, whether stored or in transit, should be attacked at every opportunity.

During the period covered by this chapter, the acts of sabotage that occurred in Norway in spite of the attitude of the Norwegian authorities in London and of *Milorg* were carried out by two groups: the Linge men, who were sent in from Britain; and the Norwegian Communists. The Linge men carried out a few actions from Britain against the production of strategically important raw materials. The raw materials in question were iron pyrites (the Orkla mines near Trondheim were attacked in February and October 1943, and the Stord mines near Bergen in January 1943); silicon carbide (Arendal foundry was attacked in November 1943); and heavy water (Norsk Hydro's works at Vemork in Rjukan were attacked in February 1943 and February 1944). The Linge men also participated in just under a dozen actions under the direction of the home leadership against *Arbeidstjenesten* and the mobilization of labor in May and June 1944.

The action against the heavy water supplies has become well-nigh world famous. It has been mentioned in many books and has been the subject of at least two films. The first attempt to destroy the works ended in tragedy. In November 1942 a British commando unit was sent to Norway in two gliders. Both crash-landed without reaching their targets, and the survivors were shot by the Germans. In February 1943 a team of six men was dropped by parachute on the Hardangervidda and joined forces with a group that had parachuted in in October 1942 to prepare the way for the commando unit. The two teams of men jointly attacked the heavy water works on the night of 27-28 February 1943, and they succeeded in destroying important parts of the machinery and the stocks of heavy water without sustaining any losses. However, the Germans set about restoring production, and the works were, in consequence, attacked on 16 November 1943 by American bombers. The heavy water installations were only partially damaged, and the Germans began to dismantle them so that they might be moved to Germany. Knud Haukelid, a Linge man who had been involved in the first action against the works, suggested to the authorities in London that the ferry *Hydro* should be sunk as it was carrying the heavy water over the lake of Tinnsjø, and this proposal was approved. On 20 February 1944 the ferry sank in deep water with its cargo of 16,000 liters of heavy water.

The British made great efforts to have ships sailing in German service sabotaged, but in relation to the efforts made, the results were modest. The Linge men entrusted with this task succeeded only in sinking or damaging just under a dozen ships, or a total of about 30,000 tons, in the period 1943-45. However, the difficulty of the undertaking should not be underestimated: a similar group that was sent to Aarhus in Jutland in September 1944 was never able to sink or damage a single German ship.

During this period arms and explosives were sent to Norway from Britain primarily for use in carrying out the tasks entrusted to the Linge men and only to a limited extent for supplying *Milorg*'s "waiting groups." Supplies were dropped by plane or brought in by sea on the so-called Shetland bus, officially called "The Norwegian Independent Naval Unit," which was based on the Shetland Islands. Established in the autumn of 1940, it sailed between the Shetlands and the west coast of Norway during the winter months, using at first small Norwegian fishing vessels and then, from the autumn of 1943, three antisubmarine boats, which the Americans had assigned to this task. In 1943, 192 containers, or about twenty tons, were dropped by plane, whereas the "Shetland bus" brought in thirty-three tons during its sailing season in the winter of 1942-43 and twenty-one tons in the winter of 1943-44. These amounts increased greatly after the Allied invasion of Normandy in June 1944, but even before that time they were considerably larger than what was sent to Denmark in the same period.

Milorg, like the home leadership as a whole, could accept the acts of sabotage initiated by the British. There were very few such acts, and they all belonged to the category of strategic sabotage. It was quite another matter to accept sabotage undertaken by the Norwegian Communists. From the very start, the Communist party had been quite distinct from the other illegal groups, and the home leadership's distrust of the party leadership, "whose intentions the military command does not know" (to quote from the minutes of the meeting in Stockholm in May 1943 which was mentioned earlier), was intense. It was suspected that Communist policy arose out of Soviet as much as Norwegian interests, or in other words that it was made in Moscow and not by the Norwegian Communists themselves. This suspicion could only be strengthened by the attitude of the Communist party toward the problem of sabotage. Under the leadership of Peder Furubotn, the party unequivocally supported an activist policy and carried out as many acts of sabotage as it could, quite irrespective of the views and directives of *Milorg*. Sometimes it failed to implement its plans, as when a Communist sabotage group in Stavanger in the summer of 1943 never got beyond the stage of issuing an illegal newspaper and drawing up great plans for sabotage before it was arrested. Sometimes it met with modest success, as when its sabotage organization (*Saborg*) executed a series of small acts of sabotage around the country against railways, the electricity supply, and various factories. And occasionally, particularly striking actions were carried out: an attack in April 1943 against one of the labor bureaus in Oslo (undertaken, strangely enough, on behalf of *Milorg*); and a train derailment near Drammen in October 1943 (the Germans responded by executing five hostages, and the sabotage did not win the approval of public opinion). The Communists won their greatest success in November 1944 when they sank or damaged six ships, or a total of 50,000 tons, in two shipyards in Oslo.

Milorg opposed the Communists' sabotage offensive on the grounds that it did not have the support of the population as a whole. This was true. Moreover, *Milorg* thought that sabotage would provoke severe German reprisals. This was also true. However, *Milorg* conceded that the acts of sabotage carried out by the Communists appealed increasingly to the desire for direct action on the part of its own "waiting groups," and this realization played a large role in altering its view on the legitimacy and necessity of sabotage in the course of 1944. This fear of division and disintegration within the ranks of *Milorg* meant that the Communists, even though they were consistently excluded, could not be regarded as a *quantité negligeable*, particularly since they consciously sought to divide the home front in the spring of 1944 by their agitation for the establishment of a Freedom Council representing a Popular Front of political forces. On this point, Danish conditions could be held up as a model worthy of emulation. Moreover, in Norway, as in all other countries, the rapidly growing prestige of the Soviet Union and admiration for the Red Army rubbed off on the local Communists, who made the most of the situation. In February 1944 a prominent Labor politician observed that "the enthusiasm for the Russian war effort is indescribable. All hopes are placed on the Russians, and this enthusiasm can be found in all social groups."

As a result of the aggressive resistance policy and the enhanced standing of the Communists, the civilian and military leaders of the resistance drew closer to each other during 1943 and finally (though this process was only completed in 1944) formed a joint *Hjemmefrontens Ledelse* (Home Front Command). Other reasons for this development were that overlapping administrative tasks were increasingly discernible; that different sets of bodies were concerning themselves with the same problems; and that there was a growing need for a coordination of the responses of the civilian and the military resistance to the measures taken by the *Nasjonal Samling* regime and the Germans. A clear example is the difficulties experienced in securing popular support for the boycott of *Arbeidstjenesten.* This was a slow process that took about nine months, partly because the mutual suspicion between the two bodies was great, especially during the first phase, and partly because a number of arrests carried out by the Germans checked the coordination and fusion of the two groups. Jens Christian Hauge, a twenty-seven-year-old lawyer, who was *Milorg*'s inspector-general for the local districts throughout 1943, played a very important role in bringing the civilian and military resistance together. During 1943 he became the dominant figure within *Milorg,* and he retained his position as its *de facto* leader until the end of the war. It was he who negotiated with the district commands on behalf of *Milorg,* and it was he who was the driving force in developing the closest possible relations between the civilian and the military resistance.

During the period covered by this chapter the resistance struggle was not particularly active in the military sphere. The struggle was conducted mainly by civilian defensive methods—ostracism, boycott, and escape. As during the preceding period (from the beginning of 1943 until late spring 1944), it was directed against the usurpation of the government and administration by *Nasjonal Samling* and against the latter's attempts to impose ideological uniformity on society. But now the struggle also included a new element: economic warfare. The fight against the national labor law was not only a political and ideological struggle but also, and perhaps primarily, an attempt to prevent the use of Norway's labor resources on the wrong side. It was therefore directed against the occupying power, which was behind the legislation to which Quisling lent his name. In the military sphere, the Germans were first to be fought when the Allies invaded the country, so until that moment came, *Milorg*'s units were to be "waiting groups."

In many parts of the country, the resistance, frightened by the thoroughgoing wave of arrests in 1942, was content with drawing up paper schemes of organization. However, Norway was, even so, far ahead of Denmark, where the systematic formation of "waiting groups" did not begin until early in 1944. Acts of sabotage were to be carried out only if they served a strategic purpose and were left to the initiative of the British and Norwegian authorities in London. In this respect, the resistance leadership had the support of public opinion, which wanted to see a sensible purpose behind acts of sabotage. A similar phenomenon can be observed in Denmark, where the popularity of sabotage among the people as a whole was a problem not only before but also after 29 August 1943, that is to say at a time when in resistance circles sabotage had long since been adopted as a suitable weapon in the fight against the Germans. Perhaps the most important objective behind the acts of sabotage carried out by the Norwegian Communists was to win the people over to this "higher form of struggle," to use Communist terminology. In the Soviet Union, the people were not allowed to content themselves with passive resistance and the right attitude. However, in Norway the people seem to have believed, as did the civilian leadership, that they had, through the successful civilian resistance struggle in 1942, gained all the self-respect that was required and that it was therefore not necessary to send "amateur soldiers" on a "children's crusade." These last two phrases were used in a communication from the civilian leadership to London in February 1943, a communication which argued against a "rising by irregular guerrilla or sabotage troops behind the German front" in the event of an invasion. No one wanted real partisan warfare, apart from the Communists. The latter called on the young men who took to the forest in May 1944 to remain there and establish camps. This call did not meet with much of a response, but the parallel with, for example, the French *maquis,* who were created in a similar situation, is clear. The *Milorg* command did not want to create a *maquis* out of the boys in the forest. It did issue a directive to the local districts, instructing them to recruit the best and toughest of the young men for the *"Milorg* cells" that were being set up in the forest, but it had the great majority reintegrated into civilian society or sent to Sweden. The civilian leadership wrote that "a tactic that may be excellent for Serbia is not appropriate in Norway," not because that country was unsuitable for partisan warfare—on the contrary, it was as well suited as Bosnia or Serbia in this respect—but because unlike Tito, neither London nor the home front was willing to see the country become the scene of violent fighting and reprisals, with all the economic and political consequences that would follow.

Finland: A Slow Adjustment to the Turn of the Tide

The northern section of the eastern front had been stable since the end of 1941. Once the Finnish army had reached Lake Onega, the river Svir (the Aunus in Finnish), and the old frontier of the interwar period on the Karelian isthmus, it discontinued offensive operations. The area overrun by Finnish forces included the old Finnish bastion against the east, Viipuri, and the capital of the Soviet Karelian Republic, Petrosavodsk, but the Finns made no attempt to interrupt the Murmansk railway, which was of great importance for the Western powers' deliveries to the Soviet Union. The Finnish army, a force of nineteen divisions or about 375,000 men, restricted its activities to patrolling and to constructing field works. The 20th German army, a force of seven divisions or about 175,000 men, was stationed in Lappland. Because of its extended line of communications, it had abandoned the idea of attacking the Murmansk railway, and its most important function was to secure the nickel mines in Petsamo, and to serve as a political guarantee of the German presence on the northernmost section of the eastern front and also, if the occasion should arise, as an instrument of political pressure on the Finns.

In 1941 and 1942 the climate of opinion in Finland had been

overwhelmingly sympathetic to the concept of a Greater Finland and, partly in consequence, also anti-Swedish. It was characteristic of Finnish attitudes at this time that the foreign minister, Rolf Witting, should have said in June 1942 that to understand Swedish policy one had to be not a professor of oceanography (his own occupation in private life) but of pathological anatomy. However, the course of the war obliged him to modify his views. Under the influence of the Allied landing in North Africa, he thought it expedient to declare in an interview with the Swedish newspaper *Social-Demokraten* in November 1942 that he was a convinced adherent of Nordic cooperation and democracy.

At the end of January 1943, when the German defeat at Stalingrad was already a reality, the American government, eagerly seconded and supported by the Swedes, sounded Moscow about the possibilities of mediating a separate Fenno-Soviet peace. Molotov indicated that the Soviet Union was prepared to make peace but did not wish to take any initiative before the Finns had presented their views on suitable peace terms. However, at this stage the leading circles in the Finnish government were not interested in anything more than a separate peace with Britain, and the Swedes regarded any feelers on this subject as pointless.

In February 1943 a presidential election was held in accordance with the terms of the Finnish constitution, although the electoral college chosen in 1937 was used again on this occasion and the presidential term of office was limited to two years instead of the six years prescribed by the constitution. The incumbent president, Risto Ryti, was reelected, and the national government was reconstructed at the beginning of March. The new prime minister, who took over from Rangell, was Edwin Linkomies, a Conservative and professor of literature, while Henrik Ramsay, a shipowner and member of the Swedish People's party, replaced Witting as foreign minsiter. The new government was less committed to the idea of a Greater Finland (Ramsay's presence was an expression of this) and less oriented toward Germany than was its predecessor. At the time of its formation, it was not regarded as a strong ministry that might prove able to make peace but rather as an interim government that would keep all doors open. It was seen as colorless by Berlin, and the German minister in Helsinki described Linkomies as "a weak and vacillating man lacking the qualities of leadership."

The change of government marked, indeed, the extent of the move

away from the dreams of a Greater Finland and cobelligerency with
Germany toward a policy oriented toward the Western powers and
the North which the events in North Africa and at Stalingrad had
caused. In March 1943, after the Germans had stabilized the situation in the southern sector of the eastern front, anxiety about the
turn events had taken abated among the decisionmakers in Helsinki.
Marshal Mannerheim, Ramsay, and the minister of defense were
agreed that a separate peace with the Soviet Union which involved
territorial losses (meaning thereby a return to the frontiers of March
1940) and which was not accompanied by guarantees from the
Western powers would place the country in a worse position than it
was at present with the Finnish army on the Svir and in occupation
of considerable areas of Soviet territory. The thinking behind this
view was that a separate Russo-German peace was not inconceivable,
in which case the Finns would stand alone, betrayed by all and at the
mercy of the Soviet Union. Another possibility was that the Russians
might by committing all their resources finally crush Germany but
that they would be gravely weakened. In either eventuality—and
neither seemed inconceivable to Helsinki in early 1943—Finland
would benefit from its army and its conquests. In line with these
attitudes, the American offer of mediation, which as we have seen
had been under consideration since the end of January and which
was presented on 20 March, was neither received with warm thanks
nor rejected out of hand. Instead, the Finns asked for details of the
peace terms. After giving this reply to the Americans, Ramsay
traveled to Berlin in order to explain the Finnish position to the
Germans in private. He did not receive a warm welcome. Ribbentrop
manifested his irritation by allowing Ramsay to wait in the anteroom
to his office for six hours and gave his Finnish opposite number a
great dressing down when he was finally admitted. Ribbentrop presented two demands: the American offer should be rejected in clear
and unequivocal terms; and Finland should sign a treaty with Germany undertaking not to conclude a separate peace.

The problems created by the first demand solved themselves. The
Americans regarded the Soviet peace terms as unacceptable, and
accordingly withdrew their offer. On 10 April they informed the
Finns that they had intended only to establish contact, not to trans-
mit peace terms. The Finnish government replied that in that case
the Finnish people had no choice but to continue their defensive
struggle until their independence, freedom, and democratic social

order had been secured and the threat against them had ceased. In these circumstances, the Finnish reply continued, the Finnish government could not enter into the negotiations proposed by the United States. The Finns flatly refused to accede to the second German demand, and it was of no avail that the Germans put pressure on Helsinki, for example by withholding grain deliveries, in an attempt to induce the Finns to give way. The Germans had to content themselves with a statement in a speech made by Linkomies in the middle of May 1943 that "the Finnish people would rather fight to the last man than surrender unconditionally to its eastern neighbor."

This attitude of the leading Finnish circles, which has been delineated in the preceding paragraphs, was not based on their continued belief in a German victory. Those days were long gone. So was the time when their interest in a warm and intimate relationship with Sweden was very limited. Furthermore, they well knew the value of good relations with the United States. Accordingly, repayment of the loan that the United States had given to Finland in the 1920s, and on which Congress had granted a two-year moratorium in 1940, was resumed in July 1943 with a payment of $170,000, and a Fenno-American association, founded in the middle of the year with broad support from all political groups except the extreme right, enjoyed official blessing in spite of the clearly expressed irritation of the Germans. The fact that the United States reduced the level of its diplomatic representation in Finland at the same time did not alter the Finnish desire to maintain the best possible relations with that country. However, the leading circles in Finland also realized that for the time being the Germans were too strong for Finland to escape from cobelligerency, and the point was underlined by the country's dependence on food imports from Germany and the German-dominated parts of Europe. For the present, no alternative to these imports could be seen. It was thought that the army should be kept intact deep in enemy territory, so that in the event of chaos in Europe Finland would dispose of one instrument of power which could bring the country safely out of this chaos. In retrospect, this may seem a delusive exaggeration of the strength of the Finnish army fostered by the fact that it stood undefeated on the Svir and outside Leningrad. However, it should also be taken into account that Finns were at the time acutely aware that their country had on two occasions, in the periods 1918-20 and 1939-40, survived a trial of strength with its mighty neighbor in the east largely by its own efforts.

At the end of July 1943 the Soviet Union sounded Helsinki about peace negotiations through the Belgian minister in Stockholm. The Finns were told that they should inform Moscow in writing of their ideas concerning peace terms, and absolute secrecy was guaranteed. The Finnish government replied orally that the borders of 1939 could serve as the basis for the negotiations, although frontier rectifications on the Karelian isthmus would be possible. This reply, which was given after the collapse of the German summer offensive on the eastern front, the Allied landing in Sicily, and the fall of Mussolini, reveals the inertia that gripped Finnish minds. The reply was unacceptable to the Soviet Union, and matters were taken no further at this stage.

In November 1943 the Russians used both the stick and the carrot on the Finns. They were told in a Finnish-language radio broadcast that the Allied demand for unconditional surrender applied to all the Axis powers and that Finland, in spite of all the groundless talk about a separate war, was an Axis power. Yet later in the month Madame Alexandra Kollontai, the Soviet minister in Stockholm, informed them through the Swedish government that they would be welcome in Moscow if they were willing to enter into peace negotiations. The government of the Soviet Union did not intend to make Finland into a province or to limit its independence unless the future course of Finnish policy made it necessary, but the Finns should first let the Russians know their proposals so that they could see whether the journey would serve any purpose. The Finns replied that they wanted peace, good neighborly relations, and neutrality, and that they believed that the frontiers of 1939 were well suited to form the basis for the realization of these goals; nonetheless, they were prepared to discuss such divergences from the 1939 frontiers as might serve to guarantee confidence and peace. Before the Russians responded to this communication, Stalin made it clear to Roosevelt and Churchill at the Teheran conference that the Soviet Union would insist on the frontiers of 1940 and on a war indemnity that corresponded to 50% of the damage the Finns had caused. No real decisions were reached on the basis of the brief conversations on this question, but Roosevelt and Churchill accepted Stalin's view and the discussions turned to what all three agreed were "much bigger things to think about." Moscow now replied on 20 December to the Finns that it regarded the 1940 frontiers as definitive and therefore did not consider the Finnish communication satisfactory. As the American ambassador in Moscow, Averell Harriman, observed on one occasion, the Russians were determined to appear the undisputed victors in their war with Finland, and proposals based on the 1939 frontiers were accordingly to no purpose.

There are a number of features in the Soviet Union's Finnish policy that are noteworthy. The peace feelers in August and November 1943 were initiated by the Russians at a time when the Soviet Union had made it clear to the Western powers that it would not welcome their involvement in the Finnish affair. Finland was also the only one of Germany's small allies that received such an offer. There is no evidence in the available sources (or from the Soviet side) that the Russians dropped parachutists into Finland to establish sabotage or partisan groups at any time during the war, and the Soviet Karelian partisans who were based on nonoccupied areas and who passed through the front line in order to carry out commando raids had no contact with the local civilian population in Finland (assuming they got that far) or in the Finnish-occupied territories. Volunteer military units of Finnish prisoners-of-war were not established in the Soviet Union, as was done with Romanian and Hungarian prisoners-of-war in October 1943 and December 1944 respectively. There were, to be sure, few Finnish prisoners-of-war from among whom volunteers could have been recruited (only 1,900 Finnish soldiers were captured throughout the war), but the Russians set up token forces elsewhere when it suited their political goals. For instance, they set up a Hungarian railway unit of about 4,000 men. All these factors could be interpreted as suggesting that the Soviet Union envisaged a special status for Finland either for domestic reasons or because of the special standing and popularity which Finland enjoyed in the United States. But whatever the nature of Soviet motives, the Russians were determined that this status should not appear to be the result of representations from or intervention by the Western powers.

The Finnish attitude in late 1943 and early 1944 was to await the invasion of northwest Europe by the Western Allies. Once this had occurred, their very presence would in itself reduce Soviet domination of the mainland. The Finnish government calculated that the country would have less to lose if it participated in a general ordering of Europe's affairs after the great war than if, after a separate peace, it had to face the Soviet Union impotent and alone. In other words, Finnish inertia continued, but it was now based on other premises than before.

The next initiative was taken by the United States, which acted of course with Soviet consent. On 30 January 1944 Washington suggested to the Finns that they take the first step toward an approach to the Soviet Union, and it was added that American good offices might help to secure a successful outcome. The Swedes also recommended an approach to Moscow, as they always did, and the Russians bombed Helsinki as if to emphasize that something should be done now. It was perhaps of equal importance that Mannerheim approved the idea of sounding out the Russians. In the middle of February Juho Paasikivi, who had made peace with the Russians before, traveled to Stockholm for discussions with Madame Kollontai. She told him that the Soviet Union was prepared to enter into negotiations concerning an armistice and peace on the understanding that the Finns were willing to disarm or intern the German troops in Finland, possibly with Soviet assistance, and that they would accept the frontiers of 1940. There would also be negotiations about a war indemnity and Petsamo, a warning that further territorial losses might be required.

At the same time that these terms were conveyed to Paasikivi, the Russians publicized them through the Swedish press and carried out further bombing attacks on Finnish territory, and it was in this atmosphere that the Finnish government and political leadership as a whole discussed what reply should be made. Parliament was divided on the question whether Finland should enter into negotiations with the Soviet Union. A small majority favored such negotiations, but if public opinion was to accept a harsh peace, it was necessary that Mannerheim should assume the leadership of the country. When Linkomies approached Mannerheim on this subject, the commander-in-chief gave a negative answer—twice over. In consequence, the government drew up a reply to the effect that it seriously sought peace but could not accept the Soviet terms and instead proposed negotiations on individual questions. However, the Swedish government, which was to convey this reply to Moscow, found it insufficiently accommodating and applied very strong pressure to the Finns in order to produce a more suitable reply. King Gustaf's "personal view of the matter" was used in this connection and was conveyed to Ryti and Mannerheim. It had some effect. The Finnish government declared that it was prepared to negotiate with the Soviet Union, but without binding itself definitely to the terms that had been transmitted to Paasikivi in Stockholm. The Swedes found this new reply satisfactory, and Madame Kollontai said that she was also satisfied by it. The Soviet government, however, declared that it was wholly unsatisfactory, and the Finns were given a week to draw up another and better reply. Such a reply was not forthcoming. On 15 March 1944 parliament endorsed unanimously, though only after much soul searching by the Social Democrats and the Swedish People's party, the Finnish government's attitude as expressed in a new communication to Moscow, saying that it could not accept in advance conditions whose meaning and contents it was not sure of.

It might have been expected that the matter would now be shelved for a while, but this did not happen. On 19 March Madame Kollontai conveyed through the Swedish government an invitation to the Finns to send a couple of delegates to Moscow to whom the terms could be explained. Kollontai maintained that the Finns would be amazed at how tolerable the Soviet terms were, and on this basis Paasikivi and Carl Enckell, a former foreign minister, traveled secretly to Moscow via Stockholm at the end of March. However, when they arrived, they found no cause for amazement at Soviet moderation. Molotov told the two Finns that "you have not come here in order to obtain concessions but to hear an explanation." The terms were, as before, the frontiers of 1940, and the cession of Petsamo was also demanded. The German troops in northern Finland were to be interned or expelled from the country by the end of May 1944, and Finland was to pay goods to the value of 600 million gold dollars as reparations. At this stage, these terms were unacceptable to the Finns, and in its reply on 15 April 1944 the government declared with the unanimous support of parliament that it had to reject the Soviet terms, since they would weaken and undermine Finland's existence as an independent state and impose burdens on the Finnish people which it could not bear.

Despite the low profile maintained and the attempts at secrecy, all these soundings and negotiations could not be concealed from the Germans, whose intelligence work in both Stockholm and Helsinki was very effective. (The day after Paasikivi and Enckell flew from Stockholm to Moscow the German legation in Stockholm was aware of their journey.) As early as the end of September 1943 a *Führerweisung* (directive from Hitler) had stated that, if Finland left the war, the 20th German army should withdraw to and hold the Karesuando-Ivalo line in order to safeguard war supplies from the nickel mines at Petsamo. In February 1944 this eventuality became more of a reality, and planning for the execution of this operation was completed (Operation *Birke*). At the same time plans were drawn up for the occupation of the Ålands with the aid of the 416th infantry division from Denmark and eight coastal batteries and for the seizure of the island of Hogland in the Gulf of Finland (Operation *Tanne*). On the diplomatic front, the first German reaction, apart from verbal pressure and reproaches, came on 3 April, when grain deliveries were suspended. The next German response was on 17 April, when deliveries of armaments were discontinued. The Germans also hinted that they might respond as they had done when they occupied Hungary in February 1944, but this was mere verbal pressure. The reality was Operations *Birke* and *Tanne*, which covered the areas for which the Germans had a strategic use and represented what they were capable of militarily. The armaments embargo was imposed when the Fenno-Soviet exchanges were already over, and was intended to manifest German displeasure at Finland's attempt to go its own way when it seemed safe to do so.

The Finnish reply of 15 April 1944 put an end to peace feelers for the time being, and the situation remained static until 9 June, when the Soviet Union launched a major offensive on the Karelian isthmus. Viipuri fell on 20 June, and at the same time the Russians started another great offensive on the Svir front and north of Lake Onega, taking Petrosavodsk on the twenty-ninth. These events destroyed the illusions on which Finnish policy had rested. The bargaining counters which the Finns had hitherto thought could be exploited in future negotiations—the undefeated army and the Finnish-occupied territories—no longer existed. It was only now that the real turn of the tide began in Finland.

This survey of developments in Finland has concentrated on the policy of the government and has left out public opinion and the atmosphere in the country, but there is no doubt that the government's attitude reflected the general view of how the country's difficult situation should be dealt with. The American journalist John Scott visited Finland in April 1944. After a stay of fourteen days in Helsinki and other parts of the country, he was left with the impression that most Finns did not feel defeated and believed that, on the contrary, the Soviet Union was not capable of overcoming Finland.

This gave them a feeling of self-confidence which did not correspond to the real political and military situation. Because of censorship, the obstinacy of the Finns as a nation, and their partisan way of thinking, they did not understand the real state of affairs.

The most uncompromising attitude was adopted by the successor of the Lapua movement, the Patriotic People's Movement (IKL), the stronghold of those who believed in a Greater Finland. In March 1943 the party did not wish to continue to participate in the national government, as reconstructed by Linkomies, if the "soft" Social Democrat Karl August Fagerholm was also to serve in it—and he did. As late as April 1944 the IKL launched a campaign designed to convince public opinion that negotiations with the Russians would be mistaken.

On the other side, there were also circles which thought that the country should escape from its ties with Germany and put its relations with the Soviet Union in order at a much more rapid pace than that adopted by the government. These circles did not include Communists. Strangely enough, the latter, according to all the available evidence, played no role either on the political or the conspiratorial-illegal level. However, there was a so-called peace opposition, which was to be found primarily in Swedish-Finnish circles and on one wing of the Social Democratic party and the trade union movement.

The peace opposition placed its hopes in Mannerheim—the collective need for father figures was great in Finland, as in other countries, during the Second World War. The peace opposition would have liked to see Mannerheim chosen as president in the election of February 1943, and he was willing to have his name put on the ballot, but only on condition that support for his candidature was so great that his election was guaranteed. When such a degree of support was not forthcoming, Mannerheim withdrew and waited for his hour to come. Ryti was then elected unanimously, but the Social Democrats accompanied their support with a resolution which declared that the country was free to leave the war when a suitable opportunity arose and when the country's freedom and independence had been ensured. This cautious appeal, that Finland should not bind its fate to that of Germany but should be ready to decamp when the chance came, was repeated during the spring of 1943 in statements by the national trade union federation and by the Swedish-Finnish members of the Social Democratic party.

The greatest sensation was caused by the appeal of "the thirty-three" in August 1943. A number of prominent figures (twenty of the thirty-three were members of parliament and nineteen of them were Swedish-Finns) emphasized in an appeal to President Ryti that it was necessary for the country's leadership to take such measures as might extricate Finland from the war and secure its freedom, independence, and peace through negotiation; the possibilities for acting along these lines should be studied without delay. Because of an indiscretion in Stockholm, the appeal was made public and provoked lively polemics in Finland, including a debate on foreign policy in parliament which ended with the passage of a vote of confidence in the government. However, this was all that occurred.

Just as too much importance should not be ascribed to the IKL and other groups supporting the idea of a Greater Finland, the significance of the peace opposition should not be overestimated. It put forward its views with caution and restraint. It did not denounce Finland's entry into "The Continuation War" and accepted the restoration of the country's frontiers to what they had been before the Winter War. It merely argued that the time had now come to get out of the war quickly and unhurt. And the government was well aware of this too.

Living conditions in Finland contributed to the inertia that gripped Finnish attitudes and policies. In the spring of 1944 John Scott had expected to see "hunger, rags and hopelessness," but he had found that the Finns were "about as well-nourished, well-clad and willing to work as the British." The value of his impressions may be doubtful, but at any rate the country had not yet experienced disaster. Moreover, it was absolutely clear, at least to the leading political circles, that as regards food supplies the country depended on Germany for grain and on German-occupied Denmark for butter and sugar. A premature break with Germany would certainly make a bad situation worse, for although Scott may have seen no hunger on his fourteen-day visit, rations were not substantial. Sweden was always very willing to provide diplomatic support and mediation, but would not go further in material assistance than to receive about 20,000 Finnish children. It was not until June 1944 that Sweden became prepared to deliver 40,000 tons of grain.

Sweden: Changing Course

Swedish neutrality and the concrete shape of Sweden's neutrality policy, which sought to balance between Germany on the one side and Britain and the United States on the other, accorded closely in 1943, as they did both in earlier and later periods, with the course of the war. The Western Allies constantly demanded that the passage by rail of German material and troops, on leave across Sweden be reduced or halted. This transit traffic was of limited albeit real advantage to the Germans, for their ability to wage war was only marginally affected by the passage of these trains through Sweden. There was more substance behind the Anglo-American demand that Sweden cease to extend credit to Germany and give only very limited amounts of credit to Finland. The practice of extending commercial credits to Germany was brought to an end as early as December 1942 during the trade negotiations between Sweden and Germany. On this occasion, Gunnar Hägglöf, the highly competent head of the commercial department of the Swedish Foreign Ministry, secured German acceptance of this demand, even though his government was vacillating and uncertain whether it should dare to present Germany with such an act of defiance. The effects of ending credit to Germany exceeded all expectations. In 1943 German deliveries to Sweden were more extensive and regular than ever before and were sufficient both to pay for current Swedish exports to Germany and to repay earlier export credits that had fallen due. This demonstrated the value of Swedish goods to Germany but also the value to Sweden of having a German trading partner that was able both to supply imports and to pay for Swedish exports.

Economic realities may have been behind the Anglo-American demands concerning the transit traffic and the giving of credit to Germany, but the demands relating to the ships *Lionel* and *Dicto* were of a purely political nature. The two ships, which were Norwegian vessels, had been forbidden by the Swedish government to leave Gothenburg for Britain. The Western powers demanded that the Swedes allow the two ships to sail and warned them that a refusal would affect the Allied agreement to import into Sweden important transoceanic commodities, above all oil (the so-called safe-conduct traffic). The Germans demanded that the *Lionel* and the *Dicto* remain in Gothenburg harbor and threatened to prevent transoceanic imports into Sweden if their wishes were not met. The Swedish attitude toward this issue, which in itself was unimportant, thus became an indicator of which side Sweden was more reluctant to offend.

The question was discussed when Erik Boheman, the permanent head of the Swedish Foreign Ministry, visited London and Washington in the autumn of 1942 in order to conduct trade negotiations and especially to secure more oil for Sweden. He returned to Sweden in December 1942 without having given in on any demand but also without having achieved anything. The climate in which the negotiations had been conducted had been harsh, and Boheman's report caused the leader of the Conservative party, Gösta Bagge, to observe that the British and Americans had in fact treated Sweden far more ruthlessly than the Germans had done. The situation rapidly became worse. A little later in December two British negotiators arrived in Stockholm with an ultimatum to the effect that, if the two ships were not released immediately, the Western powers would put an end to all imports from the West into Sweden. The Swedish government twisted and turned but ultimately gave way after three weeks of negotiations. Having won the point of principle, the British then allowed the *Lionel* and the *Dicto* to remain in Gothenburg harbor until the end of the war. The Germans reacted promptly by stopping the safe-conduct traffic from January 1943, though they immediately indicated that they were prepared to allow it to resume in return for suitable compensation for Germany, which the Swedes were unwilling to provide. Nevertheless, in May 1943 the Germans allowed the safe-conduct traffic to resume for fear that the question would impair relations between the two countries. In October 1943 they stopped the traffic again, because of the continued presence of the *Lionel* and the *Dicto* in Gothenburg, but the resumption of the safe-conduct traffic became linked with other issues, above all with the German-Swedish trade agreement for 1944, and when the latter had been successfully negotiated, resumption followed in January 1944.

The safe-conduct traffic was important for Sweden: the import of feedstuffs and fats and of raw materials for the textile and leather industries played an essential role in production. The import of coffee enjoyed the undivided support of the Swedish people, and oil was vital for the Swedish armed forces. However, when Hägglöf had to set priorities, he was obliged to note that, although oil was important for Sweden, what the Germans could offer, above all coal and coke, fertilizers and chemicals, was still more important for the Swedish economy. The country could not do without its two-way trade with Germany, even if it wanted to. The Germans were vitally interested in importing Swedish iron ore, and in the prevailing political and military situation the Swedes had no other customers to whom they might sell their ore. While Boheman was struggling with the unaccommodating Western powers, Hägglöf was concluding in December 1942 a new German-Swedish trade agreement for 1943. Under its terms, the Germans promised to continue to deliver those commodities that were important to Sweden, and at the same high level as before, and the Swedes gave a corresponding promise. This meant that the Germans could import up to 10 million tons of Swedish iron ore. In previous years this amount had never in fact been collected, but in 1943 it was. In that year Swedish exports of iron ore to Germany reached a wartime record of 10.1 million tons, which was the equivalent of 5,568,000 tons of iron or 27.5% of Germany's total supplies of iron ore.

This mutual dependence and the interest of both countries in maintaining trade are undisputable. The Swedes reacted to the course of the war in late 1942 and early 1943 by suspending, above all in their own interests, the granting of credit to Germany and by giving way to the Western powers rather than Germany over the *Lionel* and the *Dicto*. However, when it came to fundamental realities, certain soothing remarks made by Staffan Söderblom, the head of the political department of the Swedish Foreign Ministry, to a German diplomat in February 1943 were of some relevance in this connection. Söderblom explained that, even if the Germans naturally had to anticipate a more restrictive attitude on the part of Sweden in some respects, it ought to be of great value to Germany to know that a change in Sweden's general policy toward Germany was unthinkable.

The next phase in Sweden's attempt to balance between the belligerents occurred in May and June 1943, when a delegation headed by Hägglöf was in London for trade negotiations. The delegation was exposed to severe demands and was sometimes obliged to make decisions, above all when it came to making concessions, without obtaining Stockholm's prior agreement. This led Bagge to remark that Sweden too now seemed to have an exile government of its own in London. The delegation had to agree to end the German transit traffic across Sweden by 1 October at the latest and to reduce Swedish exports to the German-occupied parts of Europe. In 1944 a maximum of 7.5 million tons of iron ore and ball bearings to the value of about 30 million Swedish *kronor* could be exported to Germany. In return, the Western Allies would double Sweden's oil quota from 60,000 to 120,000 tons a year.

Traveling could be difficult in wartime. The delegation flew to London in a Swedish civil aircraft, which was shot down by the Germans on its way home, and the delegation therefore returned to Sweden by flying to the Faroes and then sailing on a safe-conduct ship to Gothenburg, a journey of about a dozen days. When he reached Stockholm, Hägglöf emphasized to the government that the outcome of the negotiations in London would hardly cause insuperable difficulties in relations with Germany. The 7.5 million tons of iron ore was such a substantial quantity that it could not create real problems. However, the prime minister, Per Albin Hansson, and the foreign minister, Christian Günther, could not accept such a sharp divergence from the course that Swedish foreign policy had hitherto followed as they thought the outcome of the London negotiations represented. Hansson declared that the ending of the transit traffic should occur, not through acceptance of the agreement reached in London but through a decision that was taken by the Swedish government quite independently and without prior negotiations with the Western powers. Günther thought that, although the course of the war dictated a policy that was more oriented toward the Western powers than before, Sweden ought not to change course with undue rapidity. The meeting of the government on 28 June ended with a decision that the transit traffic would be terminated, but that the proposed trade agreement with the Western powers could not be approved.

There was a good deal of concern for Swedish prestige behind this repudiation of Hägglöf, and during the negotiations and deliberations of the summer the Swedish government devoted much attention to saving face. There is not enough space here to describe all the details of this process. As a first step, the government told the Western powers on 12 July that it was prepared, once the transit traffic had been stopped, to make a decision concerning an agreement on the other matters that had been discussed, but that it intended until that time to conduct its commercial and financial policies in accordance with the principles worked out in London. The government then moved to put an end to the transit traffic and, when this episode was concluded, it finally decided on 24 August to approve the London agreement, though it reserved some freedom of action for the eventuality of Finland's withdrawal from the war. The Western powers could accept this, and the London agreement was finally signed and put into effect on 23 September 1943.

The termination of the transit traffic was undertaken with some anxiety: the number of Swedish men under arms was increased from the customary 170,000 to 300,000. (The Swedes did not know that German staff studies had concluded as early as the spring of 1943 that Germany was not capable of far-reaching military action against Sweden.) Sweden informed Germany on 29 July 1943 that the transit traffic had to cease. Hitler took this development calmly: it occurred at a time when he had other and greater problems, like the dismissal of Mussolini, to think about. On 5 August a joint communiqué was issued, which stated that the transit traffic would be brought to an end in the course of the month. A consideration that probably contributed to the accommodating German attitude was the fact that the transit traffic was not vital—or even necessary, as the last eighteen months of the war clearly demonstrated—to the maintenance of the German position in Norway. However, the effect of its termination on opinion in Sweden, Norway, and Denmark and among the Allies was as important as strategic realities: it was clear that Sweden was changing course.

Other indications of this change were the diplomatic representations made by Sweden in October and December 1943 because of the action taken against the Danish Jews and the deportation of the Oslo University students to Germany. The Swedish government's decision to allow the training of Norwegian and Danish "police corps" on Swedish soil was of great significance. The training of Norwegians had been taking place throughout the autumn of 1943 with the willing assistance of Swedish civil servants and the connivance of Gustav Möller, the minister of social affairs, on a far greater scale than the other Swedish ministers knew or had intended. The Danes desired similar treatment. They wanted to have a Danish police corps trained with access to stocks of Swedish armaments, and the Danish Social Democrat Vilhelm Buhl also requested of his Swedish party comrade Per Albin Hansson that two Swedish divisions be landed in Denmark at the end of the war in order to prevent a possible Communist attempt to seize power. This was far more than the Swedes could dream of undertaking. They had originally been prepared to place arms for 10,000 men in depots for the Danes but began to think along different lines when the Norwegians also asked that arms for 10,000 men be placed in depots and that the training of the police corps be extended to include about 10,000 men who would be bearing arms. The outcome in December 1943 was that the Danes were allowed to train 500 men "for the maintenance of order and the suppression of violence" at the end of the war and they were promised that material for 7,500 men would be stored in depots on their account. The Norwegians were allowed to train a police corps of 1,500 men and 8,000 reserve police, and received arms for a third of this number.

However, Sweden's changed behavior toward its two German-occupied neighbors was one thing; the government's willingness to alter radically its commercial policy toward Germany was quite another matter. Regardless of the degree of pressure the Western powers applied to bring Sweden into line with their economic warfare strategy, Swedish willingness to comply did not keep pace with their wishes. At the beginning of 1944 they asked the Swedes to reduce iron ore exports to Germany in the first six months of 1944 to 2.6 million tons, that is, by one-third. At this time the Allies evinced an even greater interest in ball bearings, an interest that was probably connected with their attempts to eliminate the German production of ball bearings at Schweinfurt. They demanded a radical reduction in Swedish exports of ball bearings to Germany and offered in return to deliver 200 Spitfires to Sweden. At the same time, Germany offered to supply Sweden with 200 Messerschmitts in order to secure an increase in the ball bearings quota for 1944 to the same level as in 1943. However, in April 1944 the Swedes rejected both ideas and stood by the quantities fixed in January 1944 in the German-Swedish trade agreement for that year: 7.1 million tons of iron ore and ball bearings to a value of about 30 million Swedish *kronor*.

The Swedes had promised during their negotiations with the Western powers in the middle of 1943 to reduce Germany's iron ore quota to 7.5 million tons, and the figure that was actually agreed upon with the Germans in January 1944 was 7.1 million tons . During the record year of 1943 the figure (as we have seen) had been 10.1 million tons. The decline from 1943 to 1944 may be taken as a quantitative expression of how far Sweden had changed course a year after the turning point in the great war. However, the change of course would not be completed until the invasion of Normandy the following summer.

Swedish public opinion was expressed through protest demonstrations and resolutions whenever the opportunity arose. One is almost tempted to say that such protests were obligatory. Opportunities for protest presented themselves in the German actions against the Jews in Denmark and against the students in Oslo. However, a steadily growing weariness with the war was equally characteristic of the general climate of opinion at this time among "*das Volk im Pension*," in the bitter phrase employed by the Germans. The sale of such German propaganda organs as *Signal, Adler,* and *Die Wehrmacht* fell by half in the course of 1943, but it was not only German propaganda that could no longer be sold. This was also true of pro-Allied works. In 1941 just under 6,000 copies of the annual collection of Churchill's war speeches were sold in Swedish translation; in 1943 the figure fell to about 1,700 copies. The activist weekly *Trots Allt*, whose attitude was that what was good for the Allies was good for Sweden, achieved its greatest circulation in the spring of 1943, when about 45,000 copies of each issue were sold, but declined steadily after that. As the war progressed the general outlook became ever more openly pro-Allied and anti-German, but it did not lead now, any more than it had done earlier, to any desire for intervention. After all, the war was going well anyway.

Foreign journalists reported home that the Swedes were more interested in the new running records set by the athlete Gunder Hägg than in events at the front. Hägg's achievements also aroused lively and widespread interest in occupied Denmark, but the real basis of this sour observation about the Swedes was the awareness that by never entering the war they had preserved for themselves the "normalcy" of the interwar period. The Swedes themselves felt the various restrictions imposed on their daily lives, but a foreigner, coming from war-ravaged Europe to this country of peace and light, felt like Alice in Wonderland. This was the impression experienced by the British journalist Gordon Young on his arrival in Sweden in March 1943; and when he witnessed normal peacetime conditions a few months later at the gala opening of Malmö's new theater, he could not avoid a sense of indignation.

The display of white ties, elbow-length gloves and evening dresses, and mass banqueting which accompanied the occasion seemed to me somehow out of place in a town which was only twelve miles across the water from Copenhagen, where just then Danes were dodging through a blackout to escape one of the Gestapo's raids for hostages.

(The Gestapo did not in fact carry out such raids in Denmark—their raids were aimed at capturing members of the resistance.)

To the extent that the Swedes were not preoccupied with the more or less ephemeral events of daily life in a country at peace, they began to take an interest in the postwar period and its political constellations as the latter's contours gradually emerged. There were signs that the Communists after a long period of isolation were about to enjoy a renaissance among the Swedish working class, and the

Social Democrats reacted to these signs with some sensitivity. Until this time a civic truce had prevailed in parliament, but the Social Democrats now began on suitable occasions to emphasize their specific profile in relation to their nonsocialist coalition partners and to move away from them. If the Social Democrats were not anticipating the coming restoration of peace, they were at any rate aware that there would be parliamentary elections in the autumn of 1944.

Concluding Remarks

In this chapter, the discussion of each of the four Nordic countries began at the same point, namely the very end of 1942. However, the concluding point is very different for all four, and this is an expression of the differing tempo at which they responded to the change in the fortunes of war. With Sweden, it is impossible to point to a definite date or striking event that marked the turn of the tide. In the field of foreign policy, Sweden changed course in a number of small steps which made its neutrality pro-Allied instead of pro-German (or as some would prefer to put it: made its neutrality active instead of passive), whereas public opinion remained equally resolved that the country should stay outside the war. Finland maintained its cobelligerency with Germany and continued its parallel war while hoping, because it had overestimated its own strength and opportunities, to achieve a favorable termination of the war through the retention of the frontiers of 1939. It was the great Soviet offensive in the midsummer of 1944 that first brought the realities of high politics home to the Finns. In Norway too there was continuity between 1942 and 1943, and in the case of the resistance perhaps even a sense of anticlimax. The lively expectation of invasion that was present in 1942 was succeeded by a disillusioned recognition of the fact that the end of the war was not imminent. But in the spring of 1944 public opinion shifted significantly when the home front's call for a boycott of *Arbeidstjenesten* suddenly evoked a response. In contrast to the situation in the other Nordic countries, the events in Denmark in August created a clear and decisive break with the policy of negotiation which had characterized the first three years of the occupation. Economic and administrative collaboration continued, to be sure, and great quantities of agricultural produce were still exported to Germany, but the Danish population, the Danish politicians, the illegal circles, not to mention the German occupation authorities believed that the situation was now quite different. The tangible manifestation of this change was the emergence of the Freedom Council as an alternative to the government that had ceased to function.

Adjusting to Allied Victory

by Berit Nøkleby

It started to become clear as early as 1943 that Germany would lose the war. The Allies were preparing for their final and decisive assault on Nazi Germany, and each of the Nordic countries began, insofar as it was possible, to ready themselves for the end of the war. Neutral Sweden, which had reacted to the changing fortunes of war by shifting from reluctant acceptance of German domination to being truly neutral, became ever more oriented toward the Western powers during this last phase. Germany's weakened ability to intervene gave greater scope for Swedish assistance to the other Nordic countries, including occupied Denmark and Norway. For Finland, 1944 was a decisive year: after yet another great military clash with the Russians, the Finns concluded an armistice with the Soviet Union in September 1944. However, this did not mean that Finnish soldiers could lay down their arms. In response to Soviet demands, the Finns had to wage war with their former German comrades-in-arms, and Finnish units were engaged in driving the last German forces out of northern Finland throughout the winter of 1944-45 and right up to April 1945. Denmark and Norway continued their fight with the Germans on the home front and along with the Allied forces in the war proper. However, the great question for them, which overshadowed all other problems, was the possibility that the large German forces in the two countries might take desperate action in the final period of the war. Would there be chaos, insurrection, and looting in Denmark? Would the *Wehrmacht* choose to continue the fight in its *Festung Norwegen* even after Germany had capitulated? And what would

The main building of the 300-year-old University of Helsinki, destroyed in the bombing in February 1944. Note Wäinö Aaltonen's damaged relief "Freedom and Youth," dated 1940. (Puolustusvoimien Kuvakeskus, Helsinki)

Sweden do in that event: would it intervene and thus finally abandon its neutrality?

Finland Leaves the War

The Fenno-Russian front largely remained calm from December 1941 to June 1944. The Finns limited themselves to defending their positions and did not want to be drawn more than was absolutely necessary into the great trial of strength between the two great powers. On the contrary, they would gladly have followed Swedish advice and withdrawn from the war. However, both the cabinet and parliament had found the Russian peace terms unacceptable in April

1944, in large part because of a military consideration: the Finnish military authorities, with Mannerheim at their head, believed it was impossible for the Finns to disarm the German troops in Finland within a month, as the Soviets demanded. Economic factors also played a role in the Finnish decision to reject the Russian terms. Not only was the figure of $600 million in reparations payments considered hopelessly high, but the Finns also had a more immediate problem to deal with. How would Finland obtain supplies if it withdrew from the war while Germany continued to control the Baltic? Germany had given a foretaste of the problems it could create in this area by suspending deliveries of grain and armaments to Finland in April 1944 in order to put pressure on Finland to remain loyal to its comrades-in-arms.

Finland also played for time. Since the Russo-Finnish front still lay far to the east of the 1940 frontier and thus included territory that did not belong to prewar Finland, there might be room for bargaining later. If still undefeated by the end of the world war, Finland might have something to offer in the peace negotiations. But that would depend on a Soviet decision to leave the Finnish question for the time being and concentrate on the main enemy — Germany. The Finns hoped that the Russian summer offensive on the eastern front would leave Finland out and give the country a period of grace.

The landings in Normandy on 6 June 1944 established the second front which the Western Allies had promised the Soviet Union, but Stalin was still somewhat suspicious as to whether this would really produce lasting relief for the Russians. Moreover, Finnish forces were only thirty kilometers from Leningrad, so he decided to resolve the Finnish problem before beginning the main assault on the eastern front. On 10 June 1944 the Red Army began a great offensive against the Finnish positions on the Karelian isthmus; the Russians quickly broke through the main Finnish line, and on the twentieth they took Viipuri. The situation was critical for the Finns, but after several weeks of desperate fighting they succeeded in stabilizing the front again both to the south and to the north of Lake Ladoga. In the meantime, the Russians had begun their offensive against the Germans on 23 June, and in consequence the pressure on the Finnish front had become less severe. The Finns also obtained some relief because of Hitler's decision, a couple of days after the Russian attack on the Finnish positions, to resume shipments of food and armaments to Finland. Furthermore, the *Luftwaffe* and the *Kriegsmarine*

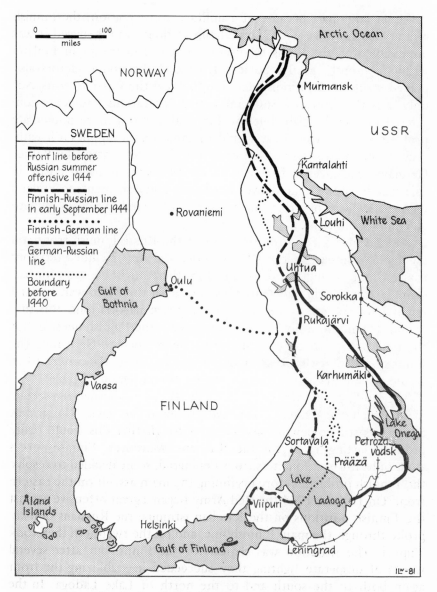

Fenno-Russian front lines in 1944. (Cartographer: Ingrid Lowzow)

were ordered to give some assistance to the Finns. "As long as the Finn fights, we will help him," said Hitler, "as soon as he begins to negotiate, we will end these shipments."

Until this time Finland had participated in the war on the German side but without entering into a formal pact with Germany. The Finns

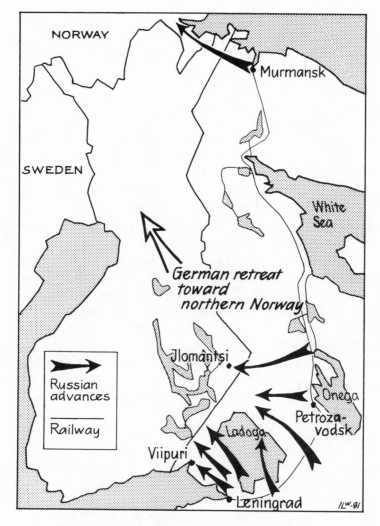

Russian advances in 1944. (Cartographer: Ingrid Lowzow)

felt that they were fighting in their own interests against the common enemy, Russia. Now, while the battle raged on the Karelian isthmus and the situation seemed desperate, German demands became more exacting. The Germans wanted some assurance that the Finns would continue the struggle. On 22 June the German foreign minister Ribbentrop arrived in Helsinki, bearing an ultimatum from Hitler: if Finland would not clearly declare that a separate peace between Finland and the Soviet Union was out of the question, Hitler would stop sending armaments to Finland and would withdraw German troops from the country. The Finns now had to come out clearly on Germany's side. It was no longer possible to maintain that they were fighting a "separate war" with Russia over Finland's borders. Meanwhile, on 23 June the Russians demanded that Finland capitulate before any peace negotiations could begin.

Unconditional surrender to the Russians or a pact with the Germans? The Finns faced a bitter choice, but Mannerheim at least had no doubts about what was the right course: the Soviet demand was unacceptable; so was the German, but if the Finns acceded to it, they would at least gain time. Finland's negotiating position at midsummer 1944 was catastrophically bad, the Finnish front being in danger of collapse. However, this situation could perhaps be rectified with German assistance, so that with the front duly stabilized Finland could enter into negotiations with the Soviet Union. Mannerheim maintained on this occasion that necessity knows no law, but the solution the Finns adopted to the dilemma they faced represented in fact a highly casuistic use of laws and democratic parliamentary practice. Under pressure from the commander-in-chief, President Ryti entered into a personal pact with Germany. He declared in a letter to Hitler that he, as president of the Finnish republic, would only make peace with the Soviet Union, or allow the government or any individual appointed by him to begin negotiations designed to lead to peace, in concert with the government of the German *Reich*. Ribbentrop returned to Berlin with this letter, which was regarded on the German side as a pact between Germany and Finland; the Germans seem to have been satisfied by Ryti's letter and not to have seen through the legal sophistry of the Finns. From the Finnish point of view, there was no formal pact between the two countries, the letter did not bind the Finnish parliament, only Ryti personally; and the agreement could therefore easily be broken by replacing the president of the republic, which is precisely what ultimately happened.

The pact led the United States to break off diplomatic relations with Finland. However, Mannerheim's assessment of the military situation proved to be accurate. Germany was not able to send troops to Finland on any significant scale, but the German supplies of armaments were of both practical and moral importance to the Finnish forces, which were able to halt the Soviet offensive and stabilize the front. Moreover, the pressure on Finland also declined as the Russians began later in the summer to divert troops from the far north to what was for them a far more important purpose: the race for Berlin. Finland had succeeded in gaining time.

Now it was time to take the next step on the tortuous road toward peace. After having ascertained that the Soviet Union was willing to negotiate with a new Finnish government and that the demand for unconditional surrender had been dropped, Ryti resigned as president. On 4 August 1944 Mannerheim was sworn in before parliament as the new president of Finland. The motive given for the replacement of Ryti was that the seriousness of the hour required the concentration of political and military power in the hands of one man and that only Mannerheim had sufficient personal prestige to hold such wide authority. However, the main purpose behind the change was to rid Finland of the pact with Germany and initiate negotiations with the Russians.

Mannerheim declared that he and Finland were not bound by Ryti's agreement with the Germans. The Finns were anxious for a time lest Hitler take retaliatory action after the unilateral Finnish abandonment of the pact, and Mannerheim therefore chose to await developments. However, it soon became clear that the Germans had their hands more than full in other areas: the Western Allies were approaching Paris, the eastern front was giving way, and Romania and Bulgaria were collapsing. A formal breach with Germany was a Soviet condition for the initiation of negotiations, as had been made clear during the preliminary contacts between Helsinki and Moscow at the end of August through the Swedish Foreign Ministry and the Soviet minister in Stockholm, Madame Kollontai. On 2 September 1944 relations between Finland and Germany were finally and formally broken off in a letter from Mannerheim to Hitler. A ceasefire followed at the front on the fourth, and a Finnish delegation arrived in Moscow on the seventh.

The Russians kept the Finnish delegates waiting for a few days before they were summoned to the Kremlin. The negotiations were conducted on the Soviet side by Molotov, and they assumed the form more of a Russian dictation than real negotiations. Britain was also represented in the discussions, but the British kept their involvement to a minimum; during the first meeting the British ambassador in Moscow, Sir Archibald Clark Kerr, spoke only once and that was to say, "I am in complete agreement with Mr. Molotov."

The Russian proposals for an agreement, as Molotov emphasized, related only to an armistice, not a peace treaty, and they were virtually an ultimatum—Molotov was most unwilling to discuss the various demands in detail. The Soviet terms were largely known to the Finns already, since they were approximately the same as those presented to Finland in April 1944, when the Finnish cabinet and a unanimous parliament had rejected them as impossible. The demands put forward in September included the following items: the 1940 frontier was to be restored; the Finns were to disarm the German forces in their country; the Finnish army was to be demobilized within two and a half months; Petsamo was to be ceded to the Soviet Union; and Finland was to pay a war indemnity of $300 million within six years. This last point represented an improvement on the terms presented in April, when the Russians had demanded $600 million. Finally, the Soviet Union now demanded that in place of Hanko, they be allowed to lease the Porkala peninsula, which lay about twenty kilometers from Helsinki, as a naval base.

These were severe terms, and it has been widely discussed in Finland whether they really represented any improvement on those put forward in April. Was the only result of the stubborn fight of the Finnish army on the Karelian isthmus a mere $300 million? However, although the texts of the two draft armistice proposals were fairly similar, the military situation in September 1944 was different from that in April 1944. In April the great stumbling block to agreement had been the Soviet demand that the Finns disarm the German troops in the country. Mannerheim (and his views carried considerable weight) regarded the demand as quite impossible. At that time, a German army of over 200,000 men, fully armed, with battle experience and excellent morale was stationed inside Finland. Germany itself was certainly in retreat, but was still the undefeated master of the greater part of the European continent. Finland was entirely dependent on Germany for supplies, and no one knew how long the war in Europe would last. In September 1944, on the other hand, the demand that the German forces in Finland be disarmed was still a severe one, but it was no longer impossible. Germany was now on the brink of collapse, and the Russians no longer insisted that the task be carried out within a fixed period of time.

At any rate, the Finnish delegation in Moscow in September 1944 believed that Finland no longer had a choice in the matter. On 19 September the delegation, headed by the foreign minister, Carl Enckell, signed the armistice agreement. Finland's war against the

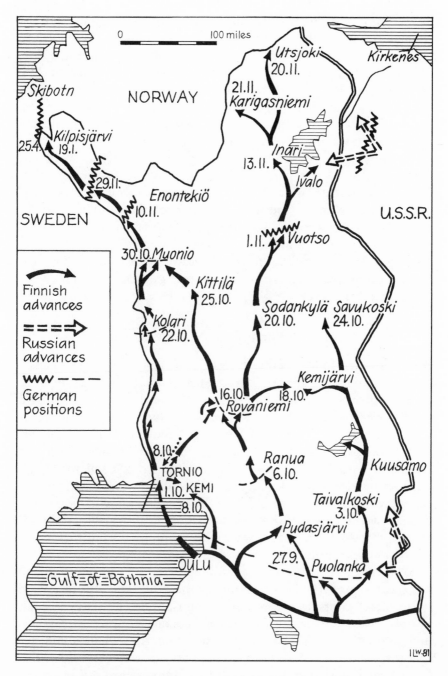

The war against the Germans in Lappland, 1944–45. Dates of Finnish recon-
quests are indicated. (Cartographer: Ingrid Lowzow)

Soviet Union was over. However, because of the demand that the German troops in the country be disarmed, Finland continued to participate in the Second World War, this time on the Allied side, against its former German comrades-in-arms and on Finnish soil. After 20 September 1944 Finnish soldiers fought to drive the Germans out of Finnish Lappland and over the frontier into northern Norway. It was not until 24 April 1945 that the Finns could announce that the country was free of German troops.

However, in the rest of Finland life returned to normal with surprising rapidity. A number of tasks created by the war or the armistice agreement certainly remained: the resettlement once again of refugees from Karelia; the demobilization of those military forces that were not required in Lappland; and the preparations for legal action against "war criminals." Finnish democracy could nonetheless begin to function again in conditions of peace—before the great war in Europe was over. For example, parliamentary elections were held in March 1945.

Sweden—Neutrality and Nordic Solidarity

Neutral Sweden followed the struggle of its neighbors against Russia or Germany with the greatest interest, partly out of genuine sympathy for the other Nordic states but also, of course, because their fate would have a great and perhaps decisive influence on the future of Sweden itself. For much of 1944 it was above all Finland that attracted Swedish attention. It was only a matter of time before the German occupation of Denmark and Norway would come to an end, but if things went really badly for Finland, Sweden might have a great power as its closest neighbor in the east, and a Russian-occupied Finland would dramatically change Sweden's strategic position. Sweden therefore wanted to see Finland withdraw from the war as quickly as possible and with its independence intact.

However, there was little that Sweden could do to help Finland in the summer of 1944, but as long as the Finns and Russians were not in direct contact, one practical contribution, now as earlier in the war, was to test the waters and conduct private discussions through the Swedish Foreign Ministry and the Russian minister Kollontai. The Swedes always did what they could to ensure that this channel for negotiation remained open and functioned satisfactorily. In June 1944 the Swedish government could hardly press the Finns to accept unconditional surrender, but when the situation became dramatically worse for Germany in July, the Swedes felt that it was high time that Finland withdrew from the war and its association with Germany, which could now only increase the risk of an occupation by the victorious Soviet troops. The Swedish government was therefore among those which urged Mannerheim to assume the presidency and lead Finland out of the war.

For its own part, Sweden still adhered firmly to neutrality albeit that its relations with the great powers were not easy as the year 1944 and the expected invasion in the west and Russian successes in the east brought the hostilities closer to Swedish territories. Germany, even when on the retreat, remained a power to be reckoned with, but the Western Allies now had the strongest cards and also a growing interest in cutting off the Germans from all the supplies that could sustain their war effort. In consequence, Sweden came under increased pressure from Britain and the United States.

The most serious result of this development for Germany was that Sweden now began to curtail trade between the two countries. On 10 January 1944 the new trade agreement between Sweden and Germany was signed, and Sweden had carried out the reductions in its exports to Germany which the London agreement of 1943 required. However, by 1944 this was no longer enough for the Western powers, which, as the date for the invasion of Normandy approached, regarded Swedish exports to Germany as an important contribution to the German war effort. Washington was particularly dissatisfied with the Swedes, especially with regard to the export of iron ore and ball bearings.

The Swedish government could not give way to this new pressure from the Western Allies if Sweden was to remain a truly neutral state. An agreement had been reached, and Sweden had fulfilled it and more. The Swedish government believed that neutrality would be endangered if it gave way again since it feared that it would not be possible later to put a stop to further concessions. Accordingly, despite quite severe threats from Washington (the United States declared itself prepared to use all means available to stop the export), Stockholm insisted on standing by the London agreement of the autumn of 1943 and the trade agreement with Germany that was based on it. More accurately, Sweden formally stood by these agreements and thus saved its neutral face; while informally and quite "unintentionally" trying to reduce exports to Germany somewhat. Serviceable methods were to delay the opening of the ore-exporting ports after the winter on the grounds that ice-breakers were unobtainable; to reduce the number of miners by mobilization; and to use similar "unfortunate coincidences"—and they were not without results.

The growing transit and transportation problems the Germans experienced should also be seen in connection with Sweden's shift toward the Western powers. Some of their special advantages had been withdrawn as early as 1943. Now even in the field of normal commercial transit, Sweden was exposed to strong pressure from the Western powers and once again, as in the case of trade, the Swedes defended their obligation as a neutral to stand by existing agreements. However, in this area too, one restriction after the other was imposed on the Germans in 1944. Germany's right to send mail and military couriers through Sweden was abruptly ended in May 1944, after the Swedish customs service had on several occasions discovered maps of Sweden among the goods in transit. At around the same time Stockholm warned Berlin that restrictions would be placed on transit via the ports of the Gulf of Bothnia to Norway. However, the Western powers, especially Washington, were not content with these moves. In their view, exports to Germany should now cease entirely. Sweden should break completely and openly with Germany.

An open breach would, of course, be quite incompatible with neutrality, and indeed this never occurred. However, events did begin to move quickly after D-day. The Germans had to accept a reduction in Swedish exports of ball bearings and a complete stop to the transportation of coal, coke, and cement through the ports of northern Sweden to Trondheim and Narvik. In August 1944 the Swedish government withdrew the war risk insurance for journeys to Germany's Baltic ports, which left Swedish ships sailing to these ports totally uninsured against any damage caused by the war actions. No shipowner would take that risk, and as a result the Swedish part of the tonnage—about 50%—that carried trade between Germany and Sweden was removed at a time when Germany desperately needed shipping, partly in order to carry supplies to Norway, supplies that increasingly had to be sent by sea in view of Swedish restrictions on transit across Sweden.

Transit through Sweden to northern Finland ended with the cease-fire of 4 September 1944, and from 9 September on the Swedes withdrew permission for any German transportation across Sweden, except for the sick and wounded. At around the same time they stopped issuing visas to Germans traveling to or from Norway. At the end of September, against the background of the Fenno-Soviet armistice agreement, Sweden closed its Baltic ports to foreign (i.e., German) shipping, because the government feared that the Russians might intervene against German vessels in Swedish territorial waters. The official reason given for this decision was that it was taken out of "regard for the entirely changed situation in and around the Baltic."

The German reaction to all this was very restrained. Germany was unable to take concrete action to defend its interests, and this became even more true as 1944 wore on. If the Germans protested at all, it was usually only in the form of polite, diplomatic protests. The most important objective for Germany now was to maintain as good relations with Sweden as possible, so as to receive such deliveries as might still be obtained for as long as possible. Accordingly, while the Swedes gradually restricted German imports and transportation facilities, there was little risk of German reprisals.

These trends continued during the last months of the war. Trade with Germany was eventually stopped without leading to a diplomatic breach. Sweden remained neutral in form to the very end, but during the last year of hostilities it was shifting toward the Western powers in pace with the fortunes of war, so that in the spring of 1945 "neutral" Sweden can justifiably be called a "pro-Allied nonbelligerent" state. However, it should be noted that this shift toward an Allied orientation was not only the outcome of a small neutral country's attempts to adjust to the prevailing balance of power in the outer world. There is no doubt that the Swedes regarded the growing likelihood of an Allied victory with sympathy, and Germany's weakened position also provided them with a welcome opportunity of increasing their assistance to the other Nordic countries—within the flexible limits of neutrality.

Swedish military circles had begun to worry about the transition from war to peace in the neighboring countries as early as December 1942. Nor could the Swedish military authorities be indifferent to the way in which this transition occurred or to the situation in these countries during the period immediately after the war. For example, it was possible that the large, well-armed German forces in Denmark, Norway, and northern Finland would create chaos in these countries after the collapse of Germany, with all the tragic consequences which this would involve for their civilian populations. An Allied invasion of Denmark or Norway might lead to one or more of the Allied great powers obtaining a foothold on Scandinavian soil, which would be contrary to Swedish interests. For example, the possibility that the Soviet Union would obtain a foothold at the entrance to the Baltic was not a particularly attractive one for Sweden.

The plans for Operations *Rädda Danmark* (Save Denmark) and *Rädda Norge* (Save Norway), which never became anything more than plans drawn up by the Swedish defense staff, were therefore based on possible Swedish military intervention to ensure that the transition from war to peace in the neighboring countries should be as peaceful as possible and that the legal authorities in Denmark and Norway should be enabled to govern their countries independently as soon as possible. In the spring of 1945 these plans were submitted to the government, which approved the guidelines behind them, though at the beginning of May 1945 planning was still incomplete and the Swedish government was still asserting a policy of neutrality and nonintervention.

At the end of 1943 and beginning of 1944 there were about 20,000 Norwegian refugees in Sweden, and about 13,000 of them were men of military age. It was, of course, clear to the Norwegian authorities in London that these men ought to be used for the good of Norway. Moreover, if a substantial proportion of these refugees could be placed in organized employment, this would undoubtedly be welcomed by the Swedish authorities, since the Norwegians who were crossing into Sweden in growing numbers were creating problems. The Swedish labor market could not accommodate a large part of them; they also made it somewhat more difficult to maintain order; and many of them, having fled Norway with a definite wish to do something for their country, found themselves loitering in Sweden, where they had no opportunity to help Norway and no way of joining the Norwegian forces in Britain. The obstacle to utilizing these manpower resources was that Swedish neutrality did not provide much scope for organizing Norwegians of draft age in a meaningful way on Swedish soil. However, in the course of 1943 certain possibilities began to be discerned—possibilities that turned out to give a satisfactory solution to the problem as Swedish neutrality shifted toward the Western powers.

Open military training was impossible, but through various plans and private discussions in both Swedish and Norwegian quarters the idea emerged that young Norwegians in Sweden could be given police training instead. The latter would fulfill some military requirements like assembling the men in camps, giving them physical training, placing them in a military organization, and giving them instruction at least in the use of small arms. The men could be employed during the transition period from war to peace as a police and security corps in the event of a German capitulation, but it was not intended that they should fight regular German troops.

Preparations began in the second half of 1943, when over 8,000 men were summoned to so-called health camps, where they were medically examined, classified, and registered by the Norwegian

A Norwegian police troop, trained at a mansion in the neighborhood of Stockholm. About 14,000 of the 50,000 Norwegians who fled to Sweden during the war were assembled in camps where they received military training. (Gullers International ab, Stockholm)

authorities. At the same time the plans for organized police training were more closely discussed with the Swedish authorities. On 3 December 1943 the Swedish government gave its permission for the establishment of a force of 1,500 *Rikspoliti* (national police), trained as policemen and intended for use solely as policemen. At the same time the Norwegians were also allowed to train 8,000 men in the so-called *Reservepoliti* (police reserve). The Norwegians envisaged, even though they did not say this openly to the Swedes, that the police corps would be trained for purely military service under the camouflage of police training. By the end of the year most of the *Rikspoliti* companies had been set up, and the training of the police reserve began on 15 January 1944.

The training of the police corps encountered many problems. One of the most serious problems was that it was not always easy to persuade Norwegian refugees to volunteer for service in the corps—and they had to be volunteers, because the Swedes insisted on this out of concern for their neutrality. However, the greatest problem concerned training in the use of arms. The Norwegians were originally allowed to give instruction only in the use of hand weapons, and even then not in all camps at the same time. In consequence, many of the recruits found it difficult to see any value in the training program they underwent, and this naturally led to poor discipline. Matters improved in the autumn of 1944. The Norwegians received permission to carry out training exercises and large-scale maneuvers in August and to use heavy arms in camps where instruction in the use of weapons was allowed (and the number of such camps was also increased) in September. Ultimately, training in the use of arms was allowed in virtually all the camps. In the autumn of 1944 the Norwegians were also allowed to increase the number of men in the police reserve to 12,000.

At first, both the Swedes and Norwegians tried to camouflage the "police training" of Norwegian refugees on Swedish soil as far as possible, but the existence of the police corps became ever more apparent. For example, from February 1945 on the members of the corps were allowed to wear uniforms outside the camps and in April of that year 6,000 Norwegians took part in maneuvers—the largest Norwegian field maneuvers since 1918.

The Danes likewise received permission on 3 December 1943 to set up a police corps on Swedish soil. After the break with Germany in August 1943 and the dissolution of the Danish armed forces, Denmark had to face the question of how it would make the transition from war to peace. The Danish government that would be set up at the end of the war would need an armed force to maintain order in a situation in which an uprising or chaos was possible. Danish circles were aware of Norwegian plans and found the example an attractive one; the question was how it could be adapted to Danish circumstances, which were rather different from those in Norway.

Danish plans and private discussions with the Swedes in the autumn of 1943 primarily concerned the reconstitution and rearmament of the disbanded and disarmed Danish army. It was thought that the whole Danish officer corps could be evacuated to Sweden so as to keep it intact. The Danes also asked the Swedes to set up weapon depots for Danish use with arms for 50,000 men, including a number of tanks, and to train Danish military personnel in the use of such weapons. The plan to evacuate the officer corps was abandoned, and the Swedish authorities proved to be reluctant about giving any promises about weapon depots. The Danish requests were extensive, and Sweden needed armaments for the Norwegians and, of course, for its own use. However, concern for neutrality was the most serious consideration. The Norwegian idea of a police corps came to apply to the Danes as well. A small number of Danish officers began to recruit volunteers for the corps among the Danish refugees who were now arriving in Sweden in growing numbers, and from a modest start of 500 men at the end of 1943 and the beginning of 1944, the Danish Brigade grew to about 5,000 men in May 1945.

The Danish police corps, like its Norwegian counterpart, benefited from the Swedish shift toward an Allied orientation. Its working conditions became steadily better through 1944: the Danes were allowed to recruit volunteers more freely among Danish refugees and to give more extensive instruction in the use of arms, including, toward the end of the year, heavy infantry weapons. The forces of the police corps had developed into regular infantry battalions.

Denmark and Norway — Occupied Allies?

At a cursory glance, there are many similarities between the fates of Denmark and Norway during the war. The most important and obvious similarity is, of course, the German occupation, which lasted in both cases from 1940 until the capitulation of the German forces in May 1945. Another similarity is that public opinion in both countries clearly and quite openly supported the Allies. Danes and Norwegians both within and outside occupied territory wished to see, and many also actively worked for, an Allied victory. However, the two countries did not have an identical relationship with the great powers.

In the case of Norway, the matter was clear: Norway was at war with Germany after 9 April 1940. The Norwegian government-in-exile was recognized by the Allies from 1940 on, and the Norwegian underground army at home (*Milorg*) was accepted in November 1941 as a part of the Norwegian armed forces that were fighting Germany. At the end of 1943 and the beginning of 1944 Norway was still fighting in the Allied camp with the means at its disposal: the Norwegian merchant marine made a significant contribution to the war effort, while Norwegian naval, air, and specialist units (commando and sabotage units, working with the Special Operations Executive, SOE, and intelligence units working with the Secret Intelligence Service) fought as more or less integrated parts of the British armed forces. There were even some military operations on Norwegian soil. Apart from the contribution made by the merchant marine, Norwegian activities on the Allied side were hardly of worldwide importance, but the cardinal point was clear and recognized by the great powers: Norway was occupied but also a fighting ally.

For occupied Denmark, the road to recognition as a fighting ally was long, difficult, and ultimately doomed to failure. Although the Danes wanted this status and the Western Allies were sympathetic to their desires, it was never achieved. Denmark's relationship to the great powers remained unclear even after the break with Germany in August 1943. Denmark was occupied by Germany but never formally at war with the occupying power, although public opinion was clearly anti-German from the very first and although it can justifiably be said that there was a *de facto* state of war between the home front and the Germans after August 1943. Danish shipping also sailed in Allied service—two-thirds of the Danish merchant marine, including its most modern vessels, operated outside the control of the Danish authorities at home. Sections of the Danish home front cooperated with and received help from British paramilitary organizations. However, Denmark was still not recognized as an ally by the three allied great powers. In the summer of 1944 the Russians went so far as to accept a recognized representative of the Danish resistance in Moscow in response to an initiative taken by the Freedom Council, but London and Washington adopted a negative attitude. One of the problems was the degree to which the Freedom

Council represented the Danish nation. This problem for the Western powers was to some extent resolved at the turn of the year 1945, when the Freedom Council and the leaders of the four largest political parties sent a joint communication to the governments of the three allied great powers. However, the Danes could not receive a reply until the big three had reached an agreement, and they had not done so before the end of the war, above all because of various considerations arising out of their own interests.

By late 1944 there were Soviet troops in northern Norway, but Norway was nonetheless clearly viewed as a British sphere of influence, even by the Russians. However, the great powers had reached no such agreement about Denmark. The British certainly wished to clarify the matter, but the Russians were hesitant, and the question had still not been resolved in March 1945. Denmark was not important enough for the British to engage in an open confrontation with the Soviet Union over its future. For their part, the Russians also did not have a great interest in the affairs of Denmark, but they did not want to tie their hands prematurely by entering into an otherwise unnecessary agreement. In consequence, all Danish and British efforts to secure allied status for Denmark were unsuccessful until it became a *fait accompli* in May 1945. At that time, Denmark was liberated and occupied by British troops, and Molotov expressed the view that Denmark should be invited to the inaugural meeting of the United Nations in San Francisco as an ally.

By the winter of 1943-44 there were active resistance movements, which carried out military and civilian resistance activity against the occupying power, in both Denmark and Norway. In Norway the years 1943 and 1944 did not bring anything radically new, but rather the further development of trends present in earlier years. In Denmark, on the other hand, the resistance movement grew rapidly after August 1943. A primary factor behind this development was that loyalty toward the democratic parties, an attitude that had sustained the policy of negotiation, no longer inhibited participation in illegal work. For many Danes, the German attempt to seize the Danish Jews removed the last barrier to approval of active struggle. The personal risk involved was greater now, because the death sentences passed by German military courts were now carried out (unless Dr. Best used his powers of reprieve, and he did so only on the basis of political considerations, using the captured resisters as hostages). On the other hand, the suppression of sabotage had become considerably less effective, since the last remnants of cooperation from the population and the Danish police now disappeared. A number of officers from the disbanded Danish army were directed into resistance work by an unofficial, clandestine group of officers known as "the little general staff." Its activities have been the subject of much debate. Although it was formally subordinate to the Freedom Council, it carried out its policies in agreement with, though not necessarily under instructions from, the politicians of the established parties. In the minds of the conservative Danish officer corps, anti-Communist activity undoubtedly was more important than fighting the Germans.

In both Denmark and Norway the resistance movement now had an organized central leadership. The Danish Freedom Council, which had been set up in September 1943, was the most important political grouping in Denmark from the summer of 1944 on, and in the Freedom Council the resistance movement had found its political leadership. Relations with the politicians (as we have seen, there was no government in Denmark after August 1943) were cool, above all because the Communists played a prominent role within the Freedom Council, a fact that aroused suspicion and apprehension in some parliamentary circles. It was feared, for example, that the Communists would exploit the Freedom Council for their own ends during the transition from war to peace. Some Danish politicians retained a lively fear of a Communist *coup d'état* right up to the German capitulation and even for a time after it. Fear of the Communists and distrust between the resistance leadership and the politicians made it difficult to reach agreement on the most suitable arrangements for the transition from war to peace in Denmark. There was a strong desire in both Denmark and Norway to place the control of government in national hands and avoid an Allied military administration during the transitional phase. However, to achieve this aim, it was necessary to produce agreement on a tenable alternative that enjoyed broad popular support. In Denmark the politicians and the resistance leadership did not reach such an agreement until 1 May 1945, whereas the corresponding Norwegian agreement was signed a year earlier in April 1944.

In Norway, mistrust between the resistance movement and the government-in-exile was by 1944 almost entirely a thing of the past. By this time the Norwegian resistance movement had a recognized stable leadership. There was still no formal body on which the leaders of all the various branches of the resistance were represented, but there were good contacts between the leaders, and a number of secret meetings with representatives of the Norwegian authorities abroad in Britain or Sweden helped to establish sufficient confidence between the home front and the government-in-exile for them to cooperate effectively. In April 1944 it proved possible to sign an agreement for the administration of the country during the transition from war to peace on the basis that the home front leadership (*Hjemmefrontens Ledelse*) would rule until the legal government of Norway could take over.

The unity between the home front and the government-in-exile was also emphasized when the popular crown prince Olav became commander of all the Norwegian armed forces on 1 July 1944, an appointment which undoubtedly enjoyed wide support in Norway. Paradoxically, as a symbol of unity and as supreme military commander, the crown prince was far more acceptable to the Communist resistance movement in Norway than even the most liberal general.

In a formal sense, the home front leadership did not become a fully organized unit until the autumn of 1944. By the end of the year this group of leaders, which consisted of representatives of the various resistance organizations, above all *Milorg* and *Sivorg* (the civilian resistance organization), was ready to make its contribution during the transition from war to peace. The Communists requested that they too be represented, but this was rejected on the grounds that the group was not a body containing representatives of the political parties. *Hjemmefrontens Ledelse* saw itself as a nonpolitical body.

Whereas the Communists occupied an important place within the leadership of the Danish resistance movement, they were thus excluded from the leadership in Norway. However, this does not mean that they played no role within the Norwegian resistance. On the contrary, they were the exponents of one of the two alternative policies pursued within the Norwegian military resistance: the activist line which involved using sabotage against the *Wehrmacht* on Norwegian soil. Many non-Communists agreed with them on this point and joined their sabotage groups. On the other hand, the *Milorg* leadership, and with it *Hjemmefrontens Ledelse*, espoused a more reserved policy, which attached the greatest weight to the preservation of Norwegian lives and assets. The *Milorg* leadership assessed the likely advantages and probable price to be paid before it sanctioned any radical step, since it argued that the war would not and could not be won on Norwegian soil. The struggle between these two conflicting views of military resistance continued during the last year of the occupation and was never really resolved, although *Milorg*'s line may be said to have been the dominant one.

D-day, 6 June 1944, when the Allies landed in Normandy, was a watershed also for illegal activity in occupied Denmark and Norway. Danes and Norwegians had long awaited the occurrence of some decisive event on the western front. At least one thing was now clear: neither Norway nor Denmark would be the stage for the Allied assault on Hitler's West Wall. Both Danes and Norwegians (and Swedes too) were relieved that at least for the time being Scandinavia was to be spared the devastation that would result from a military conflict between the great powers on Nordic soil.

Until this time the Norwegian underground army, *Milorg*, had based its preparations on the assumption that its main task would be to serve as an auxiliary force in the event of an Allied invasion of Norway. It now received the following clear communication from Eisenhower's headquarters:

No Allied military offensive operations are planned for this theatre, therefore no steps must be taken to encourage the Resistance Movement as such to overt action, since no outside support can be forthcoming. . . .

Milorg ought thus to continue to wait and to be prepared. At this time the most likely course of events in Norway seemed to be that the occupation would end through a German capitulation or a German evacuation of the country. There would be useful tasks for *Milorg* to perform in either eventuality. *Milorg*'s units would be the only Allied forces in the area until regular Allied troops arrived. Events in France and later also in Finnmark showed that the Germans would seek to leave widespread destruction behind them, if they evacuated Norway. *Milorg*'s task during the last phase of the war was therefore to be prepared to prevent such a devastation and to perform guard and auxiliary duties as required.

Preparations of this kind had already begun in Norway, and through *Milorg* they now received full Allied support. High priority was attached to supplying the home front, and during the last year of the war *Milorg* received large quantities of arms and equipment and was given instruction in their use. Supplies were also brought in from Sweden or dropped to waiting *Milorg* groups. On the west coast, most of the equipment was brought in by the so-called Shetland Bus (dubbed so because of its reliability). This transportation "service" between Shetland and Norway was at first run by small fishing vessels, but during this phase of the war it was taken over by modern American-built submarine chasers manned by Norwegian sailors and under Norwegian naval command. For safety reasons, not all arms were delivered to the *Milorg* groups here; instead arms depots were set up on uninhabited islands or in other suitable places. During the last winter of the war some members of *Milorg* were also *"på skauen"* (in the forest), that is, they had left their homes and their civilian lives and were stationed in small, remote military camps in the Norwegian forests and mountains, three of them constituting regular bases established in cooperation with SOE. The *Milorg* groups in most parts of the country were in reliable radio contact with Britain; as the commander of one of these "boys in the forest camps" observed, "we were in contact with London every day and with Oslo perhaps once a week" —and his camp was not far from Oslo. In May 1945 *Milorg* was able to mobilize 40,000 armed and relatively well-trained men.

Before the spring of 1944 *Milorg* as an organization did not engage in sabotage because the *Milorg* leadership did not want to expose the organization to the danger of large-scale arrests through such action and because it thought that this risk and also that of reprisals against the civilian population outweighed the military advantages that could be derived from sabotage. However, there was some modification of *Milorg*'s attitude in the spring of 1944. A certain level of sabotage activity was now desired in order to provide training to the *Milorg* groups and to satisfy their wish to be finally allowed "to do something"; the activist line asserted by the Communists was attractive to many young men, and continued passivity would be a threat to both morale and discipline. *Milorg* therefore carried out some acts of sabotage during the summer and autumn of 1944.

However, sabotage activity by *Milorg* depended on the approval of SHAEF (Supreme Headquarters of Allied Expeditionary Forces), and the Allied supreme command held back for a long time. Above all, it wanted to see calm and order and limited activity in Norway, since the war should first be won on the continent. Then the Allied attitude slowly began to change somewhat, partly as a result of difficulties and setbacks on the continent, and from the end of July the Allies began to express a desire for sabotage against German supplies of gas and oil in Norway. Nevertheless, at the beginning of October SHAEF was still explicitly opposed to any attempts by the resistance movement to prevent the withdrawal of German troops from Norway by such measures as the sabotage of railways. SHAEF became less hostile to such action at the end of the month, and it made a complete about-face at the beginning of December, when it expressed support for extensive sabotage against railways and roads. One reason for this change of policy may have been that SHAEF did not want to see the 20th German army moved from Finland and northern Norway to the continent.

The various branches of the resistance continued their activities during the last year of the occupation. *Milorg* and *Sivorg*; intelligence; the secret radio transmitters; the clandestine press; the illegal network transporting people out of the country; and other organizations of different kinds—all the many fields of activity that together made up the resistance—functioned as they had before. However, both civilian and military organizations also made preparations for the transition to peace. These preparations were made in cooperation with the Norwegian authorities abroad and included, in the military field, far-reaching plans to protect Norwegian property and Norwegian lives, and, in the civilian sphere, such measures as the removal of NS (*Nasjonal Samling*) members and other undesirable individuals from posts in the public sector. Illegal work continued to be dangerous, and the number of executions in 1944-45 was greater than ever: 142 Norwegian men and women faced German firing squads during this period.

However, in comparison with Denmark during the same period, the number of executions is the only indication of a harsher climate in Norway. In all other fields, the course of events was more dramatic and the climate was harsher in Denmark during this phase. Whereas activist members of the Danish resistance had in the earlier years of the war wanted to see "Norwegian conditions" in Denmark, it was now the struggle in Denmark that attracted the wrath of the occupying power and the attention of the world press. The Gestapo hardly used kid gloves in Norway, but its conduct in that country was now almost restrained in comparison with Denmark. An example is the so-called clearing murders, carried out by Danish collaborators from a list drawn up by the Germans; these were pure acts of terror and claimed 100 lives. When a zealous member of the

Gestapo tried to introduce this phenomenon into Norway in the summer of 1944, four Norwegian lives were lost as a result of his *"Blumenpflücken"* (flower picking) and his superiors put a stop to the use of this method in Norway. This was not done for humanitarian reasons, but because the employment of this weapon would be unnecessarily provocative. The Germans too did not want to see more trouble in Norway than was absolutely unavoidable for military reasons, which always had top priority since Hitler never ceased to expect an invasion in Norway.

In Denmark, on the other hand, there was trouble on a large scale. Factories and other installations were blown up to the open jubilation of the population. Sabotage played a central role for the Danish resistance. Before the government's break with the Germans in August 1943, sabotage had also been a psychological weapon designed to arouse the nation's will to resist. In Norway, acts of sabotage sometimes led during the first years of the occupation to petitions calling for an end to such "irresponsible" activity, and even during the last years of the war the attitude toward sabotage was marked by caution and a weighing of the pros and cons. In Denmark, on the other hand, it was clear as early as the summer of 1943 that sabotage was supported by a majority of the population. Sabotage in Denmark gradually became a purely military weapon, that is, a weapon used to damage the German war effort. The scale and effects of sabotage were far greater in Denmark than in Norway, but SHAEF's attitude toward sabotage in each of these two countries was also different. Whereas the Norwegians were directly forbidden to sabotage railways in the autumn of 1944, the Danes were encouraged to take vigorous action.

In the euphoric atmosphere that prevailed in Denmark after D-day, a successful act of sabotage had dramatic consequences: the inhabitants of Copenhagen went on strike. On 22 June 1944 the largest armaments factory in the country was blown up. The inhabitants of the capital were jubilant over the explosion and the huge fire it caused, and the Germans allowed themselves to be provoked into taking severe reprisals. The unrest did not diminish, however, and a state of emergency was introduced in Copenhagen on 25 June. Strikes and demonstrations began on the following day. There were many clashes between German patrols and the civilian population. The Germans fired into the crowds, and several hundred Danes were killed or wounded. In some places the enraged citizens of Copenhagen built barricades across the streets, and bonfires were lit all over the city.

From the German point of view, the strike meant both a loss of production for the German war effort and a serious threat to the calm and order which they wished above all to maintain in occupied areas. There was also the affront that the world press made much of the unrest. The Germans tried to crush the uprising by carrying out executions, but this only caused the disturbances and strikes to grow into a real people's strike. On 30 June factories, workshops, offices, and other places of business closed. The Germans responded by cutting off the city's supplies of electricity, gas, and water and by blockading Copenhagen. The situation in the city had reached a deadlock, and this state of affairs could not continue for long.

The people's strike in Copenhagen in June 1944 began spontaneously and had no leadership, but once it had started both the

German auxiliary corps, made up of Danes in German service, firing pistols on City Hall Square, Copenhagen, to break the midday silence ordered by the Danish Freedom Council on special occasions, as a protest, or an observance of an anniversary. (Museet for Danmarks Frihedskamp 1940-45, Copenhagen)

Freedom Council and the politicians tried to guide the population. There has been debate as to which of these two groups had the greatest authority with the population and could consequently take the credit for the peaceful resolution of the strike. It is at least certain that a desire for a return to normal conditions gradually became general. The Germans began to show restraint in order to avoid further provocation. In the course of a few days conditions started to return to normal in the capital. People went back to work, and the Germans lifted the state of emergency. The strike was important for the resistance movement, since it was a test of authority between the Freedom Council and the politicians. It became clear, at least to the latter, that it was necessary to initiate negotiations aimed at achieving agreement between them and the resistance. Such an agreement was, however, not reached until a few days before the liberation.

The idea of establishing an underground army in Denmark had not arisen before the Danish armed forces were disarmed in August 1943. In the winter of 1943-44 the home front received a communication from London urging it to set up an army that would be ready for action as of March 1944. Small military groups, which acquired arms by taking them from the Germans or digging up old weapons from various places of concealment, had already begun to form spontaneously by the time this message was received. However, a real underground army could not be established without considerable quantities of weapons. These weapons would have to come from outside the country, but the supply of arms to an underground Danish army was not a high priority for the Allies before the invasion in the west. The Danish resistance army therefore remained a largely paper organization until the summer of 1944. It was led by a Military Committee and divided into seven regions. According to the plans drawn up, the primary task of the Danish underground army, like that of *Milorg* in Norway, was to provide auxiliary and guard troops during the liberation itself. The Danes too had to play a waiting game: they had to move cautiously so that the Germans would not retaliate before the underground army was able to act effectively.

A question discussed at this time was who was to command this secret Danish army—the Danes themselves or the Allies. The matter was clarified in June 1944. SHAEF agreed that the underground army should be subordinate to the Freedom Council until it could be used in hostilities in or near Denmark. Allied headquarters would then take over, and the army would become an auxiliary force for the Allies. Supplies of arms began to arrive from August 1944; they were dropped by plane from Britain or brought into Denmark by fishing boats across the North Sea or from Sweden. At that time the resistance had arms for about 4,000 men; in May 1945 the Danish underground army numbered 43,000 men, and they were fairly well equipped.

The uncertainty about how the occupation would end became an ever more burning issue as the year 1944 neared its end. The Danes feared that the numerous German troops in their country would cause disturbances or even chaos, and in some circles it was also feared that the Communists might attempt a *coup d'état* during the transitional phase. The Norwegians feared that the Germans would fight on in the superb fortress they had turned the country into. A hard struggle and widespread destruction would accompany an invasion of *Festung Norwegen*, if the Germans chose to hold out in Norway after all else was lost. At the end of 1944 the Allies had other matters to think about than conditions in Scandinavia. For anxious Danes and Norwegians, the answer to the question of who should support them in these circumstances was obvious, and in 1945 Sweden came under strong Norwegian and Danish pressure to promise to intervene militarily in the neighboring countries, if necessary. In the meantime, the advancing Allied forces had reached Norwegian soil: in the autumn of 1944 Russian troops entered Finnmark in northern Norway.

Nordkalotten

Nordkalotten roughly includes the area of land north of the Arctic Circle between the Norwegian and White seas, that is to say, the northern parts of Norway, Sweden, and Finland and Murmansk in the Soviet Union. From 1940 to 1944 the greater part of this region was under more or less direct German control. Finnish nickel from Petsamo and Swedish iron ore from Kiruna were of great value to German war production. The Norwegian section of *Nordkalotten* was turned into a part of *Festung Norwegen*, containing large German forces to defend the region against an invasion that never came. A large proportion of the German surface fleet, including the battleship *Tirpitz* and the battle cruiser *Scharnhorst*, was stationed in the fjords of northern Norway. The two warships, along with other naval forces and air units took part in vain attempts to cut off the flow of supplies by sea past North Cape to Murmansk.

From 1941 the Red Army was involved in hostilities with German and Finnish forces in the Soviet part of *Nordkalotten.* As soon as a separate peace between Finland and the Soviet Union, which was the subject of ever more widespread rumors in the spring of 1944, became a possibility, Finland and Norway faced quite similar, though not identical, problems in relation to the two great powers. What would the strong German forces in the far North do in the event of a German defeat or retreat? And what territorial demands might the Soviet Union make in this region?

Under the terms of the cease-fire agreement of 19 September 1944, Finland ceded the Petsamo region to the Soviet Union and undertook to drive out the German troops that still stood undefeated in northern Finland. By this time, the Germans had begun to withdraw their troops, but considerable German forces remained and they retained their control of Petsamo.

The 20th army in Finnish Lappland and Norwegian Finnmark had a single command and constituted a single military unit that straddled the frontier. It was a question of withdrawing these well-equipped and experienced troops in a controlled and orderly manner. The Germans also had to take into account the defense of northern Norway against the Russian advance that was now expected. The Germans still had about 220,000 men north of the demarcation line at Oulu in Finland, when the Finns attacked on 20 September 1944. A struggle followed throughout the winter until April 1945, when the last German soldier crossed the frontier into Norway. The Germans used scorched earth tactics on both sides of the border in order to cover the withdrawal of these retreating forces and to prevent the Red Army from following them. In October the Russians took Petsamo and the Germans withdrew over the Norwegian border, retaining only their fortified positions along the road from Finland to Norway which ran through Kilpisjärvi to Skibotn. The battle for these positions ended on 24 April 1945. With this, the Germans had abandoned their control of Finnish Lappland and of northern Norway as far south as Lyngen fjord, north of Tromsø. They left behind them a virtually uninhabited region: people and animals had been driven out, houses burned, and bridges and roads blown up.

When the Germans began their forcible evacuation of the civilian population of northern Norway and northern Finland, the Nordic countries feared that the consequences would be catastrophic. Winter was approaching, and a mass evacuation in autumn and winter conditions in these northerly regions could easily have ended in tragedy. The Swedes therefore began preparations to receive virtually the whole population of the affected areas. Refugees from Finnish Lappland crossed the frontier on a large scale: about 50,000 people were housed and fed in Sweden for a time. There were astonishingly few refugees from Norway, only about 2,000 people, but those that came were treated well. The frontier in the far North runs largely through a wilderness, and the Swedes organized food depots, air patrols, and groups of volunteers to assist those who had to travel through it under winter conditions. The Germans forcibly evacuated two-thirds of the civilian population of northern Norway (59,000 people), but the evacuation went more smoothly than any had dared to hope and without loss of life.

On 16 May 1944 the three Allied great powers—Britain, the United States, and the Soviet Union—signed an agreement with Norway concerning the relationship between the liberating Allied forces and the Norwegian authorities during the liberation of Norway. It was agreed that Allied control of the country would last only until the Norwegians themselves were able to take over. However, this agreement did nothing to resolve the question of whether Norway should be regarded as belonging to the western or eastern sphere of influence. It certainly seemed that everyone, including the Russians, accepted what the Norwegians themselves considered natural, desirable, and necessary, namely that Norway belonged to the western, and more particularly the British, sphere of influence. However, the current situation in Finland was such that the first Allied soldiers to set foot on liberated Norwegian soil would probably be Russians. Did the Russians accept full Norwegian sovereignty over the whole of Norway or did they have special desires or demands in relation to northern Norway?

Attempts to acquire information, confirmation, or assurances from Moscow proved fruitless. The Soviet occupation of Petsamo, which lay about ten miles from the Norwegian frontier, in October 1944 was the first definite news the Norwegian government received of a Russian offensive in the north. It was on 18 October that Molotov summoned the Norwegian minister in Moscow, assured him that the Soviet Union would give the Norwegians "every assistance and political support and all that is wanted and needed," and told the minister that Russian troops were ready to advance into Norway—and in fact they did so the same day.

The Western great powers were both unable and unwilling to involve themselves in the liberation of Finnmark. They did not have troops or means of transportation to spare, and they did not want a confrontation and possible friction with the Russians in the far North. The only forces that might assist the Russians in this area therefore had to be Norwegian units. The Norwegian authorities in London and Stockholm now began to work intensively to ensure Norwegian participation in the liberation of the first bit of Norwegian soil, though they were unable to provide substantial help since their small forces comprised only the troops in Scotland, which lacked the transportation to take them to Norway, and the police corps in Sweden, which could not be moved to Norway without Swedish consent. However, some troops were sent. On 10 November 1944 the Russians welcomed the first Norwegian unit of 271 men from Scotland, which consisted of an infantry company, a military mission, and some civilian officials, to a liberated Kirkenes. The first units from the police corps did not arrive until after the new year, and altogether only 1,300 men were moved from Sweden to Finnmark, even though the Swedes had agreed in October 1944 that 2-3,000 men from the police corps should be transferred to Norway.

In spite of a certain nervousness in Norwegian circles about Soviet plans in the far North, the winter of 1944-45 passed without complications. Cooperation between the Norwegian and Soviet forces was smooth, the latter choosing to remain within a small area near the frontier and to leave patrolling and guard duties in the deserted wastes of Finnmark to the Norwegians. And when peace finally came, the Norwegians were allowed to retain their old frontier in the north without running into difficulties from the Russians. Finland, however, had been obliged to surrender its territory along the Arctic coast and was now excluded from the Barents Sea, a development which gave Norway a common frontier with the Soviet Union, and the northern parts of Finland and Norway lay uninhabited and desolate after the German retreat.

1945: the Question Remains, Last Stand or Chaos?

From the earliest years of the war the idea that the invasion in the west would take place in Norway had established itself in Hitler's mind. He never changed this view, and to meet this expected invasion Norway had been turned into a veritable fortress, *Festung Norwegen*.

310 □ BERIT NØKLEBY

Troops were certainly withdrawn from Norway during the last year of the war, but they were mainly forces that had been stationed in northern Finland or northern Norway. The rest of *Festung Norwegen* remained fully manned, and in May 1945 there were about 350,000 well-equipped and well-trained German soldiers, with full naval and air support, in Norway.

The Allied forces had their hands full on the continent. The small Allied force that had been set up in Scotland for dispatch to Norway during the liberation phase was drained of British troops who were needed elsewhere. The Norwegian Brigade, which was 4,000 men strong, remained in Scotland and continued to await an opportunity to make a contribution on Norwegian soil. It could now count on the support only of the 13,000 men of the police corps in Sweden and of *Milorg*, which had about 40,000 men and was the only Norwegian force in Norway. Extreme optimism was required to believe that the use of at best 50-60,000 more or less amateur soldiers against 350,000 men in fortified positions could lead to a happy outcome. Allied assistance would ultimately arrive, but what was to happen in the meantime? The German force in Norway was large enough to be able to hold the country for quite a long time, if it chose to fight. Norway might be laid in ruins, and no one could prevent looting or chaos, if German discipline broke down. Moreover, the *Reichskommissar* Terboven was a fanatical Nazi. Would he choose to fight on, would the *Wehrmacht* obey him, and would other Nazi leaders withdraw to the mountain fortress of Norway for a last stand?

Denmark faced similar problems. It was impossible to turn Denmark into a fortress of the kind Norway had become, but 200,000 German soldiers, even though they were not of the same quality as the troops in Norway, were quite enough to lay Denmark in ruins, if they tried. Recent Nazi behavior in Denmark, with the use of terror and violence, did not augur well for the future. Moreover, the many refugees in the country from the disintegrating German *Reich* also raised problems for Denmark. There were disturbing reports that the German high command in Denmark was making preparations to receive up to 2 million refugees. In fact, a total of about 200,000 refugees reached Denmark.

Allied troops were pouring into Germany on all sides. It seemed for a time that Denmark would be cut off from Germany. If that happened, how would the German troops in Denmark behave?

Another possibility was that Russian troops would reach Denmark before Anglo-American forces did. Would Denmark be the scene of a clash between the Red Army and the *Wehrmacht*? There was also anxiety in some Danish circles over how the Danish Communists would act during the transitional phase. Might they exploit their strong position within the resistance movement to attempt a *coup d'état*?

Danes and Norwegians reached the same conclusion: Swedish assistance in the form of military intervention would be the only answer. The Norwegian government presented its request to the Swedish government through official channels. The Danish request could not have the same correct official form, but it was supported by a united front of such Danish leaders as there were: the politicians, the military, and the Freedom Council.

Sweden was faced with a dilemma. On the one hand, the Swedes realized the danger of a catastrophe in the neighboring countries and were not lacking in a desire to help the brother peoples of Denmark and Norway. On the other hand, they wished to preserve Swedish neutrality and to avoid being drawn into the war in its last moments. Since Danish and Norwegian pressure was strong, the question of military intervention became the great problem of Swedish foreign policy during the last months of the war. The Swedish government had considered the possibility of intervention as early as November 1944, and practically all ministers had been averse to the idea. Swedish neutrality had to be preserved. The Danish and Norwegian police corps could, if necessary, be used, but not Swedish troops. This fundamental attitude was not subsequently changed: Sweden stood by its neutrality to the very end but helped the Danes and Norwegians by stretching the limits of neutrality as far as possible.

Some of the assistance was provided at the government level or at any rate with the government's consent. We have already discussed the training of the two police corps. In addition, the government agreed that a certain quantity of Allied arms might pass through Sweden to the Norwegian and Danish resistance movements. Similarly, parts of the Norwegian police corps were allowed to leave Sweden in order to participate in the liberation of Finnmark. Toward the very end of the war the Swedish government even agreed to cooperate with Eisenhower in the transportation of Allied troops across Swedish territory, if the German forces in Norway decided to fight.

However, such examples of Swedish assistance were only the tip of the iceberg. There is much to suggest that the largest and most important part of Swedish military assistance to Denmark and Norway took place unofficially, on a lower level and often between the officials directly concerned. The higher authorities were either not informed or chose to close their eyes. In this unofficial way the Swedes helped the Norwegians transport their couriers safely and quickly between the frontier and Stockholm, exchanged information with the Norwegians and Danes, and assisted the Norwegians in maintaining radio contact with the home front from Swedish territory. The Danes and Norwegians would probably have found it difficult to manage without this kind of Swedish aid.

A good example of this form of unobtrusive assistance was the Norwegian police reserve camp which was turned over to the training of members of *Milorg* in February 1945 with the consent of the Swedish minister for social affairs. The Swedish authorities made no attempt to check the identity of these young men. A couple of thousand men from the Norwegian home front crossed into Sweden, were instructed in sabotage and the use of German and British arms, and sent back to Norway again after their training was completed.

However, Sweden officially maintained its neutrality. The reply to the Danish and Norwegian requests for military intervention therefore had to be a clearly negative one. The Swedish government also refused to mobilize the Swedish armed forces or to take other open military measures to prepare for the possibility of intervention. The Norwegian government was very dissatisfied with this attitude, and there was a sharp exchange of views between the two governments on this question. The Norwegians maintained that the mobilization of the Swedish armed forces might be enough to induce the Germans in Norway to give up, while the Swedes argued that it might provoke the Germans to use harsher methods in Norway and to decide to keep fighting even after a capitulation on the continent. In the course of these somewhat unfriendly exchanges the Swedes indicated that they regarded themselves as better able to assess the situation in Norway than the legal Norwegian government, a remark which the government-in-exile took with very bad grace.

Nonetheless, the Swedish government was more concerned about the situation in Denmark and Norway than these exchanges suggest. When during the last chaotic days of the war Himmler privately inquired about the possibility of Swedish involvement in the capitulation of the German forces in Norway, the Swedes immediately seized on this opportunity to try to secure a peaceful end to the occupation of Norway. They even mentioned the possibility that the German forces in Norway might cross the frontier into Sweden and be interned in that country. However, Himmler did not become Hitler's successor, as he had assumed that he would, and Dönitz, the new *Führer*, had to accept the unalterable demands of the Allies for unconditional surrender on all fronts. There could be no question of a special arrangement for the German forces in Denmark and Norway.

The Capitulation

The last days of the Second World War were a time of extreme tension. One sensation followed the other. Hitler committed suicide. Dönitz succeeded him as *Führer*. Then, on 5 May 1945, the German forces in the Netherlands, northwest Germany, and Denmark capitulated. Denmark was free again.

The question of who would govern Denmark when the liberation occurred had been a subject of discussion between the politicians and the Freedom Council throughout the preceding winter. Agreement was reached on a list of ministers at the last moment—on 1 May 1945. The government was to consist in equal halves of parliamentary politicians and representatives of the resistance movement. At noon on 5 May the king, the new prime minister, Vilhelm Buhl, and a member of the Freedom Council gave speeches from the parliament building. Resistance groups came into the open and occupied power stations and other important installations in order to prevent their destruction by the Germans. However, the German capitulation in Denmark was carried out with the maintenance of good discipline and without great difficulties, except on Bornholm, where the German commander refused to surrender to the Soviet forces that were to occupy the island. The Germans gave up after they were subjected to a bombing attack.

Tension remained high in Norway to the very end, because the German commander-in-chief in the country, General Böhme, had not made it clear whether he would obey orders from Dönitz. On 7 May Dönitz announced Germany's unconditional surrender on all fronts, including Norway. On the same day he dismissed Terboven and transferred his powers to Böhme, who was thus given supreme authority in both the military and civil fields in Norway. Böhme was in command of considerable German forces that were, in his own words, "unde-feated and in possession of their full strength." On 7 May he ordered his troops to be vigilant and to hold their positions. The planned destruction of Norwegian installations was not begun, but nothing, on the other hand, was said about capitulation.

However, on the morning of 8 May Böhme announced that he awaited the arrival of an Allied military mission, and after that events followed the Danish pattern, that is to say they went more smoothly than anyone had dared to hope. The Germans capitulated unconditionally, withdrew to the positions they were ordered to occupy, and disarmed themselves with admirable discipline and precision. *Milorg* was mobilized and occupied important installa-tions. Its members had strict orders to avoid confrontation with the Germans, and there were no difficulties of this kind. *Hjem-mefrontens Ledelse* retained political responsibility until Crown Prince Olav, the supreme commander of all Norwegian forces, and some members of the government reached Norway on 13 May. On the following day *Hjemmefrontens Ledelse* issued a proclamation to the nation, in which it declared that its work was completed.

Danes and Norwegians abroad could now return home, and even-tually they all did. On 6 May the Danish Brigade, which contained about 4,800 men, crossed from Sweden to Denmark. On 11 May the Norwegian police corps entered Norway. Both countries extended a special welcome to people who had been imprisoned in Germany, including many who returned home from Sweden, to which just over 4,000 had been transferred from Germany in April 1945 by a Swed-ish Red Cross expedition under the leadership of Folke Bernadotte. In Norway, the climax was reached on 7 June, when the now enor-mously popular King Haakon VII again set foot on Norwegian soil after being in exile for precisely five years.

Both the Danish and Norwegian authorities still faced the problem of the German troops in their countries. Naturally, they wanted them removed as quickly as possible. The repatriation of those soldiers who were to be sent to the western occupation zones in Germany was easily accomplished and was largely completed by the end of 1945. However, about 40,000 of the troops in Norway, who were to go to the eastern zone, had to wait until the summer of 1946, since the authorities in the Russian zone could not receive them be-fore that. Meanwhile, the last Allied troops left Norway during the summer and autumn of 1945, and the situation began to return to normal. But the cost of war still had to be figured.

Assessing the Cost of War

It is impossible to draw up an exact balance sheet of profit and loss for the Second World War as a whole or for the Nordic countries during these years. Statistics can be interpreted in many ways and figures cannot begin to be a true measure of human suffering. However, the figures on the war do show certain things quite clearly, including the fact that the losses were unevenly distributed.

Finland undoubtedly suffered the most severe losses among the Nordic countries. About 85,000 Finns or approximately 2% of the country's population were lost, including civilians, sailors, and those recorded as missing; more than 90% of those killed were men between the ages of twenty and thirty-nine. In addition, about 50,000 Finns were permanently invalided. Finland lost 11% of its territory, which meant that the 420,000 Finns evacuated from the ceded areas had to be found new homes. Bombing completely or partially destroyed about 4,000 buildings, and in Lappland, which the *Wehrmacht* devastated, 16,500 buildings were destroyed, and 233 railway bridges and 516 road bridges were blown up. The national debt rose from 3.3 billion marks in 1939 to 67.3 billion marks in 1944, and war reparations of $300 million were also imposed on the country.

These were enormous losses for a country of Finland's size, but it is also possible to say that, viewed from a different perspective, the country fared remarkably well during the war. Finland was the first of the Nordic countries to be drawn into the war and also the first to leave it, if the war in Lappland is disregarded. This gave the country certain advantages. During the Winter War of 1939-40, while the western front was still quiet, Finland won a degree of goodwill and admiration in the West which it never entirely lost, even when it later became the only Nordic state to fight "on the wrong side." Moreover, when the cease-fire agreement was signed in the autumn of 1944, Finland was still an independent democracy. The great powers of both the East and the West had more than enough to do on other fronts, and Finland was given a respite in which to order its affairs before any other country could interfere in them.

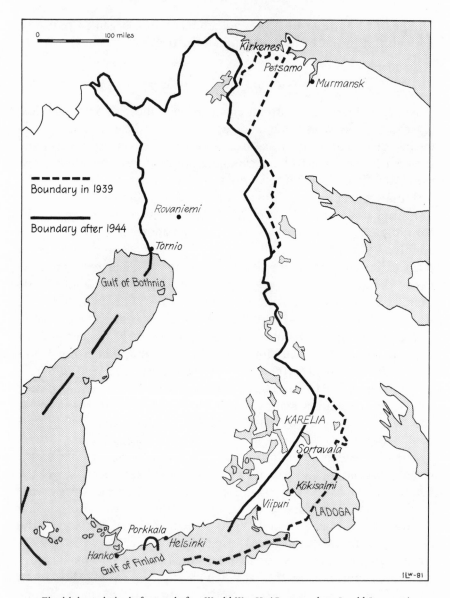

Finnish boundaries before and after World War II. (Cartographer: Ingrid Lowzow)

One unpleasant demand by the victors remained to be dealt with: the question of trying Finnish "war criminals." The Soviet Union was quite unyielding in its demand that those Finnish politicians who were "responsible for the war" should be punished, and this demand had to be met for political reasons, since there was a risk that, if it were not, the Russians would take matters into their own hands. In late 1945 and early 1946 a number of the most prominent politicians of the war years were put on trial. The Russians indicated which individuals were to be prosecuted, but the Finns themselves were responsible for the trials, the verdicts, and the sentences. Mannerheim was not involved, but eight of the nation's other leaders received prison sentences of between two and ten years. The former prime minister and president Risto Ryti was given the most severe sentence: ten years imprisonment.

It is not easy to draw up a balance sheet of profit and loss for Sweden. The country had succeeded in remaining outside the war and as a neutral maintained diplomatic relations with all parties. (On the same day that Germany capitulated, 7 May 1945, the Swedes informed the German minister in Stockholm that German-Swedish diplomatic relations had ceased.) Sweden, or rather the Swedish taxpayer, had had to provide enormous sums for defense during the long years of the war. Nonetheless, the country's military expenditure cannot, of course, be compared with that of Finland, since whereas Finnish soldiers were killed and Finnish planes were shot down, the Swedish armed forces in 1945 were intact and even perhaps too large.

Neutral Sweden with its steel and other products that were in great demand on the European market certainly profited from the war, or at any rate certain circles in Sweden did. However, it is impossible to speak with any certainty about the amount of profit or who made it. It is clear, on the other hand, that the war also placed financial burdens on Sweden, for instance in connection with assistance to the other Nordic countries.

For many victims of the war in neighboring countries Sweden was a safe haven; there were more than 193,000 refugees there in December 1944. Over 80,000 of them were Finns, mostly from Finnish Lappland, and there were also several thousand Finnish children who had been sent to Sweden from 1941 on because of the shortage of food, disease, or the impact of hostilities. About 50,000 Norwegians fled to Sweden during the war, and there were more than 43,000 Norwegian citizens in that country in May 1945. At that time, there were also 18,000 Danes there, of whom about 7,000 were Danish Jews. Other forms of assistance to the other Nordic countries were also costly. This aid consisted, apart from the supply of food, mainly of interest-free credits and loans, partly to cover needs during the war and partly for postwar reconstruction.

As occupied countries, Denmark and Norway had to pay the cost of maintaining the occupying German forces, and the occupation cost money in other ways as well; for example, it had a disruptive effect on the economy. The direct losses can therefore be calculated, though exact figures can hardly be given. The cost of the war was undoubtedly greater for Norway than for Denmark: some 21 billion *kroner* against about 8 billion *kroner.* As a percentage of the national income, the occupation cost Norway about 67% a year and Denmark about 22% a year. Moreover, during the Second World War 706 Norwegian vessels were lost at sea. These ships together constituted 2.3 million gross tons or almost half of Norway's total tonnage in December 1939. Large parts of northern Norway (Finnmark and the county of Troms as far south as Lyngen fjord) were also desolate after the *Wehrmacht's* retreat in the autumn of 1944.

More Norwegians lost their lives than did Danes. A total of 10,262 Norwegians were killed, of whom about 4,000 were seamen and 2,000 from the armed forces (835 during the 1940 campaign and about 1,100 under Allied command, mostly navy and air force). In the Norwegian resistance movement 2,091 people lost their lives, of whom 366 were executed, 162 fell in action of various kinds (this figure does not include the Norwegian campaign of 1940), 130 died in prison in Norway because of torture or from other causes, 1,340 (including 734 Norwegian Jews) did not return home from German concentration camps, and 93 disappeared while attempting to cross the North Sea to Britain. About 700 Norwegians lost their lives fighting on the German side against the Russians. The rest of the Norwegian casualties were civilians: victims of bombing (both German and Allied), passengers on Norwegian vessels sunk on the Norwegian coast, and victims of other accidents or actions of war. (The statistics on lives lost vary from source to source and are partly estimated.) The number of people permanently invalided is not known. The number of Norwegians in German prisons during the war is estimated at between 30,000 and 40,000. The exact figure will never be known, since the German Security Police (Sipo and SD) in Norway managed to burn virtually all their papers.

The Danish resistance struggle cost something like 1,300-1,400 lives; 102 were executed, and more than that number were killed in armed clashes or as a result of torture. Between 500 and 600 people did not return from German concentration camps. More than 100 Danes were killed in the so-called clearing murders, and another

500 or 600 were shot at random, the victims of a pure terror campaign.

Whereas in Finland the politicians "responsible for the war" were tried because of external pressure and to meet what might be called a foreign policy requirement, the postwar trials in both Denmark and Norway were held for reasons of domestic policy. For five long years Danes and Norwegians had carried an ill-concealed hatred of traitors, informers, and executioners, and as a result it was a clear and unavoidable popular demand in both countries after the war that accounts be settled with such "quislings."

The legal proceedings in Norway were very extensive: the behavior of 90,000 Norwegians was investigated. Since the number of people found guilty of criminal offenses before the war was under 4,000 a year, these large-scale investigations were inevitably marked by a shortage of personnel and by improvisation. The wide scope of the legal proceedings instituted has therefore been the most criticized aspect of these events: too much was attempted, with the result that the whole system functioned clumsily.

The legal basis for the trials has also been the subject of discussion in Norway. The prewar legal code allowed the death penalty only in cases of the most blatant offenses against the military criminal code in wartime, but the government-in-exile decreed that the death penalty under the military criminal code should also apply after the war and the death penalty was reintroduced into the civil criminal code (it had been abolished in 1902). Parliament supported these measures by large majorities in 1945 and 1946.

Vidkun Quisling's treachery in the month of April 1940 qualified him for the death penalty under the military penal code, but he was sentenced under the civil criminal code as well. He was put to trial on 20 August 1945 on numerous and serious charges, among them the proclamation of himself as head of government on 9 April 1940; his revocation of the mobilization order; his complicity in the deportation of the Jews; his responsibility for the execution of death sentences; and many other charges, more than enough to qualify him for a death sentence. He was found guilty on almost all counts and sentenced to death. The verdict was upheld by the Supreme Court. On 24 October 1945 he was shot by a firing squad.

The Norwegians were nonetheless restrained in the use of the death penalty: thirty Norwegians and sixteen foreigners (fifteen Germans and one Dane) were condemned to death, and of these sentences, twenty-five and twelve respectively were actually carried out. Of the twenty-five Norwegian citizens who ended their lives before a firing squad, three were "ministers" from the NS government and two of these three, Quisling and Albert Viljam Hagelin, were condemned for criminal as well as political offenses. The remaining twenty-two had all worked in the national police or the German security police. As many as ten of them had belonged to the infamous Rinnan group in Trondheim, whose members were notorious throughout the country as informers, torturers, and murderers.

There were consequently few who shed tears over those executed in Norway. However, both at the time and subsequently there was discussion and criticism of the legal proceedings, which were based on the much-debated judicial principle that membership (including even passive membership) in NS was criminal and that the members of NS were held collectively responsible for the damage their party did to the country. As a result, a number of Norwegians were punished for fairly passive "assistance to the enemy" and quite a few otherwise law-abiding citizens believed that the legal proceedings had been grossly unjust.

About half of the cases against the 90,000 Norwegians who were investigated after the war were dropped for lack of evidence. A total of about 45,000 Norwegian citizens were found guilty of betraying their country in one way or another. About 17,000 were sent to prison; another 20,000 or so were fined; and about 8,000 lost a greater or smaller proportion of their civil rights.

The postwar trials have also been the subject of discussion and criticism in Denmark, and for many of the same reasons as in Norway. There has been particularly sharp criticism of the varying severity of the sentences, a difference which depended on whether the accused was sentenced during the period immediately after the war when public opinion was most inflamed or was fortunate enough to come up for trial after tempers had had time to cool somewhat. But the total number of trials was much smaller in Denmark than in Norway. About 20,000 Danes were investigated, and about 13,000 of them were punished.

The aspect of the Danish legal proceedings that has been criticized the most was the use of retroactive legislation, whereby those who committed offenses that would have been punishable by light sentences under the normal legal code were now given much more severe sentences with retroactive force. This procedure has been defended on the grounds that it accorded with the general sense of justice and that it was needed, given the agitated mood that prevailed at the time, to prevent individuals from taking the law into their own hands. Not only were prison sentences imposed, but the profits made from excessive collaboration with the Germans were also confiscated. This was the case in Norway as well.

Both legislation and the practice of the courts distinguished between the periods before and after August 1943. Actions committed before that date could be excused to some extent because of what, to put it mildly, had been Denmark's peculiar status in international law in relation to the war and to the occupying power. The postwar legal proceedings also had the function, which they performed somewhat awkwardly, of emphasizing the legality of the "illegal" struggle. It was for this reason that there were also strong demands that the investigations include the very top of the political hierarchy. This was done through investigation by a number of parliamentary commissions, which in the following years thoroughly examined the actions of ministers during the war. In no case did their investigations lead to impeachment—it was, after all, members of parliament themselves who dealt with this matter. The most important result for posterity of the work of these commissions was the publication of the documents and statements they received in the course of their investigations.

The legal proceedings after the Second World War can even today be the subject of heated discussions in the Nordic countries, and one of the most important reasons for this is that the very principle of justice imposed by the victors can be debated. It is easier to defend the punishment of directly criminal acts, even if there were some war criminals who escaped trial simply because they wore the right uniform in 1945. However, in Nuremberg, as in Denmark and Norway, not to mention Finland, people were punished for their political views. Should one be punished for one's political convictions if one belongs to the losing side? And how should guilt and responsibility be defined and divided? History can hardly give a "verdict" on these intricate questions. It must suffice to say that those who have argued that the postwar legal proceedings in the Nordic countries were a political necessity, even if for slightly different reasons in each country, are probably right.

Sweden emerged from the Second World War with its neutrality intact. It can be said that Swedish foreign policy during the war had been successful, but also that Sweden had been able to avoid involvement in the great conflict because of both geographical factors and the policies the great powers chose to pursue. This was a piece of good fortune for Sweden, and its neighbors also had every reason to be grateful that there was a neutral country in the middle of the war-torn North. Sweden was important for the other Nordic states as a safe haven for refugees and a source of both open and concealed assistance and support.

Whether the other three Nordic countries also escaped from the ravages of war relatively unscathed is, of course, a question of what countries they are compared with. In terms of lives lost, assets destroyed, and the ravaging of their territories by foreign troops, the Nordic states fared far better than large parts of war-torn Europe. Finland lost more of its citizens than any other Nordic country, but Finland's 2.3% of the population pales in comparison with Germany's 10% or the Soviet Union's 11.6%.

The material damage inflicted on the Nordic countries was certainly considerable: northern Finland and northern Norway had been devastated, and bombing had destroyed a number of Norwegian towns in 1940 and severely damaged some Finnish towns both in the period 1939-40 and in the years 1941-44. However, of the only three belligerent capital cities in Europe that were not occupied, Moscow, London, and Helsinki, the last was the one that suffered the least damage.

The standard of living declined in all the Nordic countries during the war. The situation was the worst in Finland and Norway. There was food rationing in Denmark and its effects were unevenly distributed among the population, but there was no shortage of food in the country. There was such a direct shortage in Finland and Norway, and both depended on imports from Germany, the only available source. In the spring of 1945 all the stocks in Norway were becoming exhausted at a time when there was no possibility of getting fresh supplies from Germany.

If Finland did play a role in the outcome of the great conflict, its contribution was on the German side, even though it maintained that it was fighting its own separate war for national reasons against one of the Allied great powers. Norway and Denmark saw themselves as fighting, formally or informally, on the Allied side. Apart from the Norwegian merchant marine, which was of such a size that it clearly made a positive contribution to the Allied effort, it is difficult to determine how the other Danish and Norwegian efforts should be measured. The importance of resistance movements as "the fourth service" among the armed forces has been extensively discussed in other works and will not be dealt with here. However, it should be remembered that very many, perhaps most, of the leading figures in the Danish and Norwegian resistance movements did not attach primary importance to the specific contribution made to the war effort. They argued at the time that what was significant about the resistance movement was its role within occupied territory, in relation certainly to the occupying power but also especially to the native population. The resistance movement maintained unity and good morale among the civilian population, and it helped many victims of the war. The importance of such activities cannot be measured, but they should not be underrated.

Viewed from this perspective, the contribution of resistance activities to the outcome of the war is not a particularly significant question. Whether sabotage and intelligence work had measurable effects on the Allied war effort; whether the Danish underground army and *Milorg* in Norway were "paper tigers" or could have played a genuine role if the occupation had ended less peacefully —both these issues are less important than the daily efforts made by these and other branches of the resistance to raise Danish and Norwegian morale and preferably also to undermine that of the enemy. The Second World War was won at Stalingrad, in North Africa, Normandy, and the Pacific, but this is a different story. For the Nordic countries the supreme fact was that in 1945, as before the war, there were still four independent democracies in the far northwest corner of Europe.

Winning the Peace:
Vision and Disappointment
in Nordic Security Policy, 1945-49

by Karl Molin

VE day, 8 May 1945, is obviously a watershed in the history of warfare. It is also a turning point in the drive to create a lasting international security system, a drive which began in 1933 with the appearance of Nazism on the international scene and which ended during the spring of 1949, when a new international power structure acquired a durable shape through the formation of the Atlantic alliance and the consolidation of the Soviet bloc. The institutions and principles of collective security and international law had been seriously discredited by the demonstrated ability of a Nazi-ruled state to grow in power without hindrance. Collective agreements binding on all parties had quickly given way to bilateral nonaggression pacts, security guarantees, and treaties of military cooperation. The world had first become divided, and its divisions had then found expression in open hostilities. During the course of the war plans were devised in all camps concerning the future organization of the international community. The outcome of the war meant that some of these plans, like the Nazis' concept of *Neuropa*, were of no further significance, whereas others appeared to be more realistic or at any rate compatible with the general political ideas that the victors had proclaimed as their own.

During the first postwar years, different forms of international organization were debated and tested as the nations of the world tried to achieve a lasting peace. Ultimately, the nations were formally united in an international security organization with a very limited capacity to act, but politically divided into two antagonistic blocs which because of advances in nuclear technology disposed over almost unlimited powers of destruction. Obviously, the small Nordic states had limited opportunities for influencing the general efforts to achieve security, but they still believed that they had an obligation to seek their own security in ways that helped promote international attempts to achieve peace. This task seemed increasingly difficult as the insecurity of the postwar world became more clear and as a third world war appeared more likely.

The following pages represent an attempt to describe how the Nordic countries conceived of their role and their opportunities during this period of adaptation, a period marked by memories of the world war that had just come to an end and by presentiments of a new conflagration. The main emphasis will be on that phenomenon which in retrospect appears to characterize the whole period, namely the belief that the time was now ripe for the political ideology of democratic socialism, which sought to combine collective economic planning and equal distribution of material possessions with the freedom of the individual and democratic rights. Democratic socialists also had their own ideas on security policy, and these ideas will constitute a main theme in this essay. We therefore begin with a brief presentation of the ideas of the democratic socialists on how the peace should be won. This is followed by a survey of the foreign policies of the Nordic countries, viewed from this ideological perspective. The survey is divided into two periods and is sketched against its domestic political background; it ends with an attempt to discover why the Scandinavian countries went their separate ways in the spring of 1949. Defense policy, which is dealt with in a concluding section, is of course allied with foreign policy, but has nonetheless been awarded a section of its own in order to do justice to the special problems presented by this topic. In the case of defense policy too, the objective is to discuss briefly the relationship between ideology and policy.

Historical research into the period covered by this essay has just begun, and our knowledge of even central points is still incomplete. Accordingly, a survey of this kind must be of a preliminary nature and must sometimes content itself with identifying problems rather than solving them.

Goals of the Postwar Period

The Nordic debate about the future shape of society bore many similarities to that conducted in the rest of western Europe. Nordic politicians and publicists received important impulses from abroad, especially from Britain. The so-called Beveridge Report, presented to the British government in the summer of 1942, stimulated concrete discussion about the policy of social reform that should be pursued after the war. Yet perhaps the most important feature of Sir William Beveridge's ideas was that they gave such explicit expression to the widely held belief that the Second World War would be followed by a period of radicalism among the common people. He was convinced that the broad mass of the people would demand sweeping social and economic reforms as reward for the heavy burdens it had borne in the service of the national war effort.

The consequences of such radicalism in the field of foreign policy were not perhaps self-evident, but many thought that traditional social democratic ideals in this area would now be pursued with more vigor. Such notions were encouraged by another central British planning document, the so-called Interim Report, which was presented by the British Labour party in May 1942 under the title "The Old World and the New Society." The Interim Report was written within a traditional socialist framework: War between nations was ultimately caused by the struggles of monopoly capitalism for new markets. Thus the surest way of avoiding new wars lay in a general development in the directions of socialism. The state ought to assume the leading role within the economy, and a policy should be pursued that aimed at full employment, higher living standards, and social and cultural advance.

It is not the intention in this essay to try to deal with all the Scandinavian politicians who, in widely differing circumstances, made plans for the postwar period on the basis of ideas that resembled those in the Interim Report. A significant example, which has been fully researched by scholars, will have to suffice. This example is the group of exiled politicians who worked in Stockholm together with like-minded Swedes within an organization called the *Internationale Gruppe demokratischer Sozialisten.* Its members included not only many leading Swedish Social Democrats but also a number of prominent German and Austrian party members, among them Willy Brandt and Bruno Kreisky. Exiled politicians from Norway and Denmark, who later occupied leading positions in the political life of their own countries, also participated in the work of the group.

It was clear to the members of this "little international," as it was to the British Labour party, that the causes of the war were to be found in the prevailing arrangements concerning the ownership of the means of production. Their vision of a new and more secure world embraced most of the well-known elements present in international efforts toward cooperation during the interwar period: an international organization to safeguard world peace, disarmament, economic cooperation. However, they were convinced at the same time that none of these objectives could be achieved if the ideas of democratic socialism did not gain ground. Private capitalism and imperialism had to be replaced by collective ownership and international solidarity, and the world economy had to be subjected to planning. The increased degree of state control over economic life that had been introduced in most countries during the war had to be preserved, and there should be no return to so-called free capitalistic conditions. State control, through democratic organs, of economic activity should be a fundamental characteristic both of individual countries and of international cooperation.

In the field of security policy the group placed its main hope on the establishment of a new worldwide peace organization to replace the League of Nations. It emphasized that this organization should be strong and possess sufficient authority to settle disputes between states effectively. This new league of nations had to have the power to apply military or economic sanctions against any state that did not abide by its decisions. A critical point in this connection was naturally how this aspiration was to be reconciled with the principle of unrestricted national self-determination, a principle that the group simultaneously and forcefully asserted. For the Scandinavians in the group, this problem raised the familiar question whether it was possible to combine neutrality with international solidarity. The response of the "little international" was that the Scandinavian states ought to cast off neutrality to the extent that the latter was equivalent to isolationism. The wholehearted involvement of all countries was a vital precondition for the success of the new peace organization.

The demand that individual nations should disarm was now, as after the First World War, closely associated with the proposal that a new supranational legal organization should be set up. Disputes between states were to be settled through legal processes, not by force, and defensive military measures could serve only to tempt countries to deviate from this principle. However, these democratic socialists did not make as far-reaching demands as their counterparts had done twenty-five years earlier. The "little international" did not speak of total disarmament but explained that the objective was "a demilitarized world," an objective that was clearly less ambitious than total disarmament but also more diffuse.

Several of the demands expressed by the "little international" also appeared in the concrete work of planning carried out by the authorities and political parties in the Scandinavian countries during the last year of the war. However, they naturally placed the greatest emphasis on problems of domestic policy, and the connection between these problems and international developments was never discussed in any great depth. The social democratic parties of Denmark, Sweden, and Norway all drew up programs for the postwar period, and the major points in all of them may be summarized in the three objectives that the Danish party formulated in the pamphlet "Fremtidens Danmark" (The Denmark of the Future): full employment, social security, and efficiency and democracy in the economic sphere. Concrete proposals for the nationalization of some industries were put forward in all three countries, but at the same time the three social democratic parties moved away from orthodox socialist thinking about nationalization. The aim of the ideology of economic planning which they now formulated was an effective utilization of society's productive resources in the interests of a majority of the people, and nationalization was only one of several means to this end. Industrial democracy, that is to say worker participation in the management of industrial enterprises, was another important instrument for securing this objective that was considered in the course of the debate.

The political ideas that Scandinavian social democracy put forward during the last years of the war were in no way original. In domestic politics they represented a concrete, unifying statement of familiar demands. In the field of foreign policy they evolved out of that belief in the principle of the rule of law in international affairs which had been fundamental to efforts for peace during the interwar period before the Nazi seizure of power. In the situation in which they were now put forward, these ideas constituted a third viewpoint between the ideologies represented by the two dominant great powers. Their objective was an economic order that combined freedom with planning and a social atmosphere that was marked by solidarity instead of competition.

Hoping for International Concord, Summer 1945-Autumn 1947

Cooperation in Domestic Affairs

It was natural to see the end of the war as the catalyst for a period of great upheavals, if, like Sir William Beveridge, one believed that the demand for social justice would now be raised by the broad masses of the people with the irresistible force of a natural phenomenon. Memories from the period following the First World War were rekindled and used as historical proof that the hour of social change had now come. The "little international" speculated about the possibility that the defeat of Nazism in Germany would be followed by a revolution that would deprive the great industrialists, the Junkers, and the generals of the power they had used to sustain Nazism. A democratization would occur in both the political and the economic spheres, and an evolution in the same direction would follow in other countries.

During the first postwar years, developments in the Nordic countries, as in the rest of western Europe, seemed to some degree to confirm these predictions of a new political climate. The advance of the Communist party was one of the most striking features in the domestic politics of these four countries at this time. The four Communist parties acquired a political importance that they had not hitherto experienced. The Communists won 10.3% of the vote in Sweden at the elections held in September 1944, 11.9% in Norway in October 1945, and 12.5% in Denmark in the same month. In Finland, three communistic groupings together received 23.5% of the vote in March 1945. There was no doubt some connection between the electoral successes of Communist parties and a general admiration for the military achievements of the Soviet Union, but in Finland there were naturally enough mixed feelings on this point and the main cause of Communism's advance in that country was instead the simple fact that the party had become legal. In the autumn of 1944 the ban on Communist activities that had been in force since 1930 was rescinded in accordance with the terms of the Soviet-Finnish armistice. In Denmark and Norway the Communists had also greatly strengthened their reputation by their contributions to the resistance movement, and in Sweden they were able to derive certain advantages from their position as the only opposition party.

The Communists had certainly freed themselves from Moscow's formal influence when the Comintern was dissolved in May 1943, but political coordination remained to be accomplished. The European Communist parties now made joint efforts to establish cooperation with other parties on the basis of Popular Fronts. In the Nordic countries they demanded representation in the multiparty coalition governments that were formed after the end of the war. In Finland a four-party coalition took office on 17 March 1945, and the Communists obtained two posts, including, ominously, the ministry of the interior. In Norway a national coalition assumed power on 25 June 1945, and it also contained two Communist ministers (the minister of labor and the assistant minister for social affairs), even though the Communists at that time still had no seats in parliament. A national coalition government was also formed in Denmark, and in this case too the Communists obtained two posts; one became minister of communications and the other minister without portfolio. The new Danish government came into power on 5 May 1945. In Sweden a coalition government (with all major parties represented except the Communists) had been in power since December 1939. By summer 1945 it became evident that this government could not be kept together any longer and that a new one, dominated by the Social Democrats, would be formed. The only conceivable way that the Communists could get into the cabinet then was to enter a two-party coalition with the Social Democrats. This idea was, however, firmly turned down by the Social Democratic Party Executive. The Social Democratic minority government which assumed power on 31 July 1945 was therefore the only Nordic government with no Communist representation.

Communist participation in government was short-lived. In Denmark and Norway it came to an end when the national governments that had been in power during a transitional period after the war resigned on 1 and 7 November 1945 respectively. The Communists remained in office in Finland until July 1948, when the four-party coalition was replaced by a Social Democratic minority government. Nonetheless, the newly acquired standing of the Nordic Communist parties gave them other important advantages. A new interest was afforded to their statements, and they obtained admittance to the inner circles of parliament to a much greater degree than before. Communist members of parliament even received seats on the parliamentary committees for defense and foreign affairs.

The admittance of the Communists into the democratic community also raised the question of the unity of the working class. Attempts were made in the Scandinavian countries to unite the Communist and Social Democratic parties. However, the Social Democrats in Sweden adopted a negative attitude toward such ideas from an early stage. They reacted coldly to the news that the Communists had expressed approval of the Social Democratic postwar program and categorically rejected a Communist invitation to enter into an electoral cartel for the 1944 elections. Danish and Norwegian social democracy adopted a more open attitude: in both countries negotiations were held between the two workers' parties during the summer of 1945 concerning the possibility of amalgamation. It proved possible in both cases to establish a far-reaching degree of agreement on questions relating to party platforms, but when it came to the shape of the new party's organization and the division of authority within it, difficulties arose and the negotiations came to nothing. In Finland discussions took place between the Communists (the SKP) and groups that had left the Social Democratic party, and in October 1944 these negotiations resulted in the formation of the Popular Democratic Union of Finland (the SKDL). The intention was not to create a new party but to establish a link between different parties and organizations of a popular and democratic character. However, the evolution of the SKDL followed other paths than those originally intended. The majority group within the Social Democratic party rejected all association with the new organization, which in consequence developed into a new party dominated by the Communists. Serving as an electoral and parliamentary organization for the SKP became its main task, and the SKDL functioned in this role for the first time during the elections of March 1945.

The new strength of the Communists was not the only sign which suggested that a more radical political climate was being formed. It could also be seen in a more understanding attitude on the part of the nonsocialist parties toward the principal demands of the labor movement. In Norway all the parties represented in parliament, including the Conservatives, agreed on a joint program which included the demand for full employment and for a new organization of the economy. The leader of the Danish Conservative People's party, Christmas Møller, said in an interview in June 1945 that "we have all now become socialists." Møller was exaggerating, but this statement is indicative of a mood that was making itself felt not only in Scandinavia but also in most west European countries.

Not only center parties but also conservatives regarded full employment as a central objective that was even more important than a stable currency. They even seemed inclined to reassess their view of the role of the state within the economy.

If a new political environment was being created in which the opportunities for pursuing a radical policy were better than before, there should also have been good prospects for a foreign policy that actively sought to preserve cooperation among the great powers and in this way to promote a strong supranational organization for the maintenance of peace. However, even if the will was there, the Nordic states had limited opportunities for making such a contribution to world peace. Their scope for action was strongly circumscribed by the strategic conditions evolving in their part of Europe.

Strategic Realities

There could be no doubt as to what was the most important change from the point of view of security policy in the Europe that emerged after the end of the war in May 1945: the Soviet Union had become the dominant great power on the European continent. The traditional great powers of Europe had lost their leading position. A defeated Germany lay in ruins, while Britain and France, though among the victors, had been greatly weakened both economically and militarily. In terms of strength, the United States was now the dominant Western power. The fate of Europe would no longer be determined in Berlin, Paris, or London but in Washington and Moscow.

Some of Europe's smaller states never had to concern themselves with how they might best adapt to the new realities of power, since they had either ceased to exist as independent states (this applied to Estonia, Latvia, and Lithuania) or had been incorporated into the Soviet sphere of influence and could not pursue their own defense and foreign policies (this applied to Poland, Hungary, Romania, and Bulgaria). Austria, which was jointly occupied by the victorious powers until 1955, was also unable to act independently on the international stage. The group of independent small states able to influence the development of their own and the world's affairs had thus been decimated and now included only Switzerland, Portugal, Czechoslovakia, the Benelux countries, and the Nordic states. Within this group, Czechoslovakia and Scandinavia were the only countries whose territory was of central strategic importance, an essential common feature that caused many Scandinavians to follow the fate of Czechoslovakia with special interest.

In the situation that now prevailed in the Baltic area, it was vital for the Nordic states to have a realistic picture of how the Soviet authorities viewed their own country's security problems. During a visit to Moscow in November 1944 a Norwegian trade delegation led by the foreign minister, Trygve Lie, had received a dramatic lesson on this subject. The Norwegians had been summoned, late one night, to a meeting with the Soviet foreign minister, Viacheslav Molotov, who had unfolded a large map on the table and proceeded to demonstrate his country's confined position. Placing his clenched fist over the Dardenelles he had exclaimed, "'We are shut in here!" He had then moved his fist to the Sound between Denmark and Sweden and repeated the phrase. Finally, he had placed his hand on *Nordkalotten* and explained that an opening had existed in this region but that the war had shown that even this passage could be blocked. Molotov assured his guests that the Soviet Union would not allow this to occur in the future.

Such Soviet attitudes indicated to the Nordic countries that they lay within an area that was of critical importance for Russia's communications with the outside world. The Soviet-Finnish armistice had removed Finland from direct contact with Russia's Arctic route to the Atlantic, but it still lay along the Baltic route. Norway, on the other hand, was greatly affected by the importance of the former and Denmark by that of the latter. Sweden was not directly concerned in either of these areas but naturally still lay within the danger zone both in the north and in the south.

Not only was Finland situated along the innermost part of the Baltic passage to the Atlantic, but it also had a long land frontier with Russia. Two strategically important territorial changes were stipulated by the armistice agreement which was dictated by the Russians and signed by the Finns on 19 September 1944: the Petsamo area with its nickel mines and its harbor on the Arctic was ceded to the Soviet Union, and the Porkala peninsula close to Helsinki was leased to the Russians as a naval base for fifty years. The armistice regulation limiting the Finnish armed forces to their peacetime size and the one ending the ban on the Finnish Communist party also had implications for national security. Important too was Finland's economic obligation to pay the Soviet Union reparations of $300 billion within six years.

During the negotiations for the conclusion of a definitive peace treaty, the Finns sought to secure a mitigation of the Russian terms, especially with respect to the size of the indemnity. However, the treaty that was signed in Paris on 10 February 1947 in the main confirmed the conditions imposed in the armistice and also defined them more precisely, for example by setting maximum figures for the Finnish armed services.

The period after the conclusion of the armistice brought a number of difficult problems for Finland. In the short term the fulfillment of the Finnish promise to drive any remaining German troops from their territory was the undertaking that demanded the most sacrifices, but in the longer term the main political task of the nation was clearly the delicate management of its relations with the Soviet Union. It was a question not only of honoring contractual obligations but also of building up a new atmosphere in Finnish-Soviet relations.

Those Finns who worked for greater mutual understanding between the two countries had to contend with deep-seated anti-Russian sentiments in Finland. According to a much quoted slogan of the interwar years Finnish patriotism consisted of two indivisible elements: love of Finland and hatred of Russia. Such attitudes were perhaps rooted in that view of Russia as the archenemy of the nation, which Finland had absorbed during its time as a Swedish province. They had, however, certainly also been stimulated by more recent events, like the russification campaign that Tsarist Russia had begun in 1899 to reduce the legal rights of the Grand Duchy of Finland and, of course, the war of 1918, which was regarded by the victorious Whites as an attempt by the Russian Bolsheviks to destroy Finland's newly acquired independence. White Finland had very much shared the hostility toward the new Russian regime that prevailed in bourgeois Europe and had understood and accepted with pride the role of the West's outpost against the East and civilization's sentry against barbarism.

However, Finnish history also contained examples of another approach toward Russia. The combination of nationalist self-consciousness and strict adherence to juridical principles was replaced by an attitude that acknowledged Russia's strategic needs and that gave due consideration to the realities of high politics. One of those who had already evolved such an attitude during the struggles to preserve Finnish autonomy around the turn of the century was the jurist and economist J. K. Paasikivi. It was, to be sure, Marshal

Mannerheim who began the reorientation of Finland's policy toward Russia after his assumption of the presidency on 5 August 1944, and it has often been emphasized that his personal authority was a necessary precondition for the successful execution of the first, difficult phase of the new course. It was nonetheless Paasikivi, first as prime minister and then after March 1946 as president, who carried the task to its conclusion. Under his leadership the policy of seeking to create confidence in Russo-Finnish relations was transformed from the view of a minority that was often despised and sometimes branded as treasonous to the central tenet of foreign policy espoused by all shades of opinion.

The third of the passages linking Russia with the outside world which Molotov had pointed to with his clenched fist was that which passed over the northernmost part of Scandinavia. After the frontier changes of 1944 Norway was the only Nordic country with territory on the Arctic coast, and this proved a decisive consideration for postwar Norwegian policy.

The Soviet-Finnish armistice of September 1944 created a new task for the Soviet Union in Allied military operations: the liberation of northern Norway. The Norwegian government had foreseen such a development with a certain anxiety ever since the end of 1943, when a separate Finno-Russian peace had for the first time begun to seem possible. The Norwegian government had then sought to secure the involvement of Anglo-American forces in the operations, and when this attempt failed, it had turned to the Russians in order to seek an agreement providing for Norwegian participation in them.

The Russian response to this Norwegian approach was positive, but was delayed until 18 October 1944, the day on which the first Russian units crossed the Norwegian frontier. The Norwegian contingent that was hastily assembled had to be limited to 271 men because the ships available could not carry more than that number of passengers. Norwegian participation in the operations to liberate northern Norway consequently could be of no more than symbolic importance, but this did not lead to any disturbing Soviet initiatives. The Russian troops did not pursue the fleeing German forces, which were devastating the countryside as they retreated, but halted about sixty-five miles west of the frontier and took up defensive positions. The greater part of Finnmark and half of Troms province, an area as large as Belgium and Holland (or West Virginia), became militarily a no-man's-land.

The Russians had already given the impression that they regarded Norway as a part of the Western powers' sphere of influence during the spring of 1944, when the Allied great powers and the Norwegian government had discussed the regulations for the civil administration of liberated Norway, and this impression was fortified by their conduct during the operations in northern Norway. However, it would soon become clear that there was another area in which Norwegian and Soviet interests collided. This area was Svalbard.

The juridical position of the Svalbard islands had been regulated in 1920 by a treaty that afforded Norway sovereignty over the area but which obliged Norway to maintain its neutrality. In 1924 the Soviet Union subscribed to the treaty, which also covered Bear Island. However, Lie learned during his nocturnal conversation in Moscow in November 1944 that Molotov now wanted to revise the treaty, so that Bear Island passed to Russia and Svalbard became a Soviet-Norwegian condominium. The Norwegians had insisted that the islands were Norwegian but did enter into preliminary discussions concerning cooperation in the military field. On 9 April 1945 the two sides agreed on a secret declaration, in which Norway stated that it was prepared to accept a militarization of the islands provided that the other signatories to the treaty consented. The Norwegian government conceded that the defense of the islands was a joint Norwegian-Russian interest and declared itself willing to enter into an agreement by which the two countries would participate on an equal basis in establishing military installations there. These installations would constitute a part of a security system established by a universal international organization for the preservation of peace.

After this agreement the Svalbard question lay dormant until the peace conference began in Paris in August 1946. Until that time the Norwegian government chose deliberately to conduct the negotiations with the greatest possible discretion so that the Soviet position should not become inflexible for reasons of prestige. Britain and the United States were certainly told in July 1945 that the question might arise during the impending great-power negotiations in Potsdam, but other signatories of the 1920 treaty, such as Sweden and Denmark, were not informed. The Norwegian parliament was only told behind closed doors, and no information at all was given to the mass media. The government succeeded in maintaining secrecy because of the discretion of those who had been initiated and the loyalty of the press, which did not exploit those leaks that did occur.

The American ambassador in Oslo noticed the Norwegian attitude and reported home that a remarkable reticence prevailed. His explanation was that fear had caused the Norwegians, who were uncommunicative even under normal circumstances, to become quite mute.

In the autumn of 1946, after fifteen months of silence, the Russians again raised the Svalbard question. The new Norwegian foreign minister, Halvard Lange, continued, in conversation with Molotov, to follow the evasive and discreet line that had been pursued until then. All the signatories except Italy and Japan were now informed, but the full Norwegian parliament was not; only its foreign affairs committee was told of what was happening.

However, the policy of discretion was ruined on 10 January 1947 by an article in *The London Times*, which gave a fairly correct account of the Russian demands and the consequent negotiations. The Norwegian Foreign Ministry now confirmed in as undramatic terms as possible that negotiations were in progress, and after a *communiqué* had appeared in *Tass* setting forth the Russian viewpoint the Norwegian government declared that parliament would now have to take a stand on this question.

The proceedings in parliament concerning this matter remained secret until 15 February, when the public learned that all parties except the Communists had accepted a government recommendation to the effect that all bilateral defense measures on the islands should be rejected but that discussions concerning nonmilitary cooperation might continue. Military installations on the islands would be approved only if more states than Norway and the Soviet Union were involved. From the political point of view, the central element in parliament's decision was that it ruled out not only military cooperation with the Soviet Union but any form of bilateral cooperation. This amounted, in effect, to a Norwegian guarantee that Norway would not agree to the establishment of a base in the area by the Western powers, and it clearly satisfied the fundamental Soviet interest in the matter. There were no further discussions of this question.

Not only did the lack of clear boundaries between the operational areas of the Allied countries cause uncertainty and anxiety in Norway, it also presented an acute problem for Danish foreign policy during the last year of the war. Moreover, Denmark had good reason to be anxious about Soviet intervention, since the relations between the two countries were fairly complicated. In October 1945 the

Danish foreign minister, Christmas Møller, declared that "Russia is the country where we are worst placed." The origins of this tense situation are not hard to find: they lay in the policy followed by Denmark after the German attack on Russia in midsummer 1941. Denmark had broken off diplomatic relations with Moscow in July 1941 and had met German demands for Danish adherence to the Anti-Comintern Pact. However, since the Danish government's break with the German occupation authorities on 29 August 1943, the reestablishment of satisfactory relations with the Soviet Union had been a major objective of Danish policy.

A channel for Russo-Danish communications had been opened in April 1944, when the Danish Freedom Council was permitted to station a representative in Moscow. However, the Russians had not agreed to recognize this envoy as the representative of the Danish government as well, and in July 1944, when the Western powers issued a declaration stating that Denmark was not fighting on the Allied side, Moscow had refused to append its signature. A request for Allied status, made jointly by the Freedom Council and the government in January 1945, was also rejected. Moreover, the Danish representative in Moscow had been informed a month before that it should not be taken for granted that Denmark belonged to the Anglo-American area of operations and that it should be realized that the Soviet Union now dominated the Baltic.

Uncertainty about what Denmark might expect from the Russians was consequently great, and it was increased by the absence of clear lines of demarcation between the operational areas of the Allies in northern Europe. It was evident by the spring of 1945 that the fate of Denmark would be decided by the course of military developments in northern Germany. The power that reached Lübeck first would also liberate Denmark. In a letter to his foreign secretary Anthony Eden on 19 April, Winston Churchill emphasized how important it was that Lübeck be occupied by the Western powers first. "Denmark," he wrote, "is a country to be liberated and to have its sovereignty restored." The question was resolved on 2 May when British troops captured Lübeck.

However, even though the Western powers liberated Jutland and the major Danish islands, a part of Denmark's territory, the island of Bornholm, was drawn into the Russian zone of operations. The Red Army had already reached the line of the Oder at the end of January and the beginning of February, and in so doing it brought

Bornholm, which lay directly north of the mouth of this river, into the Soviet operational sphere. Russian troops landed on Bornholm on 9 May. One of their first statements to the Danish authorities on the island was that they would leave Bornholm at the same time the last German did. The Germans were all gone four days later, but the Russians stayed for more than ten months.

Like the Norwegians, the Danes adopted a cautious and discreet attitude in their relations with the Soviet Union. In keeping with this attitude, the Danish government on 4 June introduced a partial press censorship, which stipulated that all articles about the Soviet presence on Bornholm should be examined by the Press Office of the Foreign Ministry before publication. In addition, the Danish government attempted to convince Moscow that its desire for independence was directed against the West as well as against the East. It was clear in the question of Bornholm (as it was in that of Svalbard) that the Russians would relinquish their position only if this would not cause them to lose ground to the Western powers. Danish foreign policy adapted itself to this strategic reality. On 18 September 1945 Foreign Minister Møller declared that Denmark, like the other Nordic countries, now had to conduct its foreign policy within the framework of the United Nations and to maintain good relations with both the East and the West. This attitude was confirmed after the elections in October by the new foreign minister, Gustav Rasmussen. Another feature of these efforts was the statement, which was repeated on a number of occasions, that the Danish armed forces were now capable of defending all parts of the country by themselves. In the course of 1946 the number of British troops in Denmark was reduced to about one hundred men.

A Russian note to the Danish government in April 1946, which announced that Soviet forces would be withdrawn from Bornholm, implicitly confirmed that such attitudes accorded well with Soviet interests. It was explained in the note that the Russian withdrawal was contingent upon the Danish government immediately sending its own troops to Bornholm and establishing a purely Danish administration, in which there was no foreign participation whatsoever.

It might seem probable that Sweden's policy during the war, just like Denmark's, would have created strained relations with the Soviet Union. During the Winter War of 1939-40 Sweden had not, to be sure, sent regular troops to help Finland, but had in all other respects done practically everything to support the Soviet Union's opponent. During the Barbarossa campaign Sweden had given practical assistance to the Germans by allowing them to transport troops on Swedish railways. The circumstance that Sweden, despite these hostile acts, could enjoy a fairly untroubled relationship with Moscow, whereas Denmark had to overcome a barrier of mistrust, may be seen as a reflection of the different positions the two countries occupied in the Soviet Union's Baltic strategy. Sweden's territory was less important than Denmark's for Russia's passage to the Atlantic, and Sweden was also more independent of the Western powers than were its neighbors.

However, the absence of any sharp conflict in official Soviet-Swedish relations never caused pro-Soviet sentiments to spread to political groups that lay at all far to the right of the Communist party. There was a traditional fear of Russia in Sweden, a fear that still played an important role in shaping attitudes toward the problems of Swedish security policy. In April 1944, 45% of the Swedes interviewed in a Gallup survey believed that the Soviet Union would not rest content with the frontiers of 1941 and intended to conquer a large part of Europe; only 25% thought the Russians would be satisfied with their existing borders. This poll was taken at a time when widespread admiration for Russian military achievements probably caused Swedish opinion to be unusually well disposed toward the Soviet Union. The general attitude toward Russia was perhaps often more positive in political circles, but public opinion made it necessary to limit displays of friendliness toward the Soviet Union.

Sweden was never subjected to the dramatic strains in the field of security policy that its Nordic neighbors experienced, but on two occasions relations with the Soviet Union came to occupy a central position in the political debate. These two cases are well-known events in modern Swedish history: the repatriation of refugees from the three Baltic states who were interned in Sweden; and the conclusion of a bilateral agreement with Moscow concerning the granting of export credits.

The Baltic refugees had fought in the German armed forces and had fled to Sweden during the last stages of the war. In June 1945 the Swedish government decided in response to Soviet representations that the refugees should be handed over to the Soviet authorities which now controlled their countries of origin. In the autumn of

1945, when the time came for the execution of this decision, it was widely maintained in the Swedish press that the refugees were regarded as traitors by the Russians and that an unspeakable fate awaited them once they were in Soviet hands. An intensive campaign flared up against the decision, and it was stimulated by reports of hunger strikes and self-mutilation among the desperate refugees. The government nonetheless carried out its decision, justifying its action with the argument that the Soviet Union ought to be regarded as a state where the rule of law prevailed as in other countries and that in Russia, as elsewhere, it was possible for such humanitarian considerations as might be appropriate to make themselves felt. It was quite clear that there was little understanding among formative elements in Swedish public opinion for this picture of the Soviet Union as a state that in any Western sense was humane and guided by the principles of law and there was great hesitation even within the government. In December the foreign minister proposed that the existing decision should be rescinded, and, when a majority within the government still maintained that it should be carried out; three of its members insisted on formally recording their dissent in the official protocol of the discussion. In the last resort the decisive consideration for the government was its aspiration to maintain normal and amicable relations with the state that was undisputably the dominant power in the Baltic region. The same aspiration also colored its deliberations about Swedish exports to the Soviet Union.

During the last two years of the war the Soviets had displayed interest in buying large quantities of Swedish exports on credit. For primarily economic reasons, the Swedish government had considered these feelers in a favorable light. In Sweden, as in the rest of the Western world, many people believed that the first postwar years would be marked by an international slump and that the Swedish export industries would consequently experience difficulties in selling their products abroad. This was still the prevailing view when a concrete Soviet proposal was presented in June 1945. In these circumstances, it had been possible to achieve a high level of agreement in Sweden that the proposal, whose main feature was the granting of credits by the Swedish state to the tune of 200 billion *kronor* a year for five years, could profitably be accepted. However, the situation had changed by March 1946, when the time came for the conclusion of a final agreement. Western markets

were absorbing greater quantities of Swedish exports than had ever
been expected, and representatives of Swedish industry now explained
that they lacked the productive capacity required to provide the
proposed deliveries and that they did not regard it as economically
sound to develop it. It was at this point that political considerations
entered into the picture. In reply to demands from the nonsocialist
parties that the amount of the credits be reduced, the Social Democratic government argued that the diplomatic repercussions of a
change in policy had to be avoided. Foreign observers, like nonsocialist opinion in Sweden, thought that such reasoning confirmed suspicions that the government was weak and that the conclusion of a
disadvantageous commercial treaty demonstrated that fear and sub-
servience were the cornerstones of Swedish policy toward Russia.
The Swedish foreign minister argued, on the other hand, that an expansion of trade was an important element in efforts to achieve
peaceful and stable relations between different countries: if economic contacts could not be made to work, political relations would
also be spoiled.

Visions of an international order grounded in law instead of power
were based on a belief in the possibility of change even with regard
to fundamental features of the political systems on both the national
and international levels. True to this basic idea, democratic socialists
had manifested their faith in the possibility of internal changes in
both the superpowers. They hoped for a development toward economic democracy in the United States, but above all that political
democracy and civil rights would be given a chance in the totalitarian Soviet Union. The cooperative attitude toward Russia shown
by all the Nordic countries can be viewed in this light and may then
be seen as an attempt to encourage an evolution toward a world
united by a greater community of values. However, this policy also
involved no sacrifices whatsoever in the area of national security
policy: the requirements of vision and self-preservation were in
accord, and both demanded cooperation and the peaceful resolution
of all disputes.

Relations between the Soviet Union and the Nordic countries followed the pattern whereby a great power acts and a small state reacts.
These four small states found no scope for initiatives of their own,
only for cautious, closely considered responses to the initiatives of
others. However, the more ambitious politicians in the smaller countries did not perhaps need to feel discouraged: traditionally, they

had accomplished the most not in the area of bilateral relations but in that of international organizations.

The New Peace Organization

Those who hoped for an international order grounded in law naturally regarded plans for the reestablishment of a universal peace organization as a matter of overriding importance. The discussions of this question that were conducted in the Allied camp were also followed with great interest in the Nordic countries. However, the new organization was conceived of as a continuation of the wartime Grand Alliance, and in consequence Norway was for a long time the only Nordic state that had cause to evolve an official position on this matter.

It was the government-in-exile in London that made the first authoritative Norwegian pronouncements concerning the plans for a new organization. It declared, in a statement in May 1942 on "the guiding principles of Norwegian foreign policy," that a universal peace organization would certainly be a desirable solution but that, at least to begin with, it probably could not be given the strength that was required if it was to safeguard peace. Norway ought therefore in the first instance to seek its security in regional agreements until an effective, universal organization had been created. However, from the second half of 1942 the government-in-exile evinced an increasing interest in a universalist solution to Norway's security problems. This shift was clearly due in part to a realization by the Norwegians that the plans for a new peace organization were seriously meant, but a growing awareness that the Soviet Union would occupy a leading role in the postwar world was also a factor. It seemed necessary to establish as broad a basis as possible for contact with the new superpower, and a new organization of states seemed a suitable means of achieving this objective. Work within the new general peace organization was accordingly placed at the center of Norwegian policy in a new statement in January 1944, while regional agreements were reduced to subordinate measures of a complementary nature.

At this point, some Norwegian politicians also began to hope that a small country like Norway, which enjoyed good relations with both the East and the West, might be able to help strengthen cooperation between the great powers. However, in the concluding discussions concerning the establishment of a new international organization the Norwegians had a limited role: they gave their passive assent to the decisions of the great powers and participated in the San Francisco Conference as one of the fifty-one founding members of the United Nations.

The Danish government also thought that it was natural to have a positive attitude toward the plans for such an organization, but as long as Denmark was not recognized as an ally, it had no opportunity for influencing developments in this area. The question of Denmark's admission to the alliance was raised again in August 1945 during the San Francisco Conference. This time the Russians agreed to it, and a Danish delegation was therefore able to join the negotiations in September. In consequence, Denmark also became a founding member of the United Nations. The belief in the possibilities for mediation and conciliation which would be open to a small state played an important role in the Danish debate about the United Nations, as it did in the case of Norway.

Sweden was not able to participate in the creation of the United Nations and had to await an invitation to join once everything was decided. There was no doubt that Sweden's response would be positive, but Swedish attitudes toward the new peace organization were, at least in the beginning, by no means unambiguous.

Christian Günther, the foreign minister in the wartime national government, regarded the exclusion of nonallied states from the San Francisco Conference as an ominous sign. As perhaps the foremost representative of a foreign policy that had been based on neutrality, he now protested, albeit in veiled terms, against the discrimination to which states that had been on the wrong side or on no side at all in the great conflict were being subjected. He declared during a speech in the summer of 1945 that the problem of which states should participate in the conference had been solved purely with reference to "rather ephemeral circumstances in the prevailing political situation." Consideration ought instead to have been given to the willingness and ability of different nations to promote what was after all the high purpose of the conference: the safeguarding of world peace. The unspoken inference was, of course, that if this had been done then Sweden, a country that had been more successful in preserving peace than most others, would never have been placed in the second rank. However, Günther's irritation did not prevent him from emphasizing that active participation in the new organization would be a self-evident and important component of Swedish foreign policy in the future. This attitude was also shared by Günther's successor, Östen Undén, and Sweden's response was affirmative when, in the autumn of 1946, it received an invitation to join the United Nations.

Finland's admission to the United Nations was delayed. The Finnish government applied for membership shortly after the ratification of the peace treaty with the Soviet Union in Paris in 1947, but since the great powers could not agree on whether Finland should be admitted, it had to resign itself to a long wait. It was not until 1955 that Finland, without any great enthusiasm, joined the United Nations, which by that time was severely shaken by disputes between the great powers.

When the Nordic countries had considered joining the League of Nations at the beginning of the 1920s, the question of whether membership was compatible with neutrality had caused considerable bewilderment. The conflict between solidarity and neutrality had never been resolved and had remained an unclear point in the Nordic states' involvement in the League until the very end. However, neutrality was not a problem in the same sense when the United Nations was established. Certain conflicts of principle might occur at times, but in most cases they constituted no more than gentle collisions in a semantic haze. In practice, there was general agreement that the Nordic countries could not evade a certain measure of involvement, even in the military field, in the interests of international peace. There were, however, limits to the commitments that the Nordic states were prepared to make. If the great powers had not obtained a veto within the Security Council, membership in the United Nations would have carried with it the risk of involvement in military operations directed against one of the great powers. In such circumstances, unity among the Nordic countries could hardly have been maintained, and the internal debates about membership would surely have been considerably more heated than they were.

Up to the summer of 1947 the governments of the Nordic countries still found it possible to combine the idea of an international order grounded in law with the pursuit of short-term security interests. Caution and impartiality in bilateral relations and general support for efforts to create a multilateral international organization could be defended as serving both global concord and national security. Diverging aspirations could be combined within the same policy.

However, it must also be emphasized that there were probably only a few of the politicians of the day who saw the foreign policy of their country as a part of a consciously formed long-term plan. For most of them this was a period when foreign policy was marked by waiting and hesitation and when tasks in the field of domestic policy seemed of dominant importance. When relations between the great powers clearly became hostile, this state of relative indifference came to an end. The difficult task of trying to achieve and reconcile the dual objectives of counteracting the tendency of states to form themselves into blocs and of safeguarding one's own security now became an acute problem of central importance to the national interest.

Adapting to a Bipolar World, Summer 1947-Spring 1949

The Domestic Political Scene

In the years 1947-49, the general tendency in the domestic politics of the four Nordic countries was for differences between the political parties to become more acute and for the boundary dividing the socialist and the nonsocialist blocs to become more sharply delineated. However, before this happened the broadly based consensus of the first postwar years in favor of a pragmatic view of the state's role within the economy led to one interesting and important result: the planned reconstruction of the Norwegian economy.

Norway's economic problems at the end of the war had been overwhelming. Central branches of the economy had lost substantial parts of their real capital: 67.9% in whaling and 56.7% and 42.6% in shipping and fishing respectively. The losses within industry and agriculture were also considerable. The northernmost parts of the country had been completely devastated. The standard of living had declined.

The Norwegian economy recovered from this critical situation with astonishing rapidity. Factories and ships were repaired or replaced, and industry and trade were soon working at prewar capacity. The standard of living rose more quickly than anyone had expected. At the same time, the value of money did not fall, a circumstance that gave Norway a special position in the Western world, which generally suffered from inflation during this period. Moreover, differences in the standard of living of various social groups were reduced somewhat in Norway. These results seemed successful and impressive by most standards of comparison and were achieved within the framework of consistent economic planning. Political institutions determined the division between investment and consumption, controlled the level of incomes and prices, and promoted changes in the patterns of production and the establishment of new concerns. Private economic activity was constrained by precise regulations, but no considerable extension of state ownership occurred.

The Norwegian experience undeniably threw new light on the opportunities offered and the problems raised by economic planning. It showed that the latter could be an effective means of achieving rapid economic rehabilitation without restrictions in democratic freedoms and rights, without confiscation of private property, and without an excessively disturbing increase in the size of the state bureaucracy. It also provided examples of the difficulties and risks involved. The central authorities, who were reponsible for the direction of industry, were confronted with a number of severe problems when it came to setting priorities. In particular, how were acceptable criteria to be found for the division of resources among different branches of the economy and different companies? An overall solution to this problem was never achieved, and it often seemed as if decisions were governed by routine. It was clear in other cases that the authorities lacked the knowledge and skill in coordination which were required if their priorities were to be enforced. Capital and labor were used to some extent by branches of industry that were regarded as fairly unprofitable by the state authorities. The establishment of this so-called ashtray industry was one of the problems of economic policy during the reconstruction period.

However, it was not concrete problems of this kind which were at the center of that domestic political debate concerning state regulation of the economy which eventually developed but rather the traditional questions that had always figured in arguments about the role of the state in the economy. In the autumn of 1946, the Norwegian Conservative party (*Høvre*) gave a forewarning of what was to come: the party's parliamentary group demanded that the development toward state direction of the economy be stopped, the restrictions on economic activity abolished, and the state administration simplified. A violent political debate ensued during the following two years. The nonsocialist parties tried to cast doubt on the intentions of the Labor party in economic policy. They asserted that it wished to retain the present detailed regulations because it saw them as desirable in themselves, and argued that if Labor's policy were carried out, the country would be led into a doctrinaire system of state socialism leaving no scope for individual freedom.

Politicians and publicists in the other Nordic countries likewise soon reverted to the conflicts habitual in the interwar period. Such divisions were already apparent in Denmark during the campaign leading up to the election of October 1945. In this campaign, the Radical Liberals (*Radikale Venstre*) were particularly insistent that the change of leadership which was in progress within social democracy, represented by the emergence of a new generation at the head of the party, had important and disturbing political implications. They maintained that the Social Democrats wished to make permanent the extraordinary measures of the war years in order to create an economy directed by the state. Two years later, when the parties were again preparing for an election, this argument was a main theme in the representations of the nonsocialist parties. In Sweden an energetic campaign against economic planning, which reached its height during the election of 1948, was organized under the leadership of the Liberal party (*Folkpartiet*). As in the other Nordic countries, the Social Democrats were accused of aiming at a system of state socialism, almost on Soviet lines. In Finland political debate revolved around the question of social reform rather than the structure of the economy. Finnish conservatives now directed an ever stronger criticism at those radical forces that had imposed on the state increased expenditures for social services. This practice, they argued, was perhaps commendable in itself but could not be accepted under the prevailing economic conditions. The political conflict over the issue of exercising restraint in public spending soon became vehement.

Domestic political disputes thus became more severe in keeping with the harsher international climate that was evolving. The sharp clashes between the two blocs of parties soon eroded the memory of the unity of the war years and the early postwar period. The two sides were evenly balanced in electoral support. In the Danish election of 1947 the two socialist parties together received 46.8% of the vote and the three nonsocialist parties 46.9%. The corresponding figures in Sweden in 1948 were 52.4% against 47.5%, and in Norway in 1949 51.5% against 47.9%. In the Finnish election of 1948, the Social Democrats and Communists together obtained 46.2% of the votes and the four nonsocialist parties 42.9%, but it should be pointed out that in Finland the tendency for blocs of parties to form was counteracted by inner conflicts within the two camps.

A return to normal prewar conditions also occurred inside the socialist bloc, in the sense that the Communists again ceased to aspire seriously to the role of the leading workers' party. The electoral support the Communists had won immediately after the war did not prove durable. Their first setback came in the Danish election of October 1947, in which they received 6.8% of the votes, only about half of the total obtained two years earlier. It is noteworthy that this decline in Communist support preceded the coup in Prague in February 1948. In the autumn following the coup, elections were held in Sweden and Finland. The Swedish Communists suffered the same experience as their Danish comrades: they obtained just over 6% of the vote instead of just over 10% as in 1944. The Finnish party had labored during the period 1944-48 under the further disadvantage, above and beyond those it shared with its Scandinavian counterparts, of being suspected of planning a coup, rumors to this effect being especially rife around Easter 1948. Nonetheless, although there was a decline in electoral support, it was relatively modest: the Communists received 20% of the votes instead of the 23.5% they had won in 1945. Finally, Norway followed the Danish and Swedish pattern in the election of 1949: the Communist vote was halved and fell to just under 6%. Even if many of the votes lost by the Communists passed to the Social Democrats, the loss of votes still contributed to undermining the impression that the political tide was flowing toward the left. The pressure to adopt more radical positions, which even nonsocialist politicians appear to have felt immediately after the war, now declined.

It is difficult to describe precisely the connection between this return to normalcy on the domestic scene and the choices the Nordic countries made in the field of security policy. However, there can hardly be any doubt that the change in the internal climate weakened the global ambitions that had been entertained by the makers of foreign policy just after the war. The failure to achieve any lasting unity in domestic affairs either ideologically or in the realm of practical politics must have undermined faith in the possibility of global understanding.

The Marshall Plan

The events surrounding the institution of the Marshall Plan in the summer of 1947 furnished even more evidence that international understanding was impossible. President Truman's address to Congress on 12 March 1947, announcing his intention of giving economic support to the Greek government, had been quite generally interpreted in the Nordic countries as the beginning of a new American foreign policy with global anticommunist ambitions. Conservatives and Communists had agreed that the disputes of the superpowers had now gone so far that a division of the world into two antagonistic blocs could not be avoided. The governing Social Democrats and the Liberals had chosen a cautious and balanced approach: they did not blame exclusively one side or the other for the conflicts that had arisen, and continued to proclaim their hope that the smaller states would be able to play a mediating role. At the same time, even they had to acknowledge that the trend toward the formation of blocs had accelerated and that the United Nations' mission of preserving peace had been made considerably more difficult. Nonetheless, the foreign policy of the Nordic countries had remained unchanged.

During the summer of 1947, the European states discussed their reaction to the offer of economic assistance contained in the Marshall Plan. But preliminary discussions in Paris between Britain, France, and the Soviet Union had been broken off on 2 July after the Russians found themselves isolated in their demand that countries receiving Marshall aid undertake not to enter into any cooperation with the United States over and above that involved in providing Washington with lists setting out their needs with respect to credits and commodities. After the collapse of these discussions it was clearly quite possible that the Marshall Plan would develop into a project based on cooperation among the Western powers and that this would have important political implications.

It was by no means self-evident that the Nordic countries, faced with the prospect that the plan would become the basis for the formation of a political bloc, would accept the invitation they received to participate in further exchanges concerning the plan. However, after discussing the matter among themselves the three Scandinavian countries accepted, whereas Finland declined to take part in view of the Soviet attitude.

The decision of the three Scandinavian states might well be interpreted as an acknowledgment of the strong feeling in their countries that they were politically and culturally closest to western Europe, despite the internationalist ambitions of their foreign policies. However, there is a risk of overestimating the importance of such sentiments: the Scandinavian governments presumably also calculated that, even if participation might be seen as a step toward the West, nonparticipation would be seen as a much greater step toward the East. Moreover, it was only by taking part in the discussions that they could do anything to counteract any tendency toward the creation of a bloc which might be contained in the plan.

The Norwegian foreign minister, Halvard Lange, announced at a press conference a few days before the departure of the Scandinavian delegates for the conference that his government did not see the Marshall Plan as an attempt to create a west European bloc. It attached great importance to a passage in the Anglo-French invitation which stated that no country which wished to take part would be turned away, that there would be no interference in the internal affairs of the participating countries, and that no obstacles would be placed in the way of trade between eastern and western Europe. Lange also expressed his personal hope that long-term discussions concerning economic cooperation would be held within the framework of the permanent organs of the United Nations.

At the Paris Conference, the Scandinavian delegates acted in accordance with these ideas, accepting the American demand that recipient countries form an organization for economic cooperation but insisting that its work be restricted to examining the need for dollar credits among its members. They opposed proposals for cooperation among particular industries operating in different countries, regular economic conferences, and customs unions, and argued that all such far-reaching or long-term projects ought to be dealt with by United Nations bodies.

It seemed at first that the line promoted by the Scandinavian delegations might enjoy some success, but it became increasingly clear from the beginning of August that the Americans would not be satisfied with a list setting out European credit needs. The Scandinavian governments felt themselves under pressure and decided at the end of August to demonstrate their willingness to cooperate by appointing a joint study group to examine the possibility of establishing a Scandinavian customs union. The Danish government was now particularly worried by the prospect of having to take the responsibility for any failure to achieve practical results.

For a while longer the Scandinavian countries stuck to their view that all permanent cooperation should take place within the United Nations, that is to say with the participation of the Soviet Union.

However, once it became clear that continued opposition might lead to their exclusion from the program of assistance, they moderated their attitude. A British compromise proposal was accepted first by the Danes, then by the Norwegians, and finally by the Swedish delegation. The order in which the three Scandinavian countries gave way corresponded to differences in their economic strength. Danish agriculture had suffered severely from the restrictions on trade in food that the Allies had introduced and from the shortage of fodder and fertilizers. Optimism had prevailed in Norway during the summer of 1947 concerning the country's currency reserves, but in August the National Bank's experts reported that a dollar crisis was developing. Sweden's industrial resources had not been damaged by the war, and its position was therefore the strongest of the three, but it too experienced a rapid decline in its currency reserves and was obliged to tighten the existing restrictions on imports.

The Marshall Plan presented the Nordic countries with a situation in which their ambition to remain outside the conflicts of high politics could not be fulfilled. It was not possible to avoid taking a stand, as had often been done within the United Nations. Under the impact of American pressure and growing currency problems they had come to accept an organization with far wider political implications than they had originally been prepared to agree to. However, they did not in the autumn of 1947 regard their involvement in the Marshall Plan as a decisive departure in foreign policy. They tried to draw on their credits as little as possible and generally to ensure that their participation involved as few binding commitments as possible. They hoped that they could in this way maintain their good relations with the East.

The Finnish attitude toward the Marshall Plan largely depended on the Russian reaction. During the summer of 1947 there was strong support for Finnish participation in the plan in parliament and the press, but in July Moscow informed the Finnish government in an official démarche that a decision to take part would be interpreted as a hostile act toward the Soviet Union. The government accordingly decided to forgo American credits. To this extent Finland followed the same pattern as Russia's satellites. On the other hand, Finland was not affected by the creation of the Cominform, on 5 October 1947, as an eastern counterpart to the bloc that was forming in the West. Finland also followed its own unique path in the economic field: it was heavily dependent on the Soviet Union but without being incorporated into its immediate sphere of influence.

Finland Enters into a Pact with the Soviet Union

In connection with the formation of the Cominform, its members issued in September 1947 from Szklarska Pereba in Poland a document which asserted that the world was now divided into two camps, one of which was anti-imperialist and democratic and the other imperialist and anti-democratic. This assertion that there was a bipolar tendency in world politics was irrefutably based in reality by this time, and the tendency was reinforced by the Cominform's manifesto. It was part of a long series of confrontations, which had already begun during the days of the great wartime alliance with differences of opinion on the division of military responsibilities and the inner political structure of liberated countries. In retrospect, it is easy to see a continuous development leading to the unavoidable breach that caused the Cold War. Contemporaries found it more difficult to interpret the trend of events, and in the Nordic countries the hope that the difficulties would prove temporary and soluble survived for a long time. The decisive setbacks that caused even the most incurable optimist to capitulate were the Communist coup in Prague on 25 February 1948 and the conclusion on 17 March of a Western defense alliance between Britain, France, and the Benelux countries which was to prove the kernel of NATO.

After the reconstruction of the Czech government between 18 and 25 February and the death of Foreign Minister Jan Masaryk on 10 March, tension was great in the capitals of the world. It reached its height in Washington when General Clay, the commander of the American troops in Germany, reported by telegram that a "subtle change" in the Soviet attitude had given him "a feeling that war might come with dramatic suddenness." A war psychology was already a reality.

The feeling that Europe stood on the brink of a third world war was also widespread in the Nordic capitals. In Finland the threat of war was highly concrete: on 27 February President Paasikivi received a letter from Stalin, which proposed that their two countries should enter into a mutual defensive alliance of the kind the Soviet Union had previously concluded with Romania, Hungary, and Bulgaria. The Soviet treaties with these three of its border states contained stipulations that were seen in Finland as irreconcilable with national independence. In these treaties, the contracting parties had undertaken to support each other in any armed conflict that might break out and to consult each other about all international questions of importance that affected the interests of their two countries.

But even though Stalin's offer of a treaty was viewed in Finland as a deadly threat, the recognition of a fundamental connection between Finnish and Russian security policy was an essential element in that new outlook which had set the tone for Finnish foreign policy under Paasikivi's leadership. A logical inference from this recognition was that it was a "legitimate" Soviet interest that Finnish territory should not be used for new crusading expeditions against the East. The implications for Finnish security policy had been described in the following way by Paasikivi during a newspaper interview in February 1947: "if anyone seeks to attack the Soviet Union across our territory, we will together with the Soviet Union resist the aggressor with all our might and as long as we can."

It was a precondition of the new policy that this self-imposed task was all that the Soviet Union demanded of Finland. It was therefore disturbing to be presented with a proposed treaty that went much further than anything that had previously been discussed and which enjoyed no prospects whatsoever of being acceptable to political and public opinion in Finland. The atmosphere in Helsinki during the weeks following the receipt of Stalin's letter was extremely tense, and it is described in memoirs of the time as being comparable only to the agitated mood that prevailed during the Winter War and the final phase of the Continuation War.

Under these circumstances, the Finnish government had no choice but to tell Moscow that it would accept a treaty that contained what the president had said in February 1947—but nothing more. Yet within those circles in the Conservative, Agrarian, and Social Democratic parties that had previously been skeptical about Paasikivi's policy of conciliation there were many who now argued that Finland ought not to agree to the inclusion of any military clauses whatsoever in any treaty concluded with the Soviet Union. There were even some who were entirely opposed to entering into negotiations at all. But despite this quite widespread opposition to a military agreement with the Soviet Union, the ten-member delegation appointed by Paasikivi to participate in the negotiations contained no more than one delegate who held such attitudes. Although pursued by bitter complaints and cries of treason from the Finnish parliament, this delegation brought the negotiations to a conclusion that was extraordinarily favorable to Finland, at least when compared with the initial Russian proposals.

By the terms of the treaty, Finland undertook to defend its territory against Germany or any state allied with Germany, if necessary with the assistance of or in partnership with the Soviet Union. There would be consultations between the two countries if Finland were threatened by a military attack. The contracting parties also declared that they would develop friendly relations with each other and that they would work together to promote international peace and security in accordance with the principles of the United Nations. They confirmed the pledge made in the Peace of Paris that they would not join alliances directed at the other party, and undertook to strengthen their economic and cultural relations and not to interfere in each other's internal affairs. The Finns attached great importance to a sentence inserted in the preamble to the treaty. It stated that Finland's efforts to remain outside the conflicts of the great powers had been taken into consideration when the treaty was concluded.

By the time the Finnish delegation returned to Helsinki, it had therefore been shown that Paasikivi's conception of legitimate Russian interests could serve as a basis for Finland's foreign policy. The Finns had succeeded, to the surprise of many, in getting the Soviets to respect their views and to agree to a treaty that did not go beyond the attitude that the president had formulated earlier. When Paasikivi presented the contents of the treaty to the Finnish people in a radio broadcast on 9 April 1948, he declared that the provisions about military assistance were self-evident and could give rise to no legitimate objections. Finland itself had no enemies, but its territory might attract interest in the event of a conflict between the great powers. The essential point in the treaty was that it made it clear to a potential aggressor that, in such a situation, Finland had both the will and the capacity to defend itself. If a threat arose nevertheless, the president thought it quite natural that Finland and the Soviet Union should enter into negotiations about the form and timing of defensive measures. However, the obligation to hold consultations had been restricted as much as possible. Paasikivi also told his listeners that the final text of the treaty completely followed the wording in the original Finnish negotiating proposal.

Paasikivi emphasized the passage that acknowledged Finland's

efforts to avoid involvement in the conflicts of the great powers. The
president had stubbornly insisted on its inclusion in the text, and he
now explained its importance as a statement of principle. It sanctioned the impartial attitude that was unanimously supported by the
Finnish people and which most small states sought to adopt. He explained that Finnish neutrality was given "a complexion of its own"
by the fact that the Soviet Union had a naval base at Porkala and
rights of access to it across Finnish territory. Such arrangements were
not perhaps mentioned in handbooks on international law, but the
key to foreign policy was not to be found in books but in the real
world with all its varied nuances. Finland had taken the first step
in its arduous task of asserting its position as a neutral state.

The Scandinavian Countries Go Their Separate Ways

It was not only in Finland but in all the Nordic countries that the
weeks following the change of government in Prague were filled with
rumors and anxiety. There was a strong conviction that the smaller
states were in a difficult situation and that they ought to give serious
thought to their security problems. It was perhaps time to reconsider
their position. The reaction of the three Scandinavian governments
to the most recent international developments provided a first indication of the direction in which they were now turning.

Between 5 and 8 March a number of disturbing reports reached
Oslo from its embassies in Helsinki, Warsaw, and Moscow. They all
warned that Norway might at any time receive an offer from the
Russians similar to that which had been made to Finland. This was
an ominous piece of intelligence, not least because Norway would
soon be the only European state having a common frontier with
the Soviet Union which had not concluded some kind of treaty with
its mighty neighbor. In a warning from the Norwegian embassy in Moscow, the foreign minister was advised to study the old files relating
to the unsuccessful negotiations for a Soviet-Norwegian nonaggression
treaty that had been conducted between 1928 and 1930. This was to
be the first step taken in preparation for the negotiations which it
was expected would take place with Moscow. The second would be
the rapid approval of a grant of 100 million *kroner* to strengthen the
armed forces. The third, and in the long term most important, would
be the drafting of an appeal for help to the United States and Britain.

The Norwegian government was certainly agreed that a Russian
invitation would under all circumstances be refused, but it was

naturally still very interested in learning how Washington and London would react. Could Norway count on military assistance if the worst were to happen? The response of the American and British governments was that they supported the Norwegian government's position of refusing any Russian invitation to conclude an agreement on the Finnish model. Lange also learned that the question of Anglo-American cooperation on defense was being considered in the two countries at the highest level of government. So, though the Norwegian government never had to enter into negotiations with the Soviets, the preparations it made provided insights of great importance for the future.

The reaction in Copenhagen was less dramatic than in Oslo. For the Danes the most disturbing event in European politics was not the Soviet offer to Paasikivi but rather the coup in Prague. Czechoslovakia, just like Denmark, had been a small democratic state seeking to strike a balance between East and West, and such a policy presupposed that the aspiration to remain on the sidelines was respected or at any rate accepted by the great powers. Events in Czechoslovakia seemed to show that this precondition was absent, and this was worrisome to Denmark. The seriousness of the situation was underlined by a verbal report from Washington, which stated that responsible circles in the United States believed the Soviet Union had expansionist intentions and that it was now the turn of Italy and Denmark to fall victim to these intentions.

However, the Danish reaction was in no way spectacular. There was no discussion of increased defense spending, and no appeal to the Western powers was attempted. On the other hand, suspicion of Danish Communists reached its peak, and rumors about infiltration, secret arms dumps, and plans for a coup were rife. The level of preparedness to meet such a coup was raised by withdrawing Easter leave for about a third of the army, and general vigilance was increased. However, the Danish authorities apparently did not think there was any imminent danger of external attack.

Events in Europe also caused anxiety in Stockholm at the end of February and the beginning of March 1948, but since an isolated attack on Sweden was hardly likely, the atmosphere of crisis was somewhat less than in the other Nordic countries. Nonetheless, the armed forces increased their level of preparedness and intensified their monitoring of foreign wireless traffic. Swedish missions abroad were urged to be especially on the alert for information, and the reactions of the other Nordic countries to European developments were followed with great interest.

The Swedish government was informed of the Norwegian approach to the Western powers and realized that influential voices in Oslo were recommending a reorientation of Norwegian foreign policy in the direction of cooperation with the Western powers. It was also able to obtain a good picture of the division of opinion on this question within the Norwegian Labor party because of the contacts linking Swedish and Norwegian social democracy. It knew that a majority of the Labor parliamentary group opposed a change of policy, that the party leader and prime minister, Einar Gerhardsen, was undecided, and that a strong group in the party's Central Committee, headed by Lange and the defense minister, Jens Christian Hauge, was actively promoting an association with the Western powers. It was in these circumstances that the Swedish government raised the idea of a Scandinavian defense alliance.

The possibility of such an alliance had been discussed on several earlier occasions both before and during the war. The question was raised again at the first postwar meeting of the coordinating committee of the Nordic social democratic parties in July 1945. The Swedish delegation showed a particular interest in the matter, but no concrete decisions were made. The possibility of military cooperation between Norway and Sweden alone was discussed in February 1947 at a meeting between the foreign ministers of these two countries and at other sessions of the Social Democratic Coordinating Committee, but on these occasions too discussion remained on a general level.

However, these exchanges had at least caused the three governments concerned to begin to think about what an alliance of this kind would involve. The Swedish government considered the matter in March and April 1948. On 19 April Lange made a speech in which he emphasized the importance of Scandinavian unity but also that the approval of parliament's Foreign Affairs Committee, and on 3 May Foreign Minister Osten Unden presented Lange with a proposal for a Scandinavian defense alliance that would be unconnected with all with this prospect, Swedish plans for an alliance matured into a concrete diplomatic initiative. On 22 April the government obtained the approval of parliament's Foreign Affairs Committee, and on 3 May Foreign Minister Östen Undén presented Lange with a proposal for a Scandinavian defense alliance that would be unconnected with all outside powers. One week later the first collective negotiations between the three Scandinavian governments began.

Delegations from the three governments met seven times between May 1948 and January 1949 in an attempt to agree on a plan for a joint nonaligned defense alliance. A special expert committee worked for three months on technical defense questions. However, it proved impossible to reach agreement, and in the course of March 1949 decisions were made which finally confirmed that the Nordic countries had taken different roads. Denmark and Norway joined NATO, whereas Sweden continued to pursue a policy of nonalignment.

The negotiations revealed from the very first the existence of deep differences between the Swedish and Norwegian attitudes, and there were only a few occasions when supporters of an alliance had any reason for hope. The details of the negotiations have still not been fully clarified, and they will not be dealt with in this essay. Instead, an attempt will be made to summarize the arguments and motives that influenced the three governments concerned.

During the course of the negotiations the Swedish Social Democratic government was subjected to quite sharp criticism from sections of its own parliamentary group, which accused it of entering into a commitment that involved risks for Sweden without conferring any compensatory advantages. It is easy to understand the reasoning that lay behind this criticism. The security threat to Scandinavia was that it would be regarded as a military vacuum by the great powers. This vacuum had to be filled as a shield against isolated attack, but this could be achieved in a way fully satisfactory for Sweden if the country took care of the defense of its own territory while the Western powers helped Denmark and Norway. Moreover, it was clear that Sweden would enjoy better prospects of remaining neutral during a general war between the great powers if it was not committed to the defense of its neighbor.

However, another appraisal may have seemed more reasonable for those who believed in the ability of the nonaligned nations to reduce the risk of conflict between the great powers and therefore also the risk of war in Scandinavia. If the military defenses of the Scandinavian area were to be strengthened, as seemed unavoidable, it was better to have the Scandinavians do this by themselves than to draw one of the great powers into the area, a development that would further the tendency for blocs of states to form with the attendant increase in international tension. Seen in these terms, a Scandinavian defense alliance represented a Swedish security interest.

National security could thus be served by such an alliance, but what then of the other goal of Swedish foreign policy: the promotion of international harmony? Would international peace, apprehended in the vein of democratic socialism, be furthered by this initiative? It is possible that many Scandinavian social democrats thought that it would. In November 1947 they had participated in a conference of European social democratic parties at which a resolution directed against a foreign policy designed to divide nations into blocs had been adopted. The resolution had declared that it was the duty of social democratic parties to do all they could to promote understanding and cooperation among all countries and to resist the formation of blocs. A Scandinavian defense alliance would be in harmony with these objectives since it meant that one area in Europe excluded itself from the general trend toward bipolarity and created a haven for an alternative to both capitalism and communism. In these circumstances, the Swedish initiative can be seen as an attempt to find a policy which even in the new international political climate reconciled the interests of national security and international understanding.

Ideas of this kind could certainly arouse a response in the three social democratic parties that were then in power in the Scandinavian countries. However, as we have seen, their position was not overwhelmingly strong and the trend of events did not suggest that it would become any stronger. The proposal for a defense alliance still won wide political support because it was also sustained by other considerations. One of them, which appealed equally to all parties and had great influence on public opinion, was the feeling of affinity among the Nordic peoples.

In Sweden, such sentiments had in recent years been directed above all toward Finland, which was not, to be sure, directly affected by the new Swedish initiative but might well be indirectly affected. There was reason to suspect that Finland would be the primary victim if the confrontation between the great powers became more acute in the Nordic area, in that the Soviet hold on that country would tighten if the Western powers established themselves in Denmark and Norway. The maintenance of Scandinavian neutrality should therefore also benefit Finland. This thought was naturally not purely altruistic since Sweden, as Finland's closest neighbor in the west, would be pushed into Finland's position as a state on the very borders of the Soviet sphere, if the iron curtain were moved forward to the Gulf of Bothnia: "If Finland were not Finland, then Sweden would be Finland."

Sweden's relations with Denmark and Norway were more complicated. They had been forced to fight Nazism while Sweden had looked on, had granted transit facilities to German troops, and had for a long time refused to recognize the Norwegian government-in-exile. Sweden had certainly given material help to both Norway and Denmark but on a far smaller scale than it had to Finland. All this provided a basis for feelings of inferiority and guilt, which may have made it attractive to bind the fortunes of the three countries together. An alliance might prevent the recurrence of such an awkward situation in the future. The Swedish conscience had been soothed by many good arguments, but it is possible that it still gnawed at Swedish minds and gave the initiative for an alliance something of the character of a gesture of reparation.

The immediate impulse behind the Swedish initiative had been the realization that Norway was moving toward an association with the Western powers. Throughout the negotiations those Norwegians who favored such an association naturally regarded the policy of nonalignment promoted by the Swedes as impossible. They soon managed to convince the initially ambivalent Gerhardsen, and they also succeeded in overcoming opposition within the Labor parliamentary group. In the final reckoning, they had virtually all members of parliament except the Communists on their side.

Even the supporters of an orientation toward the Western powers were undoubtedly somewhat sympathetic to the idea that a nonaligned position would make it possible for Norway to pursue a policy aimed at mediating and reducing conflicts over security policy and ideology. This had indeed been the guiding principle of Norwegian policy since the end of the war, but the express precondition for this policy had been that the wartime understanding among the great powers would be continued and strengthened. After the Prague coup all such hopes were crushed, and it seemed impossible to achieve national security outside one of the great-powers blocs. The Norwegians therefore made some association with the Western powers, which would provide material help while Denmark and Norway were building up their defenses and an assurance of support in the event of a Soviet attack, a condition for their participation in a Scandinavian alliance. It is perhaps debatable whether a compromise between this condition and the Swedish demand for neutrality was as impossible as it might appear at first sight, but this divergence proved to be the point on which the negotiations collapsed.

The differences between Norway and Sweden in the orientation of their foreign policies were expressed in their views of the great powers. During the negotiations the Norwegians attached much greater importance than did Sweden (or Denmark) to the threat from the East. The Norwegian defense minister warned that the Soviet Union would deal with the divided democratic states one by one. He clearly feared a repetition of the pattern of the 1930s, when Hitler's expansionism had been met by the appeasement policy of the Western powers. The mistakes perpetrated by the democratic states when they had not used force to resist an aggressive dictatorship should not be repeated. The Norwegians were thus more suspicious of Soviet intentions than were the Swedes, but they were also influenced by a stronger feeling of affinity with the Western powers. The bonds that had been forged during the war were still felt to be firm. The Norwegian delegates became alarmed when it was suggested that the Scandinavian defense alliance might be submitted to the Security Council of the United Nations for its approval. If this were done, it would mean that the Soviet Union's consent was sought, and this in its turn would mean that the alliance was directed, at least formally, at the Western powers as well. Since the war years it was a common Swedish argument that a policy of neutrality could succeed only if the potential aggressor was assured that the neutral would defend itself against *all* quarters. The Norwegians could perhaps accept this nonaligned strategy in theory, but they probably still found it hard to nod agreement when Undén during the discussions formulated its practical consequences in the following way: "If the Yankees come, we'll fire."

These differences of opinion concerning the great powers can also be seen in the discussions about the alliance's prospects of being able to buy armaments from the Western powers on favorable terms. The Swedes, with their phlegmatic attitude toward the Russian threat, did not see this as an urgent problem. They also seem to have thought that the Western powers, while initially adopting a negative attitude toward supplying armaments to a neutral alliance, would prove more amenable when faced with a *fait accompli*. If Scandinavia was really an area of strategic importance, the Western powers would under all circumstances wish to see it able to defend its own independence. For the same reason, it could be assumed that they would intervene if one of the Scandinavian countries were attacked, at any rate so long as it offered resistance itself.

The Norwegians refused to accept a strategy based on expecting the assistance of the Western powers without at the same time declaring political and military solidarity with them. It is possible that they, unlike the Swedes, did not regard such a strategy as realistic, but a more important consideration was probably that they found it incompatible with fundamental moral principles. For them, nonalignment was tantamount to military nonintervention in a conflict in which they were deeply involved ideologically and emotionally. Gerhardsen explained at one of the first meetings of the Scandinavian delegations that in Norway great importance was attached to this moral aspect. It was thought that it would not be right for Norway to stand on the sidelines in a struggle between freedom and force, and Gerhardsen made it clear that he personally sympathized with this view. According to reports received by the Swedish government, Lange unreservedly supported this line. In response to a direct question, he is said to have declared that it would be morally indefensible for Norway not to participate in a new war. The Swedish minister of agriculture, who jotted down this reply, commented, "Here is an adventurous foreign minister."

Important differences had thus arisen between leading Norwegian and Swedish social democrats in their view of their countries' international mission. The negotiations were also complicated by a number of undisguised emotional reactions to the prospect of an alliance.

During the war Norway had established intimate contacts with the Western great powers, above all Britain, and had gained prestige and an international position. One of the choices Norway now had to make was whether it would rather remain a small country in the shadow of great powers or return to the more narrow Nordic circle where it would be overshadowed by another small state, namely, Sweden. It was evident that leading members of the Norwegian government preferred the first alternative. Lange clearly showed that he was one of them. "We shouldn't run every time the Swedes beckon," he explained on one occasion when he had rejected a Swedish proposal for a meeting. He also demonstrated his attitude by expressing his views publicly without first contacting his Nordic colleagues.

It is clear from contemporary diary material that such emotional manifestations on the part of the Norwegians caused considerable disappointment and irritation within the Swedish government.

Swedish suspicion of Lange, which was fueled by his opponents within his own party, gave rise to all kinds of speculation in Stockholm. It was thought that he might be playing a double game when it became known that the British were well informed of all that passed between Sweden and Norway, and it was even suspected that the dramatic Norwegian reaction to international events in February and March 1948 had been feigned in an attempt to throw the Scandinavian states into the arms of the Western powers. This hypothesis received some support from information suggesting that the reports of the Norwegian embassy in Moscow had not been nearly so alarming as Lange had intimated.

When the archives were opened, scholars were able to find several indications that the Norwegians were playing a double game during the negotiations. On four different occasions between September 1948 and January 1949 the Norwegian authorities expressly asked representatives of the American government to make it clear to the Swedes that a neutral alliance could not count on receiving supplies of American armaments. The Americans did in fact speak to the Swedes in this vein, and the Swedish proposal was naturally undermined in consequence.

The Danish representatives in the negotiations devoted their efforts to mediating between the Norwegian and Swedish positions. This was not because the Danes had no view of their own. On the contrary, it appears from both public statements and the unpublished record of the negotiations that the Danish prime minister, Hans Hedtoft, and his foreign minister, Gustaf Rasmussen, were perhaps the most zealous adherents of a nonaligned Scandinavian mutual assistance pact. They were thus in agreement with the Swedes, but it was they who assumed, in the course of negotiations, the task of trying to find practicable compromises.

The Danes also seem to have found it more natural than did the Swedes to emphasize the increased security their own country would enjoy as an argument for an alliance. They regarded their position as the most exposed, and their defense forces were the weakest among the three countries. However, they also stressed the importance of the pact as a constructive contribution to the promotion of peace: Rasmussen said that it would be "a stabilizing factor for peace and would contribute to the relaxation of international tension in general."

Rasmussen's statement perhaps suggests that some feeling for the ideological value of a neutral Scandinavian bloc was still alive among Danish Social Democrats. The same deduction can be drawn from a temperamental intervention by Hedtoft during one of the discussions. After stating that if Norway chose association with the Western powers, Denmark would be obliged to do the same, he added that he nevertheless "would curse the moment when it became clear that we, as three socialist governments, could not find another solution." This remark hints at the fear that Nordic socialism was now throwing away its opportunities of fulfilling an international mission.

Hedtoft was also moved by a strong feeling of Nordic affinity which made the idea of an alliance of self-evident value in itself. The same feeling can be seen in the public pronouncements of other members of the Danish government. They referred, as for example did Rasmussen, to the Nordic countries' spiritual kinship, their similar cultural and social development, their common outlook on life, and their shared conception of what constituted human dignity, freedom, and justice.

The strength of the Danish commitment to a Nordic solution is also shown by the Danish government's persistence in trying to create the preconditions for such a solution, even after the other two countries concerned had abandoned the attempt. It did not give up until a proposal for an alliance between Sweden and Denmark alone had been rejected by the Swedes. One feels strongly that it was more than just a formal phrase, when Hedtoft declared after the final collapse that he personally believed it was "more than tragic" that a Scandinavian solution had not been possible.

By the end of March 1949 the Nordic states had definitively taken their places in the bipolar world of the Cold War. Finland had begun its efforts within the framework of the pact with Moscow to establish its status as a neutral state. Sweden stood by the neutrality it had maintained for 135 years. Norway had joined the Western bloc, but with the express reservation that the great powers would not be allowed bases on its territory, of which it had given an assurance to the Soviet Union in a note delivered on 1 February 1949. Finally, Denmark had decided a few weeks later to follow Norway into the Western bloc, though also with the proviso that foreign bases would not be permitted on its soil.

Defense Policy

At the end of the Second World War democratic socialists dreamed of a demilitarized world in which its peoples would no longer labor under the burden of massive defense spending. Even if their program seemed radical at the time, it was moderate in comparison with the demand for total disarmament that their liberal and socialist predecessors had raised twenty-five years earlier. It is not wholly clear just how far this moderation extended, but they seem to have been prepared to accept an international peace-keeping force and even small national armies designed to resist sudden attacks.

Some observers may have believed at the end of the war that the Nordic countries had already gone a long way toward this ideal of disarmament. At any rate, this appears to have been the view of Sir Orme Sargent, the permanent under-secretary of state at the British Foreign Office. In conversation with the Swedish ambassador in London, he described the outcome of the Scandinavian defense alliance in the following way: $0 + 0 + 0 = 0$.

However, this dismissal of Scandinavian military capabilities was not entirely justified. If Swedish taxpayers had happened to learn of Sargent's observations, they would probably not have taken them in good humor. During the war income and property taxes had increased by 90%, and a purchase tax of 5% had been introduced in order to finance the expansion of Sweden's defenses. A Norwegian defense committee described this expansion as "splendid and systematic," and in fact, for a small state, Sweden by the end of the war had a strong defense.

Sargent's remarks were less unjustified in the case of the other Nordic states. There were practically no functioning defense forces in Denmark and Norway. The position was weakest in Denmark. According to the modest plan that applied before 9 April 1940, Denmark could mobilize a fully equipped army of about 100,000 men, but in reality only 10,000 men were available on 1 August 1946. The navy consisted almost entirely of supply and ancillary vessels whose value in combat would be very small. The air force had lost all its planes and practically all other material of any importance. The Norwegian armed forces, like their Danish counterpart, had been formally dissolved by the German occupation authorities. Training had therefore completely ceased during the war years, and it was only those officers and soldiers who had received military instruction from the British who had any military qualifications. As for armaments, supplies were largely limited to the weapons and ammunition left behind by the German forces in Norway after their capitulation.

Finland's defense problems had in a sense been solved by the terms of the armistice, which required the Finns to reduce their armed forces to "peacetime levels." These were numerically defined in the Treaty of Paris, the upper limit for the Finnish armed forces being set at 41,900 men: 34,400 in the army, 4,500 in the navy, and 3,000 in the air force. The last-named was not allowed to have more than sixty planes, of which none might be bombers. The Finns were also forbidden to possess nuclear weapons, guided missiles, noncontact mines, and torpedoes and submarines. This was, to be sure, a diminution of national sovereignty, but it was largely borne with equanimity since it was realized that it also had its advantages. A difficult and contentious issue of domestic politics, defense spending, disappeared from the political debate, and the country's resources could be devoted to a greater extent than would otherwise have been possible to the pursuit of peaceful economic development and increased prosperity.

The expansion of the nation's defenses was not regarded as a political task of the first rank in any of the four Nordic countries during the first postwar years. There were many other areas of activity that required economic resources and political energy, and in any case most other countries were reducing their military strength at this time. During the first years of peace the Finnish armed forces fell short of their permitted maximum by about 10,000 men. Throughout this period decisions about defense policy were made without any domestic political controversy.

In Sweden, on the other hand, quite a lively debate about defense policy, which raised important questions of principle, had begun even before the end of the war. Ever since the early interwar years social democratic and liberal circles had asserted the "elasticity principle" in their approach to defense policy. The elasticity argument was that the size of the armed forces ought to be adjusted in response to the international situation: it should increase at times of conflict and insecurity and contract during calm periods. The continued strength of such thinking was manifested during the last phase of the war: many accepted the argument that the world, after its present sufferings, would refrain from war for a long time to come and that Sweden could therefore reduce the huge sums spent on defense without risk.

When the minister of defense in the coalition government appointed a commission to study future defense arrangements, he clearly hoped that the pro-defense atmosphere of the war years would still be strong enough to resist these new calls for disarmament. However, he was to be disappointed. The commission's proposals, which were presented in November 1947, had clearly been affected by a desire for financial retrenchment. It recommended that the training period in the army be reduced from fifteen to eleven months and that the number of troops in each unit be cut by 14%. It proposed a considerable limitation on the construction of new ships for the navy and the disbandment of two wings of aircraft (i.e., about sixty planes). As compared with a maintenance of the armed forces at their existing level, these recommendations would mean savings of 290 million *kronor,* or 25%. One of the arguments advanced to justify this change in defense policy was that a "period of peace" of not inconsiderable length might now be expected. However, those who favored the "permanency principle" in defense questions, that is to say those who maintained that the armed forces should be kept on a high and even level at all times for both technical and strategic reasons, did not need to lose heart. There was a large, albeit divided, group within the commission which expressed reservations about its main proposals, and this position received considerable support, especially from the military authorities, as soon as the report of the commission was circulated.

In Denmark and Norway the proponents of disarmament faced a situation which was the exact reverse of that in Sweden. It was a question not of reducing the size of a large defense apparatus but of preventing the expansion of a small one. Both countries had been occupied before they had had time to rearm to the extent Sweden had done, and they had also asserted the antimilitarist tradition with greater force and consistency than Sweden during the interwar period. However, it was politically impossible to continue this tradition after the war and occupation had ended. A certain degree of rearmament was unavoidable, but it did prove possible to hold it within narrow limits. In September 1946 the Norwegian government proposed an expansion of the armed forces which meant that expenditure on defense would be slightly more than double that in the last prewar budget of 1940 but still would not represent more than 12% of total state spending. In Sweden that same year, defense claimed 27% of the budget.

The moderate tempo of Norwegian rearmament was justified by the argument that the country was impoverished after the war and economic reconstruction had to come first. The government's proposal met with a favorable reception in parliament, even if there were some who wondered why Norway should rearm at all when the whole world was disarming. One isolated voice from Labor's anti-militarist wing protested against the size of the recommended defense expenditure, but otherwise the proposal was generally approved, although a strikingly large number of speakers emphasized that the objective was the concentration of the world's military resources under the control of the United Nations and the disarmament of the individual member states. The minister of defense also stressed that the primary task of the defense forces was to fulfill Norway's international obligations as a member of the United Nations. The moderate degree of rearmament that occurred did not therefore necessarily represent the beginnings of a national defense of the traditional type.

In Denmark defense spending during the last interwar years had not exceeded 10% of total state expenditure. In 1940 the army consisted of 14,000 men, which represented only a quarter of its strength at the outbreak of the First World War. During the first two postwar years defense spending was increased to about the same level as in Norway: it consumed about 230 million *kroner,* or 14% of the total budget. However, the Danes did not enjoy that unity among the parties which characterized, at least outwardly, the defense debate in Norway and Sweden. The defense question resulted in the creation of a new political division when the Radical Liberals, who had about 8% of the voters behind them, together with the Communists and the Georgist so-called Justice party (*Retsforbundet,*) demanded that rearmament proceed at a slower tempo. They were opposed by an overwhelming majority in parliament, made up of the Social Democrats, the Liberals (*Venstre*), and the Conservatives. The leader of the Radicals sharply attacked the Conservative defense program as early as October 1945, during the general political debate in parliament, claiming that this program would involve greatly excessive costs. He referred to the defense debate of the interwar period and asserted that the prevailing view of those years, namely that the country could not resist the army of a great power, was still valid. Danish defense policy, he concluded, should be determined by the military obligations involved in membership in the United Nations and by nothing else.

However, when the Liberal government announced its decision to prepare a new defense plan on 1 March 1946, it did not have many friendly words for the defense debate of the interwar years. The defense minister recommended that what had been said at that time should be forgotten, since it now seemed to him both unrealistic and uninteresting.

The discussion on defense policy in the Nordic countries was strongly influenced by the recent upheavals of the war. Politicians were unable to ignore the experiences of the war years when drawing up plans for future security policy. However, interpretations of the significance of past events were often widely divergent. This applied not least to the event which from a Nordic point of view was the most revolutionary of the war, namely, the German invasion of Denmark and Norway on 9 April 1940.

During the summer of 1940 the Swedish press, which was the only one in the North by this time that could still express its views freely, discussed who was responsible for the catastrophe. Those, mostly conservative, newspapers that saw international politics as a perpetual and unchanging struggle for power regarded it as a natural phenomenon that the great powers would sooner or later fill a military and political vacuum. Responsibility for the attack therefore fell on those who had created such a vacuum in Denmark and Norway by promoting disarmament and international solidarity. One Stockholm newspaper declared that the German invasion was a correction by life itself of dangerous illusions. It threw "the light of reality onto the ruins of that castle in the air which officious and foolish people had been so eager to construct for their countrymen."

On the other hand, those who believed in the possibility of creating a rational and moral international order found it grotesque to lay the blame for what had happened on anyone but the aggressor. The low level of military preparedness in Denmark and Norway was regrettable, but it did not change the balance of guilt, indeed it only made Germany's actions still more criminal. *Weserübung* was not, according to this way of thinking, the result of some political "law of nature" but the expression of a political decision.

The same question was discussed five years later in October 1945 by the Lower Chamber of the Danish parliament. The debate, according to one of its main participants, revealed "almost a chasm of disagreement." In the recent election, the Conservatives had campaigned with a defense program declaring, under the rubric "Never again a ninth of April," that the prewar defense policy had suffered its final defeat and received a crushing judgment on that day. In the parliamentary debate, the Conservative leader went further and announced that he felt a personal sense of shame for 9 April, "shame that we were not better prepared." He wished to lay the blame for what had happened on the Danish political parties, including the Conservatives, because they had not attempted to strengthen the national defense at an earlier stage. Like his conservative colleagues in Sweden, he thought that a country which placed itself in a military vacuum could not expect to remain at peace.

A contrary view was upheld by the Radicals. Their leader denied that 9 April was an event of importance for future Danish defense policy. The German invasion had merely confirmed that, as everyone already knew, Denmark was at the mercy of any great power that chose to cross the Danish frontier in Jutland. However, the fact that it was easy to occupy the country did not justify doing so. He therefore dissociated himself from Conservative feelings of shame: "The events of 9 April were a cause of shame not to Denmark but to Germany."

In the postwar Norwegian debate 9 April did not lead to accusations and confessions in the same way as in Denmark. Memories of the German attack were marked less by the military debacle of the first days than by the resistance struggle during the years of occupation. When the Defense Ministry summarized Norway's war experiences in September 1945, it placed the resistance movement at the center of its account. It argued that events in 1940 and later had shown that the Norwegian people would fight for its freedom and independence even against an apparently invincible aggressor. Emphasis was laid less on the lack of equipment and training than on the fact that arms had been fearlessly taken up. The question of the defense policy pursued during the interwar years was pushed into the background, and the sharp differences that characterized the Danish debate could, in consequence, be avoided. However, this did not mean that complete unity prevailed concerning the interpretation of these historical experiences. The overwhelming majority in parliament thought the practical significance of the experiences was that Norway ought not once again to expose itself to the necessity of fighting without adequate means of defense. The idea that Norway should contribute to a more peaceful world by disarming was rejected with reference to the vacuum theory. But a contrary view was asserted from within the Labor party by a minority that eagerly favored disarmament. A spokesman for this group declared in parliament that the events of 9 April 1940 provided no grounds for any change of opinion. Instead, there was now, just as much as before, reason to weep over "those millions who would needlessly be sacrificed on the altar of armaments capitalism."

Despite such differences in the interpretation of experience and in psychology "the ninth of April" had the same effect, as a historical example, in both countries. The memory of violent aggression strengthened the credibility of the argument put forward by the adherents of strong defenses, namely, that security could not be obtained without military resources. It contributed to the isolation of those groups which remained skeptical of the view that strong defenses increased security.

The "little international" 's vision of a demilitarized world was thus under pressure from the start, but it was not wholly without importance. Antimilitarism was still a significant factor when the first decisions in the field of defense policy were made after the war. In conjunction with the intense desire to devote all available resources to economic reconstruction, it contributed to restricting defense spending to a comparatively low level. However, after the hopes for cooperation between the great powers and an international order grounded in law had faded, the debate over defense was conducted in a different context. In this new situation, it soon became clear that there were important differences in the three countries' ideas on the role of defense in security policy.

The change in the international climate had immediate effects on defense spending in Sweden. The rather optimistic view of international developments that had formed the basis of the defense commission's main proposal was regarded, when the latter was presented in November 1947, as totally unrealistic. The military authorities strongly criticized the proposal, and later the political authorities did so as well. The defense proposals that the cabinet submitted to parliament on 15 April 1948 completely rejected all thought of disarmament. The government emphasized in its proposal that the armed forces were being strengthened around the world and that Sweden had to follow this general development. The air force must be considerably expanded and the needs of the army and navy examined by new commissions, which would work within the terms of reference that the existing strength should be retained or extended.

The period of training ought to be one month longer than the commission had recommended.

Because of the government's repudiation of the defense commission, it was possible to maintain unity among the political parties in regard to the defense question. The party leaders were able now, as during the war, to compliment each other on their "positive interest in defense." Small groups within the Liberal and Social Democratic parties still espoused the ideal of disarmament, but they were unable to achieve more than helpless protests.

The deterioration of the international situation did not have any immediate effects on the development of the defense question in Denmark and Norway. It was unrealistic to suppose that these two countries could, with their own resources, rapidly build up defenses capable of repelling outside attack, and their main efforts were therefore directed toward obtaining security through alliance with others. In Denmark, the various government directives to the defense commission established in 1946 illustrated this absence of an immediate connection between the international situation and defense spending. The first directive envisaged a three-year plan whose annual cost would be considerably in excess of the amounts spent on defense during the first postwar years. However, in November 1947 a new Social Democratic government took office, and a few months later, in the middle of the crisis in Czechoslovakia, it issued new directives which did not, by and large, involve any increase in defense expenditure above existing levels.

The commanders of the three services, who were instructed to work out a proposal on the basis of the new directives, at first refused to follow the guidelines they had been given. When they did at last present a proposal that kept within the financial limits set, they were careful to stress that in their opinion it lacked military value and would not provide a basis for successful defense if the country's neutrality were violated.

When the negotiations for a Scandinavian defense alliance began, these Danish investigations were discontinued until the outcome of the negotiations was known. However, an isolated proposal concerning the organization of the Home Guard was presented and accepted in May 1948. The defense minister explained that an immediate decision had been made on this part of the general defense plan in order to create a favorable impression in other countries, not least in Norway and Sweden. The Danish government wished to show that the Danes also sincerely wanted to build up strong defenses.

Membership in NATO changed both the organizational and financial premises of Danish defense policy. Denmark's armed forces would now be a part of NATO's joint defense system and could therefore be built up with the help of the Western powers. Defense spending increased rapidly and soon exceeded the suggested limits which had caused the protests of the military authorities.

The harsher international climate did not have any immediate consequences for Norwegian defense planning either. The three-year plan which was approved in 1946 continued in force until 1949 at an annual cost of about 203 million *kroner*. In October 1949 a commission presented a proposal for a six-year plan, which sought to meet the demands that could be made on Norway as a member of NATO. It was suggested that annual defense spending should rise to 300 million *kroner*, but the main argument used to justify this increase was that costs could no longer be curtailed by the use of weapons, ammunition, and other supplies left behind by the Germans after their capitulation. Thus it was not, according to the commission, a question of any real extension in defense activity.

The commission was also anxious to emphasize that its proposal was not satisfactory from a purely military point of view. One of the weaknesses it pointed to was that the basic training period of nine months was too short and that later training periods in the reserve were too few and too brief. However, it had decided to regard the capacity of the Norwegian economy to support defense expenditure as the overriding consideration and had therefore tried to limit costs. A feature of the Norwegian discussion that is striking in comparison with the other Scandinavian countries is that this broad approach to the problem was shared by the military experts. The defense staff stated in its report on the proposal that it had considered arguing in favor of higher defense expenditure, which would have been justified from the military point of view, but had decided to refrain from doing so out of regard for other "important national tasks and other problems of reconstruction which Norway must solve in the future."

The presence of such attitudes within the Norwegian high command was clearly connected with the special climate that had been created by the country's strong antimilitarist tradition. The encouragement of a positive attitude toward defense among the Norwegian people still seemed an important and difficult task, and the commission had given special attention to it. The commission had emphasized that all the parties concerned ought to strive for a solution of defense problems based on "a united estimate of all the factors involved." This meant in the case of officers that they should bear in mind the relationship between the defense question and economic and social policy. Against this background, the report of the defense staff seems a deliberate step in a campaign to integrate the armed forces into a democratic society. This also doubtless provides much of the explanation for the dispassionate and largely positive spirit in which the commission's proposal was examined by the political parties and parliament.

If the development of defense policy is viewed in isolation from its context in security policy, it is difficult to reconcile the clear expressions of a will to self-defense in Denmark and Norway with their failure to react in the field of defense policy to the symptoms of international crisis. The clear connection between the Swedish debate and the course taken by outside events seems more natural for a state that did not think it had a convincing margin of security. The explanation is, of course, that Norwegian and Danish politicians saw diplomacy and not defense policy as the main instrument in their efforts to achieve security. From the point of view of military policy, the recently proposed differentiation in a country's military resources between "its own forces" and its "borrowed forces" may help to explain the situation. If these concepts are applied to Nordic developments in the years 1948-49, it can be said that Sweden sought its security mainly in its own strength and Denmark and Norway in borrowed strength obtained through an alliance with others. Finland received rather than sought borrowed strength against attack from the south or west, but had to rely on its own decimated strength against attack from the east. In the case of Norway, Denmark, and Finland, it was without doubt their borrowed strength which constituted the core of their defense and which gave it its deterrent effect. Their own armed forces primarily served the purpose of demonstrating that they were loyal members of the alliance, could resist any sudden, unexpected attack, and could organize a defense while awaiting assistance from the great powers.

The picture is more ambiguous, however, in the case of Sweden. Greater importance was undeniably attached to the country's own strength than in the other Nordic countries, and this was reflected in the greater sensitivity of the Swedish defense debate to changes in the picture of the threat from without. In consequence, Swedish defense spending, whether measured in *kronor* per inhabitant or as a percentage of the Gross National Product, was much higher than that of the other Nordic states. However, it may seem excessively optimistic for the Swedes to have believed that their armed forces, alone and without assistance, could provide security against an attack by a great power. The Swedes were able to solve this problem to their own satisfaction because they, unlike their Nordic neighbors, never thought Sweden would be exposed to isolated aggression. They believed that Sweden would only become involved in war in connection with a general European conflict and, in that event, the larger part of the forces of any aggressor would be tied down on other fronts. Swedish policy aimed at making the country's defenses so strong that a potential aggressor would have to allocate so much manpower and material for the conquest of Sweden that it would believe the costs of attack outweighed the advantages of conquest. This reasoning enabled the Swedes to keep the tasks demanded of their own forces within realistic boundaries. Moreover, there was also the consideration that a country which was not assured of outside assistance by treaty still might obtain it in practice. It was possible to calculate that such help would be forthcoming even if there were no formal alliance, and the Swedish government thought in this way with respect to the proposed Scandinavian defense pact and in all probability also with respect to Sweden alone. An indication to this effect was given during the parliamentary defense debate of 1948 when Undén stated, in reply to a direct question, that Sweden would not consider itself precluded from requesting outside help in the event of an attack. The Swedish commander-in-chief made the position clearer the following year, when he explained in a speech that Sweden's military strategy was based on holding off the enemy until outside assistance arrived. There could have been little doubt that he envisaged attack from the East and assistance from the West. So the Swedes also seem to have counted on being able in practice to obtain considerable borrowed forces.

Thus the main difference between the situations of Sweden on the one hand and Denmark and Norway on the other was that Sweden was freed of the military, political, and moral obligations of NATO membership, but had instead to bear the cost of maintaining a considerably stronger defense. However, irrespective of whether their strength was borrowed or their own, all the Scandinavian countries had now decided that large-scale defense could not be avoided. The vision of a "demilitarized world" was further than ever from realization.

Conclusion

As the Second World War came to an end, it may have seemed as if there were good prospects for creating a world that fulfilled the demand of democratic socialists for justice and security. There was reason to believe that success was more likely now than during the interwar period. The working class, the political base of the radical forces, was better organized and more articulate than before. Experiences gained in the League of Nations ought to be helpful in the work of creating a new international peace organization, and there were prospects of securing the adhesion of all nations. The two new superpowers had shown themselves capable of cooperating during the war.

During the interwar period the Nordic countries had been deeply involved in international efforts for peace, and it was natural for them now to take up where they had left off. It also seemed at first as if there would be strong and reliable domestic support for a radical peace policy. The socialist parties were riding high, and the nonsocialist ones seemed to be undergoing a process of radicalization. The first postwar elections indicated that those who had said the war would be followed by a completely new political climate had been right.

The socialist vision on the domestic plane was set out in a fairly detailed and concrete form in the postwar programs of the social democratic parties. The guiding principle of economic policy would be planning, and the forms of production would be chosen on the basis of macroeconomic criteria of efficiency. In the field of social policy, social democracy outlined an ambitious policy of reform aimed at making compassion and solidarity the dominant features of society.

However, the socialist vision in foreign policy was much less concrete. Nonetheless, in Norway, the foreign policy pursued in the first postwar years has been graced with a name of its own: bridge-building. This word describes efforts to encourage and develop harmony between the great powers and to do everything possible to give the delicate structure of the United Nations a chance of gaining strength.

Such aspirations were no doubt equally alive in the other Nordic countries, but these countries had an objection to the use of this term, an objection which has been raised often, most recently by Erik Brofoss, the Norwegian postwar minister of finance. He observed that the word "bridge-building" implies an active involvement, containing ambitions to play the role of self-appointed mediator between the great powers. Brofoss wished to make it clear that the Norwegian government at least harbored no such illusions and that, while it certainly hoped for the establishment of a strong supranational organization, hesitation and passivity were its actual policy. It is possible that in retrospect Brofoss underestimated the dreams and hopes that could not be realized, but this description of the policy the Nordic countries pursued in practice deserves consideration.

The caution, discretion, and adaptiveness that characterized Nordic relations with the dominant great power in the area, the Soviet Union, naturally exemplified to a great extent the "normal" and traditional policy adopted by a small power in relation to a potential aggressor. This is a prominent feature of Finnish policy as established by Mannerheim and Paasikivi, but it can also be seen in the way the Norwegian and Danish governments handled questions relating to Finnmark, Svalbard, and Bornholm, and in the decisions of the Swedish government concerning the repatriation of Baltic refugees and the credit agreement. Nor did the Nordic countries show much enterprise and initiative in multilateral forums. Their behavior in the United Nations was marked by successful attempts to avoid adopting controversial positions.

However, the same policy can serve more than one objective. It might be said that caution and discretion were also designed to calm Soviet suspicions that the Western powers were in the process of incorporating Scandinavia into an anti-Soviet bloc. Scandinavian policy aimed at avoiding any move that might increase mutual suspicion between the great powers. This consideration does not, however, remove the impression of passivity: the Scandinavian countries did not try to build bridges but contented themselves with not destroying what others might build.

Nonetheless, a number of possible modifications to this picture deserve examination. A small state can actively influence international developments by testing political options that are under discussion. From this angle, Finland seems in its policy toward the

Soviet Union to have given the world an example that deserves consideration. In Allied discussions concerning the principles that would govern reconstruction in the states bordering Russia, there had been a clash between the demand from Moscow that the governments of these countries be in harmony with the U.S.S.R. and the Western demand that free and democratic political systems be installed. Finland demonstrated that one and the same country could fulfill both these demands. The Paasikivi line, though in reality it aimed only at ensuring the continuance of the Finnish state, provided a practical example, for those who wished to see it, of the feasibility of a policy of international understanding.

The choices made by small states in domestic politics may also be seen as a sort of concrete contribution to international discussion. In the field of social and economic policy, Scandinavia, and especially Sweden, had already given many such contributions, which had also aroused the interest of the outside world. During the first postwar years it was above all Norway which put into practice political ideas that were under debate. The planned reconstruction of Norway provided empirical material for a discussion of possible options other than Soviet communism and American capitalism. However, the existence of an example does not necessarily mean that it is followed, and in fact Norwegian economic planning was observed and discussed in other countries only to a very small extent.

In the field of defense policy, the idea that the small states should present a good example was not an unknown one. It had often been cited by the proponents of disarmament during the interwar years as grounds for further reductions in defense spending. Such ambitions were no longer realistic after the war, but it might be said that the Scandinavian states strengthened a general European trend of holding down defense expenditure so that more resources could be devoted to economic and social rehabilitation. In the Swedish debate, quite large groups sought to justify such restraint on the basis of disarmament, but such arguments soon lost their political importance. In Denmark and Norway there were now fewer supporters of disarmament in principle and they were never able to influence the nature of the official reasons given for restraint in defense spending. Instead, economic necessity alone was cited as the motive.

If Scandinavian defense policy did embody an important principle, it was rather that the armed forces should be integrated into the democratic system. In the Swedish debate during the period of intensive rearmament between 1939 and 1942, there were repeated demands for the internal democratization of the armed forces and that officers should be recruited from a wider social base and trained to have a wider social consciousness. The Norwegian defense staff in their report of 1949 provided an example of how democratic officers should behave when explaining why it did not want to argue in favor of higher defense spending. However, any hope that such a democratization of the armed forces might contribute to global understanding was very much a long-term project whose success cannot be estimated without reference to a much longer period than that covered by this study.

The other consideration that might modify the description of Nordic foreign policy as passive is that on a few occasions the Scandinavian countries in fact played an active role. The first example of this is their ultimately unsuccessful attempt to turn the Marshall Plan into a matter of credits without political implications. When faced with a proposal that clearly conflicted with the pursuit of international harmony, they resisted. The second example is the project for a Scandinavian defense alliance. In the spring of 1948, the three countries were faced with a situation, like that in the case of the Marshall Plan, in which passivity would perhaps have implied a more emphatic stand than the degree of activity they displayed. The threat of war was felt to be strong, and both Norway and Denmark disposed of very modest defenses. Several different sets of motives can be cited to explain the idea of an alliance, and one of them was the desire to resist bipolarity and the policy of forming blocs. On the international scene, a neutral alliance would have been a concrete and constructive counterproposal to alliance with a great power, which seemed to be the only other way in which small states could safeguard their security.

Many possible explanations for the failure of the attempt to preserve Scandinavian noninvolvement in great-power alliances can be suggested. Many observers have found it natural to point to the actions of the great powers and to say that the small states had to adjust to the realities of power. Only countries like Sweden that were favored by special historical and geographical circumstances had a real possibility of remaining outside the two hostile blocs. Other observers, especially those who shared the ideological beliefs of democratic socialism, would rather point to domestic political factors, above all the development of public opinion.

It is clear that in economic and social questions the first postwar wave of radical opinion weakened a few years after the end of the war and that in consequence few changes were made in the field of economic policy. Nationalization proposals disappeared under the weight of lengthy consideration by committees, and no substantial redistribution of influence over production occurred.

It is more difficult to determine what effects the development of opinion had on foreign policy, but there can hardly be any doubt that the weakened position of the left undermined the opportunities for pursuing a visionary foreign policy. A social democratic government which was flanked by a strong Communist party on its left and radicalized nonsocialist parties on its right might perhaps have been able to refuse Marshall aid and to commit itself to a third alternative between the great powers. However, a government with a narrow majority and under heavy attack could not. It was too risky, for both the nation and the party, to pursue a policy that was supported by an uncertain parliamentary majority. Just as in the field of domestic policy, the result was that social democracy adjusted to the prevailing circumstances and postponed bold plans for reform.

The development of public opinion during the first postwar years therefore presents a central problem for scholars. It is a topic that has still not been fully researched. An essential question to be answered is whether the broadly based, radical mood which left-wing politicians and many others talked about really existed.

One of the reasons for the belief in a new, popular radicalism was the experience of the closing stages of the First World War. It was thought that the radical atmosphere that had dominated Europe at that time would return, and the electoral successes of the Communists seemed to confirm this hypothesis. Moreover, it was also believed that the sacrifices made by the working class during the war had given its political demands an overwhelming moral strength.

There is, however, reason to wonder whether such assumptions were correct. The parallel with the First World War may have been erroneous because of the considerable improvement in social conditions that had occurred during the interwar period. The temporary increase in Communist electoral support need not have been due to anything more than admiration for the military achievements of the Soviet Union and sympathy for the Communist role in the resistance movement. Large popular groups may indeed have demanded a greater share of the resources of society, but perhaps thought only in terms of a higher income and a better social security system.

So was the view that there was a strong movement toward a socialist system, both nationally and internationally, based on an overestimate of the ideological awareness of the working class or, if you will, of the propagandistic capacities of the workers' parties? The question touches upon the problem of the interaction between the masses and political visionaries, a problem that is central for any democracy. It therefore constitutes one of the most important reasons for continued research into the events surrounding the exposure of the grand plans of the postwar years to political reality.

Bibliographical Note

Bibliographical Note

The Race for Northern Europe

This subject is discussed in several excellent articles in the *Scandinavian Journal of History* 2, nos. 1-2, 1977, a special issue on "The Great Powers and the Nordic Countries, 1939-40." Recommended books on the subject include:

Bédarida, François, *La stratégie secrète de la drôle de guerre. Le Conseil Suprême Interallié, Septembre 1939-Avril 1940* (Paris, 1979).

Butler, J. R. M., *Grand Strategy*, II (London, 1957).

Derry, T. K., *The Campaign in Norway* (London, 1952). Derry's account, such as it is, is modified in his *History of Scandinavia* (London and Minneapolis, 1979).

Gemzell, Carl-Axel, *Raeder, Hitler, und Skandinavien. Der Kampf für einen maritimen Operationsplan* (Lund, 1965).

Gibbs, N. H., *Grand Strategy*, I (London, 1976).

Hubatsch, W., *Weserübung. Die deutsche Besetzung von Dänemark und Norwegen* (Göttingen, 1960).

Kersaudy, François, *Stratèges et Norvège 1940. Les jeux de la guerre et du hasard* (Paris, 1977).

Nevakivi, Jukka, *The Appeal that Was Never Made. The Allies, Scandinavia, and the Finnish Winter War, 1939-40* (London, 1976).

Salewski, Michael, *Die deutsche Seekriegsleitung, 1935-1945*, 1, 1935-1941 (Frankfurt am Main, 1970).

Woodward, Llewellyn, *British Foreign Policy in the Second World War*, I (London, 1970).

The Scandinavian Countries during the War, 1939-45

There is a chapter on Scandinavia, 1939-47 in Derry, T. K., *A History of Scandinavia* (London and Minneapolis, 1979).

DENMARK

Works in English, French, or German

General surveys of the course of events in Denmark during the Second World War are not available in English or German or French. On the other hand, a number of works have appeared on special subjects, especially the resistance movement, and we shall mention some of the more recent of these.

The English edition of Jørgen Hæstrup's pioneer studies in the history of the resistance movement is based on two major accounts, published in 1953 and 1959; the English translation by Alison Borch-Johansen is entitled *Secret Alliance*, I-III (Odense, 1976-77). The same author also discusses conditions in Denmark in *Europe Ablaze. An Analysis of the History of the European Resistance Movements, 1939-45,* translation by Alison Borch-Johansen (Odense, 1978; Danish edition, 1976).

Richard Petrow, *The Bitter Years. Invasion and Occupation of Denmark and Norway, April 1940-May 1945* (New York, 1974; London, 1975), is affected by the writer's ignorance of Danish and Norwegian; it is disjointed and unsystematic.

John Oram Thomas, *The Giant-Killers. The Story of the Danish Resistance Movement, 1940-1945* (London, 1975), indulges in the hero-worship implied by the title, focusing upon dramatic episodes; this writer too knows no Danish.

A somewhat earlier work is David Lampe, *The Savage Canary: The Story of Resistance in Denmark* (London, 1959); U.S. title: *Danish Resistance.*

While the three English writers we have named belong to the journalistic school of historiography, readers of German have available to them a scholarly monograph by Erich Thomsen, *Deutsche Besatzungspolitik in Dänemark, 1940-45* (Düsseldorf, 1971). This is constructed chiefly from German source materials and, perhaps for that reason, has become to a considerable extent an apologia for Werner Best.

Conditions in Denmark are examined, though generally to a limited degree in surveys of the European resistance movement, of which three are singled out for mention:

E. H. Cookridge allots fully twenty pages to the chapter on the "redoubtable Danes" in his *Inside SOE. The Story of Special Operations in Western Europe, 1940-45* (London, 1966). But what he writes about Denmark is full of mistakes, and readers should not accept his information without checking it for accuracy.

Henri Michel makes few and sometimes erroneous references to Denmark in his celebrated account of the resistance movement in Europe: *La guerre des ombres. La résistance en Europe* (Paris, 1970); English translation: *The Shadow War: European Resistance 1939-45* (New York, 1972).

M. R. D. Foot, *Resistance. An Analysis of European Resistance to Nazism 1940-45* (London, 1976; New York, 1977), devotes five and a half pages to Denmark, concentrating upon SOE activities.

Other subject areas have been examined in separate works:

Jeremy Bennett, *British Broadcasting and the Danish Resistance Movement, 1940-45: A Study of the Wartime Broadcasts of the BBC Danish Service* (Cambridge, 1966), is best on the BBC, weakest on Denmark.

Leni Yahil, *The Rescue of Danish Jewry: Test of a Democracy* (Philadelphia, 1969; first version in Hebrew, 1966), is a thorough piece of work with a dubious thesis (stated in the subtitle).

Robin Reilly, *The Sixth Floor* (London, 1969), is about the RAF attack on Gestapo Headquarters in Copenhagen in March 1945.

Rüdiger Eckert, *Die politische Struktur der dänischen Wiederstandsbewegung im Zweiten Weltkrieg. Eine Untersuchung über die Bedeutung der illegalen Presse und einiger repräsentativer Vertreter der Wiederstandsgruppen* (Hamburg, 1969), is a substantial work on the political structure of the resistance movement.

Erik Lund, *A Girdle of Truth. The Underground News Service Information, 1943-1945* (Copengagen, 1970, with Danish original in the same year), is important for its discussion of the clandestine press.

Two volumes of memoirs should be mentioned:

Flemming Muus, *The Spark and the Flame* (London, 1957; Danish original, 1950).

Ebbe Munck, *Sibyllegatan 13 ou La résistance danoise* (Paris, 1970; Danish original, 1967).

A bibliographical survey of Danish literature covering the period of the occupation is provided by Jørgen Hæstrup in *Revue d'histoire de la deuxième guerre mondiale* 88 October 1972).

Works in Danish

An asterisk (*) after a title denotes a work with a summary in English or German.

Directly after the Liberation in May 1945, there was a widespread interest in learning more about the dramatic years of the occupation. As a result, a number of books appeared, including major accounts of the period, descriptions of single events and local areas, and histories of the occupation in particular towns. It was natural for the books to be biased toward resistance policy, which in the final years of the occupation had supplanted the policy of negotiation. Disagreement about the policies that had been followed found expression in volumes attacking or defending particular stands that had been taken by political parties, organizations, and individuals during those five years or earlier.

The principal accounts belonging to this phase include the following:

Vilhelm la Cour, ed., *Danmark under Besættelsen*, I-III (Copenhagen, 1945-46), has a patriotic and somewhat conservative flavor, but there are individual contributions of lasting value.

Aage Friis, ed., *Danmark under Verdenskrig og Besættelse*, I-V (Copenhagen, 1946-48), includes two volumes on political developments by the former foreign minister, Peter Munch.

Hartvig Frisch, ed., *Danmark besat og befriet*, I-III (Copenhagen, 1945-48), has a definite Social Democratic bias.

P. P. Rhode et al., eds., *Frit Danmarks Hvidbog*, I-II (Copenhagen, 1945-46), contains documents, articles, etc., representing the dominant attitudes in Frit Danmark ("Free Denmark"), one of the big clandestine organizations in which conservatives and communists cooperated.

Immediately after the end of the occupation, judicial proceedings were begun against persons who had been in the service of the Germans or who had been overeager with deliveries to the *Wehrmacht*. The lawyer Niels Alkil helped the inquiries of the court by producing *Besættelsestidens Fakta*, I-II (Copenhagen, 1945-46), containing documents, articles, and surveys of various kinds.

The political side of the proceedings was in the hands of a number of commissions, appointed by the Rigsdag to inquire whether there were grounds for legal actions against politicians and persons with administrative responsibility. The hearings of the commissions and a quantity of documents and memoranda were printed in *Den Parlamentariske Kommissions Beretning* (with appendixes), I-XIV (Copenhagen 1946-53). In spite of obvious defects, these volumes must be regarded as an indispensable basis for studying the history of the occupation period.

An investigation of the persons convicted in the proceedings has been made by Karl O. Christiansen, *Landssvigerkriminaliteten i sociologisk belysning** (Copenhagen, 1955).

In the first years after the Liberation, there appeared a number of books by individuals whose position enabled them to make significant contributions to the literature:

Erling Foss, *Fra passiv til aktiv Modstand* (Copenhagen, 1946), gives the recollections of a leading resistance man, later a member of the Danish Freedom Council, and his clandestine correspondence with the BBC and persons in London. The author carried on his account into the years 1944 and 1945 in *På eget ansvar* (Copenhagen, 1958).

Oluf Pedersen, *Den politiske Modstand under Besættelsen* (Copenhagen, 1946), is chiefly a record of the author's observations as a member of the Folketing and secretary of the parliamentary interparty committee of cooperation (the Committee of Nine).

Erik Scavenius, *Forhandlingspolitiken under Besættelsen* (Copenhagen, 1948), constitutes an apologia for his policy as foreign minister (July 1940-   ) and prime minister (November 1942-   ). The book is clear, sober, and polemical.

Jørgen Hæstrup's book on the resistance movement (listed on p. 386) inspired a new start in the research into the history of the occupation period. A program of studies was introduced in 1961 under the auspices of D.N.H. (the society for publications on recent Danish history), resulting in a series of books, most of which – like those named above – figure in the bibliography of the *Revue d'histoire de la deuxième guerre mondiale*.

Jørgen Hæstrup, ed., *Christmas Møllers Londonbreve* (Copenhagen, 1974), contains the correspondence of the exiled conservative politician, written from London during the years 1942-45.

Jørgen Hæstrup, *Til landets Bedste*, I-II (Copenhagen, 1971), covers the work of the central administration, as continued in the period after 29 August 1943. The main thesis is that every sector of Danish society gradually became half-illegal during the last years of the war.

Sigurd Jensen, *Levevilkår under Besættelsen* (Copenhagen, 1971), examines the occupation period, specifically economic negotiations with Germany, rationing and regulation, and the effects on living conditions.

Hans Kirchhoff, *Augustoprøret 1943,** I-III (Copenhagen, 1979), describes the collapse of the policy of negotiation, polemically termed collaboration. It contains a penetrating study of the local strikes and disturbances, which finally convinced the central German authorities of the need to dissolve the Danish armed forces and government. The book maintains the thesis that the parliamentary politicians did not envisage breaking off the policy of negotiation until right before the moment of liberation.

Finn Løkkegaard, *Det danske gesandtskab i Washington, 1940-1942** (Copenhagen, 1968), is a study of the Danish minister in Washington, Henrik Kauffmann, of his policy as an independent envoy, and of his contribution to the making of the treaty for the defense of Greenland by the Allies and the use of the island as a base.

Peter Munch, *Erindringer*, VII-VIII, ed. D.N.H. (Copenhagen, 1967), comprise the two final volumes of Munch's memoirs; they consist of notes made at intervals of a few days or weeks by the influential politician who was foreign minister from 1929 to July 1940.

Henrik S. Nissen, *1940. Studier i Forhandlingspolitikken og Samarbejdspolitikken** (Copenhagen, 1973), examines the establishment of the policy of cooperation among the democratic parties in the Rigsdag, viewing this cooperation as the basis for the policy of negotiation. It traces the development in the first year of the occupation.

Henrik S. Nissen and Henning Poulsen, *På dansk frihends grund* (Copenhagen, 1963), is about the cooperation among the political, cultural, sports, and other youth organizations. The discussions among those cooperating and among the public reflect a number of problems in the policy of cooperation and in that of negotiation.

Henning Poulsen, *Besættelsesmagten og de danske nazister** (Copenhagen, 1970), is a study of the Danish Nazi party, its collaboration with the Germans, and its attempt to come into power with their help.

Palle Roslyng-Jensen, *Værnenes politik- politikernes værn** (Copenhagen, 1980), examines the policy conducted by leading officers in the Danish armed forces after 9 April 1940. The author shows that the actions of the commanding officers were influenced by two major considerations: 1) their loyalty to the established political system; and 2) their resolve to prevent a communist coup when the Liberation eventually occurred.

Viggo Sjøqvist, *Danmarks udenrigspolitik, 1933-1940* (Copenhagen, 1966), gives an account of Danish foreign policy from the assumption of power by the Nazis in Germany to the occupation of Denmark. The author was archivist in the Danish Foreign Ministry.

Apart from the D.N.H. program of research, other works of scholarship have appeared:

Mary Dau, *Danmark og Sovjetunionen, 1944-1949* (Copenhagen, 1969), traces the development of Denmark's relations with the Soviet Union from 1944 (when the Danish

Freedom Council and the politicians first approached the Soviet Union with a view to obtaining Denmark's recognition as an Allied nation) to 1949 (when Denmark was included in the Western alliance system).

L. Bindsløv Frederiksen, *Pressen under besættelsen* (Copenhagen, 1960), describes conditions in the legal press under the shifting and ever stricter censorship regulations.

Jørgen Hæstrup, *Krig og besættelse. Odense, 1940-1945* (Copenhagen, 1979), offers an all-round description of everyday events and the dramatic, the regular and the illegal, in a big provincial town during wartime.

Mogens Nielsen, *Socialdemokratiet og enheden i arbejderbevægelsen, 1943-1945* (Copenhagen, 1978), is a study of the preliminaries and of the actual negotiations in 1945 between the Social Democrats and the Danish Communist party regarding union or cooperation.

Ib Damgaard Petersen, *Mod-eliten. Træk af den danske modstandsbevægelses opståen og udvikling.* (Copenhagen, 1978), analyzes recruitment by the resistance movement; the work is based on the biographies of 869 freedom fighters who were killed during the war.

Viggo Sjøqvist: *Besættelsen 1940. De danske forudsætninger for 9. april* (Copenhagen, 1978), develops the thesis that those who made political decisions in Denmark before 9 April 1940 expected a German ultimatum demanding right of passage, so that it was only the attack without warning and the complete occupation that came as a surprise. The same author has also written thorough biographies of *Erik Scavenius*, I-II (Copenhagen, 1973), and *P. Munch*, I-II (Copenhagen, 1976).

Hans Snitker, *Det illegale Frit Danmark, bladet, organisationen* (Copenhagen, 1977). The Frit Danmark organization began in 1942, when conservatives outside the Rigsdag, such as Christmas Møller, and communists cooperated over the production of a clandestine paper. It developed into one of the most important organizations in the resistance movement.

Bjørn Svensson, *Derfor gik det sådan 9. april* (Copenhagen, 1969), is a well-documented attempt to clear away stab-in-the-back legends of treachery in connection with the occupation on 9 April 1940.

Aage Trommer, *Jernbanesabotagen i Danmark** (Odense, 1971), studies the sabotaging of the Danish railways and German troop movements through Denmark from the standpoint of military history. The conclusion is that the military effect of the sabotage was extremely small because of mistaken tactical assumptions.

Aage Trommer, *Modstandsarbejde i nærbillede* (Odense, 1977), provides a detailed in-depth study of the recruitment, organization, and activities of one regional unit in the resistance movement.

FINLAND

Works in English, French, or German

Blücher, Wipert von, *Gesandter zwischen Diktatur und Demokratie. Erinnerungen aus den Jahren 1935-1944* (Wiesbaden, 1951).
Erfurth, Waldemar, *Der Finnische Krieg, 1941-1944* (Wiesbaden, 1950).
Gripenberg, Georg A., *Finland and the Great Powers: Memoirs of a Diplomat* (Lincoln, Neb., 1965).
Jakobson, Max, *The Diplomacy of the Winter War. An Account of the Russo-Finnish War, 1939-1940* (Cambridge, 1961).
Jalanti, Heikki, *La Finlande dans l'étau germano-soviétique, 1940-1941*, Editions de la Baconnière (Neuchâtel, 1966).
Killinen, Kullervo, "Direction of the War in Finland during World War II," in *Revue internationale d'histoire militaire* 47 (1980), pp. 11-35.
Krosby, H. Peter, *Finland, Germany, and the Soviet Union, 1940-1941. The Petsamo Dispute* (Madison and Milwaukee, Wisc., 1968).
Lundin, D. Leonard, *Finland in the Second World War*, Indiana University Publications,

Slavic and East European series 6 (Bloomington, 1957).

Mannerheim, Carl Gustav, *The Memoirs of Marshal Mannerheim* (London, 1953; New York, 1954).

Nevakivi, Jukka, *The Appeal that Was Never Made. The Allies, Scandinavia, and the Finnish Winter War, 1939-40* (London, 1976).

Paasikivi, J. K., *Meine Moskauer Mission, 1939-41* (Hamburg, 1966).

Palm, Thede, *The Finnish-Soviet Armistice Negotiations of 1944* (Uppsala, 1971).

Tanner, Väinö, *The Winter War. Finland against Russia, 1939-1940* (Stanford, Calif., 1957).

Ueberschär, Gerd R., *Hitler und Finnland, 1939-1941. Die Deutsch-Finnischen Beziehungen während des Hitler-Stalin-Paktes*, Frankfurter Historische Abhandlungen 16 (Wiesbaden, 1978).

Upton, Anthony F., *Finland in Crisis, 1940-1941. A Study in Smallpower Politics* (London, 1964).

Wuorinen, John H., ed., *Finland and World War II, 1939-1944* (New York, 1948).

Ziemke, Karl F., *The German Northern Theater of Operations, 1940-1945* (Washington, 1960).

In addition to the bibliographies included in the Finnish and Swedish books listed in the next section, there is a very useful bibliography by Kristina Nyman: *Finland's War Years, 1939-1945. A List of Books and Articles Concerning the Winter War and the Continuation War Excluding Literature in Finnish and Russian*, Publication of the Society of Military History, 4 (Helsinki, 1973).

Beiträge zum internationalen Symposium in Hanasaari 22.-24.10. 1976 (Reports of the Research Project "Finland in the Second World War." (Helsinki, 1977), is also useful. This work contains two articles on Finland: Olli Vehviläinen, "Die Erforschung des Zweiten Weltkrieges in Finnland"; and Hannu Soikkanen, "Die Mobilisierung der Kräftreserven Finnlands während des Zweiten Weltkrieges."

In French there is M. Häikiö and A. Rusi, "La Finlande dans la seconde guerre mondiale," *Revue d'histoire de la deuxième guerre mondiale* 93 (Janvier 1974), pp. 79-88.

There are also articles in English and a bibliography for the Finnish war years in I Convegno storico italo-finlandese, *Perugia, 23-26 ottobre 1978 (Relazioni, M.A.E. Centrofotorotolitografico, 1978).*

Works in Finnish or Swedish

The literature in Finnish or Swedish includes two very useful works of a general nature. The official history of the wartime governments is *Valtioneuvoston historia,* II (Helsinki, 1977), whereas the official military history (with maps, illustrations, and tables) for the Winter War is *Talvisodan historia,* 1-4 (Helsinki, 1978-79) and for the Continuation War *Suomen sota, 1941-1944,* 1-11 (Helsinki, 1948-74). There is no comparable volume on internal developments in Finland.

Finnish foreign relations before the war are treated in Keijo Korhonen, *Turvallisuuden pettäessä* (Helsinki, 1971) and Juhani Suomi, *Talvisodan tausta,* 1 (Helsinki, 1973), both of which concentrate on Finnish-Soviet relations.

Finnish-Allied relations during the Winter War are covered in Martti Häikiö, *Maaliskuusta maaliskuuhun. Suomi Englannin politiikassa 1939-40* (Helsinki, 1976); Finnish-German relations in Risto O. Peltovuori, *Saksa ja Suomen talvisota* (Helsinki, 1975); and Mannerheim in Stig Jägerskiöld, *Fältmarskalken* (Helsingfors, 1975).

For the foreign policy in 1940-41, there is Ohto Manninen, *Toteutumaton valtioliitto* (Helsinki, 1977); Markku Reimaa, *Puun ja kuoren välissä. Rytin toinen hallitus ulkopoliittisten vaihtoehtojen edessä* (Keuruu, 1979).

On the foreign relations of Finland in 1941-47, there is a new and excellent three-volume study by Tuomo Polvinen: *Suomi kansainvälisessä politiikassa, 1941-1947,* I: 1941-1943 (Juva, 1979), II: 1944: (Juva, 1980), III: 1945-1947 (Juva, 1981). To some extent these problems are covered in another volume of the Mannerheim biography by Stig Jägerskiöld: *Marskalken av Finland* (Helsingfors, 1979).

On the war crimes trials after the war, there is Jukka Tarkka, *13. artikla* (Porvoo, 1977).

In *Suomi toisessa maailmansodassa-projektin julkaisuja 1* (Reports of the Research Project "Finland in the Second World War.") (Helsinki, 1976), there are articles and bibliographies concerning the literature on Finland's internal development and foreign policy and concerning Soviet research on the war years in Finland.

The research project "Finland in the Second World War" will shortly publish studies of Finland's foreign trade during the war (Ilkka Seppinen), of agricultural and land policy (Silvo Hietanen), and of German propaganda in Finland (Britta Hiedanniemi).

NORWAY

Works in English, French, or German

Books in the above languages on the subject of Norway during the Second World War have made their appearance quite fortuitously, many aspects having been scarcely touched. There is, however, a short but scholarly account for the general reader by Johannes Andeæs, O. Riste, and M. Skodvin: *Norway and the Second World War* (Oslo, 1966).

Most foreign writers have directed their attention to the campaign of 1940, of which the following accounts are available:

Ash, Bernard, *Norvège 1940* (Paris, 1965). Originally an English publication (London, 1964).

Bieganski, Witold, *Poles in the Battle of Narvik* (Warsaw, 1969). A translation; the Polish original dates from 1962.

Derry, T. K., *The Campaign in Norway* (London, 1952).

Hubatsch, W., *Weserübung. Die deutsche Besetzung von Dänemark und Norwegen* (Gottingen, 1960).

Macintyre, Donald, *Narvik* (London, 1971).

Mordal, J., *La campagne de Norvège* (Paris, 1948).

Moulton, J. L., *The Norwegian Campaign of 1940* (London, 1966).

Sereau, R., *L'expédition de Norvège* (Baden-Baden, 1949).

Ziemke, E. F., *The German Northern Theater of Operations* (Washington, 1959).

Both the prelude to the German invasion and political developments in the occupied area down to 25 September 1940 are discussed in an admirable account by Hans-Dietrich Loock: *Quisling, Rosenberg und Terboven. Zur Vorgeschichte und Geschichte der nationalsozialistischen Revolution in Norwegen.* (Stuttgart, 1970). Otherwise, there is no good integrated account either of the German regime in 1940-45 or of the Norwegian Nazis during the same period, whether in English, German, or French—or for that matter in Norwegian. We obtain glimpses of the German military side in the above-named book by Ziemke. Paul M. Hayes, *Quisling. The Career and Political Ideas of Vidkun Quisling, 1887-1945* (Newton Abbot, 1971), is a work of scholarship but seems neither exhaustive nor wholly satisfactory. The adherence to the Norwegian Nazi party is treated in several articles in Stein Ugelvik Larsen, ed., *Who Were the Fascists. Social Roots of European Fascism* (Bergen, 1980).

The resistance movement is described for the general reader in a short but scholarly account by Olav Riste and Berit Nøkleby: *Norway, 1940-45: The Resistance Movement* (Oslo, 1970). There is a good book by one of the participants, the Home Front leader Tore Gjelsvik, *Norwegian Resistance, 1940-1945* (London, 1979), which is a translation of *Hjemmefronten* (Oslo, 1977); this bears the stamp both of the author's personal experiences and of his examination of many sources and postwar narratives. Magne Skodvin dealt with the element of passive resistance in Norway in an article in Adam Roberts, ed., *The Strategy of Civilian Defence* (London, 1967), pp. 136-53. This has also been done by Gene Sharp in the pamphlet *Tyranny Could not Quell Them* (London, 1959).

Nils Morten Udgaard, *Great Power Politics and Norwegian Foreign Policy. A Study of Norway's Foreign Relations November 1940-February 1948.* (Oslo, 1973), concentrates upon the exiled Norwegian government in London.

Some interesting perspectives on the history of the occupation are to be found in an article by Hans-Dietrich Loock, "Zeitgeschichte Norwegens," *Vierteljahrshefte für Zeitgeschichte* no. 1 (1965):83-111.

English raids on the Norwegian coast are described in C. Buckley, *Norway, The Commandos, Dieppe* (London, 1951).

An expert study of economic conditions has been made by Alan S. Milward, *The Fascist Economy in Norway* (Oxford, 1972).

Works in Norwegian

A popular account of the period of the occupation, written by C. A. R. Christensen, is to be found in volume 9 of *Vårt folks historie* (Oslo, 1961). Edvard Bull, in volume 13 of *Norges historie* (Oslo, 1979), devotes only one long chapter to the years of the Second World War.

Some of Magne Skodvin's contributions to the extensive international debate about the great powers and Scandinavia in 1939-40 are collected in his book *Samtid og historie* (Oslo, 1975).

The Norwegian side of the campaign of 1940 has been covered by an army officer, Odd Lindbäck Larsen, in *Krigen i Norge 1940* (Oslo, 1965). It is practically a summary of a multivolume account by Forsvarets Krigshistoriske Avdeling. An insight into the mentality of the military leaders may be acquired from Otto Ruge, *Krigens dagbok* (Oslo, 1946). The Report of the Commission of Military Inquiry of 1946 has at last been published in *Norges offentlige utredninger* no. 47 (1979), with a foreword by Olav Riste.

The policy of the Germans and the Norwegian Nazis down to 25 September 1940 and the political developments at the national level during the same period have been thoroughly examined in several penetrating accounts. The latest of these, which in some respects sums up its predecessors, is the previously mentioned book by Hans-Dietrich Loock, translated into Norwegian by Astrid and Einhart Lorenz as *Quisling, Rosenberg og Terboven* (Oslo, 1972). For the rest of the war there is no comprehensive account of the policy of the Germans or of the Norwegian Nazis. Some insight into purely military matters is obtainable from the previously mentioned work by Ziemke, and it is the subject of a short article by Magne Skodvin entitled "Norges plass i Hitlers militære planer etter 7. juni 1940," *Norsk historisk tidskrift* 35, no. 7 (1951): 429-58. The German Navy's involvement in politics during the first couple of years of the war is discussed in Helge Paulsen, "Terboven i konflikt med Kriegsmarine," *Motstandskamp, strategi, og marinepolitikk.* (Oslo, 1972).

The policy of the Germans and the Norwegian Nazis in 1940-42 is presented from a particular angle in Thomas Christian Wyller, *Nyordning og motstand. En framstilling og analyse av organisasjonenes politiske funksjon under den tyske okkupasjonen, 25/9 1940-25/9 1942* (Oslo, 1958), a book with an English summary. An earlier article on approximately the same subject and period is that by Magne Skodvin: "Det store fremstøt," in Sverre Steen, ed., *Norges Krig*, II (Oslo, 1948), pp. 573-734. In spite of its title, one will find much about both Germans and Nazis in Sverre Kjeldstadli, *Hjemmestyrkene. Hovedtrekk av den militære motstanden under okkupasjonen*, I (Oslo, 1959). Snapshots as it were of German policy are to be found in Sverre Hartmann, *Nytt lys over kritiske faser i Norges historie under den annen verdenskrig* (Oslo, 1965). Some new information is made available in a short article by Helge Paulsen on relations between the Norwegian Nazi party and the Reichskommissariat in Rolf Danielsen and Stein Ugelvik Larsen, eds., *Fra idé til dom. Noen trekk fra utviklingen av Nasjonal Samling* (Oslo, 1976), pp. 196-214.

The Norwegian Nazis are the subject of an article by Magne Skodvin dating from 1962, "Den historiske bakgrunnen for landssvikoppgjeret," which is reprinted in his book *Samtid og historie* (Oslo, 1975), pp. 114-55. The Norwegians who fought on the German side are recorded by Svein Blindheim in *Nordmenn under Hitlers fane* (Oslo, 1977). A former Nazi, Odd Melsom, makes defensive representations in three works: *På nasjonal uriaspost* (Oslo, 1975); *Nasjonal Samling og fagorganisasjonen* (Oslo, 1977); and *Fra kirke-og kulturkampen under okkupasjonen* (Oslo, 1980).

A good account of the judicial settlement after the war, which also sheds light on the history of the occupation, is by Johannes Andenæs, *Det vanskelige oppgjøret* (Oslo, 1979).

The resistance movement is examined fully in three scholarly works, namely the abovementioned books by Kjeldstadli and Wyller and Ole Kristian Grimnes, *Hjemmefrontens ledelse* (Oslo, 1977). Hans Luihn, *De illegale avisene* (Oslo, 1960), examines the clandestine press. Rolf Barstad covers sabotage in *Sabotasjen i Oslo-området, 1944-45* (Oslo, 1975), while O. K. Grimnes provides a more general treatment of the same subject in two articles: "Sabotasjen i norsk og dansk motstandsbevegelse," *Motstandskamp, strategi, og marinepolitikk* (Oslo, 1972), pp. 9-36; and "Ved å pusse Quislingkoblet på befolkningen . . . .' De krogske teser om norsk okkupasjonshistorie," *Materialisten* no. 1 (1979): 4-15. In *Militær motstand i Rogaland og Vestfold* (Oslo, 1972), there are two studies of the military resistance movement at the local level, by Rolf Berg and by Peder Lindhjem. Ragnar Ulstein uses comprehensive interviews in his narrative of how people escaped from Norway during the war: *Englandsfarten*, I-II (Oslo, 1965-67), and *Svensketrafikken*, I-III (Oslo, 1974-77). A Marxist-Leninist attempt to analyse the economic situation and the Home Front leadership is Terje Valen, *De tjente på krigen* (Oslo, 1974).

There is as yet no complete account of the activities of the communists during the war. The Norwegian Communist party has published a collection of documents, *Vårt partis politikk under krigen. Krigspolitikken* (Oslo, 1945), which sheds light on policy but only to a small extent on organization and activities. Their wartime leader has found a biographer and champion in Torgrim Titlestad, the author of *Stalin midt imot. Peder Furubotn, 1938-41* (Oslo, 1977), and *I kamp, i krig. Peder Furubotn, 1942-45* (Oslo, 1977). The relations between the communists and the Home Front leadership are examined in the chapter on leadership and opposition in Ole Kristian Grimnes, *Hjemmefrontens ledelse* (Oslo, 1977).

The position of the government-in-exile is presented in the large two-volume work by Olav Riste: *"London-Regjeringa." Norge i krigsalliansen, 1940-1945. I, 1940-42: Prøvetid* (Oslo, 1973). *II, 1942-45: Vegen heim* (Oslo, 1979). He has also written two articles: "Norge i alliert strategi under 2. verdskrigen. 1940-1942," *Mellom nøytrale og allierte* (Oslo, 1968), pp. 265-92; and "Stormaktene og nordkalotten 1940-1945," *Motstandskamp, strategi, og marinepolitikk* (Oslo, 1972), pp. 37-58. The community of Norwegian exiles in Sweden is described by O. K. Grimnes in *Et flyktningesamfunn vokser fram. Nordmenn i Sverige, 1940-45* (Oslo, 1969).

The history of the Norwegian broadcasting service at home and abroad is narrated by Hans Fredrik Dahl in *"Dette er London. NRK i krig, 1940-1945* (Oslo, 1978). The same author has also expressed more general views on the history of Norway during the war in "Norsk politikk, 1940-45: Kontinuitet eller brudd," *Kontrast* nos. 1 & 2 (1971):5-23; and "Okkupasjon og integrasjon," *Norsk historisk tidsskrift* no. 3 (1972): 285-307.

The title indicates the contents of Jan Debes, *Sentraladministrasjonens historie, 1940-45* (Oslo, 1980).

Although written as early as 1950, Jens Christian Hauge, *Frigjøringen* (Oslo, 1970), can still be read with profit. In it the leader of the wartime military resistance organization (Milorg) examines developments in the final war year on the part of the Germans, the Norwegians, and the Allies. The military aspects of the liberation of the most northerly part of Norway, where the Russians moved in, is treated in Harald Sandvik, *Frigjøringen av Finnmark, 1944-45* (Oslo, 1975), whereas the political assumptions are stated in the abovenamed work of Olav Riste.

The economic and social history have so far received very slight treatment by Norwegian historians, so the English work by Alan Milward must be mentioned for a second time. Annotated statistical material is to be found in *Statistisk-økonomisk utsyn over krigsårene* published by the Central Office of Statistics (Oslo, 1945).

SWEDEN

Works in English, French, or German

The history of Sweden during the Second World War has been the subject of a special research project, from which twenty treatises have so far emerged for the following subject areas: 1) rearmament; 2) case studies in security policy; 3) domestic policy; 4) the development of public opinion; 5) humanitarian activities. A thorough and reliable summary of all these works is available for readers of German in Lothar Gruchmann, "Schweden im Zweiten Weltkrieg. Ergebnisse eines Stockholmer Forschungsprojekts," *Vierteljahrshefte für Zeitgeschichte* no. 4 (October 1977): 591-657.

Some of the most important results of the project are presented to readers of French in *Revue d'histoire de la deuxième guerre mondiale* no. 109 (January 1978). This special issue on Sweden during the Second World War contains the following papers: S. Ekman, "Introduction"; A. Johansson, "La neutralité suédoise et les puissances occidentales entre 1939 et 1945"; M. Fritz, "Les relations économiques germano-suédoises durant la seconde guerre mondiale"; K. Zetterberg, "Le transport allemand par la Suède de 1940 à 1945"; K. Molin, "Conflicts et convergences dans la politique intérieure suédoise (1939-1945)".

There is no corresponding English abridgment of the results of this research project. But nineteen of the twenty books have a four- to eight-page "Summary" in English and the remaining volume has one in German.

A comprehensive description of party activities in the Riksdag is to be found in Karl Molin, "Parliamentary Politics during World War II," in Steven Koblik, ed., *Sweden's Development from Poverty to Affluence, 1750-1970* (Minneapolis, 1975).

Apart from this research project, there have been several studies of Swedish foreign policy during the period. A detailed account from the standpoint of the Foreign Ministry is given in Wilhelm M. Carlgren, *Swedish Foreign Policy during the Second World War* (London, 1977), a standard work, written by the ministry's chief archivist. A summary argument is presented by Erik Lönnroth in "Sweden's Ambiguous Neutrality," *Scandinavian Journal of History* 2 (1977):89-105.

Sweden's relations with Germany have been the subject of two treatises, namely John M. West, "German-Swedish Relations, 1939-1942" (Ph.D. dissertation, University of Denver, 1976), and Wolfgang Wilhelmus, "Das faschistische Deutschland und Schweden im zweiten Weltkrieg" (Inaugural-dissertation, Greifswald, 1975). Both of these are well-documented and intelligent descriptions of a central problem in Swedish foreign policy, Welhelmus's treatise having a somewhat wider scope through the inclusion of cultural and economic aspects. A special study of developments during the campaign in Norway has been provided by Hans-Jürgen Lutzhöft in "Deutschland und Schweden während des Norwegenfeldzuges," *Vierteljahrshefte für Zeitgeschichte* no. 4 (1974).

Relations between the Western powers and Sweden are the theme of an article by A. Johansson in the previously mentioned special issue of *Revue d'histoire de la deuxième guerre mondiale*. The part played by Sweden in British policy during the opening phase of the world war has since been examined by two doctoral dissertations: Thomas Munch-Petersen, "British Policy towards Sweden, 1939-1940" (unpublished thesis, London School of Economics, 1979), now published as *The Strategy of Phony War. Britain, Sweden, and the Iron Ore Question, 1939-40* (Stockholm, 1981); and Patrick Salmon, "Scandinavia in British Strategy, September 1939-April 1940" (unpublished thesis, Cambridge, 1979).

The economic development of Sweden during the Second World War has been taken up in Gothenburg as a research project in economic history with the title "Under Pressure from Abroad—Sectors of the Swedish Economy, 1933-1945." The project has produced three major works, two of them in English: Martin Fritz, *German Steel and Swedish Iron Ore, 1939-1945* (Gothenburg, 1974); Sven-Olof Olsson, *German Coal and Swedish Fuel, 1939-1945* (Gothenburg, 1975).

Sweden's economic relations with Germany receive an extremely detailed and penetrating description in Klaus Wittmann, *Schwedens Wirtschaftsbeziehungen zum Dritten Reich, 1933-1945* (München, 1978).

A special problem within the framework of Swedish-German economic relationships is that of the importance of Swedish iron ore for the German armaments and war effort. An attempt by a Swedish historian to show that its importance was quite decisive provoked an animated discussion, with contributions as follows: Rolf Karlbom, "Sweden's Iron Ore Exports to Germany, 1933-1944," *The Scandinavian Economic History Review* 13 (1965): 65-93; Alan S. Milward, "Could Sweden Have Stopped the Second World War? " *ibid.* 15 (1967):127-38; Jörg-Johannes Jäger, "Sweden's Iron Ore Exports to Germany, 1933-44," *ibid.*:139-47; Rolf Karlbom, "Swedish Iron Ore Exports to Germany, 1933-44. A Reply," *ibid.* 16 (1968):171-75. A closely related problem was taken up later by Martin Fritz in "Swedish Ball-Bearings and the German War Economy," *The Scandinavian Economic History Review* 23 (1975):15-34.

Swedish neutrality became at an early date a topic of special interest to two foreign researchers. Francis La Ruche, *La neutralité de la Suède* (Paris, 1953), studies the question chiefly from the standpoint of international law, whereas Kurt Gustmann, *Die schwedische Tagespresse zur Neutralitätsfrage im zweiten Weltkrieg* (Münster, 1958), gives a good survey of the press debate on Swedish neutrality policy during the war. An early Swedish discussion of the problem is an article by Gunnar Hägglöf: "A Test of Neutrality. Sweden in the Second World War," *International Affairs* 36, no. 2 (April 1960):153-67, in which a leading diplomat tries to determine whether Sweden really did preserve its neutrality.

Works in Swedish

The special research project named in the previous section has distributed its twenty publications among the five research areas as follows:

1. Rearmament

Leif Björkman, *Sverige inför Operation Barbarossa. Svensk neutralitetspolitik, 1940-1941* (1971).

Erik Norberg, *Flyg i beredskap. Det svenska flygvapnet i omvandling och uppbyggnad, 1936-42* (1971).

Åke Holmquist, *Flottans beredskap, 1938-1940* (1972).

2. Case studies in security policy

Rune Karlsson, *Så stoppades tysktågen. Den tyska transiteringstrafiken i svensk politik, 1942-1943* (1974).

Nicolaus Rockberger, *Göteborgstrafiken. Svensk lejdtrafik under andra världskriget* (1973).

Ulf Torell, *Hjälp till Danmark. Militära och politiska förbindelser, 1943-1945* (1973).

Åke Uhlin, *Februarikrisen 1942. Svensk säkerhetspolitik och militär planering, 1941-1943* (1972).

3. Domestic policy

Kerstin Abukhanfusa, *Beredskapsfamiljernas försörjning. Krigsfamiljebidragen i teori och praktik* (1975).

Lennart Friberg, *Styre i kristid. Studier i krisförvaltningens organisation och struktur, 1939-1945* (1973).

Ann-Katrin Hatje, *Befolkningsfrågan och välfärden. Debatten om familjepolitik och nativitetsökning under 1930- och 1940- talen* (1974).

Yvonne Hirdman, *Sveriges Kommunistika Parti, 1939-1945* (1974).

Karl Molin, *Försvaret, folkhemmet, och demokratin. Socialdemokratisk riksdagspolitik, 1939-1945* (1974).

Olle Månsson, *Industriell beredskap och ekonomisk försvarsplanering inför andra världskriget* (1976).
Kent Zetterberg, *Liberalism i kris. Folkpartiet, 1939-1945* (1975).
4. The development of public opinion
Klas Åmark, *Makt eller moral. En studie i den svenska offentliga debatten om internationell politik och svensk försvars- och utrikespolitik, 1938-1939* (1973).
Louise Drangel, *Den kämpande demokratin. En studie i antinazistisk opinionsrörelse, 1939-1945* (1976).
Alf Johansson, *Finlands sak. Svensk politik och opinion under vinterkriget, 1939-1940* (1973).
Thorsten Nybom, *Motstånd-anpassning-uppslutning. Linjer i svensk debatt om utrikespolitik och internationell politik, 1940-1943* (1978).
5. Humanitarian activities
Erik Carlquist, *Solidaritet på prov. Finlandshjälp under vinterkriget* (1971).
Hans Lindberg, *Svensk flyktingpolitik under internationellt tryck, 1936-1941* (1973).
The above books have all been published by Liber Förlag, Stockholm, in a series entitled "Sverige under andra världskriget."

As regards foreign policy, Wilhelm M. Carlgren, *Svensk utrikespolitik, 1939-1945* (Stockholm, 1973), which is the basis for the previously mentioned *Swedish Foreign Policy during the Second World War*, offers a much fuller treatment than does the English version.
The role of Sweden in Finnish security policy is thoroughly examined by Krister Wahlbäck in *Finlandsfrågan i svensk politik, 1937-1940* (Stockholm, 1964). The author describes not only the diplomatic developments but also debates and attitudes in the government, the *Riksdag*, and the High Command of the armed forces. There is a summary in French.
The position taken up by the government in foreign policy, especially where Finland is concerned, is analyzed in Per G. Andreen, *De mörka åren. Perspektiv på svensk neutralitetspolitik våren 1940-nyåret 1942* (Stockholm, 1971), a book based primarily upon notes in ministers' private diaries.
The economic aspect of the military preparations is discussed in Ulf Olsson, *Upprustning och verkstadsindustri i Sverige under det andra världskriget* (Gothenburg, 1973), a publication in the research project "Under Pressure from Abroad—Sectors of the Swedish Economy, 1933-45."
There are no comprehensive publications of source material for Swedish policy during the Second World War. Particular diplomatic events have occasioned White Books, published by the Foreign Ministry, which may be found by those interested in the series: *Aktstycken utgivna av Kungl. Utrikesdepartementet. Handlingar rörande Sveriges politik under andra världskriget.*
A selection from the copious diary material, arranged by topics, is provided in Krister Wahlbäck, *Regeringen och kriget. Ur statsrådens dagböcker, 1939-1941* (Stockholm, 1972), with the main emphasis on decisions in foreign policy. Krister Wahlbäck and Göran Boberg, *Sveriges sak är vår. Svensk utrikespolitik, 1939-1945 i dokument* (Stockholm, 1966), is similarly directed, but it came out while important diary sequences were still inaccessible.

Nordic Security Policy, 1945-49

Works in English or German

Research into Scandinavian policies in the postwar era is still in its infancy, and the few available works in English or German cover only part of a large and complicated range of problems.
The most recent work is by the Norwegian scholar Geir Lundestad: *America, Scandinavia, and the Cold War, 1945-1949* (Oslo, 1980).

Barbara G. Haskel, *The Scandinavian Option. Opportunities and Opportunity Costs in Postwar Scandinavian Foreign Policies* (Oslo, 1976), applies the terms of cost-benefit estimation to three problems in the postwar history of Scandinavia, one of them being the plans for a defense alliance, but the factual account is slight.

Another work that is relevant to all the Scandinavian countries is Klaus Misgeld, *Die "Internationale Gruppe demokratischer Sozialisten" in Stockholm, 1942-1945. Zur sozialistischen Friedensdiskussione während des Zweiten Weltkrieges* (Uppsala, 1976).

The separate countries are covered by some general accounts: Max Jakobson, *Finnish Neutrality. A Study of Finnish Foreign Policy since the Second World War* (London, 1968), is authored by a leading diplomat and may be regarded as representing the official views of the Finnish government. Nevertheless, it is an unusually elegant and well-written account which cannot be ignored.

For Denmark we have Eric S. Einhorn, "The Reluctant Ally: Danish Security Policy, 1945-49," *Journal of Contemporary History* 10, no. 3 (1975):493-512, which gives the background to the final course chosen by the Danish government in March 1949.

The policy of the Norwegian government down to the final discussions of an alliance are thoroughly examined in Nils M. Udgaard, *Great Power Politics and Norwegian Foreign Policy. A Study of Norway's Foreign Relations, November 1940-February 1948* (Oslo, 1973). A special problem of considerable weight is discussed in Helge Ø. Pharo, "Bridgebuilding and Reconstruction. Norway Faces the Marshall Plan," *Scandinavian Journal of History* 1 (1976):125-53. A short rejoinder was made in "The Marshall Plan and Norway's Hesitation," *Scandinavian Journal of History* 2 (1977):241-42, by Erik Brofoss, who took part as minister of finance in the Norwegian government's decision making.

As regards Swedish policy, we can only state that no account is available in a foreign language.

Works in Danish, Norwegian, or Swedish

To date, comprehensive research into postwar history is to be found only in Norway, where a good introduction to the present state of inquiry is in Trond Bergh et al., *Vekst og velstand. Norsk politisk historie, 1945-1965* (Oslö, 1977). The volume contains seven essays offering a synthesis of such subjects as "Norway in Cooperation with the West" and "Norwegian Industrial Policy, 1945-65"; there is also a bibliography.

Norway's entry into NATO is the subject of two basic studies: Magne Skodvin, *Norden eller NATO. Utenriksdepartementet og alliansespørsmålet, 1947-1949* (Oslo, 1971), founded mainly on the archives of the Foreign Ministry, and Knut Einar Eriksen, *DNA og NATO. Striden om norsk NATO-medlemskap innen regjeringspartiet, 1948-49* (Oslo, 1972).

The American documents concerning the North Atlantic cooperation which were published in 1975 are commented on, with particular reference to the role of Norway and Scandinavia generally, in Helge Pharo, "Det nordatlantiske samarbeid—og Norge, 1948-49," *Internasjonal politikk* no. 4 (1976):859-97.

For the other Scandinavian countries, only isolated inquires are to be had. The development of Danish security policy is clearly described in two papers: Jørn Aarup Kristensen, "Danmarks sikkerhedspolitik 1945 og omsvinget 48-49" and John Danstrup, "Danmarks situation 1945-70 set fra et sikkerhedsmæssigt synspunkt," which are included in the anthology, *Dansk sikkerhedspolitik* (Copenhagen, 1970).

Denmark's sensitive relationship with the Soviet Union is examined in Mary Dau, *Danmark og Sovjetunionen, 1944-49* (Copenhagen, 1969), and central documents in foreign policy have been collected in the volume *Dansk sikkerhedspolitik, 1948-1966* (Copenhagen, 1968).

A survey of Swedish foreign policy during this period has been published in Nils Andrén and Åke Landqvist, *Svensk utrikespolitik efter 1945* (Stockholm, 1965), a collection of documents with introductory sections.

Sweden's role in the negotiations for a defense alliance has been discussed by two writers: 1) Krister Wahlbäck, "Norden och blockuppdelningen, 1948-49," the series *Internationella studier* häfte B 1973; and "USA i Skandinavien, 1948-49," the journal *Internationella studier* no. 5 (1976):192-98 and no. 1 (1977):26-30; and 2) Gustaf Jonasson, *Per Edvin Sköld, 1946-1951* (Uppsala, 1976). The latter work contains seven studies in modern political history, based to a great extent upon notes that Sköld made when he was a member of the government; one of these is on the Nordic defense alliance.

The reorientation of Finnish policy after the Second World War is among the problems examined in Krister Wahlbäck, *Från Mannerheim till Kekkonen. Huvudlinjer i finländsk politik, 1917-1967* (Malmö, 1967), which discusses the changing interpretations of developments which the Finns have debated. A dramatic description of how the pact of friendship and mutual assistance came about in Moscow in the spring of 1948 is given in *Tre resor till Moskva* (Helsingfors, 1970), by Johan Söderhjelm, who was a member of the Finnish delegation for the negotiations.

Index

Index

Aalborg, 230, 231, 233
Aaltonen, Wäinö, 280
Äänislinna, *see* Petrozavodsk
Aarhus, 230, 231, 232, 233, 254
Agrarian party: Denmark (*Bondepartiet,
Det Frie Folkeparti*, LS), 26, 31, 32,
223; Finland (*Agrarförbundet*), 26, 28,
31, 162, 354; Norway (*Bondepartiet*),
26, 27; Sweden (*Bondeförbundet*), 26,
27, 109
Åland Islands, 41, 43, 54, 55, 64, 87, 146,
246
Åndalsnes, 93, 96
Archangel, 139, 159, 161, 173
Arendal, 253
Atlantic Ocean, 10, 221, 333, 340
Aunus, *see* Svir
Australia, 166, 168
Austria, 235, 332

Bagge, Gösta, 270, 271
Balkans, 69, 71, 147
Baltic, 6, 10, 42, 43, 45, 54, 55, 59, 62,
160, 168, 175, 181, 290, 291, 292, 333,
338, 340, 341
Baltic states, 41, 56, 63, 66, 72, 176, 179
Barents Sea, 309
Bear Island, 336
Belgium, 335
Benelux, 332, 353
Bergen, 82, 93, 94, 252, 253
Berggrav, Eivind, 198

Berlin, 89, 143, 145, 147, 179, 221, 223,
239, 285, 332
Bernadotte, Folke, 314
Bernadotte, Jean Babtiste (Karl XIV Johan,
king of Sweden), 5
Bessarabia, 57
Best, Werner, 126, 224, 227, 235-39, 245,
297
Beveridge, William, 326, 329
Bismarck, Otto von, 8
Boheman, Erik, 79, 269, 270
Böhme, Franz, 313, 314
Bopa, 213, 214, 227
Bornholm, 313, 338, 339, 378
Bosnia, 258
Bothnia, Gulf of, 47, 87, 102, 103, 290,
361
Brandt, Willy, 326
Bräuer, Curt, 95, 97, 117
Brofoss, Erik, 378
Brussels, 59
Buhl, Vilhelm (Danish prime minister), 214,
236, 240, 273, 313
Bulgaria, 168, 285, 332, 353

Cajander, A. K., 28, 43, 65
Canada, 167, 168, 173
Caucasus, 179, 222
Chamberlain, Neville, 89
Christensen, I. E., 97
Christian Frederik (Danish crown prince,
later Christian VIII), 5

Christian X (king of Denmark), 92, 122-25 passim
Churchill, Winston, 61, 62, 90, 167, 172, 173, 174, 262, 275, 338
Clandestine press, 204, 206, 213, 215, 216, 218, 224, 227, 244, 302
Clandestine press in Denmark: *Aarhus Ekko*, 234; *De Frie Danske*, 215; *Fribedsstøtten*, 215; *Frit Danmark*, 215, 216, 218, 219, 222, 233, 241; *Land og Folk*, 213; *Når Danmark atter er frit*, 243; *Trods Alt*, 233; *Vædderen*, 215
Clandestine press in Norway: *Bulletinen*, 250; *Krigens Gang*, 204; *London-Nytt*, 204; *London-Radio*, 204; *Radio-Nytt*, 204
Clausen, Fritz, 25
Clay, Lucius Du Bignon, 353
Committee of Nine (*Rigsdagens Samarbejdsudvalg*) (Denmark), 121, 237
Communism (Bolshevism), 25, 27, 128, 151, 167, 184, 189, 246, 248. 329. 330, 331, 334, 349, 350, 353, 360, 379, 381: Denmark, 25, 26, 124, 154, 211-16, 218, 222, 225, 227-29, 233, 236, 241-43, 273, 297, 306, 310, 329-31, 333, 348, 349; Finland, 8, 25, 28, 44, 52, 178, 183, 267, 329-31, 333, 348, 349; Norway, 25, 195, 205, 215, 253, 255-58, 299, 301, 329-31, 337, 349, 361; Sweden, 25, 79, 127, 128, 131, 132, 275, 329-31, 340, 349
Conservative party, 26, 30, 32, 50, 332, 350: Denmark, 26, 31, 119, 216, 219, 220, 222, 331, 369, 370, 371; Finland, 26, 162, 348, 354; Norway (*Høyre*), 26, 31, 331, 347; Sweden, 26, 31, 109, 130-32, 270
Cooperation Committee, *see* Committee of Nine
Coordination Committee (Norway), 198, 199, 248, 249
Copenhagen, 5, 59, 60, 92, 125, 177, 211-13, 217, 218, 223, 227, 230, 232, 233, 234, 236, 238, 240, 241, 275, 303-5, 357
Corbin, Charles, 71
Croatia, 168, 179
Czechoslovakia, 54, 235, 332, 333, 357, 373

Danmarks Fribedsråd, see Freedom Council

Dansk Samling, 26, 124, 217, 218, 222, 228, 241, 242, 243
Dardenelles, 333
Dietl, Edouard, 95, 105, 171
Dönitz, Karl, 313
Drammen, 255
Duckwitz, Georg Ferdinand, 239

Eden, Anthony, 338
Egypt, 221
Eidsvold, 5, 6
Eisenhower, Dwight, 300, 310
El-Alamein, 126, 221
Elverum, 96
Enckell, Carl, 265, 286
Engelbrecht, Erwin, 109, 110, 153, 156, 160
Erkko, Eljas, 80, 85
Esbjerg, 93, 229-34 passim
Estonia, 56, 59, 63, 332

Fåborg, 232
Fagerholm, Karl August, 267
Falkenhorst, Nikolaus von, 161, 171, 246
Faroe Islands, 10, 271
Fascism, *see* Nazism
Finland, Gulf of, 44, 64, 65, 86, 87, 140, 150, 157, 164, 266
Finnmark, 306, 307, 309, 310, 318, 378
Fishermen's peninsula, 64, 65, 86
Fog, Mogens, 243
Food, 308: agricultural production, 12-13; agricultural trade, 13, 14, 135, 145, 168, 260, 266, 268, 276-77, 281, 352; consumption of, 20-21; rationing, 13, 136, 322; shortages, 169, 204, 317, 322
Fornebu, 94
Fredericia, 230, 232
Frederikshavn, 230
Freedom Council (Denmark), 243-45, 250, 277, 296-98, 304, 310, 313, 338
Furubotn, Peter, 255
Fyn, 213, 227, 230, 232, 241

Galicia, 179
Gällivare, 93, 95
Gamelin, Maurice G., 83
Ganeval, Jean, 84
Gerhardsen, Einar, 358, 361, 363
Göring, Herman, 103, 134, 143
Gothenburg, 133, 240, 269-71
Greece, 160, 161, 242, 350

Greenland, 10, 46
Günther, Christian, 76, 78, 79, 80, 85, 103, 105, 109, 153, 179, 272, 344, 345
Gustav V (king of Sweden), 109, 147, 153, 264

Haakon VII (king of Norway), 6, 96, 97, 99, 111, 117, 118, 186, 193, 195, 314
Haderslev, 230, 232
Hagelin, Albert Viljam, 74, 75, 123, 192, 250, 320
Hägg, Gunder, 275
Hägglöf, Gunnar, 269-72
Hague, The, 10
Halder, Franz, 91, 145
Halifax, Lord (Sir Edward Wood, Viscount of Halifax), 71, 72
Hamar, 96
Hamburg, 222
Hamsun, Knut, 178
Hanko, 64, 65, 68, 86, 102, 140, 155, 156, 186
Hanneken, Hermann von, 225, 227, 229, 235-39 passim
Hansson, Per Albin, 27, 47, 64, 81, 85, 106, 109, 129, 130, 272, 273
Hardangervidda, 253
Harriman, Averell, 262
Hauge, Jens Christian (Norwegian Defense Minister), 256, 358, 362
Haukelid, Knut, 254
Hedtoft (Hansen), Hans, 364, 365
Heinrichs, Erik, 145, 156
Helsingborg, 240
Helsinki, 66, 147, 148, 260, 265, 266, 280, 286, 322, 333, 354, 355, 356
Himmler, Heinrich, 176, 224, 238, 312, 313
Hitler, Adolf, 49, 62, 74, 75, 90, 91, 95, 103, 110, 122, 125, 126, 133, 137, 139-42 passim, 144, 147, 149, 150, 158, 161, 165, 166, 169, 171, 173-77 passim, 179, 211, 236, 238, 239, 246, 265, 273, 281, 283-84, 285, 300, 303, 309, 313, 362
Hjemmefrontens Ledelse (Home Front Command) (Norway), 256, 299, 314
Hjørring, 230
Hoare, Samuel, 83
Hogland, 266
Holland, 42, 235, 313, 335
Holma, Harri, 76, 79, 85
Holstein, 8

Horsens, 230
Houmann, Børge, 243
Hungary, 239, 266, 332, 353

Iberian peninsula, 173
Iceland, 10, 161
IKL, see Lapua movement
Ilvalo, 265
India, 168
Ingria, province of, 165
Iran (Persia), 161, 173
Iron ore, 47, 61, 62, 72, 73, 75, 80-82, 84, 89, 90, 108, 135, 136, 270-72, 274, 289, 290, 306
Italy, 42, 167, 337, 357

Jakobsen, Frode, 243
Jänisjärvi, 156
Japan, 167, 337
Jartsev, Boris, 55
Jews, 32: Danish, 114, 238-40, 273, 274, 297, 318; Norwegian, 246, 318, 319
Jodl, Alfred, 91
Jutland, 49, 213, 225, 227, 230, 233, 235, 242, 254, 338, 371

Käkisalmi, 86
Kantalahti, 148, 159, 160, 161, 171
Karelia, 44, 66, 88, 155-57, 161-64, 166, 169, 170, 262, 288
Karelian isthmus, 49, 55, 64-66, 69, 84-86, 104, 155-59, 161, 258, 262, 266, 281, 283, 286
Karesuando, 265
Karhumäki, 159, 168
Kauffmann, Henrik, 113
Keitel, Wilhelm, 149, 156
Kemi, 161, 171
Kemijärvi, 160
Kerr, Archibald Clark, 285
Kiestinki, 68, 159, 160, 171
Kilpisjärvi, 307
Kirkenes, 173, 309
Kiruna, 306
Kivimäki, Toivo M., 43, 148, 149
Koht, Halvdan, 76, 78
Kola peninsula, 159, 164, 165
Kolding, 230, 232, 233
Kollontai, Alexandra, 79, 85, 262, 264, 265, 285, 288
Korsør, 230
Kreisky, Bruno, 326

Kretsen (The Circle) (Norway), 199
Kummetz, K., 94
Kuolajärvi, 86
Kupa, *see* Bopa
Kursk, 221
Kuusinen, O. W., 66, 67, 84, 163

Labor movement, *see* Social Democratic
    party; Trade unions
la Cour, Vilhelm, 220
Ladoga, Lake, 64, 86, 87, 140, 154-58,
    164, 172, 281
Lange, Halvard, 337, 351, 356-58, 363, 364
Lappland, 146, 148, 156, 159, 160, 171,
    180, 181, 258, 288, 307, 308, 315, 317
Lappvik, 64
Lapua movement (IKL [Patriotic People's
    Movement]) (Finland), 8, 25, 26, 28,
    32, 102, 162, 267, 268
Larsen, Gunnar, 121
Latvia, 56, 59, 63, 332
Leningrad, 4, 44, 64, 68, 151, 156-59, 161,
    163, 165, 170-72, 179, 181, 261, 281
Liberal party, 26, 30, 50, 350: Denmark
    (*Venstre*), 31, 119, 222, 369; Finland,
    28, 31; Norway (*Venstre*), 6, 27, 30;
    Sweden (*Folkepartiet*), 30, 31, 103, 109,
    130-32, 348, 367, 373
Lie, Trygve, 208, 333, 336
Ling, Christopher George, 84, 85
Linge, Martin Jensen, 251-54
Linia, 221
Linkomies, Edwin, 259, 261, 264, 267
Lipola-Koivisto district, 64
Lisa River, 159
Lithuania, 56, 59, 63, 332
Lofoten, 141, 142, 174
Loivisto, 64
London, 19, 113, 131, 200, 202, 204, 222,
    244, 251, 257, 269, 271, 272, 292, 309,
    322, 332, 343, 366
Louhi, 161
Lübeck, 338
Luleå, 60, 93
Lyngen fjord, 307, 318

Mainila, 66
Malmø, 240
Mannerheim, Carl Gustav, 7, 86, 143, 144,
    147, 156-59, 161-63, 166, 169, 171,
    175, 260, 264, 267, 281, 284-86, 289,
    297, 317, 335, 378

Märkäjärvi, 86
Masaryk, Jan, 353
Milorg (Norway), 200-205, 251-58, 296,
    299-302, 305, 310, 312, 314, 323
Möller, Gustav (Swedish minister of social
    affairs), 273, 312
Møller, John Christmas, 124, 216, 219, 220,
    222, 331, 338, 339, 371
Molotov, Vyacheslav M., 57, 59, 64, 85,
    143, 174, 259, 265, 285, 286, 308, 333,
    335-37
Moscow, 32, 86, 131, 158, 159, 166, 174,
    255, 265, 286, 296, 308, 322, 332, 333,
    336, 338, 356, 364
Munch, Ebbe, 211
Munch, Peter, 27, 45, 49, 112, 113, 119
Murmansk, 87, 139-42, 159-62, 170-72,
    174, 175, 258, 306
Mussolini, Benitto, 262, 273
Muus, Flemming B., 228, 244

Nakskov, 228
Namsos, 93, 96
Nanking China, 168
Narew, 57
Narvik, 47, 60, 80, 81, 92, 95, 96, 99, 105,
    106, 110, 290
Nazism, 30, 32, 38, 46, 100, 116, 129, 133,
    137-39, 178, 185, 186, 189-91, 193,
    199, 210, 216, 324, 328, 329, 361: Den-
    mark (DNSAP), 25, 121, 124, 126, 176,
    209, 215, 223, 230, 243; Norway (*Nas-
    jonal Samling*), 25, 38, 118, 186-93,
    195-97, 204, 205, 210, 211, 248, 249,
    256, 257, 302, 320; Sweden, 25, 127,
    128, 132
"Negotiation, Policy of," 94, 111-16, 119,
    124, 126, 138, 184-86, 191, 208-10,
    215-19, 222, 224, 229, 234-36, 245,
    276, 297
Neutrality, 18, 53, 59, 60, 61-62, 129, 132,
    135, 327, 345: Denmark, 9, 46, 60, 94,
    112-13, 126; Finland, 99, 146, 150, 151,
    165, 262, 356; during interwar period,
    40-43, 46; Norway, 46, 95; and postwar
    alliance of Scandinavian states, 359-65;
    Sweden, 3, 47, 80, 104, 105-7, 110-11,
    138, 142, 153, 160, 183, 268, 276, 278,
    288-92, 294, 295, 311, 312, 317, 322,
    344
Neva, 164
New Zealand, 166, 168

Nordkalotten, 306, 307, 333
Normandy, 274, 281, 289, 300, 323
North Africa, 175, 221, 222, 259, 260, 323
North Cape, 306
Nuremberg, 321
Nygaardsvold, Johan, 27, 116, 117, 118

Odense, 230-34 passim
Oder, 338
Olav V (Norwegian crown prince), 299, 314
Olonets (Aunus), 159, 162
Onega, Lake, 159, 171, 258, 266
Oscarsborg, 94
Oslo, 6, 94, 95, 106, 118, 153, 187, 196-98, 200-202, 205, 245, 246, 250, 252, 255, 337, 356, 358
Østlandet, 252
Oulu, 307
Oxelösund, 60

Paasikivi, Juho Kusti, 64, 104, 264, 265, 334, 335, 353-55, 357, 378, 379
Pacific Ocean, 323
Pakaslahti, Aaro, 76, 79
Pancke, Günther, 238
Paris, 83, 113, 285, 332, 336, 345, 350
Parliament: Denmark (Rigsdag), 24, 98, 115, 121, 124, 154, 208, 216, 223, 225, 228, 234, 236, 313, 321, 348, 369, 370; Finland (Eduskunta, Riksdag), 43, 102, 104, 149, 151, 162, 264, 265, 267, 268, 280, 286, 288, 348, 349, 352, 354; Norway (Stortinget), 6, 96, 117, 319, 331, 336, 337, 348, 369, 371, 372, 375; Sweden (Riksdag), 24, 25, 26, 106, 127, 128, 276, 348, 358, 372, 376
Persia, see Iran
Petrozavodsk (Äänislinna), 68, 87, 159, 258, 266
Petsamo, 82, 87, 102, 110, 133, 139-41, 145, 149, 159, 170, 172-74, 246, 258, 264, 265, 286, 306-8, 333
Poland, 54-57, 59, 62, 65, 90, 332, 353
Porajärvi, 64
Porkala, 286, 333, 356
Portugal, 332
Potsdam, 336
Prague, 349, 353, 356, 357, 361
Pskov, 156

Quisling, Vidkun, 25, 73-75, 89, 95, 96, 116-18, 180, 187, 188, 191, 197, 198, 246, 248, 250, 257, 319, 320

Raade, 69
Radical Left (Det Radikale Venstre) (Denmark), 26, 27, 31, 222, 338, 369, 371
Raeder, Erich, 62, 73-75, 90
Ramsay, Henrik, 259, 260
Rangell, Johan Wilhelm, 144, 151, 259
Rasmussen, Gustav, 339, 364, 365
Renthe-Fink, Cecil von, 117, 124
Repola, 64
Resistance, 242, 381: Denmark, 124, 126, 183, 208-19, 222, 227, 230, 231, 238-44, 275, 277, 296-98, 304, 305, 311, 313, 318, 321, 329; Norway, 96, 118, 119, 138, 183, 186-207, 210, 245-58, 276, 297-302, 311, 312, 314, 318, 329, 371; phenomenon of, 182-86; and "policy of negotiation," 184-85; significance of, 323; Swedes assist movement, 183. See also Clandestine press; Sabotage; Strikes
Ribbentrop, Joachim von, 57, 59, 112, 134, 148, 167, 260, 283, 284
Rinnan, Henry Oliver, 320
Ritter, Karl, 134
Rjukan, 253
Romania, 54, 168, 285, 332, 353
Rome, 6, 112
Rommei, Ervin, 125
Roosevelt, Franklin, 49, 174, 262
Rosenberg, Alfred, 74, 75
Roskilde, 230
Rostov, 179
Rosyth, 92
Ryti, Risto, 67, 84, 143, 144, 148, 158, 162-67 passim, 169, 175, 176, 259, 264, 267, 284, 315

Sabotage, 185, 323: Denmark, 213, 214, 216-18, 227-32, 236, 238, 241, 242, 244, 298, 303; Finland, 183, 268; Norway, 199, 201-3, 206, 246, 252-55, 257, 296, 299, 301, 302, 312
Sæby, 230
Salla, 64, 159, 160, 165
Salzburg, 147
Samarbejdsudvalg, see Committee of Nine
San (Polish), 57
San Francisco, 297, 344
Sandler, Rickard, 27, 47
Sargent, Orme, 366

Scavenius, Erik, 98, 121, 126, 133, 154, 167, 178, 213, 218, 224, 229, 236
Schalburg, Count C. F., 177, 180
Schleswig, 8, 9, 92, 122, 223
Schnurre, Karl, 109, 147, 153, 179
Schweinfurt, 274
Scotland, 92, 309, 310
Scott, John, 266, 268
Seeds, William, 66
Serbia, 258
Shetland Islands, 254, 301
Siberia, 161
Sicily, 222, 262
Skagen, 230
Skagerak, 132
Skibotn, 307
Sköld, Per Edvin (Swedish minister of agriculture, defense minister), 363, 368
Slovakia, 168
Social Democratic party (Labor movement), 22, 24, 26, 27, 29, 30, 50, 51, 328, 330, 331, 349, 350, 358, 360, 377, 381: Denmark, 27, 98, 120, 213, 224, 228, 233, 234, 236, 242-44, 328, 348, 365, 369, 373; Finland, 28, 30, 31, 43, 163-65, 169, 265, 267, 330, 348, 354; Norway (*Det Norske Arbeiderparti*), 27, 46, 195, 206, 215, 256, 347, 358, 361, 363, 372; Sweden, 27, 103, 106, 108, 109, 110, 130-32, 276, 330, 331, 341, 348, 358, 363, 367, 373
Söderblom, Staffan, 271
SOE (Special Operations Executive) (Great Britain), 202, 203, 212, 216-19, 228, 242, 244, 245, 251, 252, 296, 301
Sørensen, Arne, 242
Sorokka, 161, 162, 171, 172
Sortavala, 68, 86, 87, 156
Sound, The, 239, 333
South Africa, 166
Spain, 32
Srednij, 86
Stalin, Joseph Vissarionovich, 63, 64, 170, 172-74, 262, 353, 354
Stalingrad, 125, 171, 176, 221, 222, 259, 260, 323
Stauning, Thorvald, 27, 45, 92, 98, 119, 121
Stavanger, 82, 93, 252, 255
Stein, Boris, 55
Stockholm, 6, 54, 110, 118, 179, 200, 208, 211, 212, 232, 239, 252, 255, 262, 264,

265, 268, 271, 293, 309, 312, 315, 357, 364
Strikes, 28, 228-36, 238, 303-5
Sudetenland, 54
Summa, 69
Suojärvi, 86
Suomussalmi, 69
Svalbard, 336, 337, 339, 378
Svendborg, 230-32
Svenningsen, Nils, 237
Svir, 157-59, 161, 164, 170, 171, 258, 260, 261, 266
Svolvær, 141
Switzerland, 42, 332
Sydlandet, 251, 252
Szklarska Pereba, 353

Taipale, 69
Tali, 86
Talvela, Paavo, 143, 145
Tanner, Väinö, 64, 67, 78, 84, 85, 164
Teheran, 262
Terboven, Joseph, 97, 117-19, 122, 137, 186-89, 193-96, 246, 310, 313
Theresienstadt, 239
Thyssen, Fritz, 72
Tihvin, 159
Tinnsjø, 254
Tito, Joseph Broz, 179, 258
Trade unions, 22, 23, 28, 29, 30, 34, 36, 120, 194-96, 198, 199, 229, 234, 267
Trelleborg, 106
Tromsø, 307, 315, 335
Trøndelag, 201, 251, 252
Trondheim, 74, 82, 93, 94, 96, 99, 174, 246, 253, 290, 320
Truman, Harry S., 350
Tunis, 221, 222

Ukraine, 179, 221
Undén, Östen, 341, 342, 345, 358, 362, 376
United Nations, 297, 339, 344, 345, 350-52, 355, 362, 369, 377, 378

Vejle, 230
Veltjens, Joseph, 103
Vemork, 253
Vereker, Gordon, 85
Vestfjord, 95
Vestlandet, 251, 252

Vichy, 121, 222
Viipuri (Viborg), 68, 86, 87, 157, 258, 266, 281
Voroshilov, Klimenti, 156

Warburton-Lee, B. A. M., 95
Warsaw, 356
Washington, D.C., 269, 332, 353, 357
Weichel, 57
Westman, Karl Gustav, 106, 128, 129

White Sea, 140, 141, 148, 162, 164, 306
Wied, Victor, Prince of (German minister in Sweden), 129
Wigfors, Ernst, 27
Witting, Rolf, 166, 167, 259

Young, Gordon, 275
Yugoslavia, 242

Zealand, (Sjælland), 230